Visions of Heaven

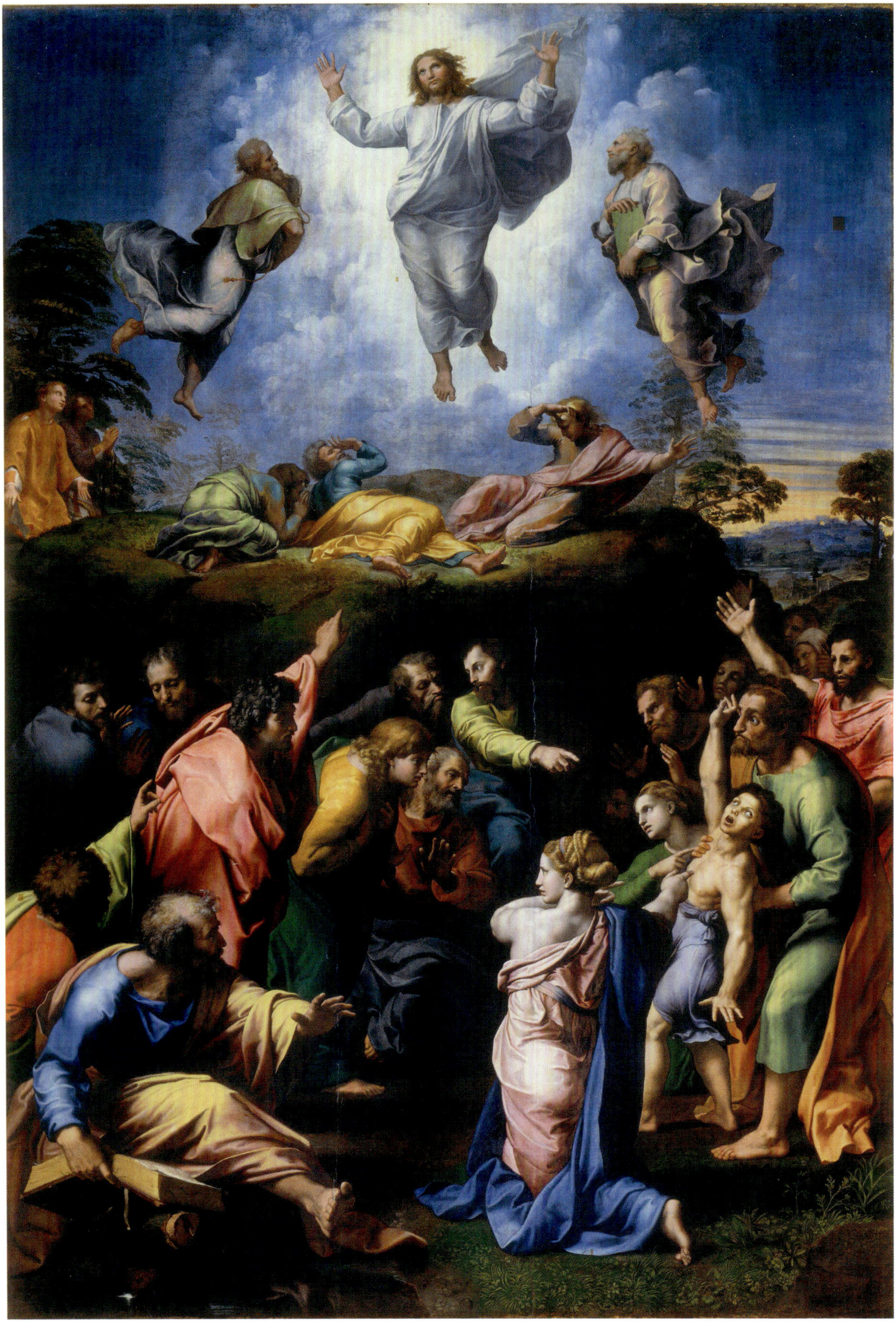

VISIONS OF HEAVEN

Dante and the Art of Divine Light

Martin Kemp

LUND HUMPHRIES

First published in 2021 by Lund Humphries

Lund Humphries
Office 3, Book House
261A City Road
London EC1V 1JX
UK

www.lundhumphries.com

ISBN: 978-1-84822-467-4

A Cataloguing-in-Publication record for this book is available from the British Library

Designed by Crow Books
Typeset in Centaur Mt and Jupiter Pro
Printed in Slovenia

FRONTISPIECE
Raphael, *The Transfiguration of Christ*, Rome, Vatican
COVER
Front: Giovanni Battista Gaulli (Baciccio), detail of *The Triumph of the Holy Name of Jesus*, Il Gesù, Rome;
Back: Titian, detail of *Assumption of the Virgin*, Santa Maria Gloriosa dei Frari, Venice

Contents

Acknowledgements

If I were to list everyone since the 1970s who has benefitted my thinking on the depiction of light in paintings, my memory would be tapped well beyond its limits and serious damage would be done to the word-count for the book. I will limit my thanks here to the immediate build-up to the present book, with two exceptions. I was fortunate to be taught and mentored by two great art historians, John Shearman and Ernst Gombrich, and it is a pleasure to include their works in my bibliography and to be reminded that they sowed seeds that are still growing.

Writing during the lockdown in the face of Covid-19, with no direct access to libraries, I have relied more than normal upon colleagues and friends who have been willing to share their knowledge and opinions. They are not of course responsible for things I have got wrong. This reliance has certainly been the case with scholarship on Dante. Simon Gilson of Oxford University lent me a precious copy of his book on Dante and optics, and has read the relevant passages, making valuable suggestions. Maria Pavlova of Warwick University, who provided valuable assistance on Renaissance poetry for the monograph on *Mona Lisa* by Giuseppe Pallanti and myself, has helped me feel less vulnerable in what I have been trying to say about the *Paradiso*. There is a cliché that a teacher learns more from her or his best students than vice versa. That is unquestionably true of Alessandra Buccheri, whose doctoral thesis and resulting book on Renaissance and early Baroque theatre and painting, has been crucial for two of my chapters, and she supplied important photographs that she had taken. She has been kind enough to read the chapters and make suggestions. Father Justin of St Catherine's Monastery in Sinai kindly sent us his own image of the *Transfiguration*, after its recent conservation, which gets the book off to a light-filled start. Late in the generation of the text, Miles Chappell provided important clarifications about Ludovico Cigoli. Piet Lombaerde shared his unrivalled expertise and provided images for the Jesuit Church in Antwerp. Arthur Becker, who has been photographing domes for a planned book, has been kind enough let me use some of his images. The challenge of photographing illusionistic painting on curved surfaces is notably demanding. Aimee Ng of the Frick provided help with the Bellini, though she will not quite agree with at least one aspect of my interpretation. Filippo Camerota assisted with access to the Cigoli treatise. Martin Gayford drew my attention to the 'Giorgione Dante'. The Oxford Bodleian Library Scan and Deliver service came to my rescue at a vital moment.

I have 'tested' the drafts for the whole or chapters of the book on willing friends, including Marina Wallace, my long-term collaborator, Samantha Jessel, who has supported my efforts enthusiastically, and Tania Coreia, who brought her logical powers to bear on how the book was working. I have been talking to Robert Hollingworth, founder and director of *I Fagiolini*, about a CD/concert centred on Dante, matching the one we created for Leonardo's 500th anniversary. Whether or not it comes off in present circumstances, I draw continued inspiration from having worked with Robert and his superb vocal ensemble.

I am most grateful to Margaret Michniewicz for her wise advice about the best publisher. It has been a pleasure working with Lund Humphries, who combine adventure with the kind of traditional values that are being surrendered by many publishers. Nigel Farrow provided vital liaison in locating the book with Lund Humphries, and Lucy Myers has been enthusiastically committed to the book since its submission, providing unstinted support.

Sarah Thorowgood has supportively guided the text through its editorial, design and production stages and has skilfully exercised her expertise on the way that the text and illustrations operate in concert. Louise Tucker has been a highly engaged and accomplished copy editor, mopping up my mistakes and introducing improvements and Kate Parker provided meticulous scrutiny of the final proofs. The elegance of the design is the responsibility of Lucie Worboys of Crow Books.

Picture research has been undertaken by Sandra Assersohn with the skill and efficiency that she has applied to other of my books, even in the face of the Covid-19 closures of libraries and museums. Some of the pictures were notably difficult to obtain. Judd Flogdell, my PA, has provided committed support in all respects, not least after an operation on my spine compromised my mobility for some weeks. As previously, she has compiled a really useful index. I have long been talking to my agent Caroline Dawnay (with Kat Aitken) about a book on light. This is not the book that she expected, but she has as always applied her sharp eye to contractual matters.

Another kind of gratitude goes to B. Roy Chaudhary, spine surgeon *par excellence*, whose skill in sorting out the compressed nerves in my back ensured that I could continue writing in the immediate aftermath of the operation and could make a full recovery.

As always, my greatest gratitude is to anyone who cares to read this book. I am still surprised when people buy one of my books or pay to come to one of the associated events.

List of Illustrations

Introduction

A New Paragone

The competitive comparison of the various arts – most notably painting, sculpture, poetry and music – became a learned and courtly pursuit in the Renaissance. Leonardo da Vinci is the most famous proponent of the *paragone*, advocating the utter supremacy of painting (of course), but he was not the only disputant. Michelangelo participated when asked to do so, promoting sculpture as the beacon for painting and making rude remarks about Leonardo along the way. The present book is in part about Dante Alighieri's understanding of light and the legacy of his *Paradiso*. This involves both the direct sense of the considerable impact of his extraordinary vision, and also the general diffusion of his literary portrayal of the extraterrestrial realm of spiritual light. But it is also a *paragone* study in what poetry can do and what painting can do. We will see Dante and the painters mutually striving to meet one of the greatest of all visual challenges. That challenge was how to describe extremities of divine light that were beyond the scope of our earth-bound sense of sight.

A key stimulus for my journey has been the 700th anniversary of Dante's death. The year 2019 marked 500 years after Leonardo's death, and 2020 was Raphael's 500th, sadly underplayed during the Covid-19 virus pandemic. Raphael is at the centre of this book in 2021, and I am pleased to offer the present tribute to an artist who once occupied the peak position in the canon of painters, but who wrongly seems no longer to rival the individualistic giants in the history of art.

There is also a personal dimension. My large study of optics in art, *The Science of Art: Optical Themes in Western Art from Brunelleschi to Seurat*, was published as long ago as 1990. This concentrated on the optical foundations of European naturalism – perspective, optical devices and colour theory. I also published a more specialised essay on divine light in the Renaissance 25 years ago: 'In the Light of Dante: Meditations on Natural Light and Divine Light in Piero della Francesca, Raphael and Michelangelo'. This looked at the dilemma of depicting divine light within images that aspired to capture the full range of natural light, and at certain painters' ingenious ways of meeting the challenge. I have long been considering writing a synoptic history of light across world cultures, and this present essay may be regarded as a highly focused aspect of the wider and somewhat improbable study.

Taking Dante as the touchstone for divine light in Renaissance and Baroque painting needs no apology. Dante, Cervantes, Shakespeare, Voltaire and Goethe are arguably the greatest writers in the major European languages. They share not only untrammelled imaginative capacities, but also a huge base in learning, including the sciences. None were more 'scientific' than Dante and Goethe. All the great authors paint compelling visual pictures which have been realised by successive generations of what may be loosely described as illustrators. It was Dante who enjoyed the most immediate succession in the visual arts.

I am taking the theme of the 1996 essay about divine light and expanding it onto a much broader stage, embracing a range of images from small but radiant manuscript illuminations to the great celestial conflagrations on the vaults of High Baroque churches. Dante's accounts of the blinding heavens rely upon a special blend of science and spirituality that characterises his unique vision and sets the tone for painting the unseeable. This motif runs as a theme through this book's chapters, from the Renaissance to the 17th century, and is ultimately reconfigured in a postscript chapter on the known and the unknown in Mediaeval and modern sciences of seeing. The whole book is an essay on the underlying theme of the *paragone*, drawing upon a highly select number of works of art, a good proportion of which are amongst the most notable ever created.

The method I have adopted transcends the customary search for chains of 'influence'. I am naturally interested when there is evidence of Dante's impact on the artists – an issue that will not go away – and I am also dealing with a more general diffusion of Dante's vision. His *Divina Commedia* plays a role like that of Einstein's $E = mc^2$ or Watson and Crick's DNA (two scientific icons about which I wrote in my book *Christ to Coke*). Contemporary researchers in nuclear physics or genetics might never have studied the Einstein papers of 1905 or the brief 1953 essay on DNA, but everything flows from these iconic achievements. Above all in the broader context of the *paragone*, Dante will set the challenge at the highest level and will serve as *the* continued point of reference as to what may potentially be achieved.

I cannot but be alert to the demands made by some of the material in the first two chapters, centred respectively on Mediaeval optics and Dante's poetic expression of the science of seeing. The Mediaeval ideas about the functioning of the sense of sight are complicated and notably different from ours. For his part, Dante never stints on the demands he makes on his readers. I have aspired to present the optical content as lucidly as possible. Amongst the large body of writing on optics in the Middle Ages, I have picked out two classic texts, the first by the Islamic philosopher Ibn al-Haytham (Alhazen), who laid the foundation for European writing on optics as a revered science. The second is by John Pecham, the British archbishop, who wrote a succinct 'textbook' on optics, the science then known as *perspectiva*. In looking at the texts, I have concentrated particularly on light that cannot be comfortably seen, a recurrent feature in Dante.

In the second chapter we pick up the optical themes expressed in Dante's writing, the *Vita Nova* or *Vita Nuova* (*New Life*) and the *Convivio* (*Banquet*), both of which are accompanied by the poet's own commentary, and the magisterial and massive *Divina Commedia* (*Divine Comedy*), which does not have a commentary. Throughout, I am using the Italian titles for Dante's writings, which have a music that English lacks. It should be said that the epithetic *divina* was not part of the early title for the poem, but appeared on the frontispiece of the printed edition of 1555, edited by Ludovico Dolce, the major Venetian author who wrote compellingly about art. *Commedia* was the name for a diverting narrative that did not end in tragedy. My concentration on mechanisms of sight in Dante means that I cannot claim to provide any kind of overview of his achievement. However, light is a theme that exemplifies how the poet used his prodigious learning and imagination.

The third chapter is concerned with direct illustrations of the *Paradiso*, which is the most difficult of the three canticles to translate into visual form, since it is more about light and spiritual abstractions than picturesque incidents that lend themselves to naturalistic rendering. I pick out just four manuscripts and one printed edition – works that were conveniently online in a period of lockdown – that present different modes of providing visual support for Dante's text. The hero of the chapter is Botticelli, whose remarkable series of unfinished folios has the courage to emulate the visual abstraction of Dante's description of the heavenly realms and the flames of the disembodied spirits he encounters.

The two central chapters on the Renaissance and Baroque present a glorious parade of major painters who have faced the Dantesque challenge with high intellectual and visual skill. With figures like Piero della Francesca, Botticelli, Bellini, Raphael and Titian, I naturally feel at home, having looked carefully at their paintings, instructed students about the delights of Renaissance art and written about their achievements over several decades. With their Netherlandish contemporaries, they were the first artists to face the dilemma of how to characterise divine light within a naturalistic framework. The decision to include Grünewald at the end of the fourth chapter is based less upon historical logic than an instinctive sense that he belongs alongside the great Italian masters, in spite of his geographical remove. His inclusion was triggered by a query from a friend.

The High Baroque has not been my natural home, and I have suffered from that ingrained Anglo-Saxon sense that all the florid spirituality is going a bit far. Working on the images of the extraordinary dome and vault decorations, above all those in Rome, has totally demolished this attitude. Coming at the great Catholic explosions of light, colour and space from the perspective of Dante's *Paradiso*, with its extremity of spiritual vision, has transformed my way of looking at them. I have concentrated on the Catholic reform movements, exemplified by the Jesuits, as an expansive and belligerent reaction to the Protestant revolution. One of the problems regarding the appreciation of the art of Pietro da Cortona, Giovanni Battista Gaulli and their fellow masters of large-scale illusion is that their major achievements can only to be seen *in situ* and not in galleries and museums – or in reproduction. At least Bernini is famous, but he is predominantly concerned with sculpture. Whether or not Gaulli and co. realised that they were emulating Dante, they did so with astonishing and improbable success.

My initial expectation was that I would look at Caravaggio and those artists in succession after late Leonardo who exploited extremes of light and shade in the service of spiritual drama. This would have embraced Rembrandt, amongst others. However, the European craze for Caravaggesque effects is a major topic in its own right, potentially of book length. The paintings do not for the most part fit the rubric 'Visions of Heaven', and they would take us too far from Dante. Caravaggio and his succession would also have entailed looking at Neoplatonic light 'metaphysics' in the 17th century, a major topic which features less than I expected. If Rembrandt is excluded, Rubens is not. I decided to follow Rubens to Antwerp where his major decorations in the Church of St Ignatius were an early expression of Catholic reform outside Italy. He had also experienced formative years in Italy as a young artist. In addition, Rubens serves to introduce us to the grand book on optics by François de Aguilón, which provided an important extension to the treatises we encountered earlier. The book was handsomely illustrated by Rubens.

The division of labour between the chapter on Baroque decorations and that on manifestations of heaven in theatrical spectaculars is rather fluid, and was determined partly on the basis of how the narrative of the chapters worked out. Art historians generally pay too little heed to the great ephemeral displays in sacred and secular venues, given the lack of compelling visual records, particularly before the 17th century. But the theatrical displays were demonstrably in dynamic relationship with contemporary paintings. The great compositions of cloud-borne denizens of heaven in the staged events, with their extraordinary machinery and arrays of light, were emulated in painted domes and vaults. The same artists were often involved. The integrated decorations of churches and chapels that included dramatic architecture, dynamic sculpture, illusionistic painting and 'magic' light effects comprised a form of visual theatre and were sometimes called *teatri*.

The last chapter is not really a chapter at all, and it is certainly not a conclusion. I tend not to like conclusions, and have a sense that it is best if the end is left rather open. In this case, I am picking up one of the underlying themes of our Dantesque exercise, namely the relationship of the known to the unknown, of the seen to the unseeable – and to the likely existence of things that are definitively unknowable. I enter this question through the writings of the most original philosopher of light in the Middle Ages, Robert Grosseteste, and two of the great scientific thinkers of the 20th century, Werner Heisenberg and Kurt Gödel. I finish with Cusanus, the great German philosopher of the 15th century, whose treatise *On Learned Ignorance* is strikingly relevant to my underlying theme. Historians can harbour hopes, if not expectations, that their subject and their research will strike some resonant notes over a longish historical span and reverberate in our present culture. In our present endeavour, I hope that my belief in such 'relevance' is not an unsupportable conceit.

Finally, it is worth saying that the book is shaped by the circumstances of its writing, during the peak months of the rampage of the Covid-19 virus. It would be rather trite to say that writing about the joys of *Paradiso* during this fraught period in human history has dispelled some of the darkness, but the reverse is certainly true. The agonies of *Inferno* as described so vividly by Dante would have been harrowing. During the weeks of lockdown, the positive absence of distractions was accompanied by the unavailability of institutional resources, those of libraries, museums and galleries in particular. The remarkable resources of the internet came into play very strongly, but the overall picture is very patchy. There are a number of good Dante sites, and many libraries have digitised key manuscripts and early books. Museums and galleries are quite uneven in what they offer online and their search tools are sometimes ill thought out from the standpoint of the user. I remain hugely grateful to those who provide very high-resolution images that allow detailed explorations of artworks and of the sites where they are or were located.

I am not sure this is quite the book I set out to write. Dante, like Leonardo, has the habit of telling his students in which direction to go, and the great works of art we have encountered have an impetus of their own. To ride the crests of the creative waves offered by those who have featured in the book is a great privilege.

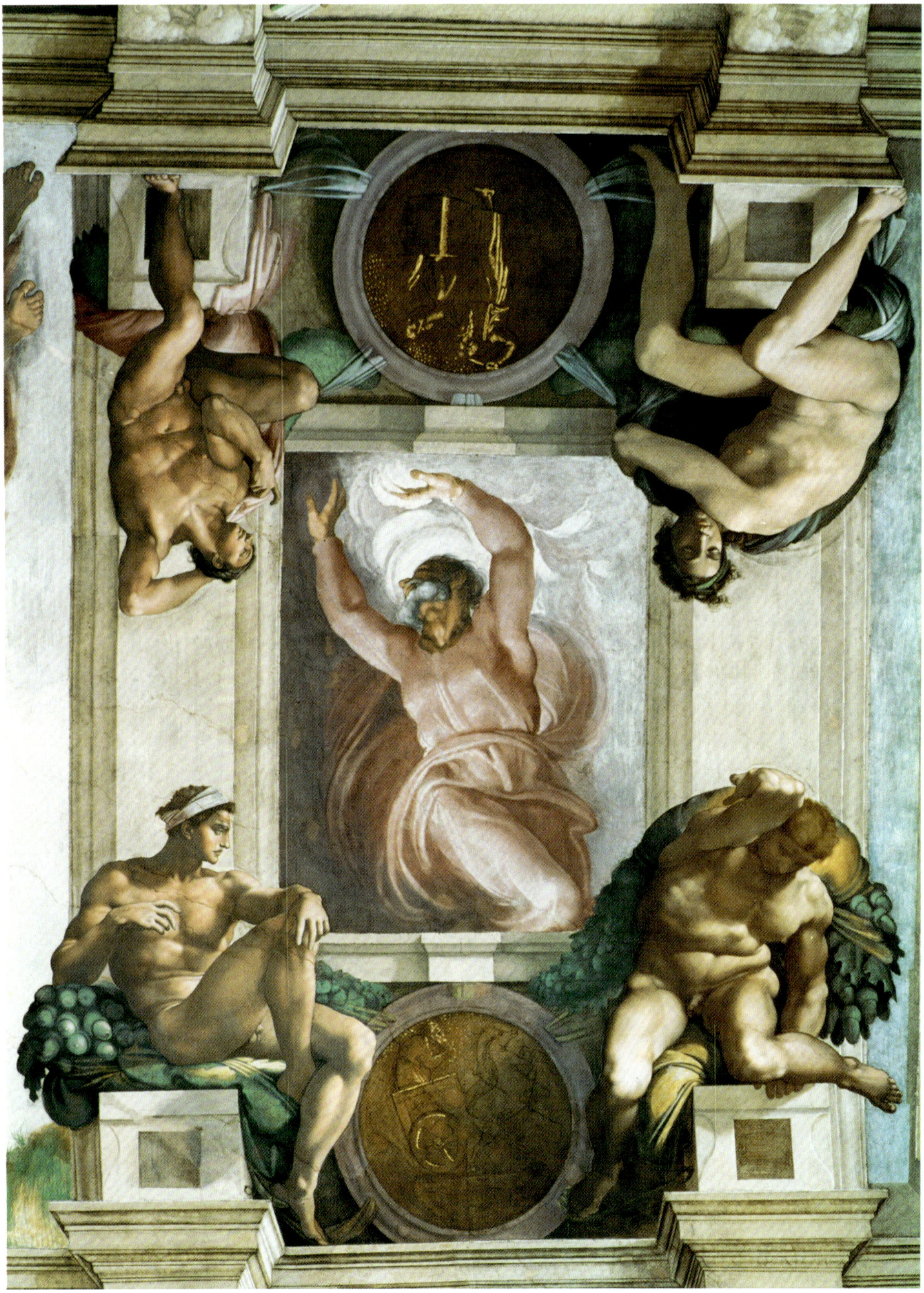

1

Divine Optics, Christian and Islamic

Light is a primary sign of divinity in many world religions. We only need to think of Diwali, the Hindu five-day autumn festival of lights, or the Jewish holiday of Hanukkah over the course of eight days and nights. For our present purposes, I will take as given the universal association of light with the divine. Here I will focus on Christianity and Islam – not so much for the traditional purpose of contrast, but to pick up common factors that converge precisely on the point at which the main story takes off. This point is where Dante brilliantly exploits an optical science that was founded in its modern guise by Islamic philosophers. Light remains central to the two big monotheisms, which presently dominate much of world culture.

At the very start of Genesis, God's separation of light and darkness is one of the primal acts of creation:

> In the beginning God created the heaven and the earth. And the earth was without form, and void; and darkness was upon the face of the deep. And the Spirit of God moved upon the face of the waters. And God said, Let there be light: and there was light. And God saw the light, that it was good: and God divided the light from the darkness. And God called the light Day, and the darkness he called Night.[1]

This means that God is not light in himself. He is the maker of light.

In Exodus, the presence of God is signalled on a number of occasions by a luminous cloud, most notably when Moses climbed Mount Sinai to receive the tablets of the commandments.

> Moses went up into the mount, and a cloud covered the mount. And the glory of the Lord abode upon mount Sinai, and the cloud covered it six days: and the seventh day he called unto Moses out of the midst of the cloud. And the sight of the glory of the Lord was like devouring fire on the top of the mount in the eyes of the children of Israel.[2]

Christ, as God's son, does identify himself directly as light. In the Gospel of St John, we are told that 'In him was life; and the life was the light of men. And the light shineth in the darkness; and the darkness comprehended it not.'[3] Later in the same gospel, Christ himself proclaims, 'I am the light [*lux*] of the world: he that followeth me shall not walk in darkness, but will have the light [*lumen*] of life.'[4] We will see that this distinction between light as *lux* and light as *lumen* plays an important role in Dante's optics. When Christ miraculously restores sight to a blind man, he declares that, 'As long as I am in the world, I am the light of the world.'[5] In the Gospel of St James, he goes further: 'Do not err, my beloved brethren. Every good gift and every perfect gift is from above, and cometh down from the Father of lights, with whom is no variableness, neither shadow of turning.'[6]

There is also the key incident of the Transfiguration on Mount Tabor. The face of Christ

Michelangelo, *The Separation of Light from the Darkness*, Rome, Vatican, Sistine Chapel

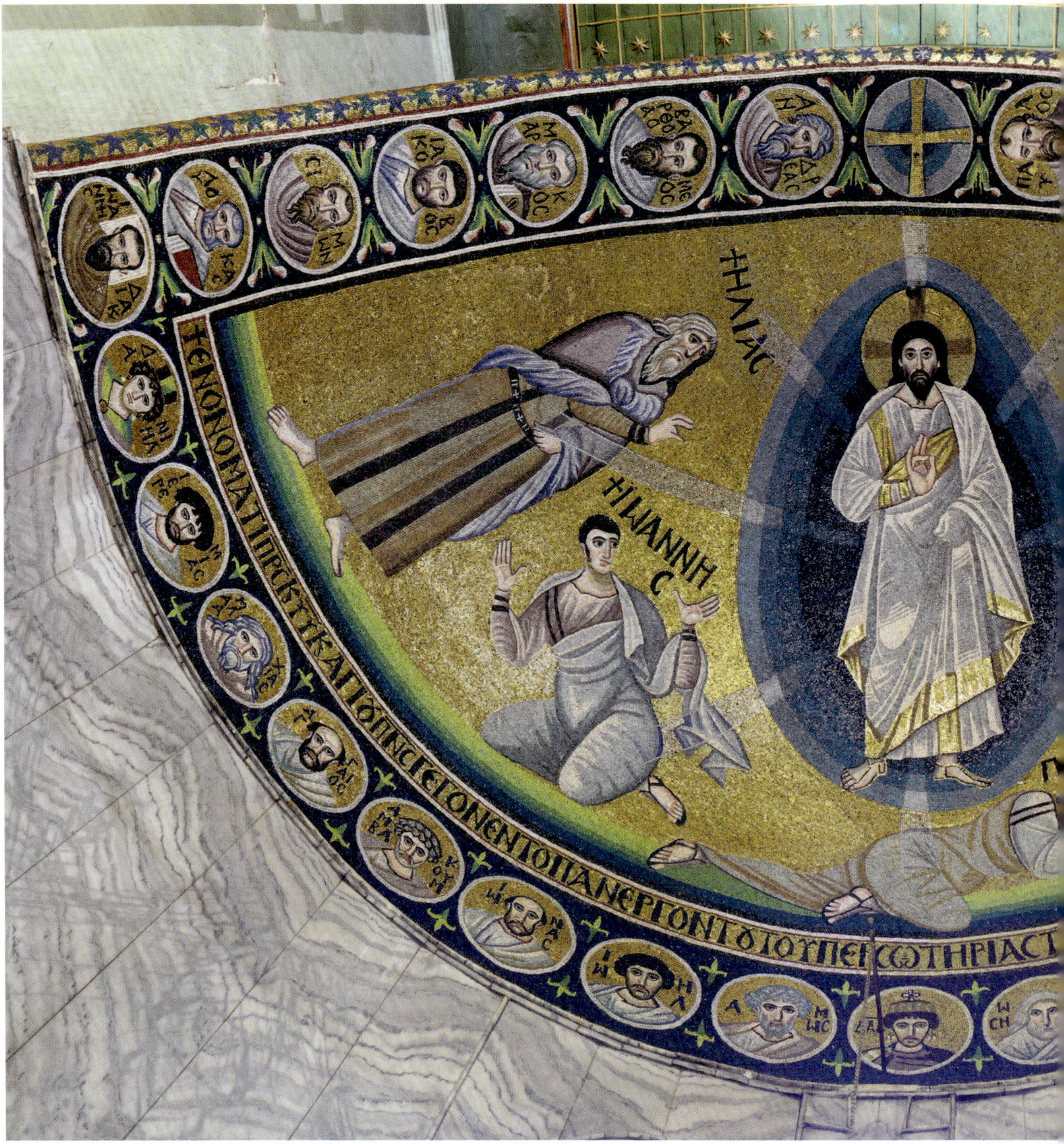
+ΗΛΙΑΣ
+ΙΩΑΝΝΗΣ

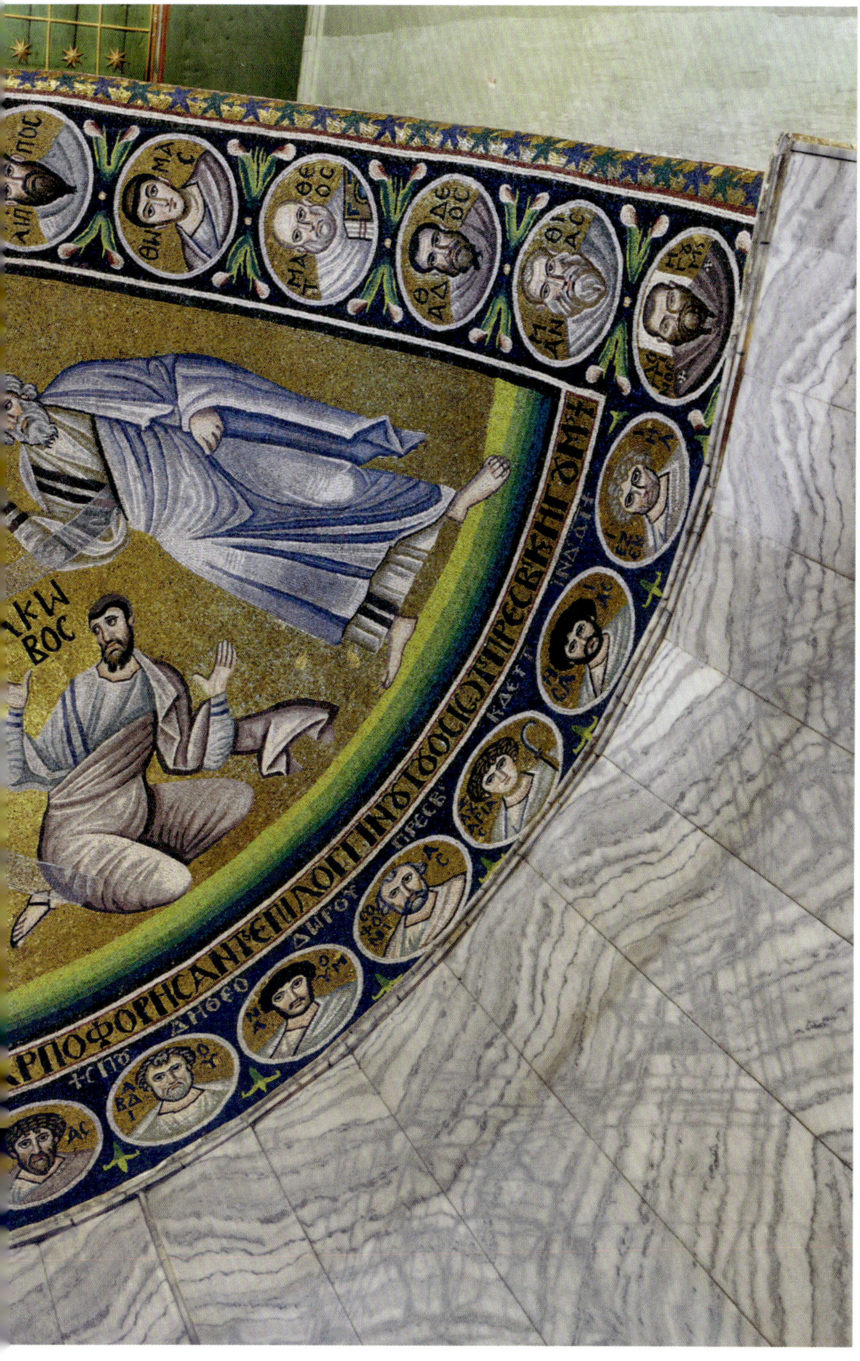

1 *The Transfiguration of Christ*, sixth-century mosaic, Church of the Monastery of St Catherine, Sinai

did shine as the sun, and his raiment was white as the light. And, behold, there appeared unto them Moses and Elias talking with him. Then answered Peter, and said unto Jesus, Lord, it is good for us to be here ... While he yet spake, behold, a bright cloud overshadowed them: and behold a voice out of the cloud, which said, This is my beloved Son, in whom I am well pleased; hear ye him.[7]

An exceptional early representation of the scene is in the sixth-century semi-dome of the Church of the Monastery of St Catherine, Sinai, the basilica at the foot of Mount Sinai in Egypt (fig.1). Christ, dressed in pure white with glittering gold decoration, is framed by a mandorla and transmits beams of light specifically towards the two prophets and the three disciples, the latter of whom collapse in the face of the startling vision. The reflective *tesserae* of the golden mosaic acts as an ideal medium for a narrative of divine light, particularly after its very recent restoration, which has made the rays of light more emphatic. The Transfiguration is a subject we will re-encounter in the Renaissance.

Light later becomes one of the major distinguishing features of Gothic architecture and art, as over the years, the walls were pierced by progressively ever-larger windows, flooding the interiors with light. The windows themselves became significant vehicles for imagery, both for the portrayal of holy figures and for narratives from the Bible and saints' lives. Light streaming though the brilliant colours of stained glass inculcates the glories of God's kingdom even for those who do not follow the intricate symbolism and often complex narratives. An ambitiously theological reading of the function of windows was given by the first book of *Rationale divinorum officiorum* (*The Rationale of Divine Offices*) written by Bishop Durandus in the 13th century:

The glass windows in a church are Holy Scriptures, which repel the wind and the rain, that is all things hurtful, but they transmit the light of the true Sun, that is to say God, into the hearts of the faithful. Windows are wider within than without, because mystical insight is broader, and precedes the literal meaning. Also, by the windows the senses of the body are signified, in that they should be closed to the vanities of this world, and open to receive spiritual gifts with complete freedom. By the tracery of the windows, we understand the prophets or other less known teachers in the Church Militant.[8]

Thinking more broadly about the presence of light within major Gothic churches of the period, our eyes would have feasted on a range of dazzling light effects – banks of flickering candles, glittering artefacts in gold and silver and the shimmering vestments of the priests. Relics, credited with miraculous powers, were viewed in precious rock crystal containers or housed in caskets glistening with gold and enamel. We will find that Dante and the optical sources on which he drew were fully alert to such glorious effects.

The cathedral in Florence, the home city of Dante, became an elaborate showpiece for Renaissance stained glass – albeit a century after Dante's cruel exile. Lorenzo Ghiberti, Donatello, Paolo Uccello and Andrea del Castagno were all involved as designers (though not as the actual executants of the glass windows). The example illustrated here is by Lorenzo Ghiberti, who began as a painter and became famed as a sculptor, not least for the gilded *Porta dell Paradiso* on the baptistery facing the cathedral. In his *Commentaries*, written towards the end of his life, Ghiberti appended a collage of Mediaeval writings on optics, drawing upon the same tradition as Dante. He seems to have gained access to an Italian translation of Ibn al-Haytham's *De Aspectibus*, a treatise that will play a conspicuous role in what follows. In his large rose window of the *Assumption of the Virgin*, Mary ascends in a starburst of intense light, sharply golden against the brilliant blue, while Christ waits in an aura of light to effect her coronation (fig.2). Her emphatic eyes are designed to have a dramatic impact high above

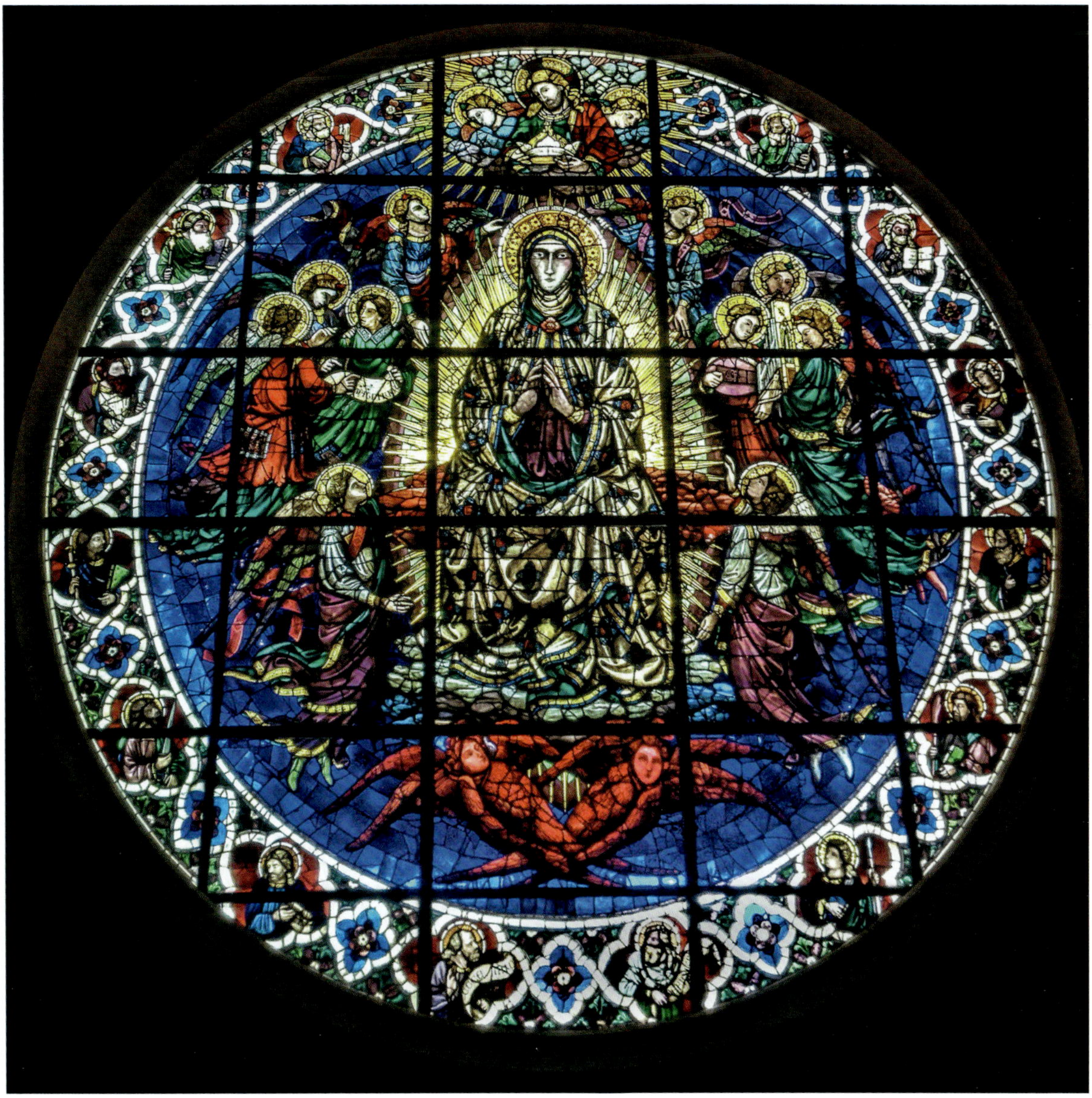

2 Lorenzo Ghiberti (designer) and Nicolò do Piero Tedescho, *Assumption of the Virgin*, 1405, Florence Cathedral

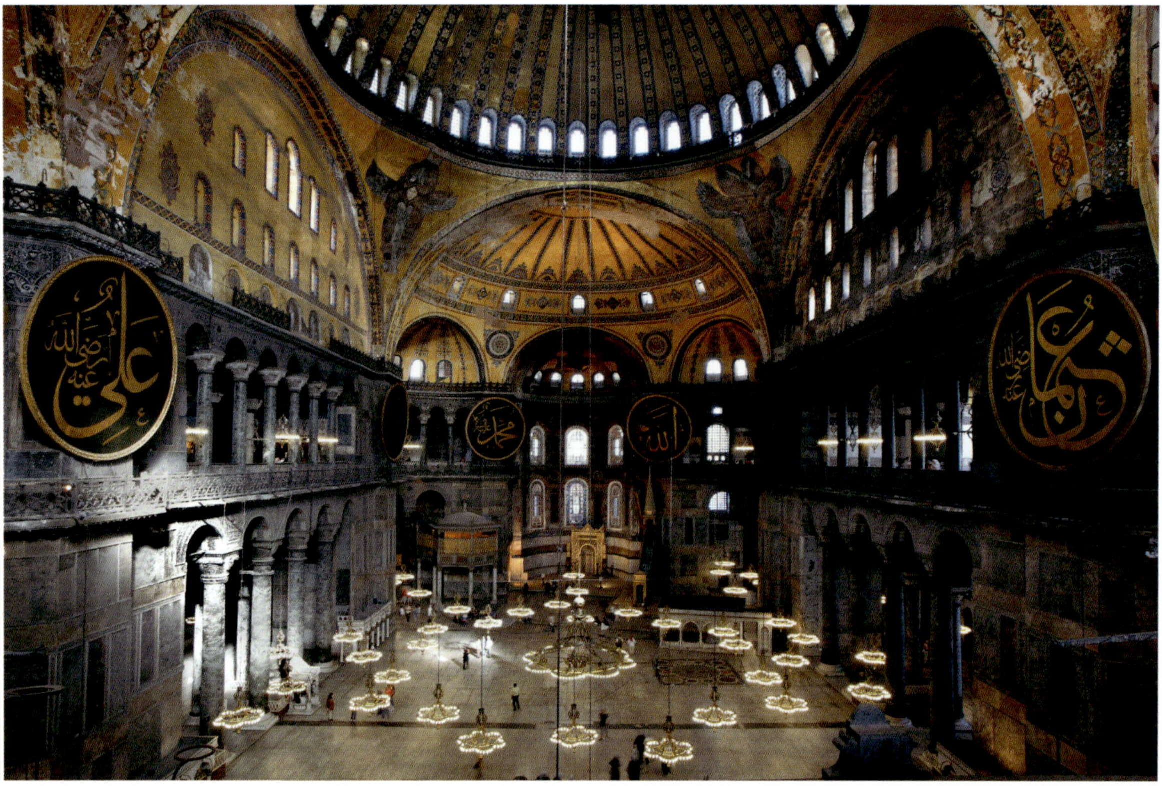

3 Hagia Sofia, interior, Istanbul

the heads of spectators – though these days most visitors look at features in the cathedral other than the brilliantly designed and executed windows.

When we turn to Islam, the truly magnificent domed space of Hagia Sophia, Istanbul, will provide a good starting point, since it was constructed by the Emperor Justinian I in the sixth century as the seat of the Christian Patriarch of Constantinople, before passing in successive periods through the hands of the Catholic Church (briefly) to the Ottomans from 1453 onwards. From 1935 it served a museum, as a world site of cultural pilgrimage, but in 2020 it was reclaimed solely for Islam by the Turkish president in defiance of much international opinion. In its earliest Eastern Orthodox incarnation it did not contain figurative images. Awesome space, the dome of heaven and brilliantly orchestrated light conveyed the sublime nature of the divine (fig.3). The architects, Isidorus of Miletus and Anthemius of Tralles, were both renowned as mathematicians. Looking at the truly extraordinary architecture, there is no shortage of features where mathematics could have been productively employed: the harmonic combinations of geometrical solids, rectilinear and curved; the engineering acumen needed to ensure that this grandest structure of its age would stand up; the calculated distribution of windows to irradiate the interior, particularly at key times of the day; and even the logistics to accomplish the construction. It was a building that subsequently served Islamic devotion superbly as a theatre of divine light – as the greatest mosque of all.

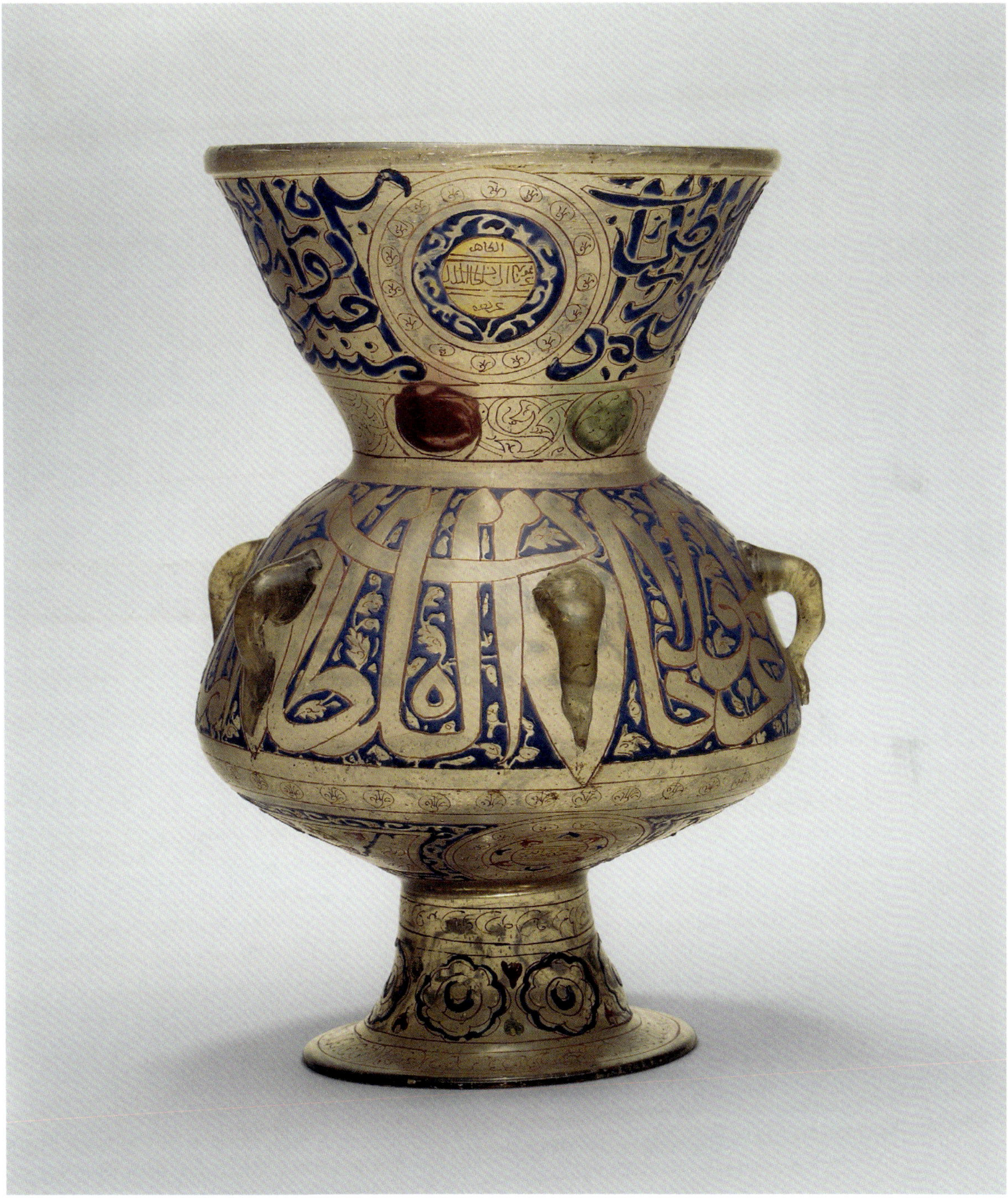

4 *Mosque Lamp of Sultan Barquq*, New York, Metropolitan Museum, enamelled and gilded glass

Islam is characterised by the same proscription of figurative images as occurs in Judaism and in various phases of Christianity. In Islam, we do not see God dividing light from the darkness; rather, God is light. This idea is seen most clearly in hugely prestigious, technically sophisticated and beautiful mosque lamps, which are typically inscribed with texts extracted from the account of God as light in the Quran.

> God is the Light of the heavens and earth. His Light is like this: there is a niche, and in it a lamp, the lamp inside a glass, a glass like a glittering star, fuelled from a blessed olive tree from neither east nor west, whose oil almost gives light even when no fire touches it – light upon light – God guides whoever He will to his Light; God draws such comparisons for people; God has full knowledge of everything – shining out in houses of worship. God has ordained that they be raised high and that His name be remembered in them, with men in them celebrating His glory morning and evening.[9]

The lamps from the Mamluk era are also typically inscribed with the name of the distinguished person for whom they were made, sometimes to be placed in their funerary chambers as a vital aid to salvation. The lamps in the Hagia Sophia were conceived as a gift of light to the mosque and hung in series from great circular chandeliers. A lamp in New York's Metropolitan Museum from the later 14th century records with pride that it was made for 'the Sultan, the Victorious King, Abu Said, may God make him triumphant' (fig.4). Amongst the calligraphic inscriptions, that on the neck of the lamp reads, 'God is the Light of the heavens and earth. His Light is like this: there is a niche, and in it a lamp'. Seen *en masse* in their original settings, with the light of the burning oil radiating through the coloured glass, the lamps perform their roles very differently from when they are housed in the glass cases of museums with external illumination.

By looking at a mosque lamp from Islam and a stained-glass window from Florence by Ghiberti, we have embarked on a converging track for our encounter with the kind of optical science with which Dante was familiar. The link with Italian art is not so unexpected: the role of Islam is more surprising. We will find that the superb text on optics by Ibn al-Haytham (often called Alhazen) laid the foundations for the theories that Dante absorbed. Both traditions, the Christian and the Islamic, were nourished by the divinity of light.

RULES, ANCIENT AND MODERN

Since classical antiquity, optics has been a prominent and much admired science. Nowhere in nature was mathematics more apparent than in the rules obeyed by light in direct vision, reflection and refraction. The two giants of Greek philosophy, Plato and Aristotle, devoted due attention to acts of seeing – and laid the foundation for a vigorously enduring dispute. Did the eye see by taking light in from outside, the Aristotelian position, or, as Plato maintained, by emitting an inner visual fire that merges with external light to produce vision? In retrospect the answer seems so obvious as to brook no disagreement. However, if we have to explain how the eye creates order from the continuous deluge of light and colour that surrounds us, and we have no conception of the lens of the eye focusing orderly 'pictures' onto the retina, the idea that the eye sends out purposeful probes does not seem so implausible. Broadly speaking, those students of optics in classical antiquity who favoured an organic and physical approach advocated the intromission of light into the eyes, while those who revered and practised geometry were inclined to support the extramission of rays from the eye.

The geometrical tradition was established by the greatest of all geometers, Euclid. His *Optics* succinctly lays the grounds for the geometrical discernment of size and distance, courtesy of the visual cone or pyramid, which has its base in what is seen and its apex in the eye. The straight rays in the cone operate as measuring devices, detecting whether something is seen at a greater or lesser angle. The cone was to become crucial for later optics and for the calculation of perspective by painters. Euclid begins by assuming that 'the rectilinear rays proceeding from the eye diverge indefinitely', but he does not engage directly with the intromission and extramission debates, which do not affect the basic geometry of seeing.[10] The mathematical aspects received fuller treatment in the surviving extracts from the *Optics* of Ptolemy, who stressed the primacy of the central axis of the visual cone, an idea that was certainly transmitted to Dante. Ptolemy was also the first person to define the three standard parts of optics: direct vision, reflection and refraction.

The third tradition looks at the actual anatomy of the eye, and is most fully expressed in the writings of the Alexandrian philosopher and anatomist Galen. According to him, the eye is a geometrically designed instrument of some complexity that emits rays and uses the air as a sensory agent. He describes the 'crystalline humour' (an early term for the lens), located in the anterior portion of the eye, as the site of vision, supported and surrounded by a complex array of roughly concentric coats and internal humours of varied consistency. The optic nerves that depart from the rear of the eye are hollow and designed to emit *pneuma* (a kind of spirit) into the air in such way that it could interact with the visual faculties in the brain.

In the Mediaeval tradition, with which we are primarily concerned here, the physical, geometrical and anatomical came to be worked into various kinds of syntheses. The writings of Islamic philosophers of the ninth and tenth centuries were crucial to bringing together various traditions. In looking at how this big, sustained and complex synthesis became integral to Christian 'natural science' in the Middle Ages, I will draw particular attention to two key texts. The first is the extensive treatise on optics by the major philosopher Ibn al-Haytham and known in Latin translation as *De Aspectibus* (*On Sight*) or *Perspectiva*. The second is the *Perspectiva communis* (*Standard Optics*) by John Pecham (or Peckham). These choices do not mean that they were direct sources for Dante (as will become apparent), but that they serve to define the kind of optics that so richly informed Dante's writings. The first work is one of the finest texts in the history of science, written in Egypt in the earlier part of the 11th century and collating a wide array of classical and Islamic science. It stands in a great Arab tradition that includes the powerful refutation of the extramission theory by Avicenna (Ibn Sina), and Al-Kindi's comprehensive review of optical science in which he defends extramission. The second book is by an English 13th-century Franciscan who became Archbishop of Canterbury, and it was intended as a compact synthesis of optical knowledge gleaned from a wide variety of sources, not least Ibn al-Haytham. The number of manuscript and (later) of printed editions indicate that Pecham's treatise came to serve as a textbook. The two texts will serve to frame our introduction to Mediaeval optics. I will treat Ibn al-Haytham at greater length, because he established the foundations for the European philosophers, including Pecham.

A comprehensive resumé of Ibn al-Haytham's *De Aspectibus* lies beyond the scope of this introductory chapter. I will concentrate on some aspects of his treatment of direct vision that feed into the subsequent sections of this book.

The first thing to say is that *De Aspectibus* contains some remarkable science. It allies ingenious optical mathematics with the structure of the eye, optical experiments and real-life observations, all conducted with rigorous logic. The opening book of Ibn al-Haytham's very large treatise is devoted to the 'manner of vision in general', dealing with the properties of light, sight and the way that we see, including the anatomy of the eye. This immediately announces that he is merging the mathematical, physical and anatomical aspects of earlier traditions, with the addition of his own experimental bent. Some of his experiments involve the admission of light into 'dark chambers' through varied apertures, to demonstrate the tracks of light in straight lines. He is led to conclude that 'from every part of every self-luminous body, light radiates in every straight line radiating from that part'.[11] This will present Ibn al-Haytham with the task of saying how the eye can cope coherently with this bombardment of rays.

Ibn al-Haytham continues in the second book to 'visible properties, their causes and manner of perception', defining no less than 21 of them, including light and colour, distance, size, number, motion and rest, darkness, beauty and ugliness. Each property is treated in turn. This sounds like a recipe for a Leonardo, who similarly listed multiple visual properties on more than one occasion.

The third book is dedicated to 'errors of direct vision and their causes', picking up a theme extensively explored by Ptolemy. Errors arise from the limitation of sight in the face of extreme light effects that lie 'outside the range of moderateness', as when something is too far away, too fast or visible for too short a time. Examples of things that move briskly in such a way as not to be clearly perceived include a spinning top and a revolving millstone.[12]

Particularly relevant to our present quest is an error that he mentions in the first book:

> *On the Effect of Light upon Sight*
> We find that when the eye looks at extremely strong lights it is pained and distressed by them. Thus when an observer looks at the body of the sun he cannot bear to gaze at it ... Similarly, when he looks at a polished mirror irradiated by sunlight, with his eyes at the point to which the light is reflected from the mirror ... he is unable to open them to meet it.
>
> We also find that when the observer looks for some length of time at a whole body irradiated by sunlight, then turns his eye from it to an obscure or dimly lit place, he can hardly gain a true perception of the visible objects in that place, as if experiencing a screen between himself and them.[13]

The 'pain' experienced by the eye was not a new observation by al-Haytham, but he subsequently expressed the effect of 'after-images' of bright objects with considerable subtlety. The painful effect of strong light *entering* the eye became an important argument in favour of the intromission theory. We will find that Dante not only experienced the 'pain' on a number of occasions in the *Divina Commedia*, but also the slow adjustment of sight after the light had overwhelmed him. More generally, the 'errors of direct vision' as defined by al-Haytham are of great relevance to Dante's struggles to understand what he seems to be seeing.

Al-Haytham's account of the structure of the eye is largely drawn from Galen, though with a few divergences. An image of the structure is shown here from a printed edition (fig.5). The outer coat is the protective *conjunctiva* occupying the eye socket (labelled *tunica adhaerens* in the illustration). It is of a white and greasy consistency and is penetrated at its anterior surface to allow light to enter. Next comes the *cornea*, which is thin, tough and transparent. Inside is the *albigineous* (or *aqueous*) humour, which is liquid and transparent and is contained by the *uvea*, which is black and penetrated at the front by the pupil. Inside and towards the middle of the eye are the *crystalline humour* and the *vitreous humour*, configured as portions of spheres (not accurately portrayed in the woodcut) and enclosed by a delicate membrane, the *aranea*. The crystalline humour is translucent but of sufficient density to pick up the images that are registered by the 'visual spirit' coming from the brain via the optic nerves. The incoming and converging rays are refracted before the visual cone tapers to a point. Although later accounts work variations on this structure, they share the basic constituents of coats (or 'tunics') and humours.

This is all very well, but we may recall that, 'from every part of every self-luminous body, light radiates in every straight line radiating from that part', which means that each point on the crystalline humour will receive light from the whole field in front of the eye.[14]

How can orderly images result from this? An answer is needed if the intromission theory is to survive. Al-Haytham's answer lies in the geometry of the eyeball and the laws of refraction. At any point on the anterior surface of the eye's sphere only one ray of the many that arrive will impact perpendicularly and will be unrefracted.

> Only one among all the points confronting the eye, which have simultaneously arrived at that point on the surface of the eye, will have travelled along the perpendicular to that point on the eye's surface, while the forms of all the other points reach that point along the eye's surface along inclined lines … Only the form of a single point among all of them will rectilinearly pass through the transparency of the eye's coats, namely the point at the extremity of the perpendicular drawn to that point on the eye's surface.[15]

Refraction – and the one unrefracted ray at each point on the curved surfaces in the eye – acts to select what is registered in the crystalline humour by the visual spirit. This optical-geometrical mechanism accomplishes what the focusing lens would achieve more effectively in Johannes Kepler's account of vision in the early 17th century. It became standard in later accounts of optics, including those known to Dante. His own account of the structure of the eye in his *Convivio* is a neatly simplified version of the complex Mediaeval eye, and he certainly understood the primacy of the unrefracted ray as we will see in chapter 2.

Before passing on to optics in the Middle Ages in Europe, it is worth pausing to say that it is not automatic for a culture which has developed sophisticated optical science to favour representations that are based on optical naturalism. Only in a culture in which figurative images are based in some way upon natural appearance can the optics of seeing come into play. This is where the Islamic proscription of images of God and of the Prophet creates a sharp divergence

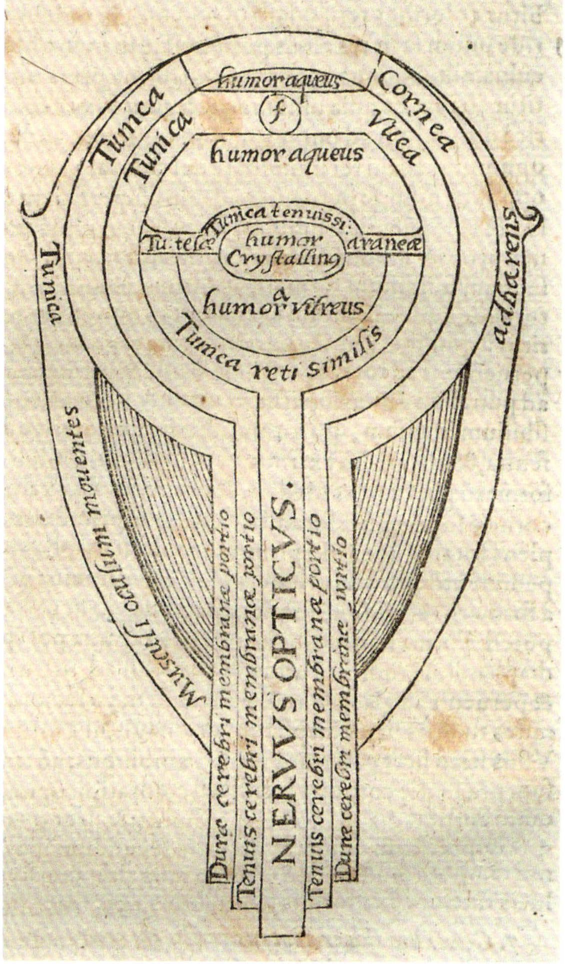

5 Ibn al-Haytham, *The Tunics and Humours of the Eye*, in *Opticae thesaurus*, ed. F. Risner, Basel, 1572

from the figurative tradition that occupies the rest of this book.

Our second exemplar is one of three English Franciscans who made distinguished contributions to the science of optics. Pecham learnt much from his monastic colleague Roger Bacon, who included substantial treatments of optics in his *Opus majus*, his ambitious compendium of universal learning. Part five of Bacon's grand treatise sometimes appeared separately

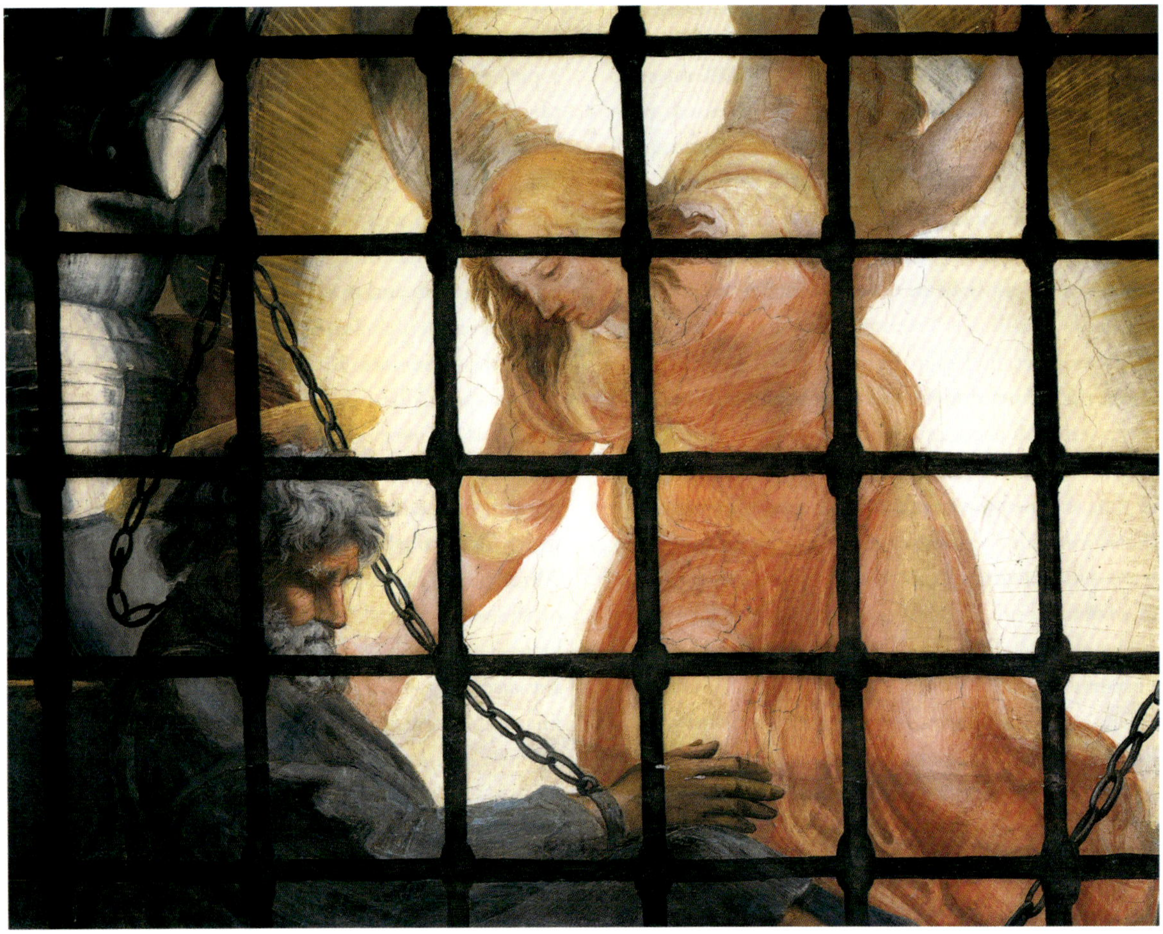

Raphael, *St Peter in Prison* (detail), Rome, Vatican

2

Dante's Dazzle

Paradiso by Dante Alighieri is the most dazzling evocation of divine light in any artform from any period. It comprises the third 'book' (or canticle) of his *Divina Commedia*, written during the first and second decades of the 14th century while in exile from Florence. His expulsion from his beloved city is neatly described by Giovanni di Paolo in one of his illustrations for *Paradiso* (fig.6). Dante had been highly active in the shifting world of Florentine politics, and his faction ended up on the wrong side of power. This greatest of all poems was probably begun around 1307 and we know that *Inferno* was finished by 1317. *Paradiso* may not have been finished until close to his death in 1321. The complete work is huge by poetic standards, particularly for a poem in the Italian vernacular. A much-respected modern translation contains well over fifty-five thousand words.[1] It consists of 14,233 lines. Each canticle – *Inferno*, *Purgatorio* and *Paradiso* – is divided into 33 cantos with an additional introductory canto in the *Inferno*, making 100 in all. Each of the cantos comprises sets of three lines, in each of which the first rhymes with the third, in what is called a *terza rima*.

Along his monumental journey the poet is conducted successively on tours of Hell and Purgatory by the revered Roman poet Virgil, who is a pagan, and finally guided into the spiritual realms of Paradise by his beloved Beatrice, almost certainly the daughter of Folco Portinari. The poet had idolised her from a distance in Florence and had accorded her a quasi-divine status after her early death in 1290 at the age of 25.

Inferno, the first of the three canticles, is the most vivid, replete with a strikingly varied repertoire of notable sins and picturesque sinners – in keeping with the cliché that the devil has the best tunes. The constantly tortured sinners inhabit the terraces of a deep, conical well from which there is no escape. *Purgatorio*, the subject of the canticle that follows, does not feature in the Bible. It was conceived in the Middle Ages as a halfway house in which certain sinners who had not adequately repented can nevertheless be redeemed for admission to heaven, even if they had been excommunicated by the Church authorities of the time. Purgatory, as pictured by Dante, is also terraced, but this time as a tapering mountain, the peak of which is the Garden of Eden or Earthly Paradise and provides access to the heavenly Paradise. The time spent in Purgatory, which was far from comfortable, was proportionate to the nature of the subject's sins. In Dante, it is also peopled by characters with memorable stories to tell. The sublime realm of heavenly *Paradiso* is less varied visually, as Dante and Beatrice ascend though the planetary and heavenly spheres of spiritual wonder to the ultimate vision of divinity (as far as this is possible for an earthly man).

High virtue is less varied than inventive sins. The inner spheres are those occupied by the celestial bodies: the

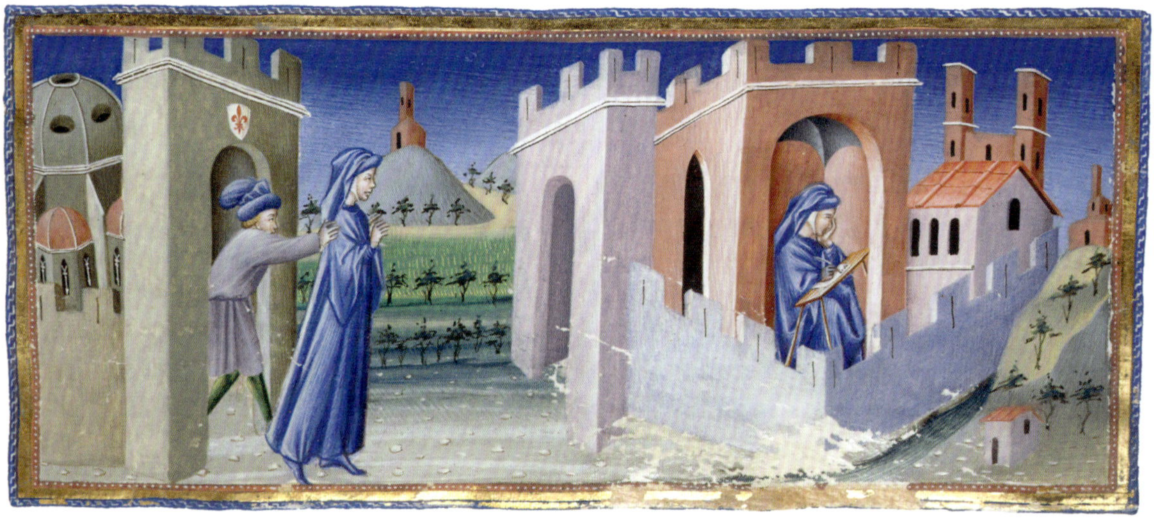

6 Giovanni di Paolo, *Dante Expelled from Florence and Writing in Exile*, in Dante Alighieri, *Divina Commedia*, British Library, Yates Thompson, 36, fol. 159

Moon, Mercury, Venus, the Sun, Mars, Jupiter, Saturn, and the fixed stars. Outside this is the *Primum Mobile*, the source of motion for the whole system, which is in turn surrounded by the *Empyrean*, the ineffable realm of pure light occupied by God and the blessed. The spirits of the saints whom Dante encounters, such as St James, St Thomas Aquinas and St Bernard of Clairvaux, instruct him in subtle questions of theology. The divine and elect spirits inhabit upper zones radiant with glowing displays of ever greater luminosity, infused by sweet sounds. Ultimately Dante's human faculties, which Beatrice repeatedly helps him to transcend, are overwhelmed.

Dante is the most scientific, philosophical, theological and visionary of poets. His treatment of light in *Paradiso* is the supreme manifestation of this complex conjunction of deep learning and soaring imagination. On the one hand his understanding of light as a phenomenon is what we would call scientific – based on a considerable grasp of the kind of Mediaeval optics we have already encountered. On the other, his poetic and theological vision of light is full of effusive rapture. As with Leonardo da Vinci, one does not 'influence' the other. Imagination and learning are somehow simultaneously present and valid within the unified compass of their minds. To describe what is happening in their own Italian, which is more musical than English, *intelletto* and *fantasia* (imagination) are acting in concert. The result is a union of *scienza* and *poesia*, an astonishing compact that few have ever achieved. Where Dante differs decisively from Leonardo is that the behaviour of divine light in *Paradiso* is quite different from that dictated by terrestrial optics. For Leonardo, optical science is as full a manifestation of the divine as we can experience.

THE VITA NOVA AND CONVIVIO

Light and optical phenomena feature prominently in the two sets of commentaries on his own poems that Dante wrote before the *Commedia*. The first is the *Vita Nova* or *Vita Nuova* (*New Life*) which was composed about 1292; the second is the *Convivio* (*Banquet*), written in the early years of the next century. They both consist of poetic verses imbedded in prose texts that comment on them, not least from a biographical standpoint. The *Vita Nova* is more visionary and metaphysical, accompanied by fervent biographical reflections. Its verses are far less affected by science than his later writings, though Dante does draw some astronomy and philosophy into the prose comments. Two visual themes are already present as seeds that are to undergo vigorous germination in the *Convivio* and the *Commedia*. The first words that deal with the subject of the *Vita Nova* introduce us to the primacy of light in the sublime machinery of the visible heavens:

> Nine times, the heaven of the light had already returned to where it was at my birth, almost to the same point according to its orbit, when the glorious lady of my mind first appeared before my eyes ... She had already been in this life long enough for the heaven of the fixed stars to have moved toward the east a twelfth of a degree since she was born, so that she was at the beginning of her ninth year when she appeared to me.[2]

This is an astronomically portentous way of saying that Dante himself was almost nine years old when he first saw Beatrice; she was four months older than eight years.

In the first of the three *canzoni* (poems) in the *Vita Nova*, the second of the big motifs appears, the failure of sight to withstand the highest stimulus, in this case the light of the beloved lady's eyes.

> From out of her eyes, according to how they move,
> Come spirits aflame with Love;
> They strike the eyes of anyone who looks at that moment
> And penetrate in such a way that each one finds the heart;
> There you will see Love painted on her face.
> Where no-one may fix his attention.[3]

Such a failure, whether of the senses or the mind, whether involving the beauty of his lady's eyes or the most radiant forms of light, is a recurrent feature of the sublime and transcendent sights and sounds that the poet experiences.

Dante also gives his first acknowledgement that there is a special direct (perpendicular) ray that penetrates our sight more than any other. He speaks of 'the woman who had been situated midpoint in the straight line that proceeded from that most gracious lady, Beatrice, and reached its end in my eyes'.[4] This was to become an important motif.

The *Convivio* adopts a comparable format of poems imbedded in the discursive text, but the whole is far more overtly learned, and the commentaries frequently develop a life of their own, springing from the content of the poems into wide-ranging expositions of philosophical matters. The opening sentence immediately signals this ambition: 'As the Philosopher says at the beginning of the *First Philosophy*, all men by nature desire to know'. The 'Philosopher', as he was known in the Middle Ages, was Aristotle, the ancient Greek authority whose encyclopaedic thoughts had been integrated into much of Mediaeval philosophy. The *First Philosophy* was what we now know as the *Metaphysics*. The subsequent texts are rich in philosophical and theological name-dropping. Dante's reading of the ancients and moderns must have been prodigious, even if we allow for some citing of authors he had not read at first hand.

Optics, comprising both the phenomena of light and the operation of the eye, feature prominently, enlarging substantially on the two themes we identified in the *Vita Nova*, namely the primacy of light in the universe and the limitations of our apparatus of vision. The third *trattato* (treatise or book) of the *Convivio*, which contains his learned commentaries on the second of the three of the *canzoni* (literally 'songs', but signalling a poem) is especially rich in its poetic evoking and intellectual analysis of light and sight. Along the way he cites the ancients, including Pythagoras and Plato, the Islamic philosopher Avicenna, the giant of European Mediaeval thought Albertus Magnus – and, of course, Aristotle on a repeated basis. It is unclear how much of this learning actually went into the making of the poems and how much was cleverly drawn out of them. In the *Convivio* Dante wears his learning conspicuously and not always lightly. Let us look in turn at light and the eye.

As a basic proposition, Dante insists that only colour and light are the primary subjects of sight. In his commentary on the line in the poem 'You know the sky is always bright and clear' (even if the dispositions of the heavenly bodies sometimes make it appear dark), he reminds us that

> Here we should know strictly speaking that what is visible is colour and light, as Aristotle argues in the second book of his *On the Soul* and in his treatise *On Sense and the Sensibles*.[5]

The study of the behaviour of light is the science of *perspettiva* (or *prospettiva*) from the Latin *perspectiva*. It is a mathematical discipline of high status, gaining dignity from geometry.

> As Euclid says, the point is the beginning of this [geometry], and, as he says, the circle is its most perfect figure, which must therefore be adopted as its end. As between its beginning and end, geometry moves between the point and the circle and these two are inimical to certainty; for the point in itself cannot be measured because of its indivisibility, and it is impossible to square the circle perfectly because of its curvature, and so it cannot be measured precisely. Geometry is furthermore the most inviolate [most white] in that it is without the stain of error and is most certain both in itself and in its handmaid, which is called *perspettiva*.[6]

The point and the circle therefore share a kind of ineffability since they are not subject to precise, enumerated measure.

Optics is integral to the geometry we witness in the planets, the precise positions of which are 'manifest and determined, according to the discipline called *perspettiva*, and arithmetic and geometry, seen by sense and reason, and by other sensory experiences'.[7] Like his Mediaeval predecessors, Dante saw optics as the most important terrestrial science. It demonstrated God's perfection as a geometer, both in itself and as the tool with which to observe the geometry of the heavens, which stood as the most sublime demonstration of the virtue that God has infused into his creation. As we are told in the biblical 'Wisdom of Solomon', God has 'ordered all things in measure and number and weight'.[8] This divine order was literally reflected by his radiant angels, whom Beatrice is now emulating.

> Here we must further know that the first agent, namely God, instils his power into things by means of direct radiance or by means of reflected light. Thus the divine light sends rays forth into the Intelligences without mediation, and is reflected into the other things by these Intelligences which are first illuminated.[9]

The mention of reflected light prompts Dante to distinguish between three types of 'light', citing Avicenna:

> Philosophers are accustomed to call light '*luce*', when it is considered in its source, '*raggio*' [ray] when it is considered in the medium from its origin to the body at which it is terminated, and '*splendore*' when it strikes some other illuminated area.[10]

Splendore is a tricky term. It refers to the brightness of light on a surface, and can partake of the nature of illumination, highlight, gleam or shine according to the qualities of the surface.

This distinction between the actual source of light, say, the sun or a candle, the rays that pass through the air carrying the likenesses of things, and the resulting illumination when the rays 'percuss' a surface is crucial for understanding the conceptions of light within the science and art of the Middle Ages, Baroque and Renaissance. *Splendore* would be particularly vivid on shiny bodies. Dante discusses this with reference to Albertus Magnus.[11]

> We see the sun's light, derived from one source, received diversely by bodies, as Albert says in his book *On the Intellect*. Because of the high degree of transparent clearness mixed within them, certain bodies become so luminous as soon as the sun sees them that by multiplying the light inside them and on their surfaces they render a great splendour [*splendore*] upon other bodies, as do gold and other stones. There are others which, because they are entirely transparent, not only receive the light but do not impede it, rather rendering it to other things, coloured with their own colour. And there are others so assertive in the purity of their transparency as to become so radiant that they overwhelm the harmonious operation of the eye and cannot be looked upon without exhausting our vision, as occurs with mirrors.[12]

We have already encountered this notion of sight being overwhelmed, and it will become a signal theme in the *Paradiso*.

This optical discourse is triggered by lines in Dante's second *canzone*: 'Love that speaks to me within my mind'. He tells us that 'Into her [Beatrice] descends a celestial power / As it does into an angel that sees him [God]'. This infused power is radiated by her eyes directly into the ravaged heart of the besotted lover. The poem continues:

> In her countenance appear such things
> As exhibit a part of the joy of Paradise.
> I mean in her eyes and in her sweet smile,
> For here Love bears them as if to his lair.
> They overwhelm our intellect,
> As a ray of sunlight does weak vision.[13]

Dante's commentary enlarges on this collapse of intellect, which is analogous to the overwhelming of sight by excessive stimulation.

> Then when it says *They overwhelm our intellect*, I excuse myself by saying that I can say little about these things because of their transcendence. Here we must understand that in a certain way these things dazzle our intellect, in as much as certain things are affirmed to exist which our intellect cannot observe, that is to say God, eternity, and primal matter, things which most certainly are known to exist and are with full faith believed to exist. But given the nature of their essence we cannot understand them.[14]

In the arena of our earthbound senses, within the context of the physical phenomena of the material world, there are extremes that lie outside the scope of our vision, as Ibn al-Haytham and subsequent authors had recognised. This shortcoming provides a ready analogy that can help us understand the inaccessible nature of supreme truths to our 'dazzled' intellect.

There is a personal dimension to this failure of sight. Dante concludes this section of the commentary with an effective account of his own experience:

> In the same year in which this *canzone* was born by greatly straining my vision through studious reading, I so weakened my visual spirits that the stars seemed to me completely overshadowed by a kind of white haze. And by resting at length in dark and cool places and by cooling the balls of my eyes with clear water, I regained that power that had degraded, so that I returned to my former state of vision.[15]

For Dante, his damaged sight offers just one instance of how something might not appear as it is, given the variability of our visual faculty and the complexity of visual phenomena.

The eye itself needs to be understood if we are to grasp how sight operates. The passage in which Dante describes his own eye problems is preceded by a detailed account of the eye's functioning, gleaned from Mediaeval texts (including commentaries on Aristotle by Thomas

Aquinas and Albertus Magnus) in which the analogies of the mirror and the ball were widely used.

> These visible things … come into the eye – I do not mean the things themselves but their 'forms' – through the diaphanous medium, not in reality but as a potentiality, as if through transparent glass. The passage that the visible form makes through this medium is completed in the water within the pupil of the eye, because that water has a boundary – almost like a mirror, which is glass backed by lead – so that it cannot pass any further but is arrested there like a ball that is stopped when it strikes something, so that the 'form', which cannot be seen in the transparent medium, now appears lucid and defined. This is why an image is seen in leaded glass, and not in any other glass. The visual spirit, which passes from the pupil to the front of the brain where is the sensitive power, and where it is represented without passage of time, and thus we see it.[16]

Dante's anatomy of the eye is a good deal simpler than that of the specialist authors on perspective. The 'forms' that are transmitted are images, corresponding to the 'species' or 'semblances' that radiate from illuminated objects, as characterised in earlier optical theory.

Earlier, when commenting on the way that the flames of Beatrice's eye penetrate unimpeded to his heart, he again draws upon the physiology of the eye.

> Here it should be known that although many things can enter the eye at the same time, it is true that whatever enters along a straight line into the centre of the pupil is truly seen and is the only one that imprints itself upon the imagination. This is because the nerve along which the visual spirit runs is orientated to this part. And therefore one eye cannot really look into another eye unless it is seen by it, just as the one who aims their sight receives the form in the pupil along a straight line, so along that same line its own form departs into the one it aims at; and many times along the extension of this line is discharged the bow of him against whom all weapons are feeble.[17]

The Mediaeval texts characterised the image imprinted on the receptive aspects of our 'imagination' as similar to the impression of a seal on the wax used to secure a letter or certify a document – an analogy that derives ultimately from Aristotle's *De Anima*.[18]

The axial ray, which locks the lovers' eyes into rectilinear combat, was crucial to the Mediaeval theory of vision, as we have noted. In Leon Battista Alberti's little book, *On Painting* (1435/6), it is called the 'prince of rays', and where it strikes the picture plane will be the 'point of convergence' of the perspective construction. The remorseless directness of the ray that passes directly to the centre of the pupil is both a source of strength to our visual system and leaves it vulnerable to extreme stimulus. Cupid's special skill is to shoot his arrow straight and true into the pupil and optic nerve of the lover, a motif we have already noticed in the *Vita Nova*.

INFERNO AND *PURGATORIO*

In contrast to the *Vita Nova* and the *Convivio*, the mighty text of the *Divina Commedia* stands on its own, without the author's elaborate and erudite guidance. It is of course a great literary masterpiece – none is definitely greater – but it is also a visual masterpiece. This applies above all to the actual act of seeing. Repeatedly Dante tells us how he turned his eyes on one of the characters or scenes that he encounters on his journey with Virgil and latterly with Beatrice. His seeing ranges from the uncertainties of foggy darkness to the struggles of his eyes to withstand the most brilliant of heavenly light. The word for eye – *occhio* and the plural *occhi* – features on 263 occasions in the *Commedia*. By contrast, God warrants 133 mentions. There are lovely observations of seeing. A typical one occurs in the 15th canto of *Inferno* when Dante tells how

... we encountered a troop of spirits
Who came along the bank, and each one of them
Looked at us, just as one might do at evening,
To see someone under a new noon;
They peered at us with knitted brows,
As an old tailor does, threading a needle.[19]

There is a real dilemma in how to handle Dante's incredibly rich array of observations about acts of seeing and the light that enables us to perform these acts in the *Divina Commedia*. My solution is to track the course of his journey more or less in sequence across the three realms, picking out some prominent signposts and landmarks along the way. These will be chosen specifically for their resonance with the way artists tackled the task of portraying divine light.

As we might expect, *Inferno* is a place of shades, dark and gloomy, as with the 'black air' which castigates one set of sinners.[20] There are occasional discomforting flashes of lurid illumination: 'the weeping earth exudes a wind that flames with vermilion light and triumphs over all my senses'.[21] The oppressive air was not conducive to clear seeing. The most dramatic instance of false seeing in the foggy gloom is when Dante thinks he percieves a 'cluster of high towers' and wonders which city they are approaching. Virgil explains that 'because your sight must travel through the darkness from too great a distance, your imagination becomes confused'.[22] It transpires that the towers are fearsome giants, buried up to their waists in a well. Just as Dante is too confused by dazzle in *Paradiso*, so his sight is befuddled by heavy shade. Both extremes lie outside the 'range of moderateness' that Ibn al-Haytham had defined. Again, the 'imagination' to which Dante refers is the kind that Mediaeval brain science characterised as responsible for receiving impressions.

Purgatorio is realm of modest natural light, tempered by some anticipatory glimpses of the divine light inhabitants could expect if they performed their penance in the stipulated manner. It opens with an act of encouraging seeing:

Sweet colour of oriental sapphire,
Which hover in the serene aspect
Of the medium, pure up to the first orbit,
Brought back pleasure to my eyes
Once I had left the deathly aura
That had afflicted my eyes and breast.
The lovely planet that gives comfort with love
Made all the east to smile
...
I turned towards the right, and fixed my mind
On the other pole, and there I saw four stars,
Never seen except by the first people.[23]

Dante is observing the planet Venus. The four stars, seen only by Adam and Eve before their fall, are the four cardinal Virtues: Justice, Prudence, Temperance and Fortitude. The first two cantos are characterised by modulations of light of various kinds, affecting both what is seen and Dante's emotions.

Divine brightness could operate more directly in *Purgatorio*, as when an angel he encounters in the second canto initially appears in the distance as an aggregation of incoherent whiteness before crystallising visually as a 'divine bird' whose radiance Dante's eyes (typically) could not withstand.[24] The same kind of radiance occurs a little later when two angels with flaming swords arrive whose bright faces 'confound' Dante's sight.[25] In the next canto an angel's inherent light is so powerful that even its reflection from the angel's sword repeatedly repel the poet's 'vain' attempts to look at it.[26] Another such heavenly apparition beyond Dante's sight 'veils its figure in a superfluity of light ... and with its light conceals himself'.[27] Later Dante describes the luminosity of another dazzling angel as greater even than that of 'glass or metal in a furnace, so luminous and red'.[28]

On one occasion, the wondrous light performs in an optical manner analogous to that on earth – or that at least is what Dante thinks is happening. He is subject once more to the dazzling light of an angel and he raises his hand to shade his eyes. The light still gets to him, apparently by reflection from some other surface.

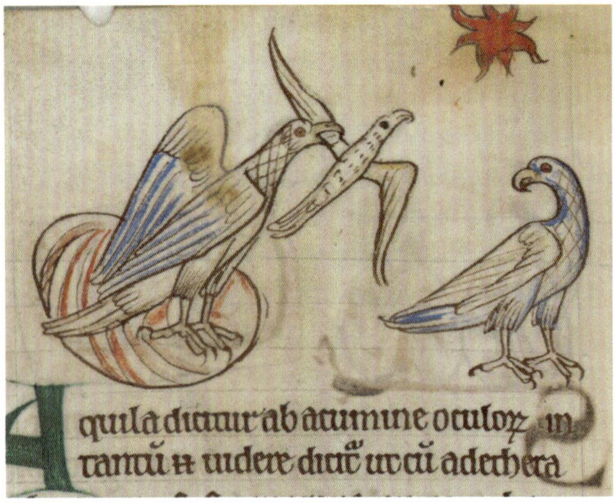

7 *An Eaglet Being Trained to Look at the Sun*, in *Isidori etymologiae et synonyma, bestiarius etc.* 12th century, Corpus Christi College, Cambridge, CCCC MS 22 fol. 166v

as 'submerged in error'. One of her counter-arguments actually relies upon the kind of optics with which Dante was familiar, using 'experiment [*esperienza*] ... which is the only source for the streams of your learned disciplines [*arti*].'[41] He is told to take three mirrors, two at equal distance in front of him, and a third further away. A light is to be placed behind Dante in such a way that it strikes all the mirrors, which are visible to him. Though the size of the image in the more distant mirror will be smaller than in the others, its brightness will not be less. Beatrice's explanation is intended to 'reform your [Dante's] intellect, and serve to inform you with a light so vivid that you will tremble at its appearance.'[42] Beatrice's conclusive argument is essentially theological, adducing the diverse 'essences' of the heavenly bodies according to divine creation. The moon and the other heavenly bodies are diverse because that is how God has conceived them. The explanation is a matter of divine will rather than yielding to Dante's optical logic.

This does not mean that Dante can resist resorting to optics. In the third canto he encounters pale and elusive faces, which he assumes are reflections.

As through a glass which is transparent and polished,
Or through limpid and tranquil water,
Not so deep that its bed is lost from view,
The details of our faces are reflected
So faintly, that a pearl on a white forehead
Does not come less strongly to our pupils.
...
Thinking that they were reflected images,
I turned my eyes to see to see whose they were;
And saw nothing ...[43]

Since the faces are those of immaterial and ephemeral spirits, Dante's optical assumptions are confounded. Characteristically, the physics of reflection is translated into poetic mythology when the poet alludes to 'the man in love with the pool'; that is to say, Narcissus who fell fatally in love with his own watery reflection. As always, Dante's visual instincts are pictorially alert.

Some of the divine spirits remain visible only as lights so bright that their form is not otherwise discernible.

Just as the sun conceals itself
In too much light, when its heat has gnawed away
The thick and tempering vapours around it,
So with increasing joy the sacred figure
Hid the holy form from me within its rays.[44]

There are passages in *Paradiso* that are very taxing, dealing with erudite niceties of Mediaeval theology to which very few of us now have access. Following a long discourse by St Thomas, Beatrice and the learned saint expound complex theological truths as to whether the light with which the spirits now glow can endure when they are resurrected in the flesh – not least whether their light would be bearable to themselves. The answer by St Thomas is that there is yet another level of radiance to come.

... the effulgence that encircles us now
will be overcome in appearance by the flesh
that all the earth still covers.[45]

Dante is assured that the organs of the resurrected bodies will be capable of withstanding the new radiance. This almost certainly refers to St Augustine's argument in his fifth-century treatise the *City of God* that the resurrected will be supplied with new eyes capable of withstanding celestial light.[46] The chorus of those who accordingly desire their bodies is succeeded by an ecstatic display of spiritual lights and Beatrice's beauty that typically test the capacity of Dante's mortal eyes, before she and he ascend to the higher heaven of Mars, the red planet that was the fourth in succession from Earth. There Dante bears witness to 'those rays in the depth of Mars that form the venerable sign from the crossing of the fourth parts (quadrants) of the circle'; that is to say a cross inscribed within a circle.[47] In this cross Dante is dazzled by a vision of Christ that definitively exceeds his descriptive talent. It becomes increasingly evident as he ascends through the spheres in Paradise that his literary skills and even his words will fall short in the same way that his senses have done.

In evoking the vision of the cross, which glitters with internal scintillations of light, he turns to a physical analogy to which those of us on earth can relate (providing we are clever enough).

From side to side and from top to bottom
Moved the lights, sparkling strongly
As they met together and passed.
Thus are they seen straight and twisted,
Swift and slow, changing appearance,
Bodies of minute dimensions
Moving through the rays of light which sometimes
Streak across the shadow, which, for our protection,
Human ingenuity and skill produce.[48]

Like some other of Dante's 'scientific' analogies, this text requires quite a lot of imagination and knowledge on the part of the reader. He is referring to the beams of light that seep through partially open shutters (ingeniously made for our 'protection' from the summer sun) in which we can see leaping points of light, caused by tiny specks of airborne dust catching the illumination. As Dante may not have known, the Roman poet-philosopher Lucretius had adduced this phenomenon to support the idea that all things in nature were composed of 'atoms'.[49] It is described in Mediaeval texts, including some commentaries on Aristotle and the notable encyclopaedia by Isidore of Seville.[50] There is no sign that Dante supported atomic theory, which indeed found limited support in classical antiquity, but the beguiling optics of the brilliant and mobile particles obviously appealed to his visual imagination.

As we ascend with Dante and Beatrice though the planetary spheres, we regularly encounter the now familiar motif of the poet's sight becoming overwhelmed. Somehow Dante manages to keep the incidents fresh and varied. At one point, Beatrice forebears to smile because he 'would become what Semele became, when she was turned to ashes'.[51] The legend was that the thunderbolts of Jupiter, Semele's lover, reduced her to a pile of ashes, and from these ashes was born Bacchus, the god of wine. Beatrice goes on to say that were the brilliant light of her beauty not tempered, Dante would resemble 'a branch split apart by thunder'.[52]

Later, witnessing the hosts of Christ's triumph, manifested as thousands of lamps, he is irradiated by 'a living light through which shone a luminance so bright in my eyes that they could not bear it'.[53] Again, Dante is reliant on his beloved companion to rescue his powers of vision. There follow successive incidents of this kind, triggered by divine light or Beatrice's beauty, each subtly varied in circumstance and language.[54] Probably his longest period of non-seeing occurs when his sight is overwhelmed by St John the Evangelist; Dante compares this to observing the sun when it is only partially eclipsed. It is only after sustained theological instruction from St John and St James that he regains his sight in the following canto.[55]

Reflections in the eyes of Beatrice allow him to see a discernible vision of God's light and that emanating from the nine circles of the orders of angels. When he turns to look at the real thing,

I saw a point that radiated a light
So intense that the sight it burnt on
Had to close because of the powerful brilliance.[56]

The innermost circle, that of the Seraphim revolves so rapidly around the central point that it forms a 'circle of fire', a blurring of the sort explained in optical science as an 'error' of vision arising from excess speed. Dante is confused to see that the speed of the circles increases the nearer they are to the centre, because he knows that the closer a point is to the axle of a wheel the slower it moves. Again, Beatrice explains that the poet's terrestrial physics is not applicable in the heavenly realm.

Canto 30 brings all the dazzling motifs together in a wonderfully sustained ecstasy of sweet seeing. Dante's sight, after initially faltering, manages to cope with much of what is presented to him. Some excerpts will give a flavour of the vision he sees. It centres upon the massive sempiternal (all-enduring) rose, transcendently white, with thousands of petals that serve as thrones for the souls of the redeemed, including Beatrice. Angels circle around the rose like honey bees performing their sweet duties.

... as the sun does to the weakest eyes,
So the remembrance of her sweet smile
Did to my mind, as if cut off from myself
...
Just as a sudden flash of lightning which scatters
Visual spirits, and so deprives the eye
Of the ability to see even the most conspicuous
objects,
So did the living light shine around me;
And left me draped in such a veil of radiance
That nothing was visible to me.
'Always the love which makes this heaven quiet
Offers greetings with a salutation like this
To make the candle ready for the flame'.
These brief words had no sooner entered me
Than I became aware that I had
Surmounted above and beyond my powers;
And I was so fortified with new sight
That there was no light, however clear,
Which my eyes could not resist.
I saw light in the form of a flowing stream
Of radiance, between two banks,
painted with the marvels of springtime.
...
O splendour of God, through which I saw
The exalted triumph of the true kingdom,
Grant me the power to say how I saw it!
The light up there renders visible
The creator of that creature
Who only finds peace in seeing him.
...
So, rising above the light and all around it,
I saw it mirrored in more than a thousand tiers
the numbers of us who had returned on high.
And if the lowest tier encloses
So great a light, what is the full size
of this rose extending to its furthest petals?
My sight in breadth and height
Was not confounded, but took in
The full extent and nature of the jubilation.
Nearness and distance add nothing, take away
nothing,
because where God governs without an intermediary
natural law holds no sway.[57]

Not only can Dante's refreshed sight withstand this radiant vision, his ability to see those far away is not compromised, because the natural laws of perspective do not apply in heaven. His vision of Beatrice is unaffected by how far she is from him on her petal throne, not least since there is no intervening atmosphere.[58]

We then learn that that the faces of the fluttering angels 'were of living flame', while their bodies exhibit 'whiteness of a level never met by any snow'.[59] At the centre of the rose, he sees; 'with wings outspread, more than a thousand festive angels each distinct in radiance and accomplishment'.[60] This progressive ability to see

ever more inaccessible visions has a downside. His powers of verbal description prove inadequate to the increasingly demanding task at hand. He admits, 'now my fable will fall far short'.[61]

The final vision in the *Commedia* is sublimely abstract, ineffable and eternal, ultimately lying beyond the power of words and the compass of Dante's mind. It involves three circles, identifiable as the Father, the Son and the Holy Ghost. It is worth quoting the last 31 lines of the great poem.[62]

> In the profundity of the clear substance
> Of the lofty light, appeared to me three circles
> Of three colours and of equal extent;
> And one appeared reflected in the other,
> As a rainbow is by a rainbow, and the third
> Seemed like a flame breathed equally from both.
> O how my how short speech falls, and how faint it is
> My conception! And what I saw was such
> That it does not suffice to call my account 'little'.
> O eternal light, existing in yourself alone,
> Known yourself alone, and, known to yourself,
> And intelligible to yourself, loving yourself and smiling.
> That encircling which was so conceived,
> Appeared in you as a reflected light
> When my eyes inspected it rather more.
> Within itself, and of its own colour,
> It seemed to be painted with our effigy;
> It totally occupied my sight.
> Like a geometer who sets himself
> To measure the area of a circle, and, pondering,
> Is unable to think of the rule he lacks,
> So I was faced with this new vision:
> I wanted to see how the image could come together
> With the circle, and how it could be insinuated there;
> But that was not a flight for my own wings:
> Except that my mind was struck by a flash
> In which what is desired came to it.
> At this point my high imagination failed;
> But already my desire and my will
> Were being turned like a wheel, all at one speed,
> By the love which moves the sun and the other stars.

Dante is at once striving to tell what he saw, while consciously failing to bring the image of the Trinity into visual focus as something we can 'see' in any normal manner. The circle of Christ is like the second, reversed rainbow that sometimes appears. That of the Holy Ghost is all flame. His quest to define the undefinable is like that of geometers who are obsessed with squaring the circle (he talks of 'measuring' the circle; that is to say, defining its area precisely in terms of an equivalent square). Dante sensed that the long-sought solution was not at hand, having fretted the finest minds of ancient and modern mathematicians. Within the reflected circle of Christ, he discerns what he calls 'our effigy' (*la nostra effige*) which compels his attention but he cannot tell how it co-exists with the circle. He is not explicit about what 'our effigy' represents. It may be an image of man, as conceived within God's mind. The form of this man is to be adopted by the incarnate Christ. But Dante can neither see it precisely, nor describe or locate it ... At the very last, faced with the supreme mystery, even Dante's highest poetic capacity – his *alta fantasia* – fails, and he surrenders his will to divine fate.

Dante can write of the unseeable. Our imagination can follow. A painter, of course, has no choice but to transform what is seen or imagined into a concrete image. This lies at the heart of our *paragone*. At the same time, artists who served the Church and religiously motivated patrons needed to create pictures that could somehow transcend their mundane materiality and prosaic optical presence. How (and to what extent) they did so, is the story of the chapters that follow.

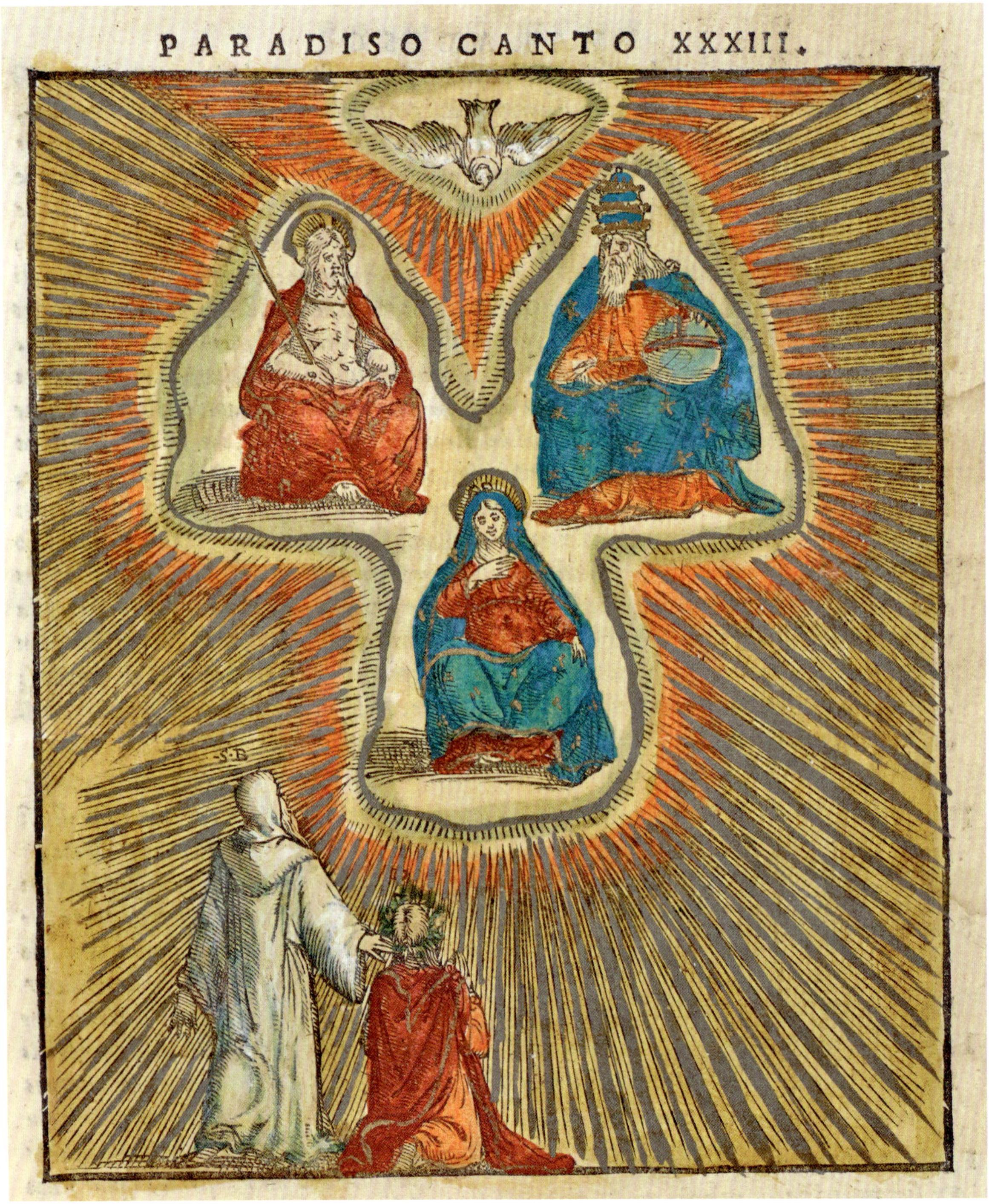

St Bernard and Dante Witness a Vision of the Trinity with the Virgin, from *La comedia di Dante Aligieri*, commentary by Alessandro Vellutello, published by Francesco Marcolini, Venice, 1544, Canto XXXIII

3

Illuminated and Illustrated

Dante's *Divina Commedia* was recognised as extraordinary when it emerged into the light of day, in the era before printed books. Over 800 manuscripts survive from an estimated 2000. The first printed edition in 1472 (some 151 years after the poet's death) was followed by more than 30. Illustrated volumes are very much another matter. Many manuscripts have illuminated initials and decorative motifs, but fully illustrated manuscripts with free-standing narrative scenes are in a small minority. Some sets of illustrations are unfinished, as the process of illumination ran out of steam, sometimes before reaching *Paradiso*. A number of the printed editions have varying quantities of illustrations of varied quality, culminating in the edition of 1544, published by Francesco Marcolini in Venice, which is fully illustrated with some in the commentary. What stands outside this count is a remarkable copy of the important 1481 Florentine printed edition that has been lavishly and ingeniously illustrated by hand and heavily annotated.[1] The more than 400 illuminated pages were probably produced by Antonio Griffo. The volume was destined for Galeazzo Sanseverino in Milan, a patron of Leonardo da Vinci.

Given Dante's vivid word-painting, it may seem surprising that most of the manuscript and printed editions did not contain illustrations of the poet's extraordinary journey. There are two main reasons: the first is practical. If, say, the illustrator was to produce one image per canto, this would mean 100 systematically drawn and painted illuminations, or the production of 100 drawings and corresponding woodcuts or engravings. Either form of illustration was very time-consuming and expensive. The other reason involves the sheer difficulty of transforming the images that well up in the mind of the reader – by turn horrendous, sad, joyous, visionary and logic-defying – into fixed pictures on the page. Dante seems to invite the *paragone*, but sets the challenge at an intimidating level. Both these reasons have deterred all but the intrepid over the centuries.

In the discussion that follows, my approach will continue the policy of selecting and sampling on the basis of examples that best speak to our present theme of divine light, that are in themselves representative of the larger group of texts, and that operate at the highest level – in this case visual. As an example of an early illustrated manuscript, I have chosen one that may have originated in Genoa not long after 1350. Currently in the Bodleian Library of Oxford, it had been added to the library at Holkham Hall in Norfolk by Thomas Coke, the Earl of Leicester and owner of a major manuscript on water, geology and astronomy by Leonardo da Vinci.[2] From the next century I have chosen, unsurprisingly, the scintillating illustrations by Giovanni di Paolo, the

+ Dissell anoi non sapre questa calla

si mosse e io dirieto inver laltura.
Lector tu uedi ben comio innalço
la mia materia e po con piu arte
nom meraviglar sio la rincalço.
Noi ciappressiamo e eravamo i parte
cola doue parcami prima rotto
pur comun fesso che muro di parte
Vidi una porta e tre gradi disotto
per gradissa di color diuersi
e un portier che ancor non facea motto.
Et come larchio piu e piu uapsi
uidil seder sopra lgrado souvrano
tal ne la faccia chio nolo soffersi.
Et una spada nuda avea i mano
he riflectecua i raggi si uer noi
ki dirizçava spesso il uiso in uano.
Dicel cosinci che uolete uoi
comincio elli a dir oue la scorta
guardate che l uenir su nonui noi.
Donna del ciel di queste cose accorta
rispose l mio maestro a llui pur dinançi
ne disse andate la quivi e la porta.
Et ella i passi uostri in bene avançi
ricominciol cortese portinaio
uenite dunque ai nostri gradi inançi.
La ue uenimmo alo scallion primaio
bianco marmo era e si polito e terso
chi mi specchiai in esso qual io paio.
Eral secondo tinto piu che perso
duna petrina ruuida e arsiccia
crepata per lo lungo e per trauerso.
Lo terço che di sopra samassiccia
porfido mi parea si fiammeggiante
come sangue che fuor di uena spiccia.
Soura questo tenea ambo le piante
langel di dio sedendo in su la soglia

che mi sembiava pietra di diamante.
Per li tre gradi su di buona uoglia
mi trasse l duca mio dicendo chiedi
humilemente che l serrame scioglia.
Diuoto mi gittai ai sancti piedi
misericordia chiesi che ma prisse
ma pria nel pecto tre fiate mi diedi.
Septe .p. nella fronte mi descripse
col punton dela spada e fa che lavi
quando se dentro queste piaghe disse.
Cener o terra che secca si cavi
dun color fora col suo uestimento
e di sotto da quel trasse due chiavi.
Luna era doro e laltera dargento
pria con la bianca e poscia colla gialla
fece ala porta si chio fui contento.
Qualunche luna delle chiavi falla
che non si uolga diricta per la toppa
+ darte e dingegno avante che disserri.
Piu cara e luna ma laltra uol troppo
darte e dingegno avante che disserri
per quella e quella che nodo disgroppa.
Da pier le tegno e dissemi chio erri
ançi adaprir che tenerla serrata
pur che la gente a piedi mi satterri.
Poi pinse luscio ala porta sacrata
dicendo intrate ma facciovi accorti
che di fuor torna chi dietro si guata.
Et quando fur ne cardini distorti
li spigoli di quella gente stan rege
che di metallo son sonanti e forti.
Non ruggio si ne si mostro si acra
tarpea quando tolto le fu l bono
metello per che poi rimase macra.
Io mi riuolsi attento al primo tono
e te deum laudamus mi parea

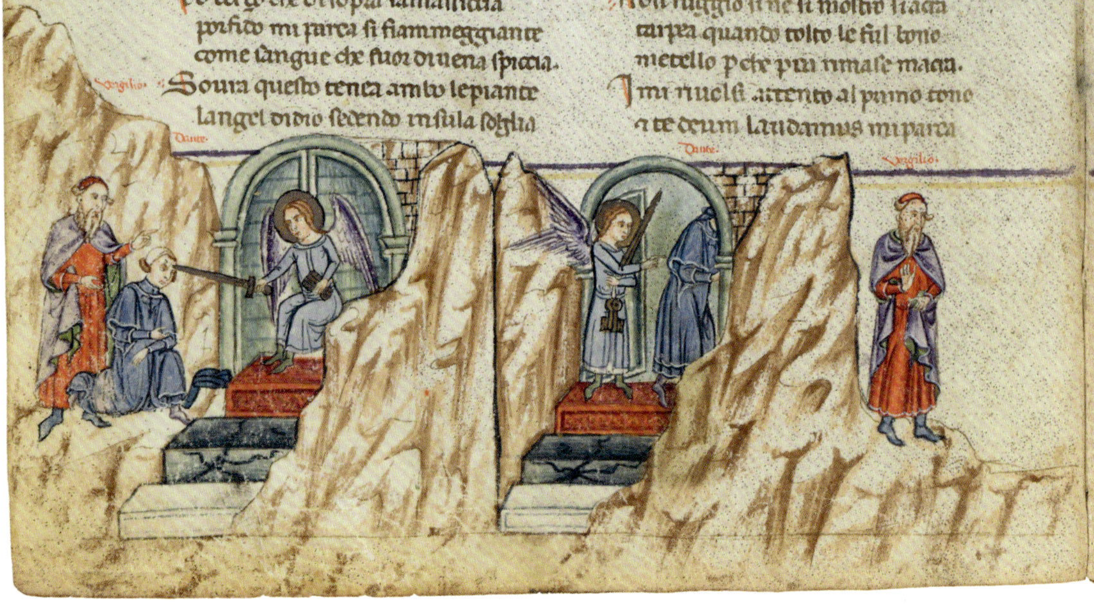

Sienese master whose elegant refinement and visual radiance are well-matched to *Paradiso,* which is the canticle of the *Commedia* that he illuminated. The Renaissance will be represented by the visionary drawings by Sandro Botticelli for an edition that was never published or even finished, although 19 designs by Botticelli (rather inelegantly rendered in woodcut) had previously appeared in the *Inferno* in the Florentine edition of 1481, that contained Cristoforo Landino's important commentary. We will also visit one of the finest of all Renaissance Dantes, made for the great patron Federico da Montefeltro, Duke of Urbino, though the illuminations in *Paradiso* were added some years later.

The illustrations that appeared in the printed editions, even if they realised some of the imagery in *Inferno* and *Purgatorio* quite effectively, were able to make little of the light show in *Paradiso*. Generally, the linear and monochrome medium of woodcut could do little more than present a prosaic series of divergent ink rays to indicate bursts of sublime radiance. The printed edition which we will be looking at was published by Marcolini in Venice in 1544, with a combative commentary by Alessandro Vellutello, and no less than 87 woodcuts. The illustrations were pirated in a number of later editions.

THE HOLKHAM DANTE

As with other Mediaeval manuscripts (for instance those dealing with medicine) we should not expect a full pictorial rendering of the scenes or subjects they serve. In the margin at the foot of each page, the illuminator neatly introduces the main protagonists (who are labelled with their names or initials) – and most of the scenes are accorded a short title. The gist of the action is spelt out in each case, with an economical indication of the setting. The function of the images is very much linked to a process of visualisation that serves to signal and clarify events and participants, not least for our memory.

In the episode in *Purgatorio* when Dante and Virgil encounter the angel with a sword who is sternly guarding a gate that protects an aperture in the rocky cliff, the left side of the illumination shows the two travellers outside the door, while on the right Dante is passing through to join Virgil on the other side (fig.8).[3] The sword, we may recall, glowed so intently with brilliant reflections that Dante's sight was overwhelmed. There is no hint of the glare of the sword in the image, and the illuminator has instead chosen to show a later incident in the canto when the angel uses his sword to mark out seven letter Ps on the poet's forehead. Each P signifies a wound left by each of the seven mortal sins, which would necessarily be purged in *Purgatorio.*

Once Dante and Beatrice begin their ascent though the heavenly spheres, the setting becomes more or less standardised. They stand on a horizontal expanse of heavenly blue, while above them is a blue firmament twinkling with stars. Frequently, only the two main protagonists are depicted as Beatrice delivers her instructional speeches to the cowed poet. Sometimes they are joined by residents of the heavens. Beatrice's assertive lecture on the mottled appearance of the moon is one scene in which they are unaccompanied (fig.9). As always in the manuscript, Beatrice is granted a spiky gold nimbus of rays, which signals the angelic radiance that Dante often strains to bear. The illuminator shows the three mirrors of the 'experiment' that she describes, each mirror floating in the air as a crescent moon, but without any real understanding of the set-up, and with no light positioned behind Dante. As we saw, Dante's account of the three mirrors is difficult to follow, and if the reader of the Holkham Dante was struggling at this point, the illustration would have done nothing to help. It is only fair to say that none of the illuminations I have seen in the original or in reproduction convey the set-up of the experiment.

A little earlier, at the very beginning of *Paradiso,* we see the voyagers ascending towards the bright heavens with Dante literally clinging to the coat tails of Beatrice as

8 *Dante and Virgil Encounter the Angel Guarding the Gate,* in Dante, *Divina Commedia,* Oxford, Bodleian Library, MS Holkham misc. 48, p.74

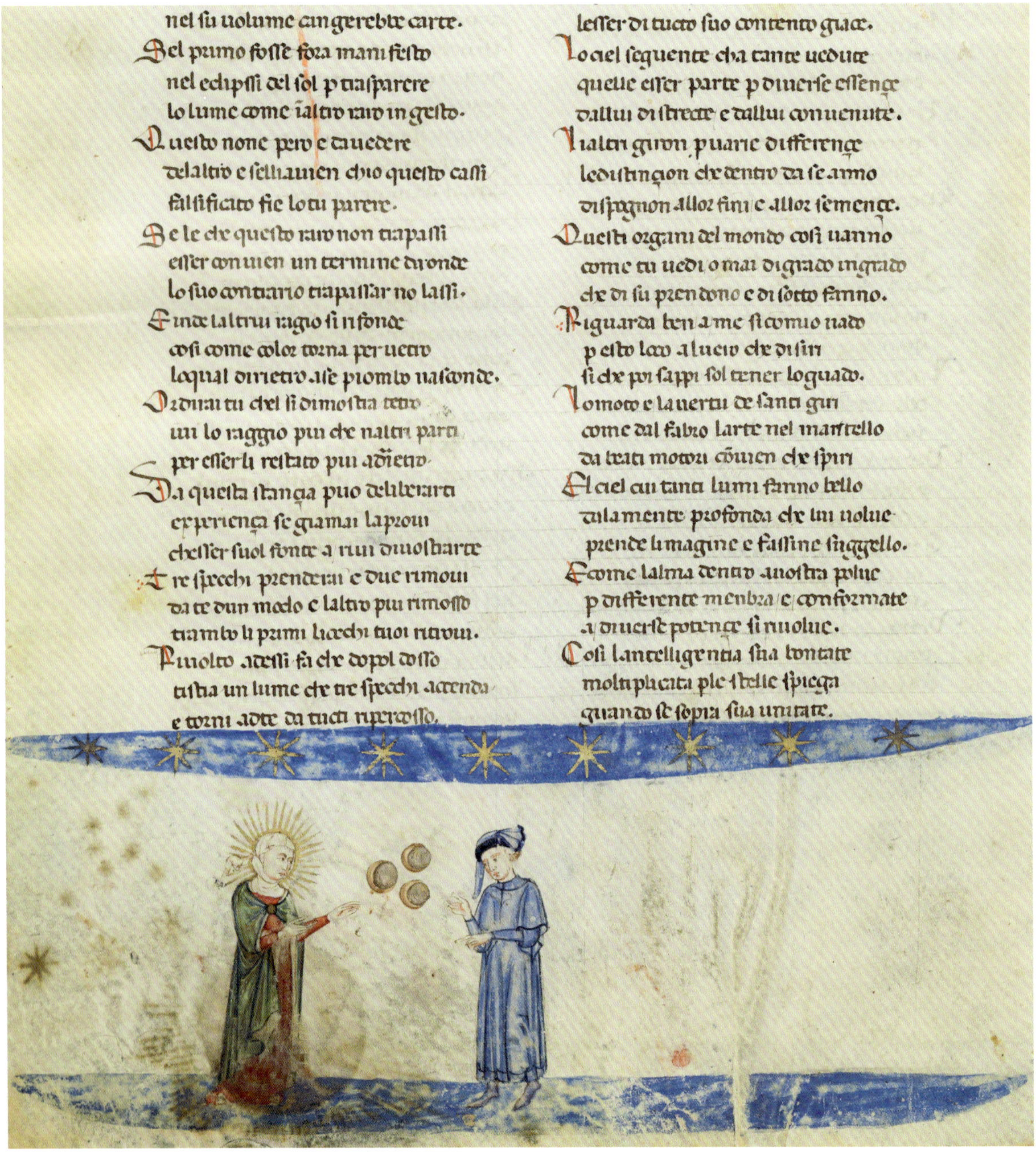

9 *Beatrice Explains the Three-Mirror 'Experiment'*, in Dante, *Divina Commedia*, Oxford, Bodleian Library, MS Holkham misc. 48, p.124

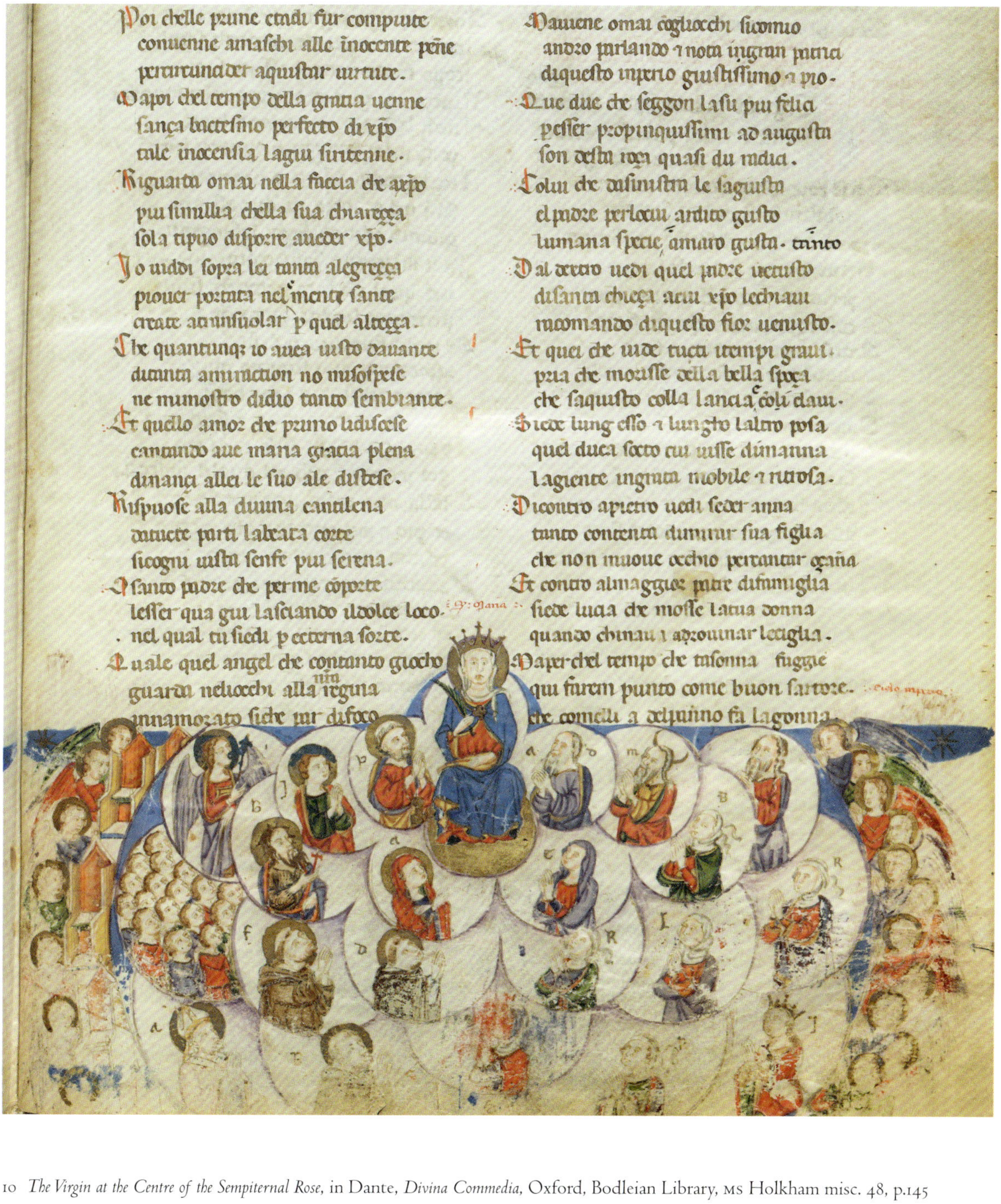

10 *The Virgin at the Centre of the Sempiternal Rose,* in Dante, *Divina Commedia,* Oxford, Bodleian Library, MS Holkham misc. 48, p.145

Cotal son io che quasi tucta cessa
mia visione et ancor midistilla
nel core il dolce che nacque dacessa.
Cosi la neve al sol sidisigilla
cosi al vento nelle fogli levi
siperdea la sentença di sibilla.
O soma luce che tanto tilevi
da concepti mortali alla mia mente
ripsta unpoco diquel che parevi
Et fa la lingua mia tanto possente
chuna favilla sol della tua gloria
possa lasciare alla futura gente.
Che per tornare alquanto amia memoria
et per sonare unpoco inquesti versi
piu siconcepera di tua victoria.
Io credo placume chio sofferisi
del vivo raggio chio sarei smarito
se gliocchi miei dalui fossor aversi.
Et mi ricorda chio fui piu ardito
per questo asostener tanto chio giunsi
laspecto mio col valor infenito
O abondonante gratia ondio presunsi
ficcar lo viso p la luce eterna
tanto che la veduta viconsumsi.
Nel suo profondo viddio chi sinterna
legato conamore in un volume
cio che per luniverso sisquaderna.
Sustançe et accidençe et lor costume
quasi conflate insieme pertal modo
che cio chio dico e un simplice lume.
La forma universal diquesto nodo
credo chio vidi perche piu dilargho
dicendo questo misento chio godo.
Un punto solo me maggior letargho
che .xxv. secoli alla impresa
che fe neptuno admirar lombra dargho

Cosi la mente mia tucta sospesa
mirava fisa imobile et actenta
et sempre dimirar faciesi accesa.
A quella luce cotal sidiventa
che volgersi dalei paltro aspecto
e impossibil che mai siconsenta.
Pero del ben che del voler obiecto
tucto saccoglie in lei et for di quella
e defectivo cio che li perfecto.
Omai sara piu corta mia favella
pur aquel chio ricordo chi dun fante
che bagni ancor la lingua alla mamella.
Non per che piu chun simplice sembiante
fosse nel vivo lume chio mirava
che tal e sempre qual sera davante
Ma pla vista che si avalorava
ime guardando una sola pvença
mutando mio ame si travagliava
Nela pfonda et chiara sussistença
dellalto lume parvemi tre giri
ditre colori et duna contigneça.
Et lun dalaltro come iri da iri
parea reflexo el terço parea fuocho
che quindi et quindi egualmente sispiri.
O quanto e corto il dir et come fiocho
almio concepto et questo aquel chio vidi
et tanto che non basta addicer poco.
O luce eterna che solo inte sidi
sola tintendi et date intellecta
et intendente te ami et arridi.
Quella circulactione che si concepta
parevia inte come lume reflexo
dagliocchi miei alquanto circunspecta.
Dentro dase del su colore stesso
miparve pinta della nostra effigie
perchello mio viso inlei tucto era messo.

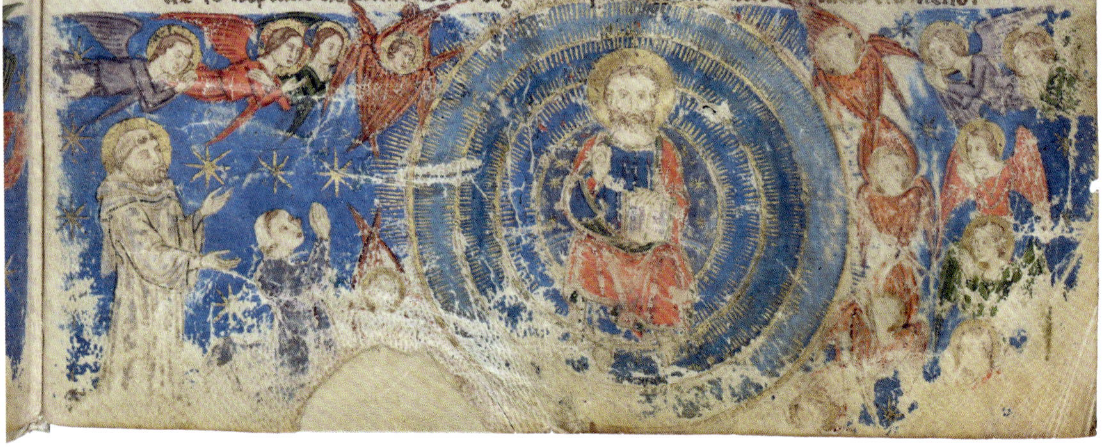

they swoosh against the current of a cascade of gold rays emanating from a badly damaged area near the right edge of the sheet. There is certain irony in the illegibility of the source of light. The opening lines read:

> The glory of him who moves everything
> Penetrates the universe and shines
> More in one part and less in another.
> I was in the heaven that takes most of his light
> Where I saw things that cannot possibly be told
> By anyone who descends from there.[4]

When it comes to the depiction if the glowing petals of the white sempiternal rose, the limitations of the illustrative system become evident (fig.10). The array of saints around the Virgin, who is seated on a gold orb, works well enough. Each is denoted by his or her initials: P for Peter, M for Moses (with his horns of light), A for Anne, D for Dominic, and so on. At the bottom of the page, towards the left, we can recognise St Bernard, who has taken over as the poet's guide for the culminating visions. This much helps the reader envisage what Dante witnesses. However, the petals of the actual rose are more geometrical than floral, and the background tone of the parchment cannot lift the lightness of the white petals above that of the whole sheet. This was a problem that was to be triumphantly solved by Giovanni di Paolo.

The rather damaged final illustration of Dante's ultimate vision is ingeniously realised (fig.11). The diminutive figure of the kneeling poet raises his hands in fervent prayer, and is presented by St Bernard, who necessarily facilitates the vision of the vision. Here we see the three concentric circles of the Trinity, though they are of varying shades of blue rather than different colours, flanked by seraphim and angels. It is labelled *Cielo imperio* (imperial heaven). The sharp spokes of golden rays emanating from the edges of each circle serve to emphasise the dense radiance of each *trinitarian* (rainbow). Seated at the very centre, in the pose of a blessing Christ, is a figure with the three faces of the Trinity: God the Father, God the Son, and the Holy Ghost. Is this what the illuminator understands by 'our effigy'? If so, it is a clever idea, the efficacy of which can still be appreciated in spite of the wear and tear of this climactic sheet.

GIOVANNI DI PAOLO

Giovanni di Paolo di Grazia was a hugely accomplished painter and miniaturist in the Sienese 14th-century tradition of Duccio di Buoninsegna, Simone Martini and the Lorenzetti brothers, Pietro and Ambrogio. He shares their compositional grace, elegant characterisation, eloquent story-telling and their meticulous craftsmanship, not least in tooled gilding that makes their panel paintings glow with light (fig.36). Yet he was actually born in the early years of the 15th century and died in 1482, when Leonardo was already 30 years old. It would be easy to characterise him as essentially an old-fashioned Gothic artist during the century that saw the birth of the Renaissance in Florence. But such labelling does not allow for the complexity of artistic trends in the 15th century, and the demands from patrons (particularly the monastic orders) for images that satisfied devotional expectations of a long-standing kind. He clearly had little or no taste for the kind of direct naturalism pioneered by the Florentines, or the system of optical perspective that Masaccio introduced into painting. In Siena, Giovanni was successful and well regarded, and was elected Rector of the Painters' Guild in 1441. He clearly had a sense, as did those who commissioned his highly refined altarpieces, that a picture of, say, the Madonna with saints should manifest a certain set of visual qualities if it was to do its job for the worshipper. The holy figures were holy figures and should not look like people off the street, either in themselves or in the style with which the painter had rendered them.

It was these characteristics that Giovanni brought to the magnificent Dante manuscript that was in the

11 *St Bernard presents Dante to the Trinity*, in Dante, *Divina Commedia*, Oxford, Bodleian Library, MS Holkham misc. 48, p.147

12 Giovanni di Paolo, *Dante and Beatrice Witness the Spheres and Crosses, the Spheres of the Heavens with Love, a Fishing Mermaid, Neptune and Creatures in the Sea of Being*, in Dante, *Divina Commedia*, British Library, Yates Thompson, 38, fol. 130

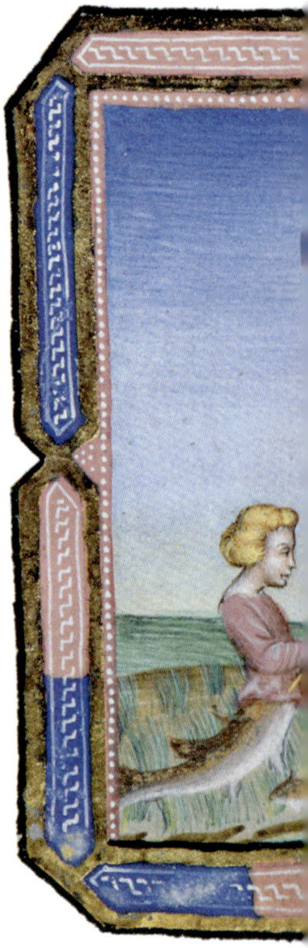

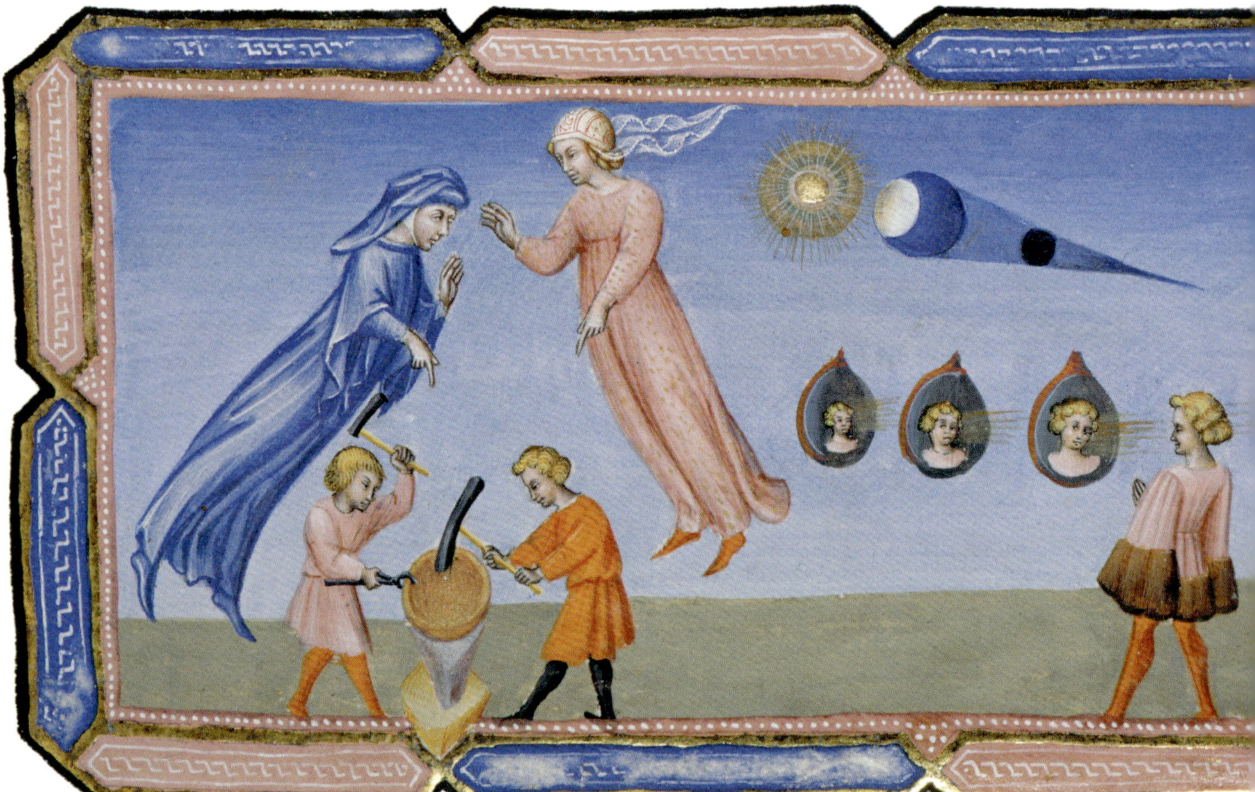

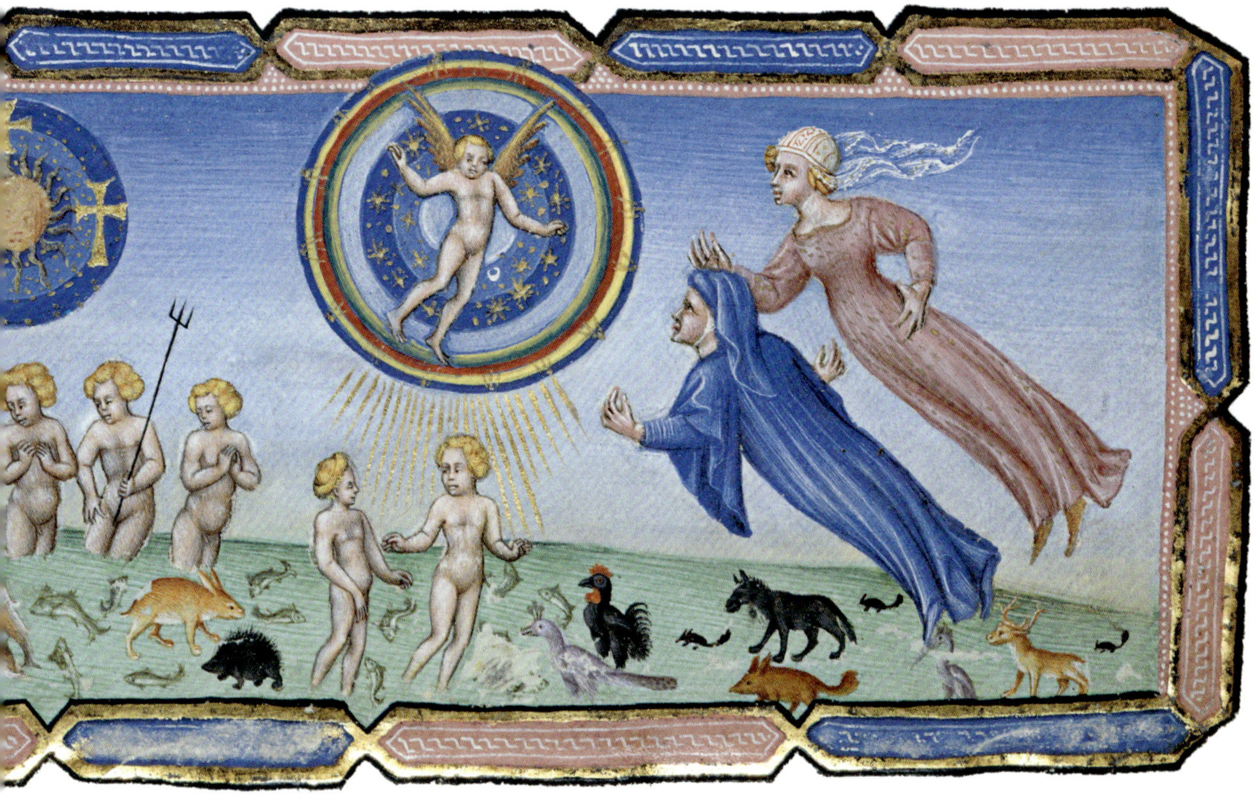

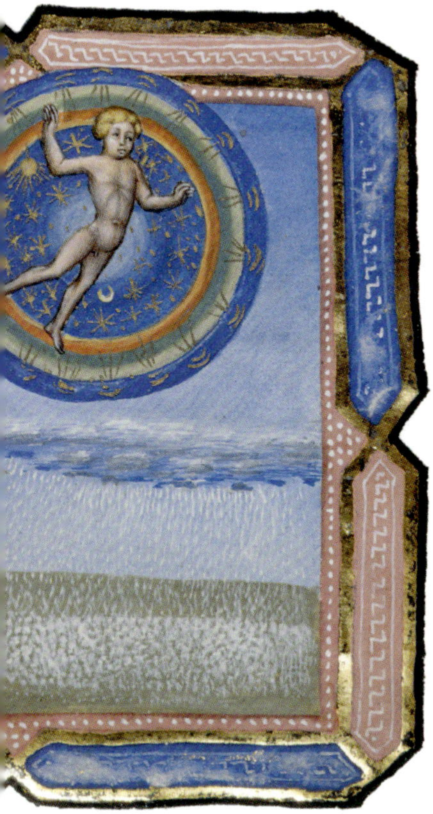

13 Giovanni di Paolo, *Beatrice Explains the Three-Mirror 'Experiment', with Smiths at an Anvil, and Eclipse of the Sun, the Spheres of the Heavens and a Snowfall*, in Dante, *Divina Commedia*, British Library, Yates Thompson, 38, fol. 132

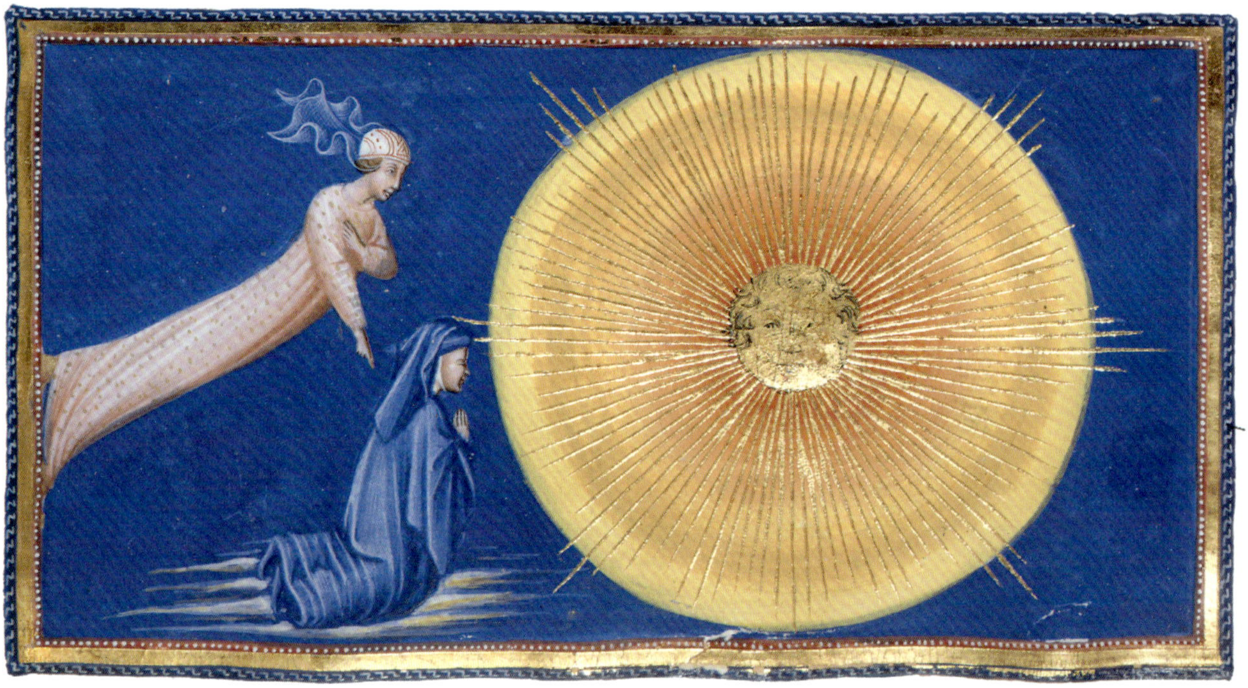

15 Giovanni di Paolo, *Dante and Beatrice Witness the Heaven of Mars, with the Bright Cross of Warriors,* in Dante, *Divina Commedia,* British Library, Yates Thompson, 38, fol. 160

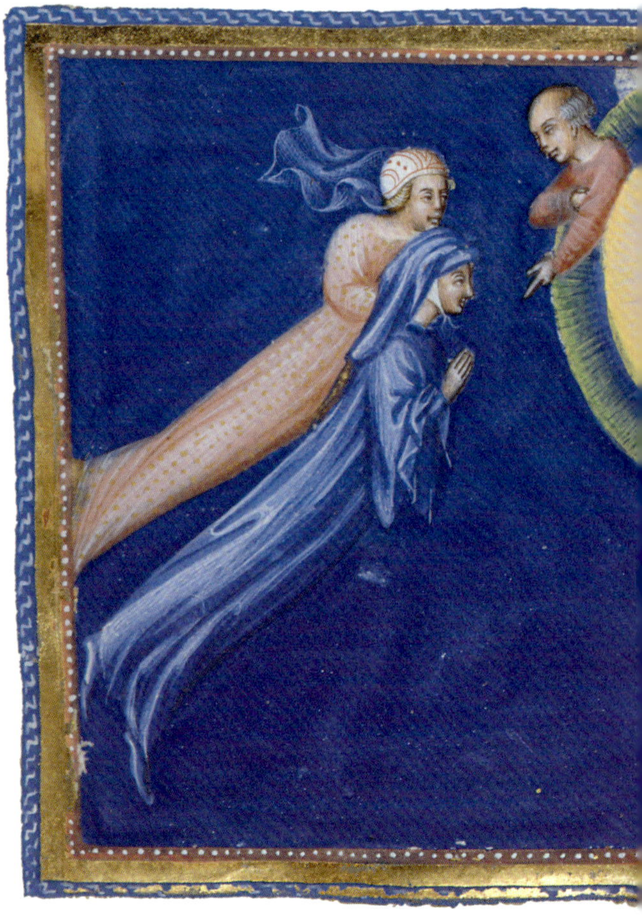

14 Giovanni di Paolo, *Dante and Beatrice Witness the Light of the Primum Mobile*, in Dante, *Divina Commedia*, British Library, Yates Thompson, 38, fol. 147

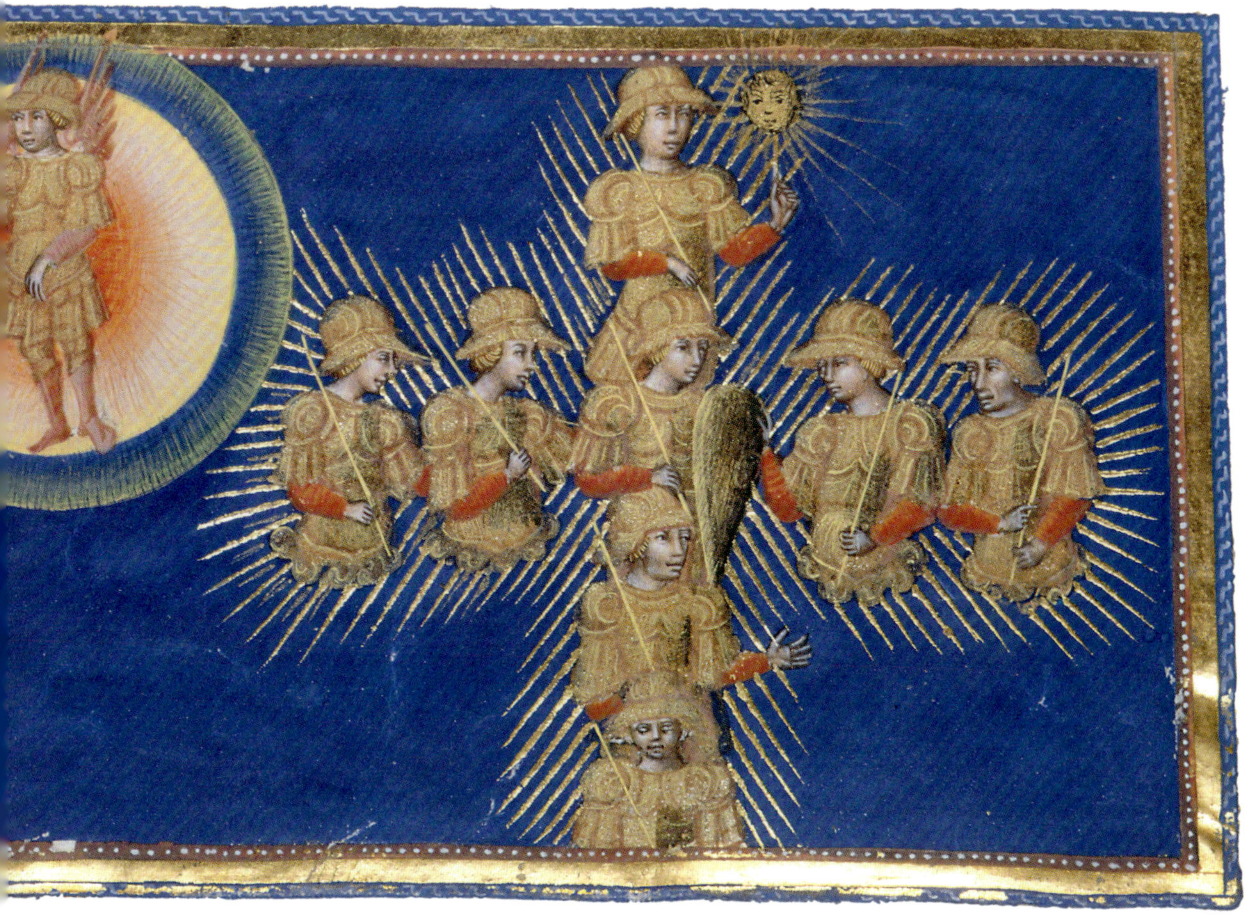

library of Alfonso I, King of Naples (Alfonso V of Aragon), who was almost certainly its commissioner. The manuscript boasts some 110 large and highly coloured miniatures in rectangular frames. The images in *Inferno* and *Purgatorio* are by another Sienese artist, Priamo della Quercia, brother of the famous sculptor, Jacopo. Giovanni di Paolo's contributions to the manuscript probably date from *c.*1450.

Giovanni's first contribution occurs at the start of *Paradiso*, in which Beatrice gazes, eagle-like, at 'the lamp of the world'. The position of the sun in the heavenly cycle was such that 'four circles and three crosses' coincide (fig.12). The three circles are those on an armillary sphere (marking the equator, the ecliptic and the colure) at the point they cross the band of the horizon. Giovanni takes the crosses and sphere very literally.

Dante describes how 'another sun' arrived, in this case the nine spheres of the heavens, which are shown under the rule of love. The fishing mermaid on the left is accompanied by golden-haired nudes (one of whom brandishes a trident and is identifiable as Neptune) and a merry cast of creatures. These nudes and animals allude to Beatrice's exposition of universal order in which all the various natures of things arise from 'the great sea of being', ranging from the animalistic nature of animals to those higher creatures governed by 'intellect and love'.[5] It is characteristic of Giovanni that he does not fight shy of trying to illustrate theological notions.

The layout of this first illumination sets the tone for many of those that follow, with Beatrice and Dante ascending diagonally through the heavens with a slender grace that is underlined by their delicately sinuous draperies. It also exemplifies Giovanni's refined skills with pen and brush, and his virtuosity with pigments and gilding on the parchment of the manuscript. Sometimes the narrative of their ascent to light is expressed simply, as when they experience the high radiance of the *Primum Mobile* (fig.14).

The same basic layout is at work when Giovanni illustrates Beatrice's three-mirror 'experiment' to disprove Dante's view that the substance of the moon is of varied transparency (fig.13). Giovanni does understand that the three mirrors are in front of the observer (an elegant youth), with the light behind him, though the mirrors reflect the youth's face rather than the light. The two artisans to whom Beatrice and Dante point appear to be hammering out a concave mirror on an anvil. This picks up a passing and rather obscure reference to the effect that the actions of the 'angelic movers' of the heavens are comparable to the 'science of the hammer that comes from the smith'. Above the mirrors is an eclipse of the sun, which casts a conical shadow over the diminutive earth. This refers to Beatrice's argument that were the moon to be semi-translucent in part, this should be apparent when it stands between us and the sun. Below the spheres of the heavens, a cloud is precipitating a light covering of snow. This seems to allude to Beatrice's claim that the warm light of Dante's eventual understanding is like the melting of snow, which rids us of cold. The four motifs of the forge, eclipse, mirrors and snow indicate a close reading of the text, whether by Giovanni himself or an adviser. The subject-matter of all the illuminations is quite varied. We encounter the stories of particular characters or saints and incidents from classical antiquity. There are also some 'political' references to events in Dante's time, including his own expulsion from Florence (fig.6).

When Beatrice and Dante rise serenely to the sphere of Mars, they witness the vision of the cross that results from the astronomical position of the red planet (fig.15). We may recall that the cross was composed of mobile sparkles of light that were compared to specks of dust dancing in a beam of light. Again, this image is difficult, conceptually and visually. Giovanni limits himself to three conventional crosses (fig.12), and no illuminator comes close to realising the 'atoms'. There is a certain prudence in not trying to emulate every aspect of Dante's vision in all its learned and poetic subtlety.

Giovanni is more readily drawn to the vision of the cross that follows in canto XVIII just before they ascend from the sphere of Mars to that of Jupiter. In this case the cross is composed of eight warrior-saints in the guise of radiant Martians, one of whom holds a bright sun-face to the upper right. The speaking figure who emerges from Mars's glowing sphere is Cacciaguida, Dante's great-grandfather, a knight and crusader who died in battle against the 'infidel'. Dante and his distinguished ancestor express pride in their Florentine heritage and lament the current state of their beloved city. Cacciaguida forecasts the poet's exile (fig.6). The message of martial power is nicely conveyed within the limits of Giovanni's charming pictorial vocabulary, which is stronger on beauty than battles.

As we move via the heaven of Saturn, the sphere of the fixed stars and the *Primum Mobile* to the climax of *Paradiso*, we encounter three images of the sempiternal rose, shining with irresistible luminosity, which is very much within Giovanni's compass, though he understandably does not aspire to show thousands of petal-thrones. He concentrates instead on the very centre of the rose (fig.16). In this folio, we see the seated Virgin with her Child, accompanied by high-status saints (not least those in Dante's own pantheon), including St Peter with his golden key. The recumbent and naked woman with a fashionable headdress, who provides Mary's footrest, does not seemingly feature in Dante's text. Presumably she represents everything the Virgin is not. A curious feature is that by this time Beatrice has taken up place on her allocated petal-throne, and it is St Bernard who actually guides the poet through the final ecstatic revelations. Indeed, one of Giovanni's miniatures shows Dante being presented to the Virgin by St Bernard.[6]

Beatrice is still present in the last of the illuminations, which does not attempt to grapple with the elusive sublimity of Dante's final vision. Instead, they witness the Virgin in her fullest majesty, frontal and hierarchical in a gold-flecked dress and radiating an aura of multiple gold rays (fig.17). Dante is apparently able to bear the assault on his eyes. To the right we unexpectedly see a buoyant galleon in full sail on a wavy sea and a near-naked Neptune. The source is the last of the classical allusions that lace Dante's text. Overwhelmed by the magnitude of what is being presented to him, he loses track, suspended in time.

> A single point in time cost me a greater hiatus
> Than the twenty-five centuries since the enterprise
> Which made Neptune marvel at the shadow of
> Argo.[7]

The *Argo* was the ship built for Jason – sometimes regarded as the first of all ships – for his heroic voyage with the Argonauts from Greece to Colchis to obtain the golden fleece. In some versions of the legend, the gods carried the *Argo* into the sky in honour of Jason, placing it beside Sirius as a constellation. Neptune was astonished at the shadow of the *Argo* as it passed over his domain. As elsewhere, Dante is making stiff demands on his readers – and seeking tolerance for what seems like a strange aside in the great narrative. In any event, Giovanni has accorded *Argo* surprising prominence, and was careful to represent the cast shadow that Dante wrote about. Perhaps he felt that an image of travel was a suitable point at which to complete his visual account of the poet's journey.

Giovanni di Paolo's illustrations, of which we have only seen a selection of those concerned with light, are full of narrative charm, sometimes showing obvious images of Dante and his companions, while in others picking out themes or persons of a more unexpected kind. Occasionally, he has the kind of trouble with Dante's texts that most of his readers experience. Above all, his illustrations are infused with visual intelligence, whether entirely of Giovanni's own doing or in collaboration with a Dantista.

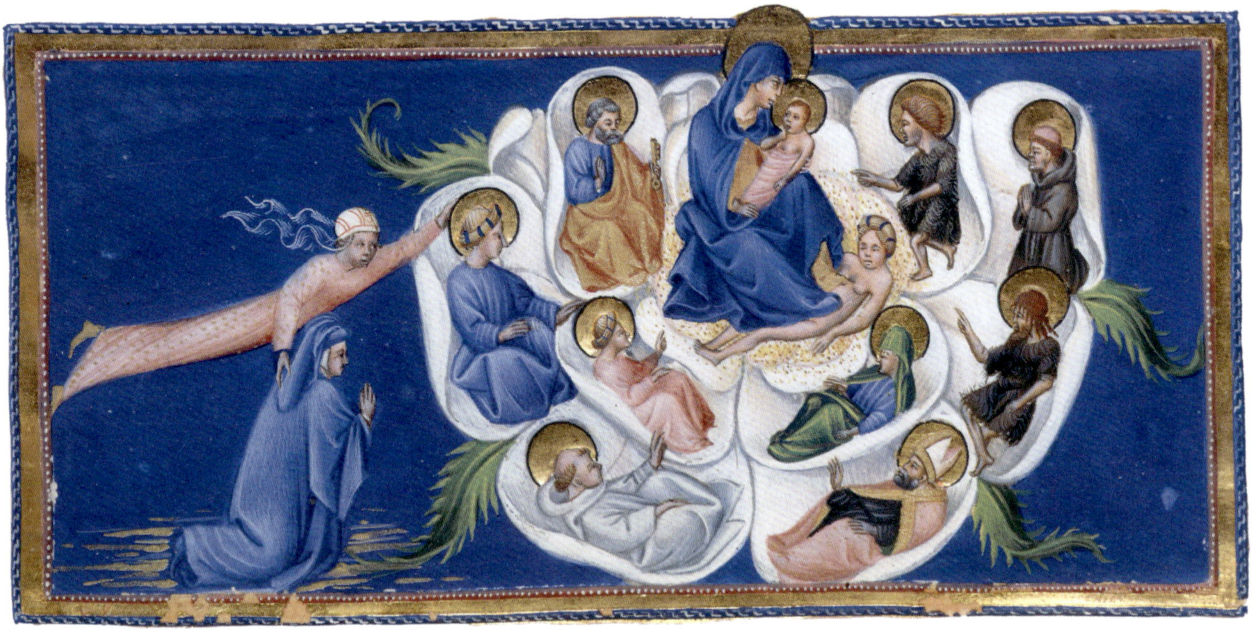

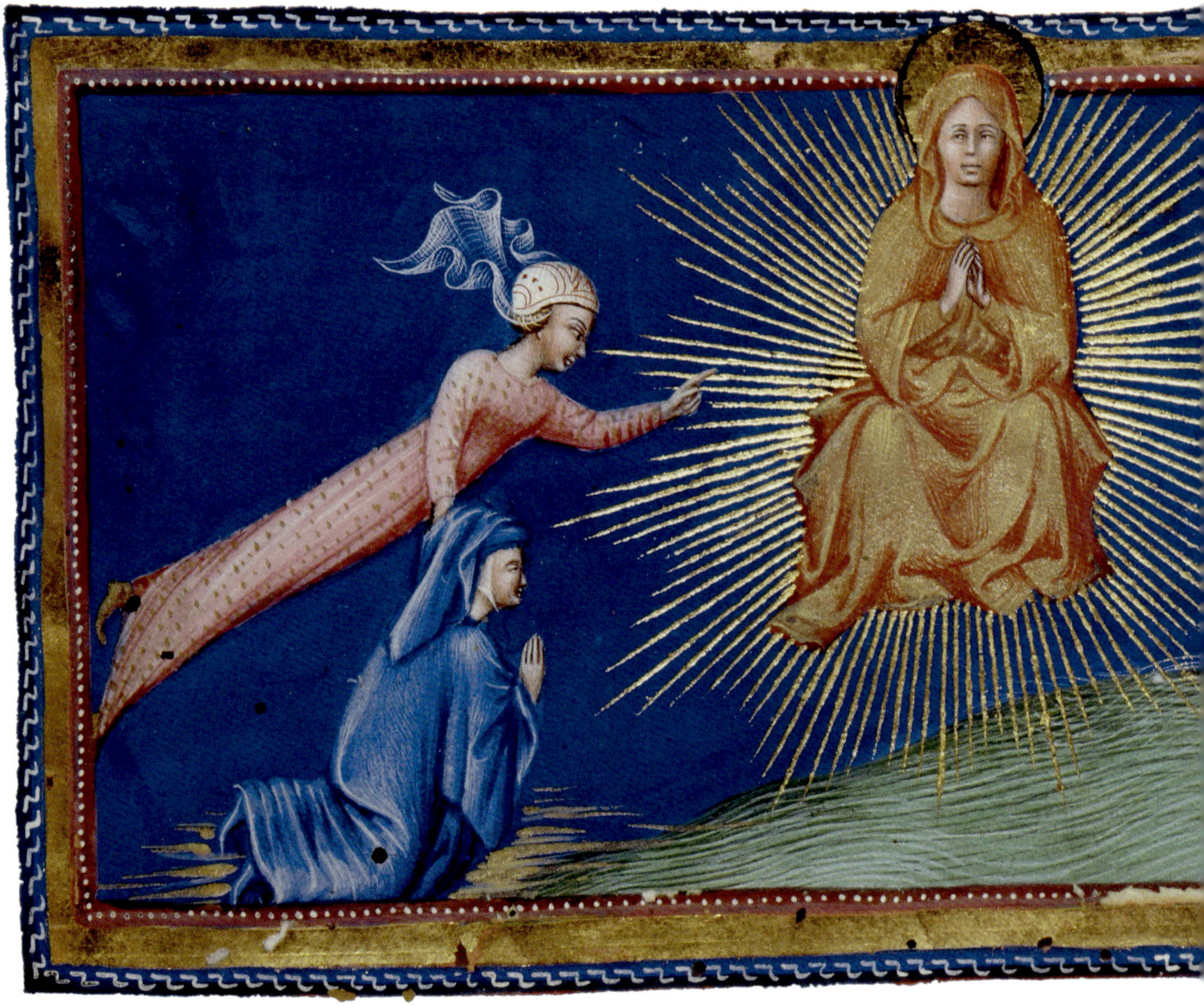

16 Giovanni di Paolo, *Dante and Beatrice Witness the Virgin in the Sempiternal Rose*, in Dante, *Divina Commedia*, British Library, Yates Thompson, 38, fol. 187

17 Giovanni di Paolo, *Dante and Beatrice Witness the Virgin, with the Ship Argo and Neptune*, in Dante, *Divina Commedia*, British Library, Yates Thompson, 38, fol. 190

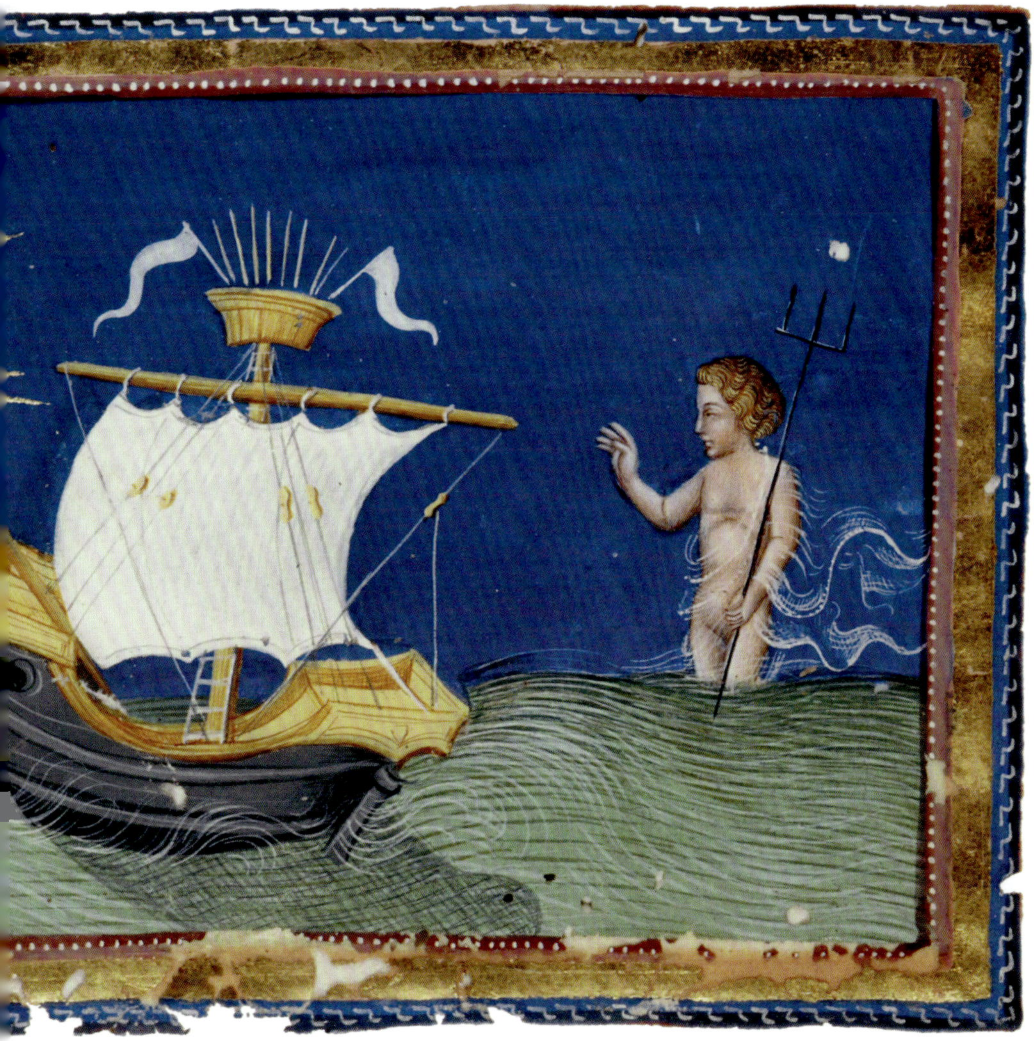

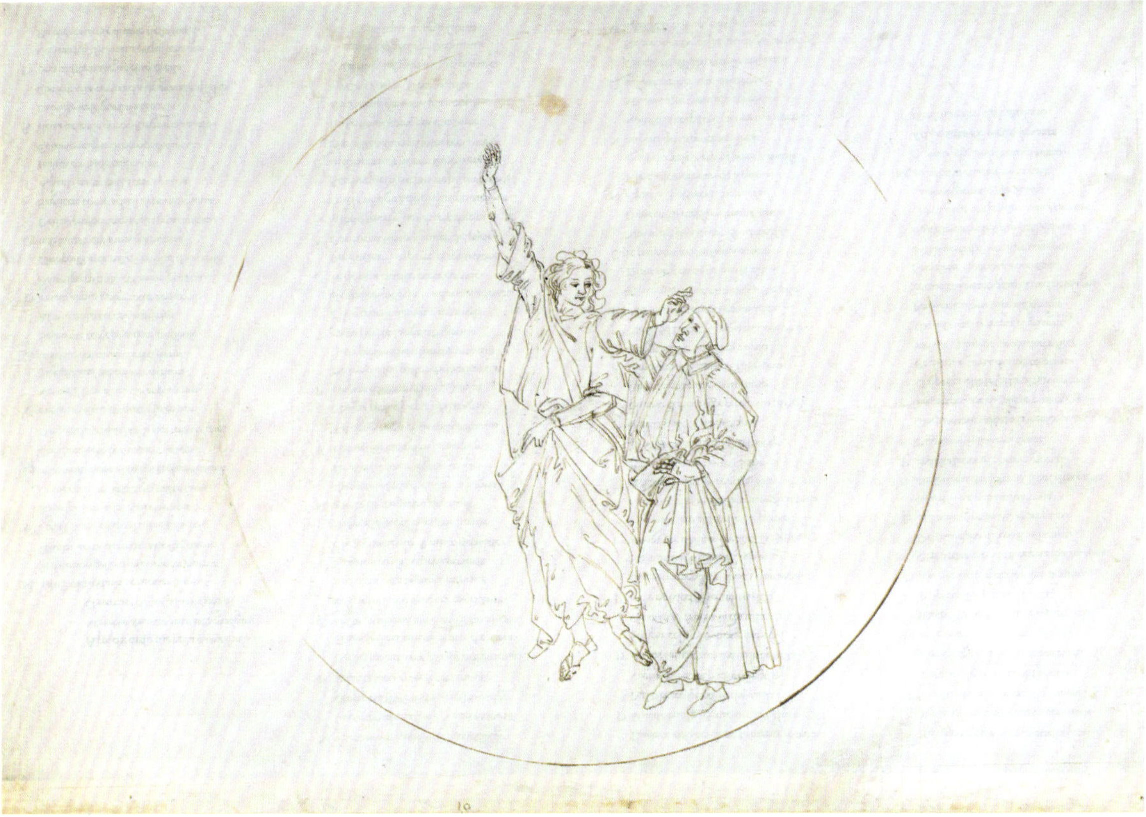

18 Sandro Botticelli, *Beatrice and Dante Who Shades his Eyes, in the Heaven of the Sun,* in Dante, *Divina Commedia, Paradiso,* Canto IX, Berlin, Staatliche Museen, Kupferstichkabinett

SANDRO BOTTICELLI

If any artist was to illustrate the *Divina Commedia* in the later 15th century, Botticelli was the obvious candidate. He was the leading painter of mythological subjects at the Medici 'court' – just think of *Primavera* (Spring) and *The Birth of Venus* – and adept at religious imagery. He was master of what Dante called *fantasia,* poetic imagination. He was also notably fertile in *invenzione* (invention). The 'court' of Lorenzo de' Medici (*Il Magnifico*) was much concerned with the promotion of Florence as the beacon of Renaissance culture and establishing Tuscan as the leading intellectual and literary language. Cristoforo Landino, the tutor of Lorenzo and a prominent philosopher and poet, was the author of the first full commentary on Dante's *Commedia.* He viewed the great poem very much through the eyes of the group of Renaissance intellectuals who comprised an informal Florentine academy. Their ideal philosopher was Plato.

Landino's preface leaves us in no doubt about the roots of his enterprise.

> I affirm only this, that I have liberated our citizen Dante from the barbarity of many foreign idioms in which he had been corrupted by many commentators, and thus so pure and simple it seemed to me my duty to present him to you, our illustrious lords, so that into the hands of that magistrate which is most high in the Florentine

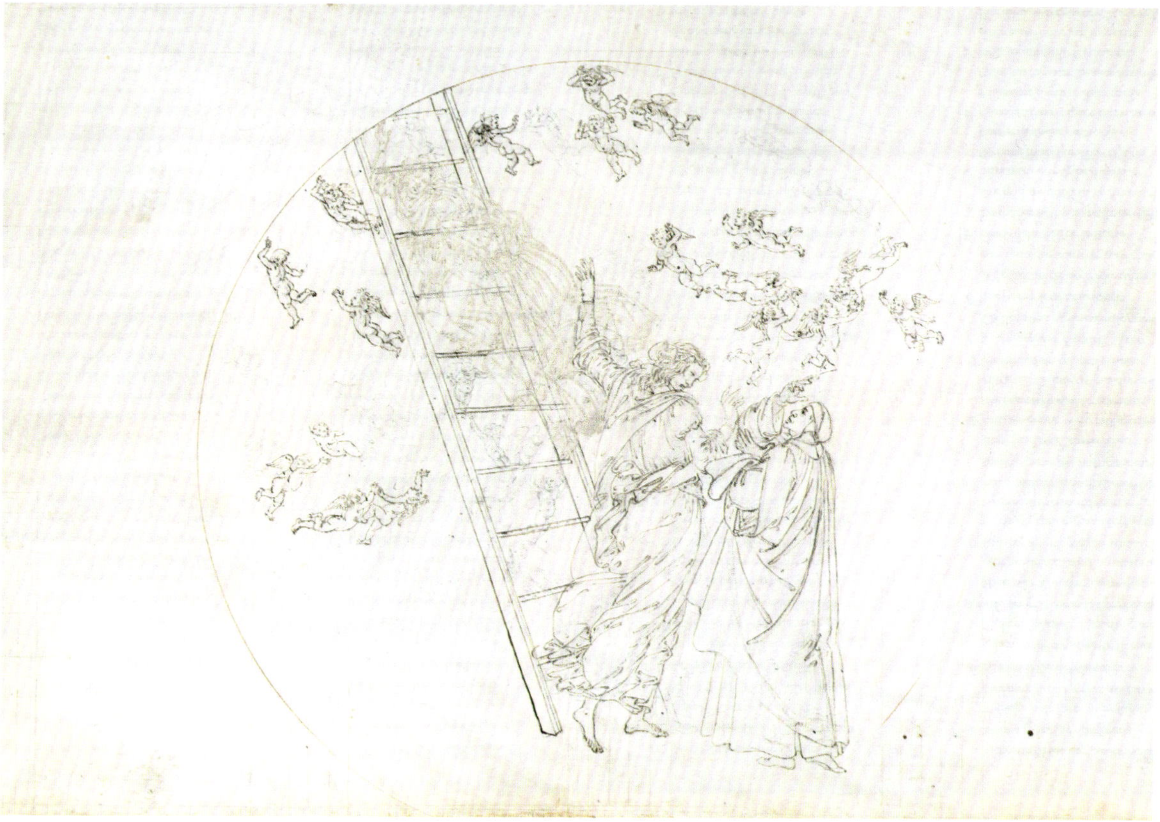

19 Sandro Botticelli, *Jacob's Ladder*, in Dante, *Divina Commedia, Paradiso*, Canto XXI, Berlin, Staatliche Museen, Kupferstichkabinett

Republic, he should be restored to his homeland after long exile and not recognized as *romagnolo* or *lombardo* nor any of the languages of those who have glossed him, but simple Florentine, a language which is greater than any other Italian idiom, as is shown clearly by the fact that no one ever expressed genius or doctrine nor wrote verses or prose, who did not attempt to use the Florentine idiom.[8]

The massive printed edition – on each page Dante's original text appears as a smallish island in a great ocean of surrounding commentary – was presented to the Florentine authorities in 1481 as a kind of reparation for Dante's exile. The edition was meant to be illustrated. Space was left for a printed illustration for each canto. However, only 19 plates for the *Inferno* were ever engraved, and of these only two or three are integral to the book as printed. Others, if they appeared at all, were pasted in. Giorgio Vasari, author of the *Lives of the Most Excellent Painters, Sculptors, and Architects*, who worked at the Medici court 50 years later, testified that Botticelli was their designer – in which case, the engraver, Baccio Baldini, has done a good job in failing to render the quality of Botticelli's draughtsmanship. An anonymous and well-informed author in the early 16th century tells us that another set of illustrations was commissioned by *Il Magnifico's* cousin, Lorenzino de' Medici, who was the patron of the *Primavera*. This set is one of the most remarkable ever made from any period.

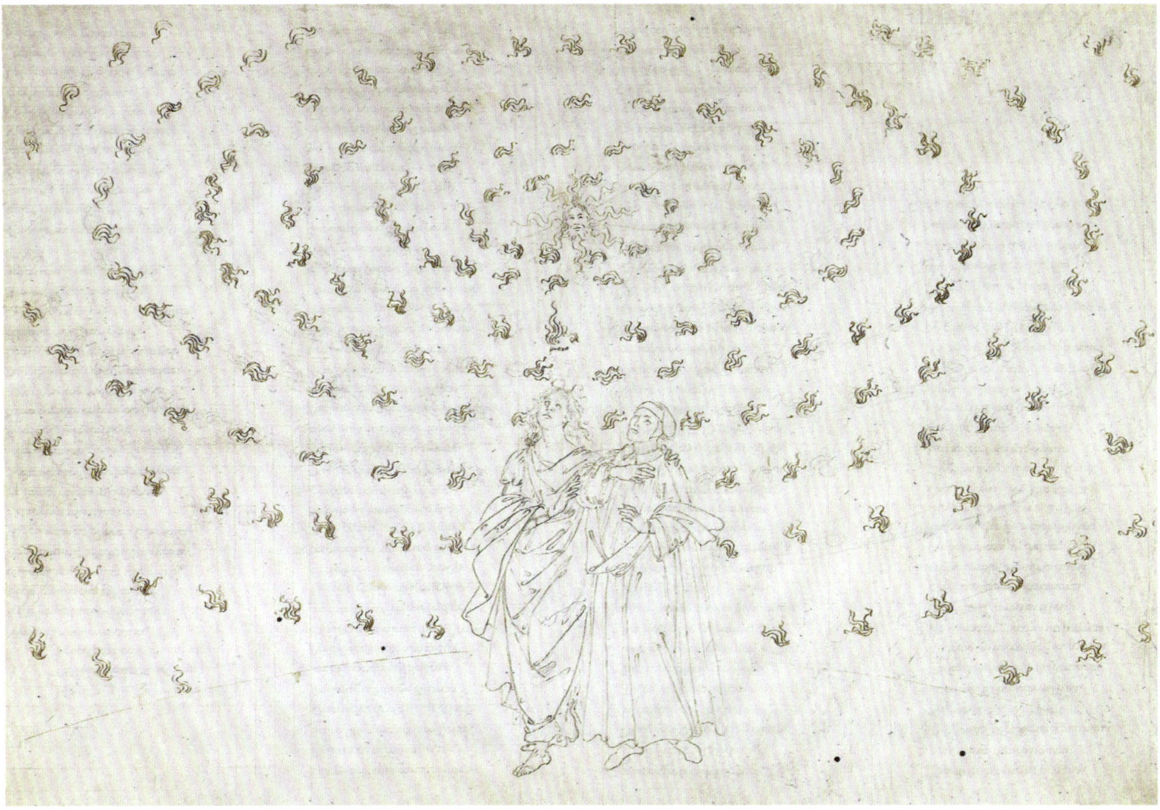

20 Sandro Botticelli, *Dante and Beatrice Converse with St Peter*, in Dante, *Divina Commedia*, *Paradiso*, Canto XXIV, Berlin, Staatliche Museen, Kupferstichkabinett

The surviving illustrations, 92 in number, are drawn on the smooth (flesh) side of large sheets of parchment, 32 cm high by 47 cm wide (12.6 × 18.5 in). The sheets are in two collections, 85 sheets are in Berlin, with seven in the Vatican. Exceptionally, the sheets are orientated horizontally. The texts, written by the hand of Niccolò Mangona, were laid out in four columns on the reverse (follicle) side of each sheet. The intention would have been that each time the pages in the volume were opened, they would have displayed texts next to relevant illustrations. They were probably to be bound along one of their long sides. The illustrations are unfinished, and only three of the pages have been fully coloured, plus another that is partially so. Botticelli began with delicate metal-point lines, some of which have been inked in.

The illustrations for *Inferno* and *Purgatorio* adopt complex narrative modes, like some of the Mediaeval manuscripts, in which Dante and Virgil not infrequently feature two or three times on the same sheet, at different stages in their laborious journey. The compositions are notably varied, with considerable freedom in how the space is handled, often in a non-perspectival manner. It is clear that Botticelli has read the text with close attention. The drawings for *Paradiso* are startlingly different. They are dominated by beautifully drawn and characterised images of Beatrice and Dante conversing, frequently with no other setting than a heavenly circle drawn with compasses (fig.18). Fifteen illustrations included no more these three elements. A further seven added orbiting tongues of

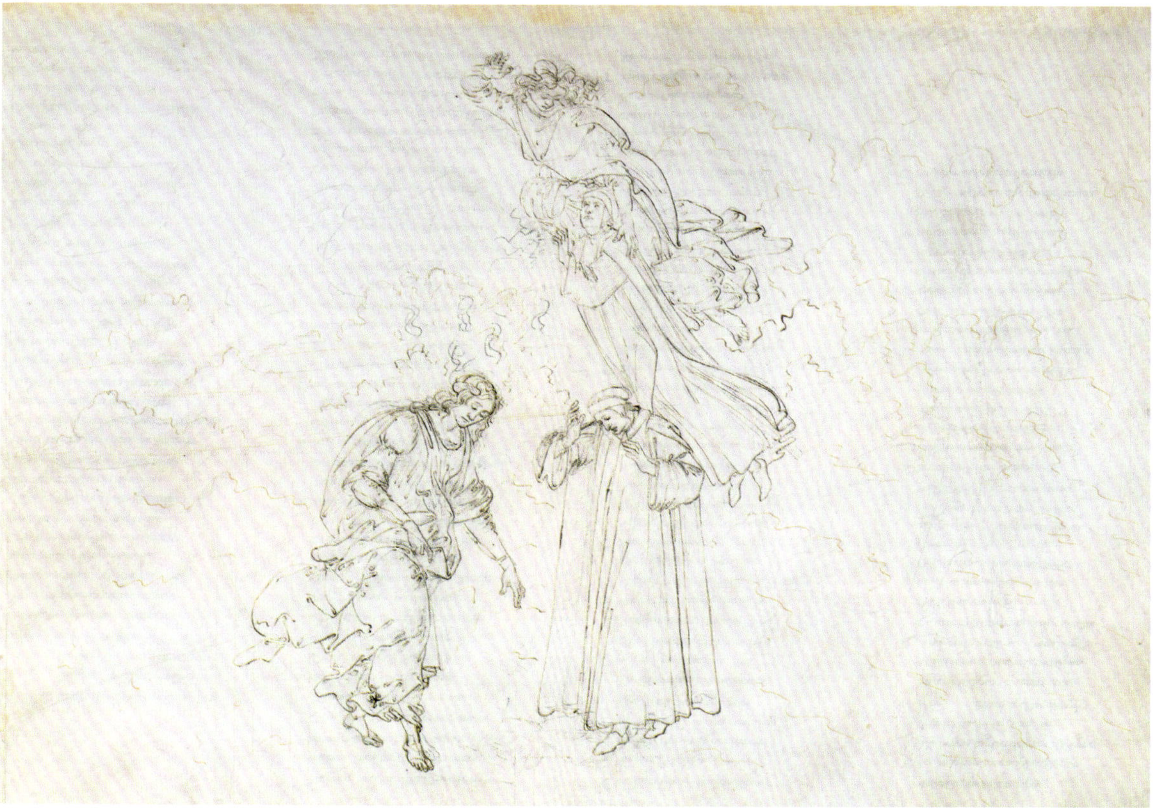

21 Sandro Botticelli, *Dante and Beatrice Look Downwards*, in Dante, *Divina Commedia, Paradiso*, Canto XXVII, Berlin, Staatliche Museen, Kupferstichkabinett

flame to this basic format (fig.20). Five images show airborne angels, including a heavenly choir in massed ranks in what is an unusually dense image (fig.22). This leaves two with slightly more elaborate settings, and one so unfinished as to be indeterminate. Had the illustrations been finished, we may imagine that the circles (spheres of the heavens), the gesticulating figures and the backgrounds would have been coloured in, but there is no indication that most of what Dante described would have been included.

Compared to the Holkham and Giovanni di Paolo manuscripts, there are no standard images of the Virgin and Child, no recognisable saints, no planetary deities, no ancillary figures such as the fishing mermaid, no 'experiment' with the three mirrors …

What is Botticelli saying? In the most radical way, he is not letting us envisage Dante's visions in the normal figurative manner. Dante nowhere says that he saw the saints in heaven as the kind of people in clothes that we see on earth. The rings of flaming light, translated into pure love, are the visible manifestations of the saints, and it is in this form that they speak and are identified. On seven occasions we see Dante and Beatrice encircled by nine heavenly circles of flames 'like comets'. In the illustration to Canto XXIV (fig.20), the mighty St Peter questions Dante on his level of faith. Beatrice intervenes on her companion's behalf. The largest of the flames one rank above Beatrice's searching gaze is labelled '*pietro*'. At the centre of the whirling flames is a radiant sun-face,

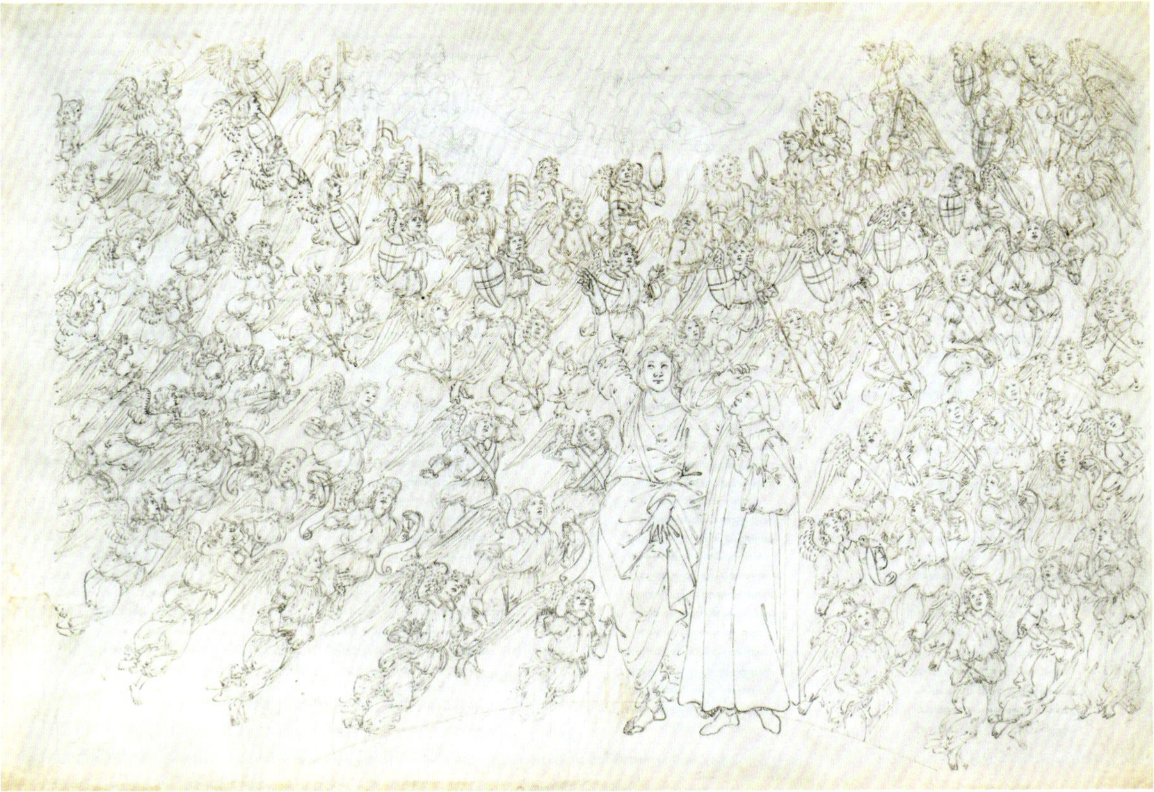

22 Sandro Botticelli, *Dante and Beatrice and the Host of Angels*, in Dante, *Divina Commedia, Paradiso*, Canto XXVIII, Berlin, Staatliche Museen, Kupferstichkabinett

that of Christ, of supreme brightness but not embodied. The various types of angels are, however, shown; we do see them on occasion. They are intermediate figures, messengers sent to earth and operating in Purgatory. To make sense of Botticelli's minimalist representations of the saints and holy figures, we have to imagine the sound of the text being read. The speaking flames emit voices.

The sequential figures of Beatrice and Dante in each drawing move in an almost cinematic manner. Typically, Dante's gestures, glances and expressions are more limited than his companion's. He predominantly reacts in a docile manner. When he raises his hands it is to ward off unbearable brightness or to express surprise and bewilderment. Beatrice, who sometimes seems to look at us, points instructively upwards and downwards, guiding Dante visually and physically. A particularly telling moment is in Canto XXI, when they have reached the seventh and outermost sphere of the planets (fig.19). The ladder of Jacob is placed to conduct them to the sphere of the fixed stars. Beatrice, graceful and light-footed, signals the climb they should undertake. At one point, Botticelli was thinking about also showing their actual ascent, but this has been partially erased and becomes the subject of the next drawing, in which Beatrice actively lifts the timorous poet. When they have ascended even further to the *Primum Mobile*, she instructs Dante to look downwards to see how magnificently far they have risen (fig.21). They have ascended to a place of 'triumphant mists', from which they then levitate spiritually to the final zone of God's heaven.

The last of Botticelli's illustrations is for the penultimate canto. It is very unfinished and shows a very small and distant sketch of the stigmatised Christ and the Virgin, just visible in corporal form at last, with an attendant angel, but there are only a few hints as to how in his abstract mode he could have described the massive celestial rose and its teeming population. For the last canto, with its vision of the Trinity, nothing survives.

In his *Paradiso* illustrations Botticelli's abstinence is heroic and profound – even taking into account that his drawings would have been coloured. No-one comes near his daring level of spiritual minimalism. Other illustrators feel a need to embody the speaking flames of the saints' spirits. John Flaxman, the neoclassical sculptor in the late 18th century, used spare and simple lines with great economy in his set of refined illustrations, but even he felt obliged to give corporeal and costumed form to some of the major saints and holy figures.

It seems impossible that the illustrations could have been realised in a printed book of such size and orientation. We are dealing with specially commissioned images for a discerning private patron. If that patron was indeed Lorenzino, he is to be congratulated on stimulating the greatest of all the illustrated Dantes – but also offered commiserations that the majestic project was never finished.

THE URBINO DANTE

One of the most sumptuous Dante manuscripts was made for Federico da Montefeltro, the great military commander and patron of the arts in Urbino. The opening page of the *Paradiso*, with 'FE[DERICO] DUX' inscribed on the base of the columns, and a cluster of Montefeltro emblems, leaves no doubt about the commissioner's identity (fig.23). Written in a very accomplished hand by Matteo Contugi, the first 72 folios were handsomely illuminated by Guglielmo Giraldi of Ferrara. It was begun in the late 1470s, but we know that things went slowly. Other illuminators were brought in. Finally, after an interval of some years – certainly after the death of Federico – the illustrations for the latter part of *Purgatorio* and the whole of *Paradiso* were added by an unknown artist. Looking at the page that contains the start of *Paradiso*, we can see that the ornamental framework and text were laid in by one of the earlier illuminators. The later artist then added the hyper-elegant Beatrice and dapper Dante. Dante looks enquiringly at Beatrice, as he so often does in the text, while she points to a just-discernible sun-face radiating a powerful golden light, in keeping with the vision of light in the opening lines of *Paradiso*. It is a pity that we do not know the name of the artist, since the illustrations are carried out in a stylish and intelligent manner. The refined figures with their curvilinear grace, the 16th-century equivalents of Giovanni di Paolo's poised participants, are quite similar to those of the Sienese painter Domenico Beccafumi.

At the opening of Canto II in the heaven of the moon, the interlocutors are remarkably set in front of a ghostly female face, as if composed of cloud (fig.24). The same setting occurs in the next two cantos, also based in the moon. The white face does not seem to correspond literally to anything in the cantos, but may allude to the illusive visual effect that Dante describes.

> As through a glass which is transparent and
> polished,
> Or through limpid and tranquil and water,
> Not so deep that its bed is lost from view,
> The details of our faces are reflected
> So faintly, that a pearl on a white forehead
> Does not come less strongly to our pupils.
> . . .
> Thinking that they were reflected images,
> I turned my eyes to see to see whose they were;
> And saw nothing . . .[9]

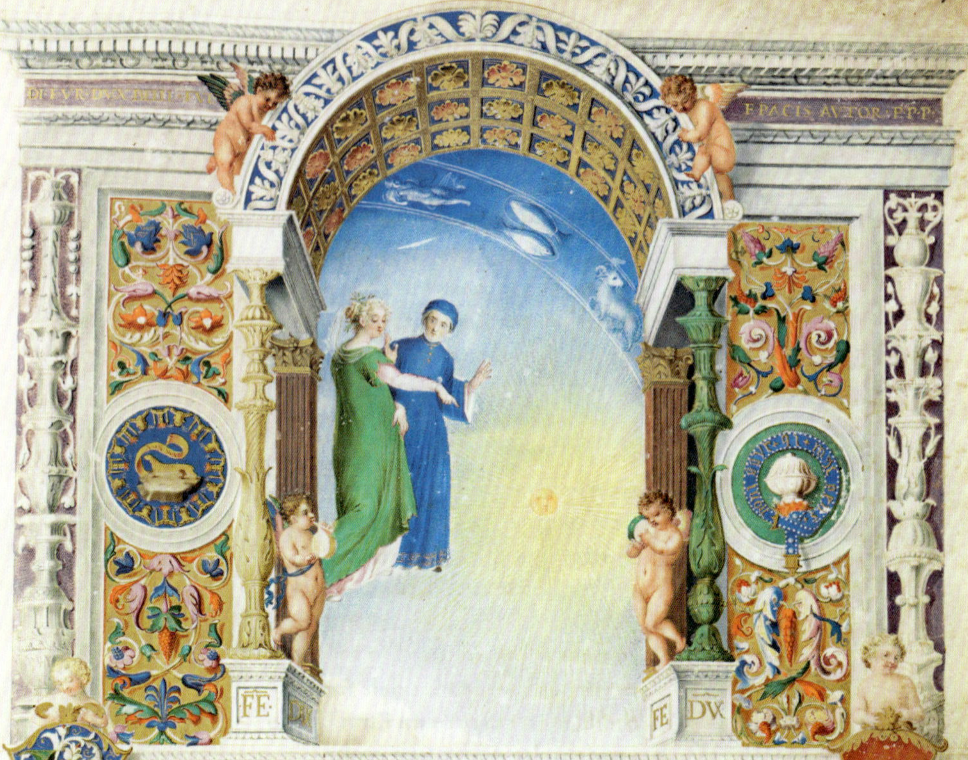

A gloria di colui che tutto muoue
per l'uniuerso penetra et risplende
in una parte piu et meno altroue
Nel ciel che piu de la sua luce rende
fu io. et uidi cose che ridire
ne sa ne puo chi di la su discende
Per che appressandosi al suo disire
nostro intellecto si profonda tanto
che dietro la memoria non puo ire

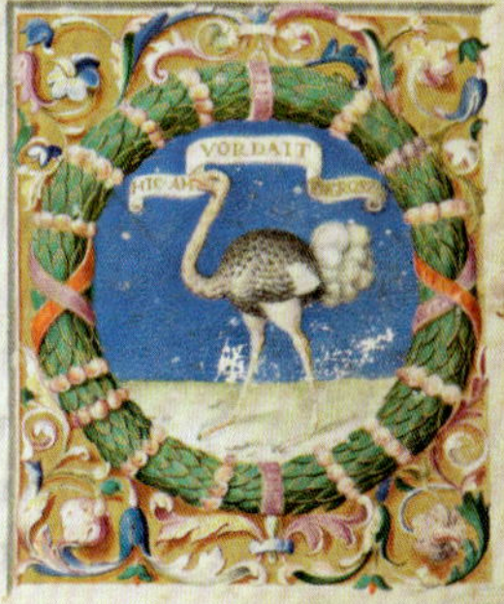

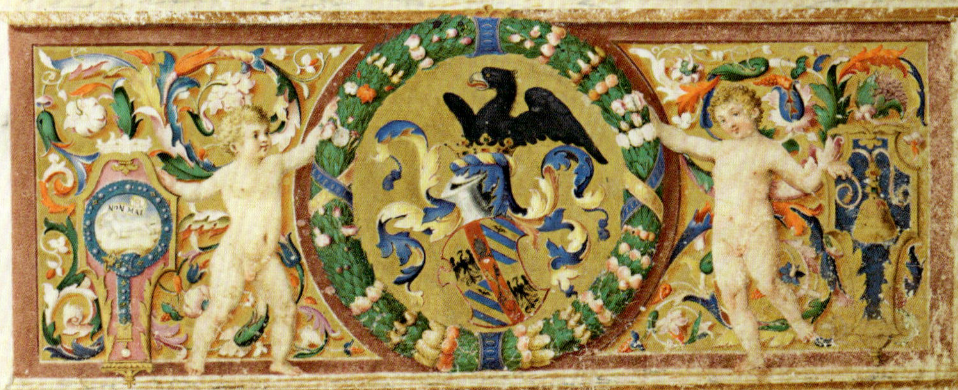

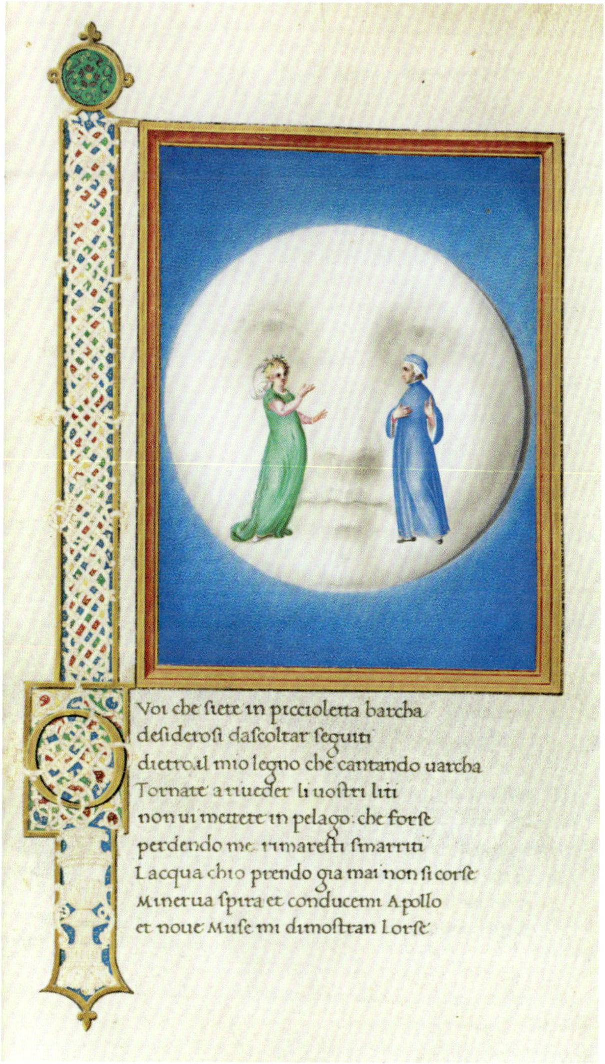

24 *Beatrice and Dante in the Heaven of the Moon*, in Dante, *Divina Commedia*, Rome, Biblioteca Vaticana, MS Codex Urbinas Latinas 365, fol. 200r. © 2020 Biblioteca Apostolica Vaticana

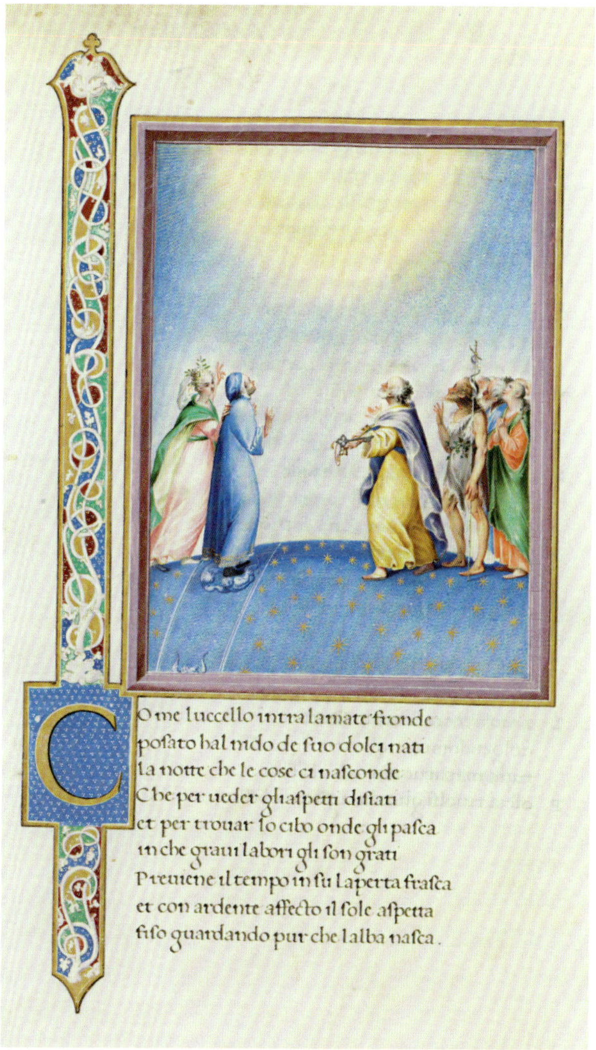

25 *Beatrice, Dante and the Saints and the Vision of Christ's Light*, in Dante, *Divina Commedia*, Rome, Biblioteca Vaticana, MS Codex Urbinas Latinas 365, fol. 262v. © 2020 Biblioteca Apostolica Vaticana

23 (OPPOSITE) *Opening Page of the Paradiso*, in Dante, *Divina Commedia*, Rome, Biblioteca Vaticana, MS Codex Urbinas Latinas 365, fol. 197r. © 2020 Biblioteca Apostolica Vaticana

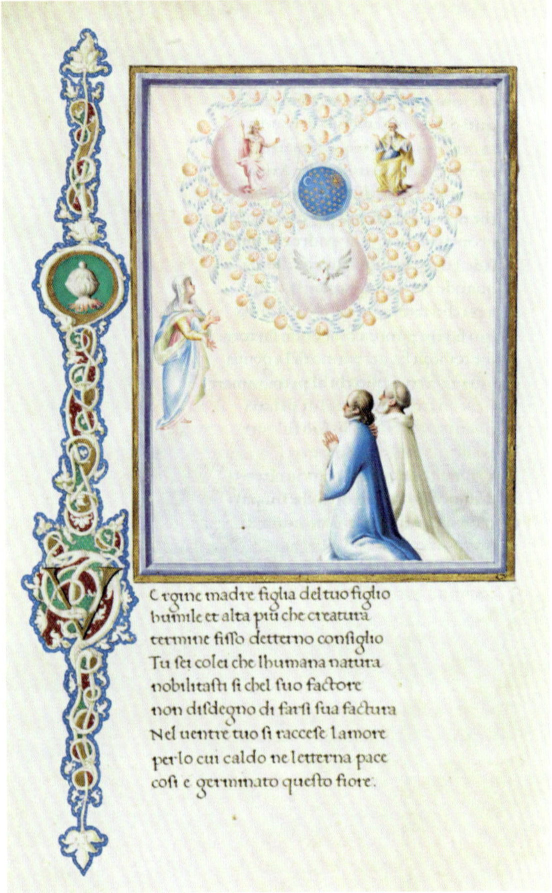

26 *Dante, St Bernard and the Virgin Witness the Trinity*, in Dante, *Divina Commedia*, Rome, Biblioteca Vaticana, MS Codex Urbinas Latinas 365, fol. 292v. © 2020 Biblioteca Apostolica Vaticana

In any event, the subtle face is a notable invention by the illuminator. It is presumably intended as an image of *luna*, the moon, the celestial body they are visiting.

In each of the subsequent cantos that are devoted to visits by Beatrice and Dante to the heavens of the other planets, the action is set within a planetary sphere adorned with 12 points of light. Then, as they leave Saturn, the fields in which the figures move assume rectangular shapes. They and other participants stand on the sphere of the fixed stars to witness ineffable bursts of intense light and pious exchanges between the residents of heaven (fig.25). In the final illustration, Dante, St Bernard and the Virgin see the privileged vision of the Trinity set in an orb of cherubim at the centre of which is a celestial globe containing the moon and the sun (fig.26).

THE MARCOLINI EDITION, 1544

The leading Venetian printer Francesco Marcolini da Forlì, published a large new edition with a commentary by Alessandro Vellutello and no less than 87 woodcuts, including some for the commentary. To include such a comprehensive set of plates was a bold move, and even bolder was the ousting of Landino's commentary. Vellutello, from Lucca, was resident in Venice from 1525 and established himself as an authority of ancient and Renaissance literature. He also seems to have invested heavily in the expensive new edition on his own account. The obvious illustrator was the engraver Giovanni Britto, who had already worked for Marcolini and made a number of effective prints after Titian paintings. However, the level of skill of the Dante illustrations seems to fall somewhat short of Britto's norm. It has been suggested that Vellutello himself was the designer. In the absence of independent evidence that Vellutello had the capacity to design such a large set of plates, the authorship of the designs and woodcuts must remain open. Compared to the Renaissance illustrations we have looked at, those in the Marcolini edition are impressive in number and ambition, while rather limited in artistic sophistication. The edition illustrated here is hand-coloured, increasing the overall cost.

The prints for *Inferno* and *Paradiso* are much concerned with the topography and scenography of the journey, picking up a long-standing interest in calculating actual measurements for the strange realms that Dante describes. As we will see, in chapter six, Galileo became involved in a dispute about the

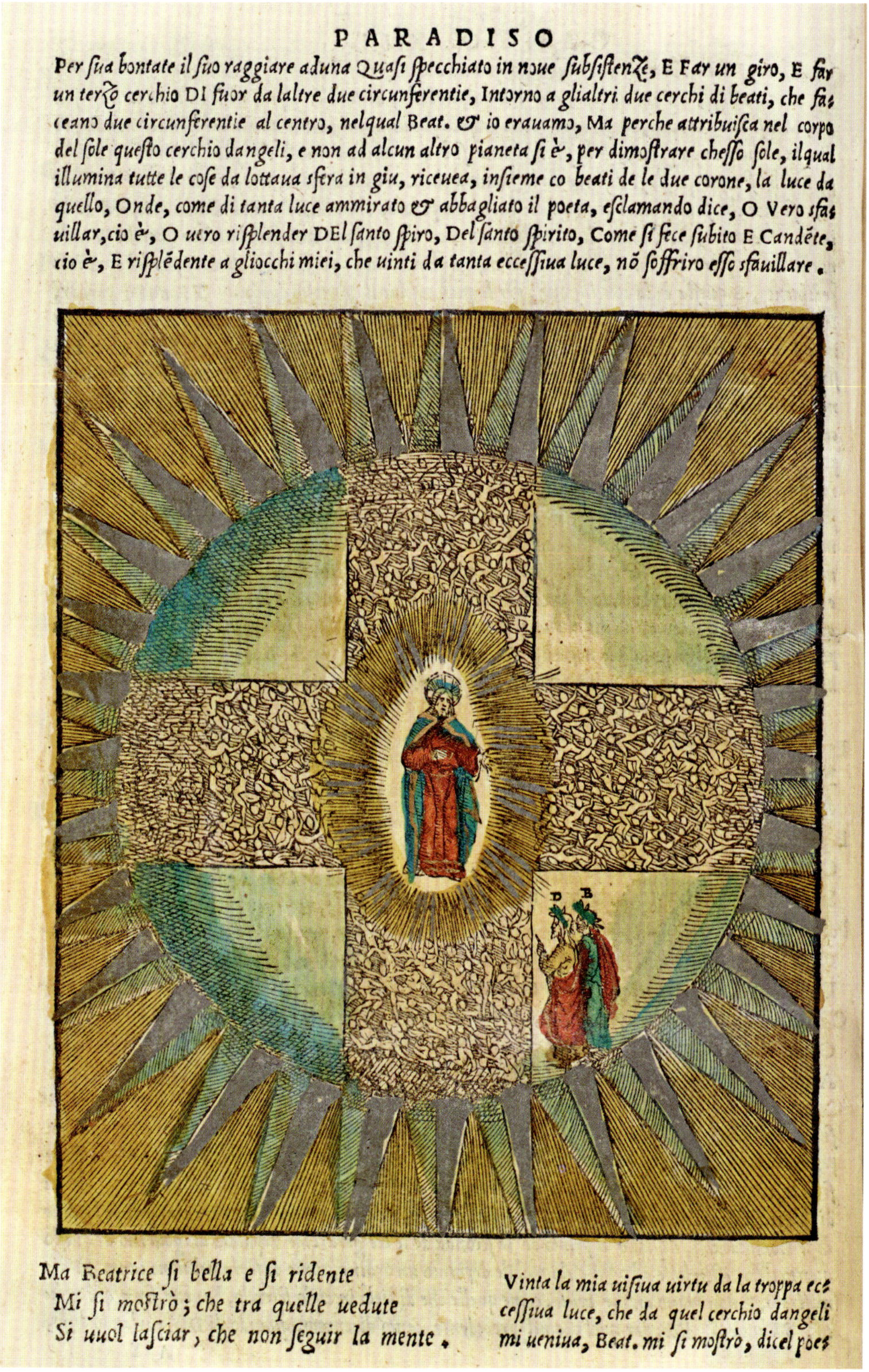

PARADISO

Per sua bontate il suo raggiare aduna Quasi specchiato in noue subsistenze, E Far un giro, E far un terzo cerchio DI fuor da laltre due circunferentie, Intorno a glialtri due cerchi di beati, che faceano due circunferentie al centro, nelqual Beat. & io erauamo, Ma perche attribuisca nel corpo del sole questo cerchio dangeli, e non ad alcun altro pianeta si è, per dimostrare chesso sole, ilqual illumina tutte le cose da lottaua sfera in giu, riceuea, insieme co beati de le due corone, la luce da quello, Onde, come di tanta luce ammirato & abbagliato il poeta, esclamando dice, O Vero sfauillar, cio è, O uero risplender DEl santo spiro, Del santo spirito, Come si fece subito E Candēte, cio è, E risplēdente a gliocchi miei, che uinti da tanta eccessiua luce, nō soffriro esso sfauillare.

Ma Beatrice si bella e si ridente
Mi si mostrò; che tra quelle uedute
Si uuol lasciar, che non seguir la mente.

Vinta la mia uisiua uirtu da la troppa eccessiua luce, che da quel cerchio dangeli mi ueniua, Beat. mi si mostrò, dicel poet

27 *The Vision of the Cross in the Heaven of Mars,* in *La comedia di Dante Aligieri,* commentary by Alessandro Vellutello, published by Francesco Marcolini, Venice, 1544, Canto XIV

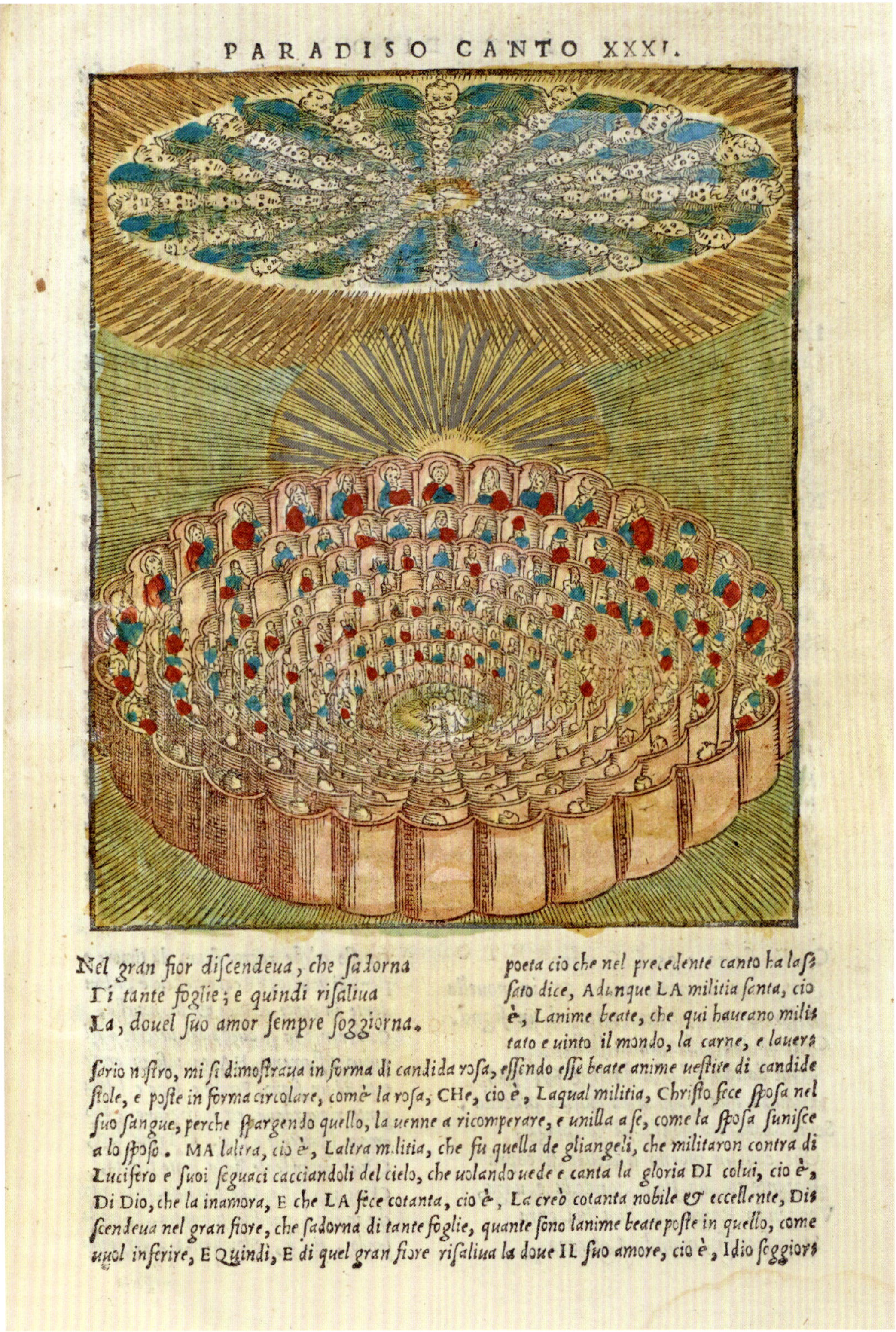
PARADISO CANTO XXXI.

Nel gran fior discendeua, che sadorna
Di tante foglie; e quindi risaliua
La, douel suo amor sempre soggiorna.

poeta cio che nel precedente canto ha lassato dice, Adunque LA militia santa, cio è, Lanime beate, che qui haueano militato e uinto il mondo, la carne, e lauersario nostro, mi si dimostraua in forma di candida rosa, essendo esse beate anime uestite di candide stole, e poste in forma circolare, comè la rosa, CHe, cio è, Laqual militia, Christo fece sposa nel suo sangue, perche spargendo quello, la uenne a ricomperare, e unilla a se, come la sposa sunisce a lo sposo. MA laltra, cio è, Laltra militia, che fu quella de gliangeli, che militaron contra di Lucifero e suoi seguaci cacciandoli del cielo, che uolando uede e canta la gloria DI colui, cio è, Di Dio, che la inamora, E che LA fece cotanta, cio è, La creò cotanta nobile & eccellente, Discendeua nel gran fiore, che sadorna di tante foglie, quante sono lanime beate poste in quello, come uuol inferire, E Quindi, E di quel gran fiore risaliua la doue IL suo amore, cio è, Idio soggiorn

28 *The Sempiternal Rose with Rings of Angels*, in *La comedia di Dante Aligieri*, commentary by Alessandro Vellutello, published by Francesco Marcolini, Venice, 1544, Canto XXVI

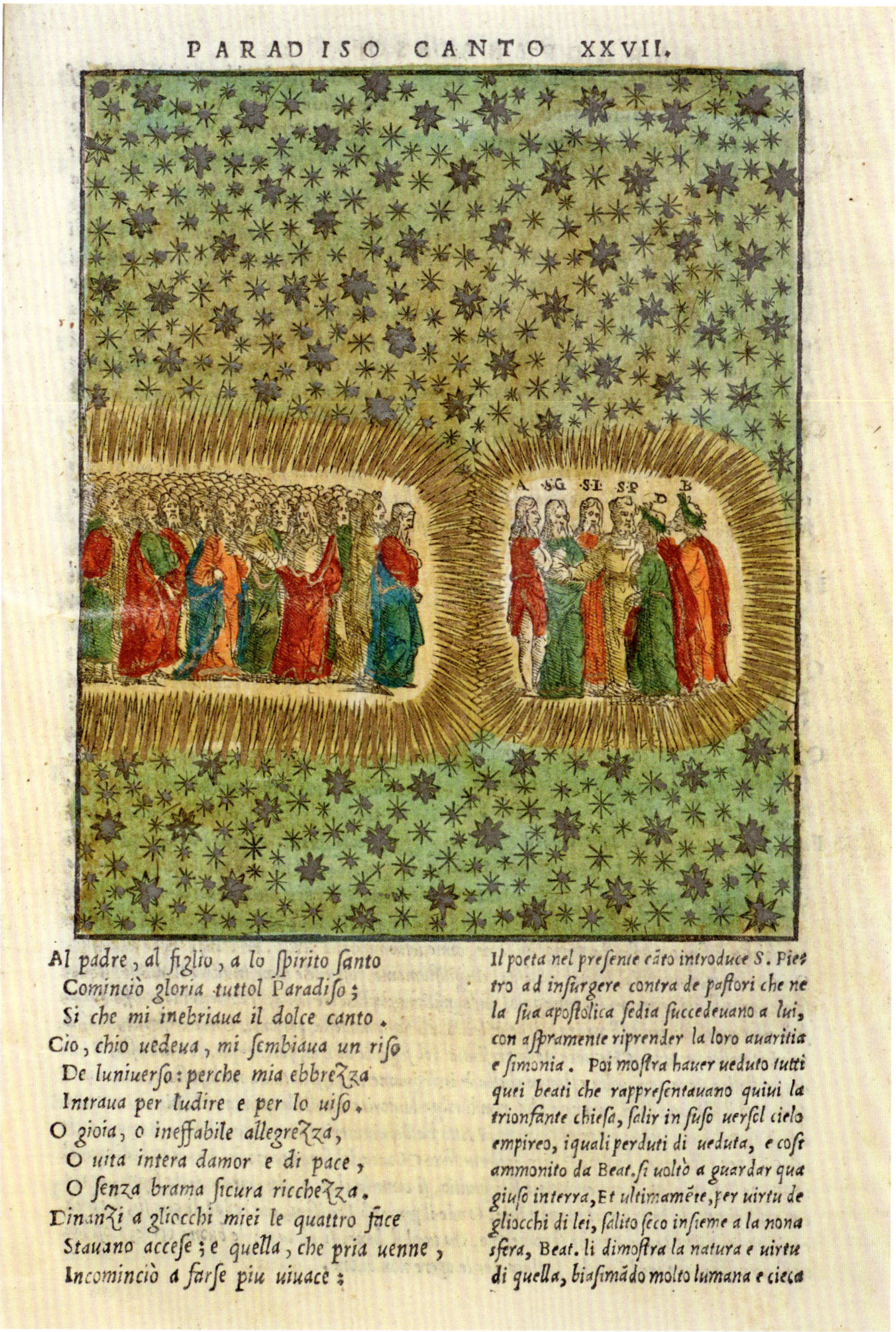
PARADISO CANTO XXVII.

Al padre, al figlio, a lo spirito santo
Cominciò gloria tuttol Paradiso;
Si che mi inebriaua il dolce canto.
Cio, chio uedeua, mi sembiaua un riso
De luniuerso: perche mia ebbrezza
Intraua per ludire e per lo uiso.
O gioia, o ineffabile allegrezza,
O uita intera damor e di pace,
O senza brama sicura ricchezza.
Dinanzi a gliocchi miei le quattro face
Stauano accese; e quella, che pria uenne,
Incominciò a farse piu uiuace:

Il poeta nel presente cãto introduce S. Pietro ad insurgere contra de pastori che ne la sua apostolica sedia succedeuano a lui, con aspramente riprender la loro auaritia e simonia. Poi mostra hauer ueduto tutti quei beati che rappresentauano quiui la trionfante chiesa, salir in suso uersel cielo empireo, iquali perduti di ueduta, e cosi ammonito da Beat. si uoltò a guardar qua giuso interra, Et ultimamẽte, per uirtu de gliocchi di lei, salito seco insieme a la nona sfera, Beat. li dimostra la natura e uirtu di quella, biasimãdo molto lumana e cieca

29 *St Peter Denounces Pope Boniface VIII*, in *La comedia di Dante Aligieri*, commentary by Alessandro Vellutello, published by Francesco Marcolini, Venice, 1544, Canto XXVIII

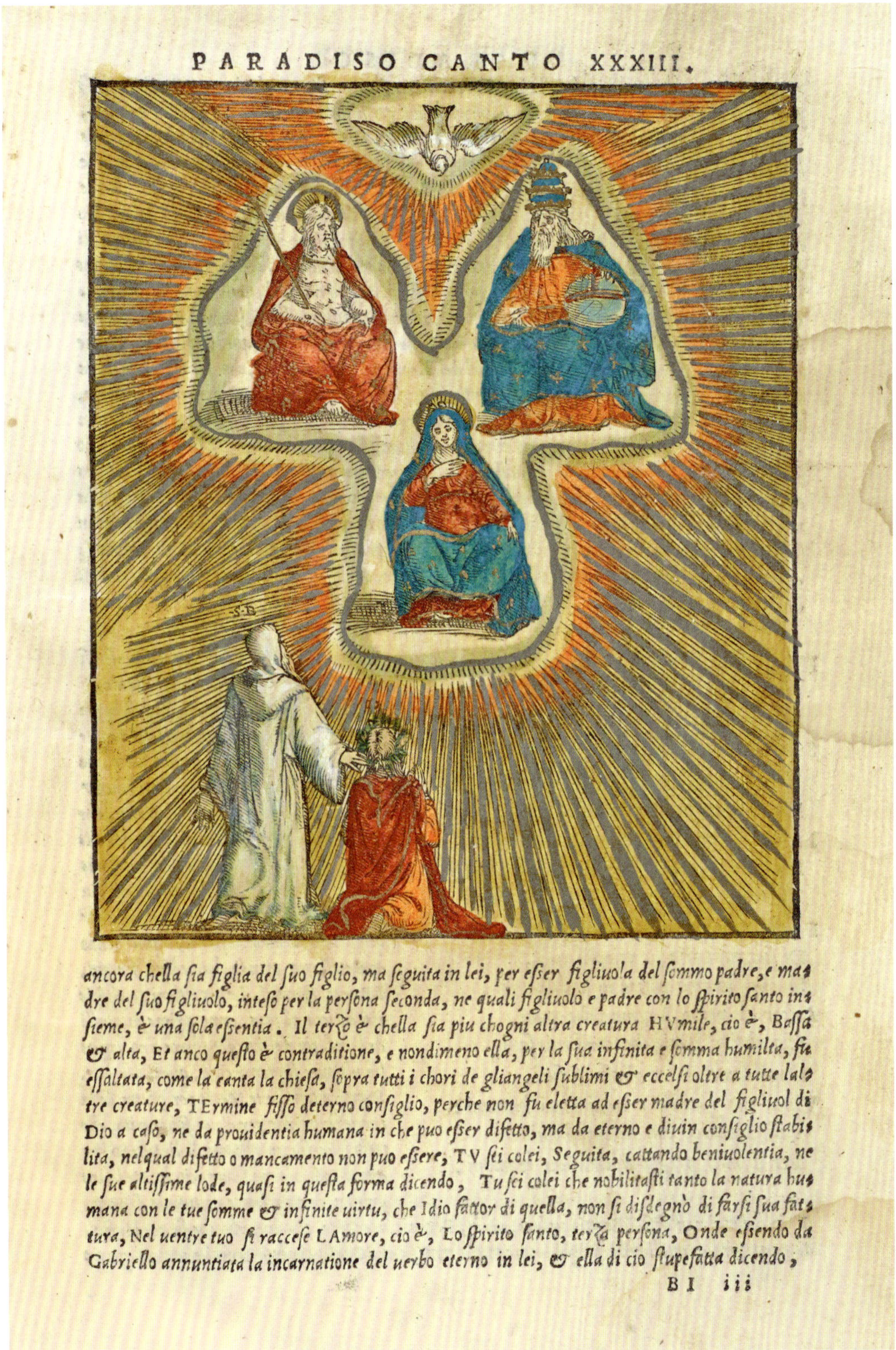

PARADISO CANTO XXXIII.

ancora chella sia figlia del suo figlio, ma seguita in lei, per esser figliuola del sommo padre, e ma-
dre del suo figliuolo, inteso per la persona seconda, ne quali figliuolo e padre con lo spirito santo in-
sieme, è una sola essentia. Il terzo è chella sia piu chogni altra creatura HVmile, cio è, Bassa
& alta, Et anco questo è contraditione, e nondimeno ella, per la sua infinita e somma humilta, fu
essaltata, come la canta la chiesa, sopra tutti i chori de gliangeli sublimi & eccelsi oltre a tutte lal-
tre creature, TErmine fisso deterno consiglio, perche non fu eletta ad esser madre del figliuol di
Dio a caso, ne da prouidentia humana in che puo esser difetto, ma da eterno e diuin consiglio stabi-
lita, nelqual difetto o mancamento non puo essere, TV sei colei, Seguita, cattando beniuolentia, ne
le sue altissime lode, quasi in questa forma dicendo, Tu sei colei che nobilitasti tanto la natura hu-
mana con le tue somme & infinite uirtu, che Idio fattor di quella, non si disdegnò di farsi sua fat-
tura, Nel uentre tuo si raccese LAmore, cio è, Lo spirito santo, terza persona, Onde essendo da
Gabriello annuntiata la incarnatione del uerbo eterno in lei, & ella di cio stupefatta dicendo,

BI iii

30 *St Bernard and Dante Witness a Vision of the Trinity with the Virgin*, in *La comedia di Dante Aligieri*, commentary by Alessandro Vellutello, published by Francesco Marcolini, Venice, 1544, Canto XXXII

dimensions of Hell and Purgatory. By contrast, the *Paradiso* plates devoted to the heavens of the planets settle on a stock formula of a luminous sphere surrounded by a corona of rays, within which the incidents are set. The image of the cross in the heaven of Mars is typical (fig.27). Dante and Beatrice are labelled D and B, as they are throughout, which hardly seems necessary. The image of Christ, elusive and fleeting in the text, is fully realised in a mandorla of light. The 'atoms' of dust that Dante likened to the moving lights within the cross are rendered, rather cleverly, as tangles of tiny figures, presumably signifying the souls of the redeemed.

The sempiternal rose is effectively rendered as a kind of circular, terraced auditorium, with orbiting ranks of angels overhead (fig.28). The overt geometry of the composition is a feature of many of the plates. Once the various protagonists are in the realm of the fixed stars, they stand in luminous islands set within an untidy firmament. In Canto XXVII, for example, a space inhabited by a throng of saints is flanked by a separate group of Adam, St James, St John and St Peter – labelled by initials – with Dante and Beatrice (fig.29). St Peter has embarked on the tirade in which he disowns the incumbent of the throne of St Peter in Rome, Pope Boniface VIII, who ranks at the top of Dante's pantheon of despised contemporaries. Given the unsophisticated literalness of the illustrations, we should not be surprised to find the final image of the Trinity is rather literally illustrative (fig.30). 'S.B[ernardino].', St Bernard, presents the kneeling Dante. The illustrator has tried his hardest to flood the plate with divine rays to signal that this final vision of light overtops all the others to which Dante has been subject. Oddly, the Trinity has become a quaternity with the admission of the Virgin to their light-filled realm. Perhaps she counts as 'our effigy', as described by Dante in the final elusive and overwhelming vision.

By concentrating on divine light in *Paradiso*, we have not generally allowed the illustrators to stretch their wings. We may well sense that they relished the creative devilry of *Inferno* and the vivid miseries of the sinners in *Purgatorio* considerably more than the succession of divine radiances in *Paradiso*. All our illustrators have realised that light is the key to illustrating Dante's experiences in the planetary and celestial heavens. However, differentiating one burst of light from another – and progressively upping the light levels – taxes the visual resources available to even the best illuminators. To do so without recourse to colour is even more taxing. This makes it all the more extraordinary how Botticelli, in drawings for what were intended to become coloured plates, had the courage to leave abstract visual spaces into which we can project the visions that the poet recounts in words. Botticelli, compared to the others, was an artist of the highest imagination and talent. In the following chapters we will see how other painters of genius painted the unpaintable.

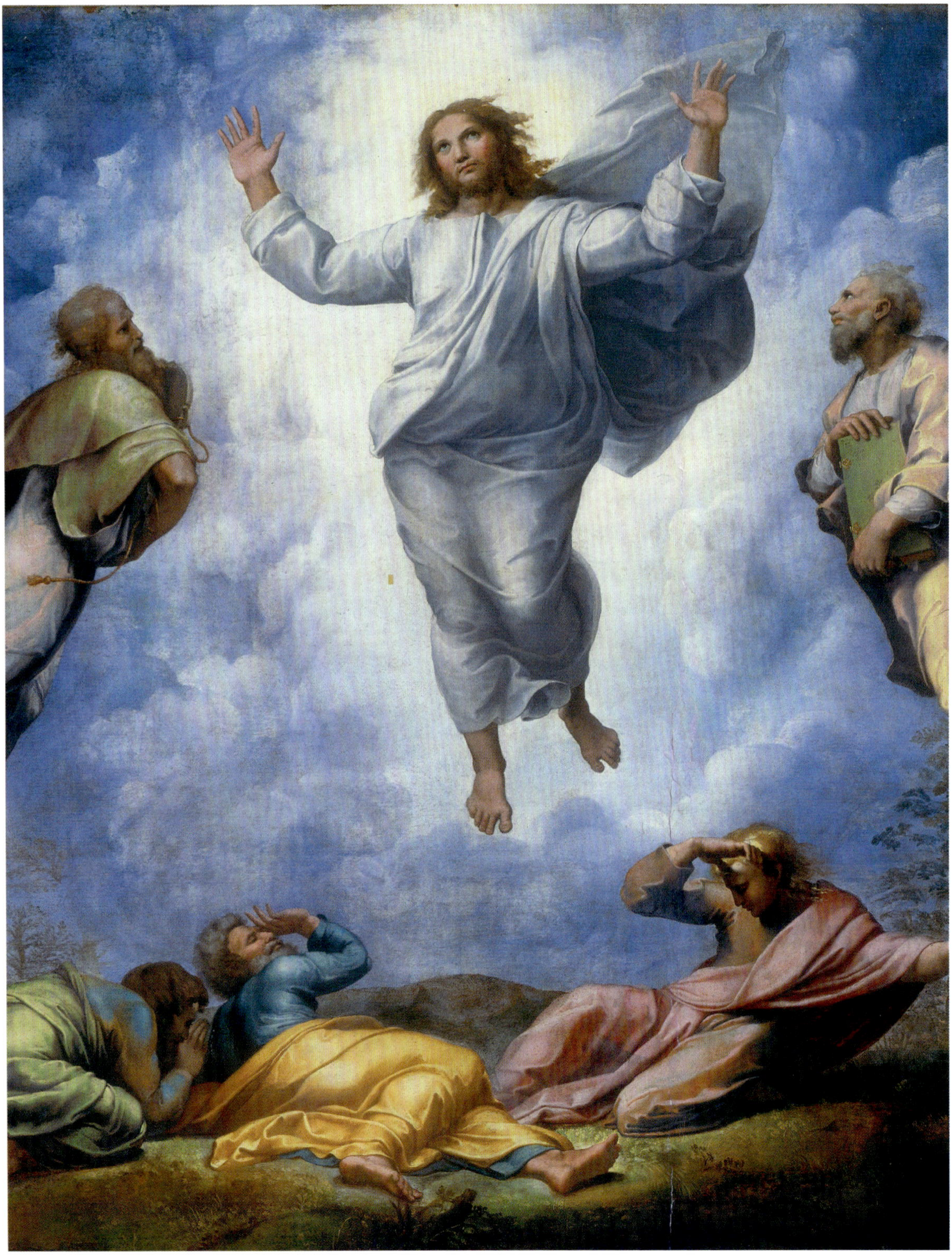

4

Dantesque Dramas: from Giotto to Titian

Dante set the standards of our *paragone* as high as they could be, both through what he described and what he was unable to describe. In the chapters that follow on Renaissance and Baroque art we will encounter a series of major masters. This is not simply because they are very good and belong to the canon of 'great artists', but because it takes visionary artists of substantial intellectual, imaginative and manual accomplishments to take on the challenge of Dante – whether or not they were consciously doing so.

GIOTTO AND THE RADIANCE OF GOLD

The obvious place to begin is with a contemporary painter of whom Dante was aware, Giotto di Bondone. In *Purgatorio*, in a section devoted to pride, Dante notes that

> In painting Cimabue thought he held
> The field, and now 'Giotto' is the cry
> And the fame of former is overshadowed.[1]

We cannot doubt that Giotto reciprocated this knowledge and was aware of Dante. It is probable that a likeness of the poet featured in a lost mural in Palazzo del Podestà (palace of the chief law officer in Florence, now the Bargello), painted by the studio of Giotto. The much-touted 'portrait of Dante' on the altar wall of the chapel in the palace is almost certainly not the painting mentioned in the early sources.

The most Dantesque of the paintings by Giotto himself is not in Florence but in Padua, where he was commissioned to decorate a free-standing chapel built by the financier Enrico Scrovegni, whose father, Reginaldo, unhappily features as a usurer in the *Inferno*. It may be that Enrico built the chapel because he felt that he had a debt to pay to heaven. The murals were finished before Dante had completed the *Commedia*. We can best see the two artists as drawing upon visual and theological sources of the early 14th century in comparably brilliant ways.

In Giotto's magisterial mural *The Last Judgement*, painted on the east wall of the chapel and finished by 1305, we see (at the bottom, left of centre) Enrico presenting his benefaction to three women with halos, identifiable as the Three Marys (the Virgin Mary, Mary Magdalene and, probably, Mary of Clopas), while a monk assumes their physical burden (fig.31). The monk's white habit suggests that he is a Benedictine, in recognition of Pope Benedict XI's 1304 grant of indulgences (time off from Purgatory) to those who worshipped in the chapel. Christ presides over the process that determines who is selected for heavenly bliss and who is eternally

Raphael, *The Transfiguration of Christ* (detail), Rome Vatican

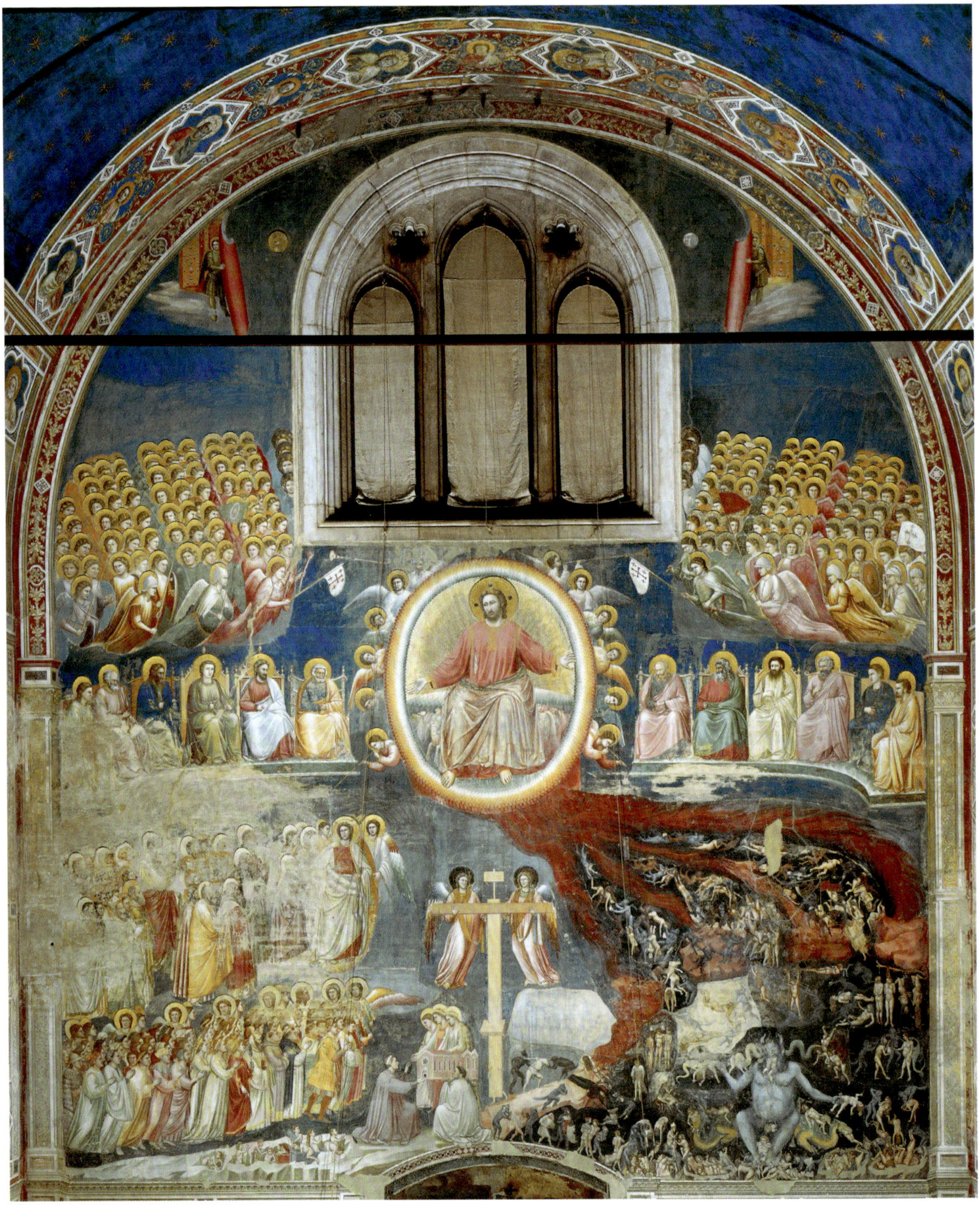

31 Giotto, *The Last Judgement*, Padua, Scrovegni (or Arena) Chapel

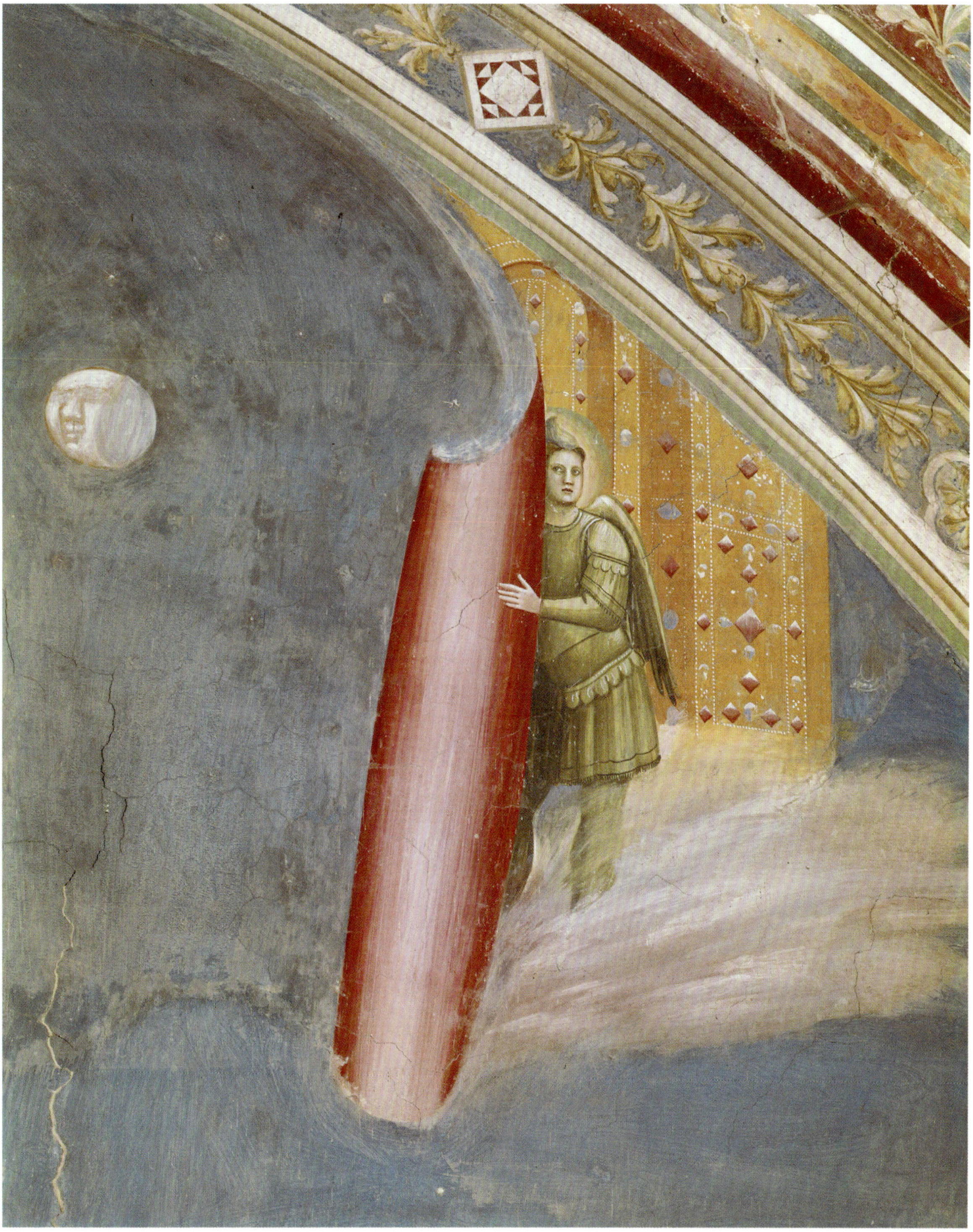

32 Giotto, *The Last Judgement*, detail of the angel on the right rolling back the plaster, Padua, Scrovegni (or Arena) Chapel

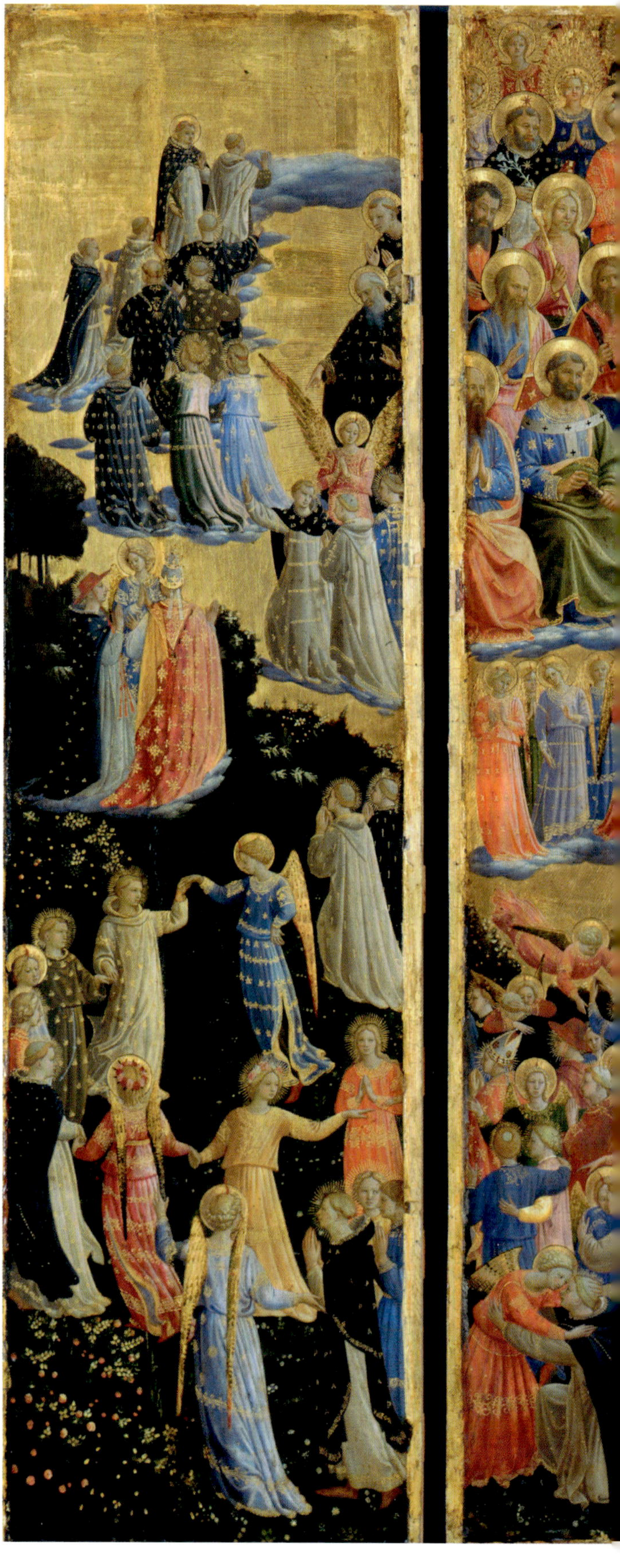

33 Fra Angelico, *The Last Judgement*, Berlin, Gemäldegalerie

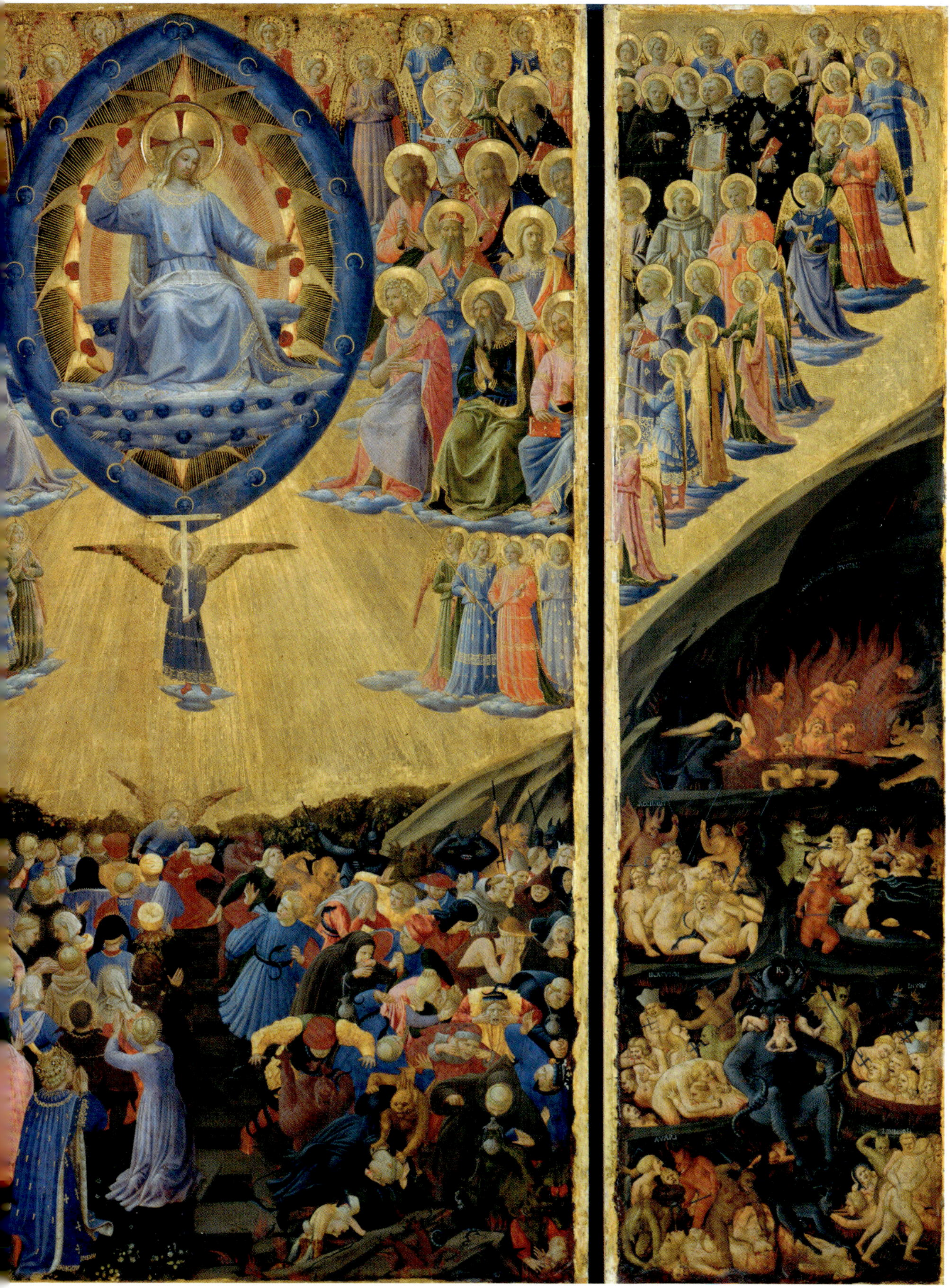

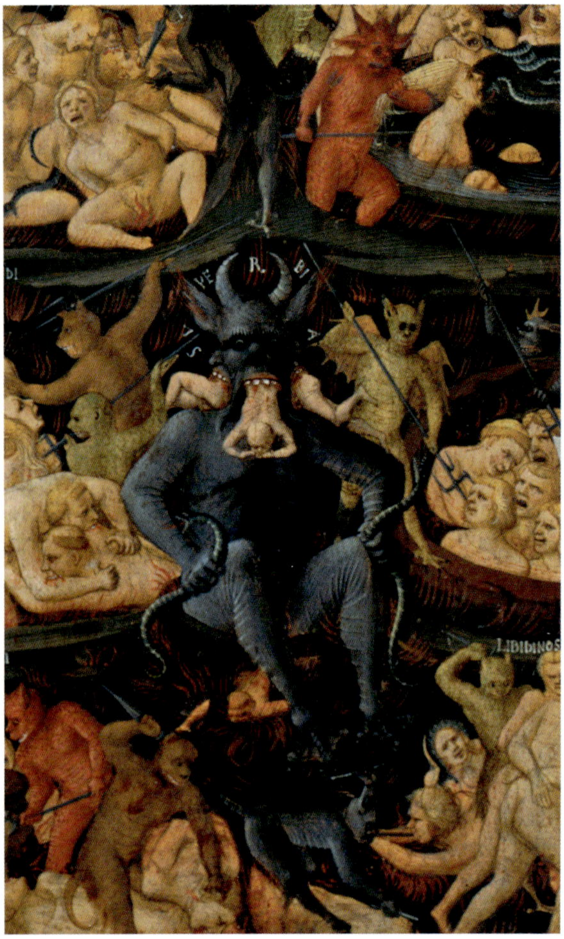

34 Fra Angelico, *The Last Judgement*, detail of Satan and punished sinners, Berlin, Gemäldegalerie

condemned to hideous punishment in a realm of gloom. Giotto's monstrous Satan, ingesting and egesting sinners in a disgusting manner, is a more dominant master of his realm than Dante's diminished but still sinister rival to God. Christ himself, though realised in a more enduring, concrete and corporeal form than Dante ever imagined, is a powerful source of incised rays of golden light and is surrounded by a faceted mandorla in rainbow colours. Above the curved row of seated disciples, angels lead the blessed in groups of three in seven rings. They comprise something like the sempiternal rose, but without its petals. The massed ranks of the undifferentiated blessed – less than exciting for artists and writers – feature in the works of both Giotto and Dante.

Perhaps the most telling parallel between Giotto and Dante is their sophisticated self-consciousness as artists. Dante is immersed in his text and overtly conscious of its nature as poetry – and of the limitations of his art. Giotto, in an unprecedented move, shows two armoured angels near the top of the actual window rolling back the *intonaco* (the upper layer of smooth plaster) on which he painted the sky (fig.32). We catch two tantalising glimpses of the entrance to God's exclusive mansion, the walls of which are gilded and decorated in the manner of embossed and stamped leather. Giotto is in effect declaring that his presentation of the Last Judgement is indeed a representation that he, as an artist, has invented – it is an *imago*.

Essentially the same ingredients are visible well into the next century with Fra Angelico's *Last Judgement* in Berlin, one of a number of versions by the Dominican monk (fig.33). It would be easy to characterise the cloistered and pious Fra Angelico as conservative, compared to the overtly radical Masaccio or even Uccello, but this would be a mistake. Fra Angelico worked under the direct patronage of Cosimo de' Medici, complementing the Renaissance architecture of the Florentine church and convent of San Marco with a series of altarpieces and frescoes that applied the latest style to traditional devotional subjects. An earlier *Last Judgement* had been commissioned from Fra Angelico by the leading humanist Ambrogio Traversari for the nearby church of Santa Maria degli Angeli, designed by Filippo Brunelleschi as a centralised 'temple' in the very latest manner. Fra Angelico was also a prominent figure in the Dominican hierarchy in Tuscany, serving as vicar of the monastery of San Domenico in Fiesole, the monks from which took over San Marco in 1437 under the patronage of Cosimo de' Medici. It is highly likely,

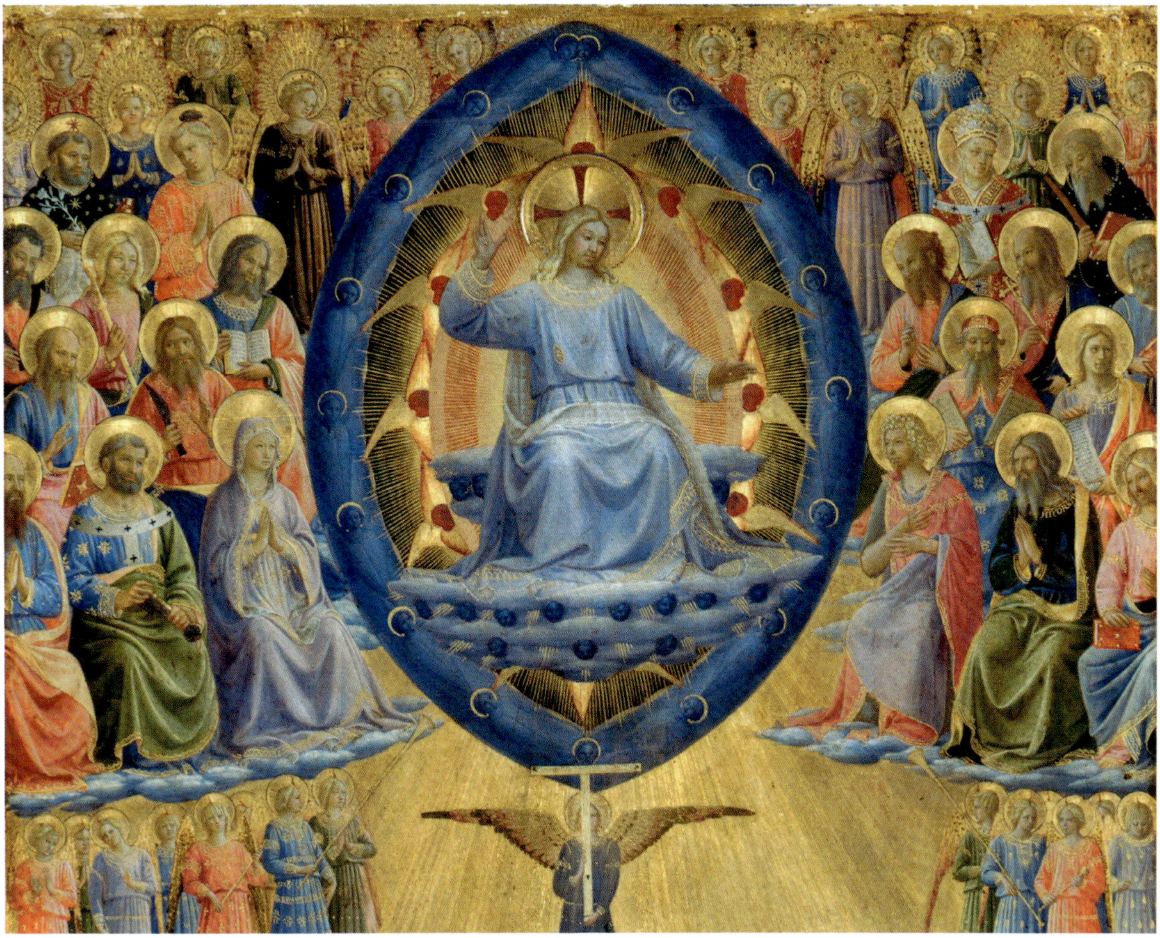

35 Fra Angelico, *The Last Judgement*, detail of Christ and the saints in Heaven, Berlin, Gemäldegalerie

given this sophisticated and high-powered context for his career, that Fra Angelico was well acquainted with the Florentine tradition of the *Commedia*.

The Berlin *Last Judgement*, probably painted in the late 1430s, pulls out the traditional stops and a good number of the modern ones. The perspectival sequence of open graves, from which the elect rise and the damned are expelled, and the controlled diminution of the more distant figures throughout the paradisiacal and heavenly realms, reveals an artist fully versed in the new spatial techniques. The strata of hell obey no such obvious spatial rules and are piled up as Dantesque terraces in zones labelled with the seven sins for which the tortured souls are condemned. For example, to the left of Satan, who is ingesting and egesting, the *iracundi* (the wrathful) viciously bite and claw each other and themselves until the end of time (fig.34).

Again, as was necessary in a painted image, Christ is realised in concrete visual form, softly modelled in light and shade, while the divine light that he emits is pitched as high as possible (fig.35). The large areas of burnished gold are densely incised with rays. The rays penetrate a succession of curved mandorlas, including two formed by cunningly designed cherubim and seraphim. The emanations of light radiate insistently from a common centre, as Dante describes:

> I saw a point that radiated a light
> So intense that the sight it burnt on
> Had to close because of the powerful brilliance.[2]

This extract raises the question about when this way of describing divine light was invented. A circular or mandorla-shaped surround for Christ is common enough in Mediaeval art but not a highly geometrical radiance of rays from a single point. The emission of light in straight lines (*raggi*) that radiate from the original source (*luce*), to cast their luminance (*splendore*) on solid bodies, originates as the foundation of Mediaeval optics. There were certainly earlier images in which bands or beams of light were characterised, as in the Sinai *Transfiguration* (fig.1), but not as densely incised 'spokes' from a common centre. Is the motif an invention in the age of Dante? It is apparent to a limited degree in Giotto's works. As with Dante, the centralised radiance in Fra Angelico's picture casts its *splendore* on the angels and saints, not least on the angels with peacock arrays of gold at the summit of the picture (fig.35).

We will not be surprised that Giovanni di Paolo, luminous illustrator of Dante, was a master of gilded light in his panel paintings. Take, for instance, the *Madonna and Child* that he painted as the central panel in a large altarpiece for the Branchini family chapel in San Domenico in Siena in 1427 (fig.36). At the bottom of the panel we read that 'Giovanni of Siena son of Paolo painted it in 1427'. The pious painter offered a personal prayer in Mary's halo: 'I painted this for you. O Virgin, Protect this man.' In 1427, Giovanni was in his early twenties and it was a year after Masaccio's austere and perspectival *Pisa Madonna*. Giovanni's painting is a stylistic and technical *tour de force*. More than half the surface area of the panel is brightly gilded. Fluttering cherubim and a pretty scattering of plants are painted in glazes over the gold. The Virgin's halo is richly tooled, as is her radiant explosion of light, which rather overwhelms God the Father and the dove. Her crown is modelled in plaster and adorned with glass jewels, while her dress and the skirt of Christ exploit a spectacular melange of paint and gold. We may recall Dante quoting Albertus Magnus, who observed that 'certain bodies become so luminous as soon as the sun sees them that by multiplying the light inside them and on their surfaces they render a great splendour [*splendore*] upon other bodies, as do gold and other stones.'[3] Giovanni di Paolo subscribes to this world of optical wonder as a fitting way to show the divinity of Mary, Queen of Heaven. It was a choice he continued to make up to his death 55 years later.

THE LOGIC OF LIGHT

In the meantime, Leon Battista Alberti, in his book *On Painting* in 1435/6, had set out the new ideal of rigorous naturalism. Alberti was a classically educated humanist and friend of the artists in Florence who were forging the latest Renaissance style in painting, sculpture and architecture. In his short but revolutionary book, in both Italian and Latin versions, he argued that a good painting should convince the viewers that it was acting as a window on a scene that corresponds to our vision of actual forms in space. This applied even if what the viewers witness involves characters and settings they could not expect to see in reality. This goal could be achieved through the description of space according to the geometrical rules of perspective and the systematic imitation of light and shade on solid bodies. The effect of glare on a shiny object in a painting could be imitated through the skilful use of paint.

36 Giovanni di Paolo, *Madonna and Child*, 1427, Pasadena, the Norton Simon Foundation

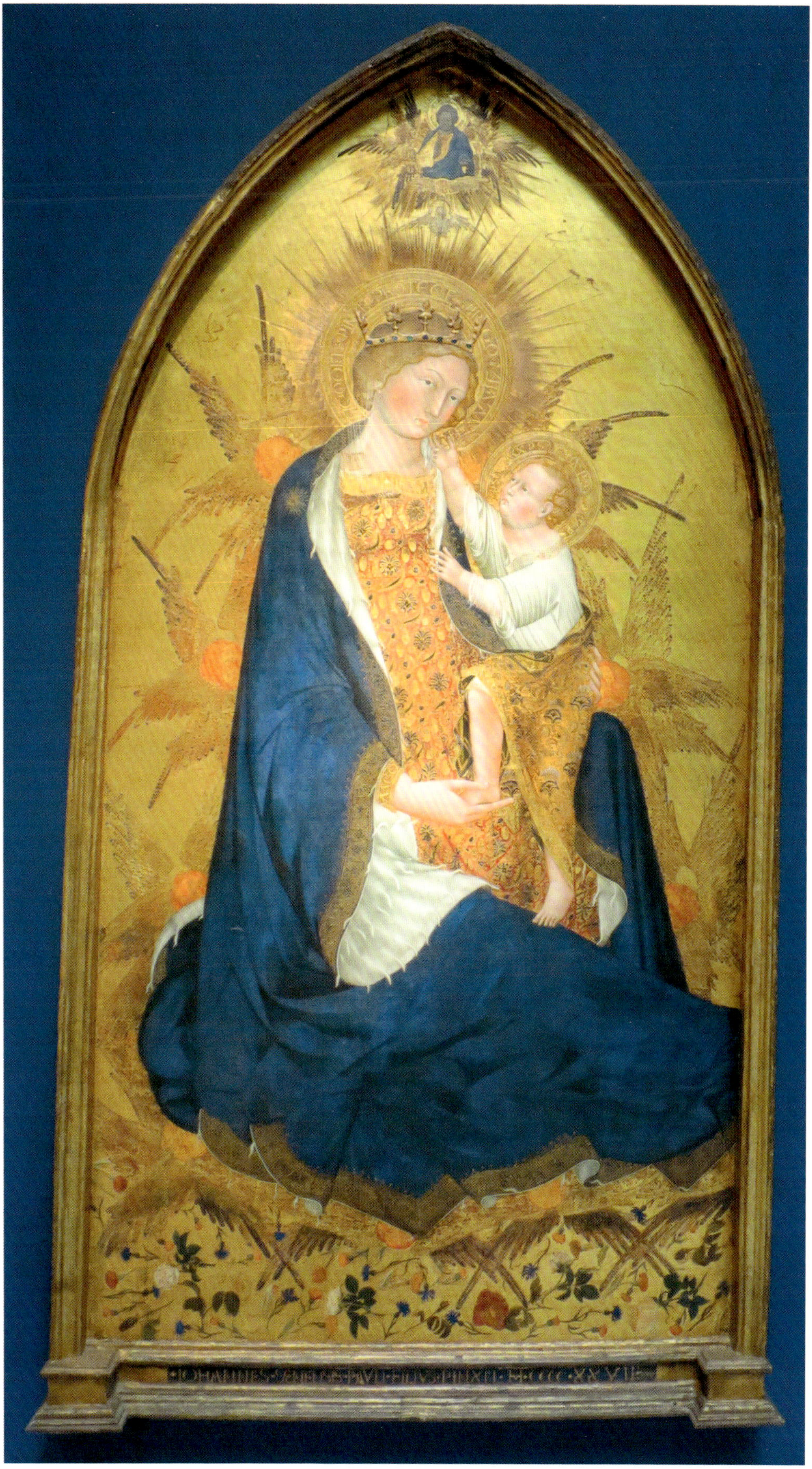

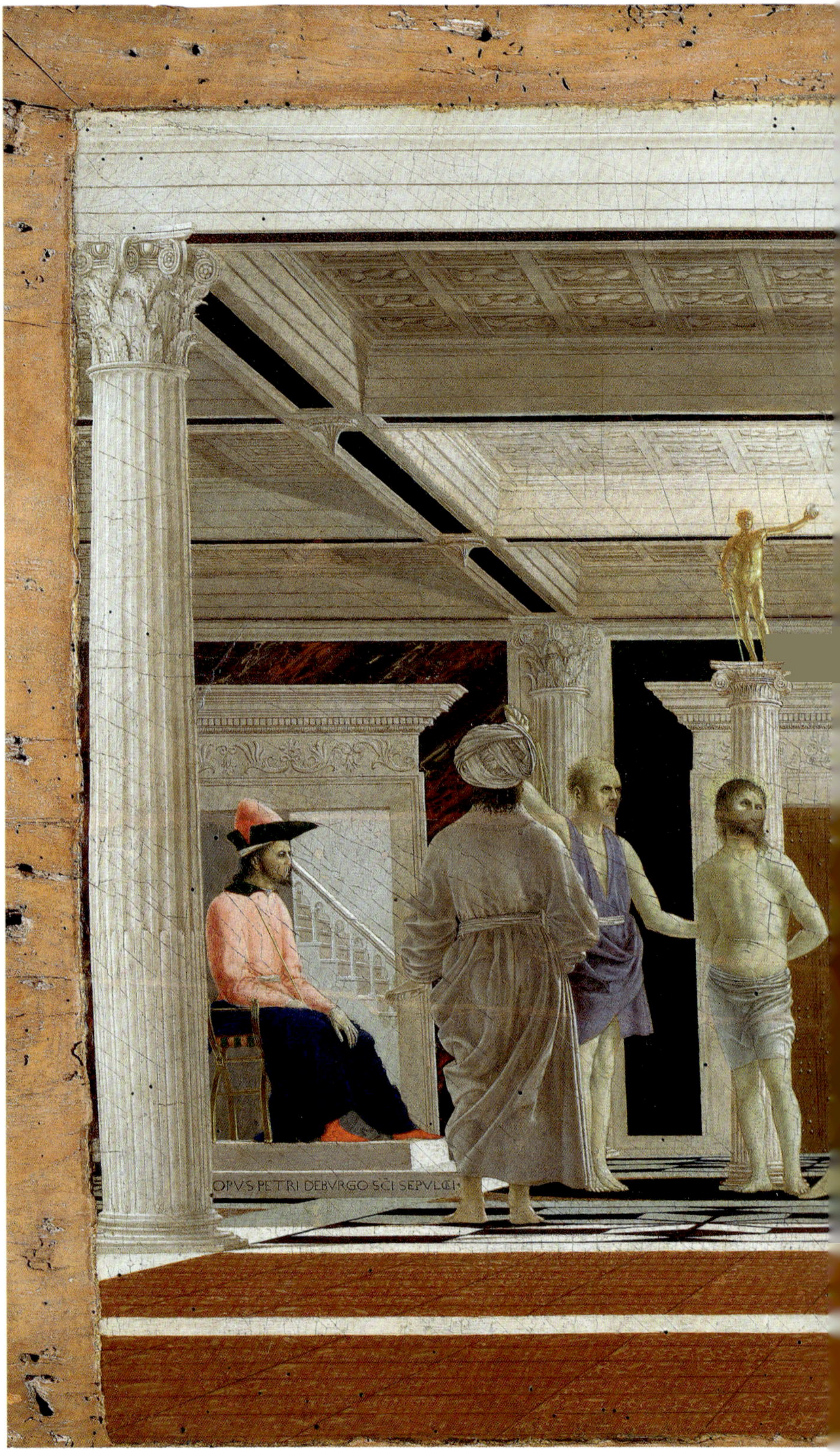

37 Piero della Francesca, *The Flagellation of Christ*, Urbino, Galleria Nazionale delle Marche

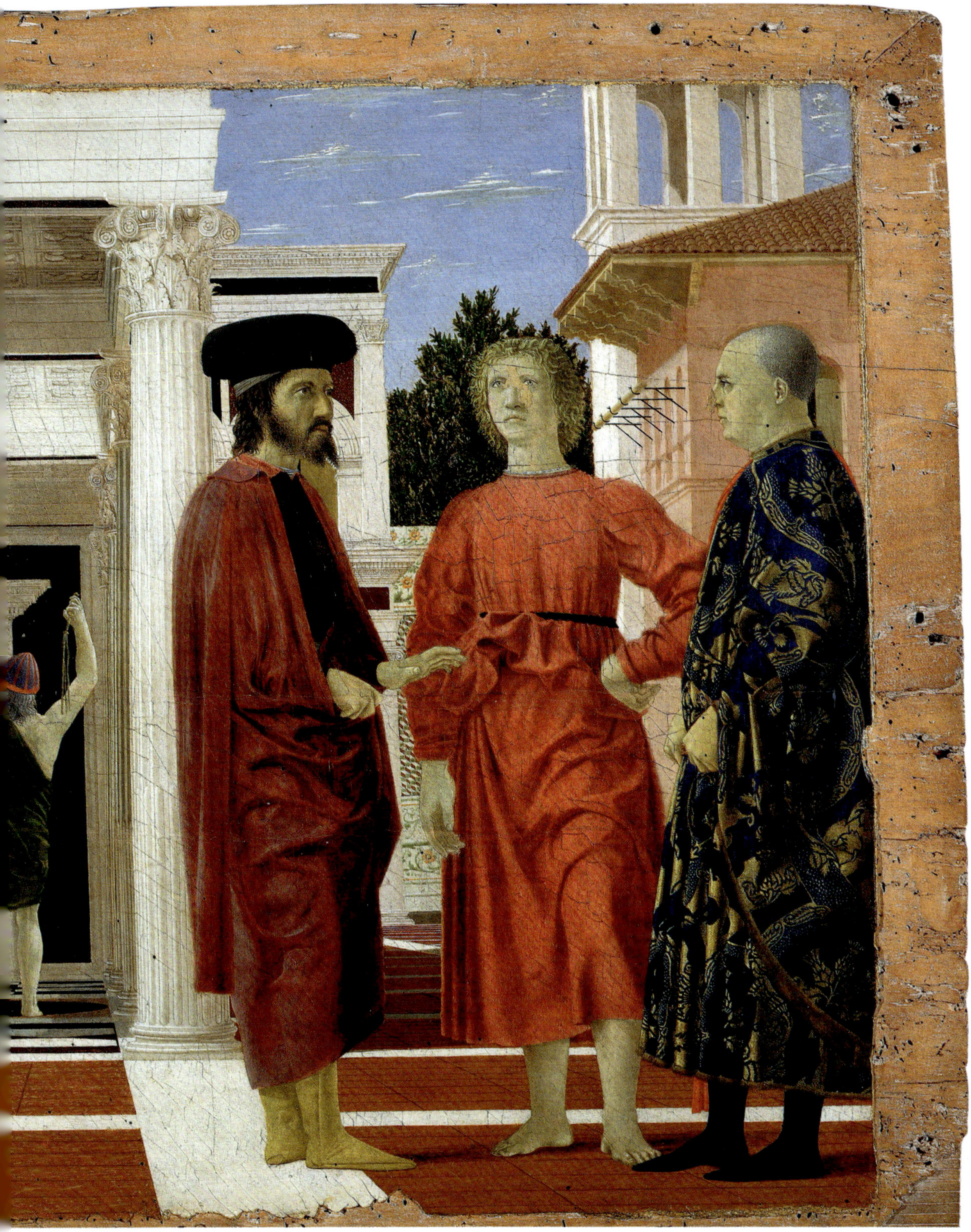

> There are some who make excessive use of gold, because they think it lends a certain majesty to painting. I would not praise them at all. Even if I wanted to paint Virgil's Dido with her quiver of gold, her hair tied up in gold, her gown fastened with a golden clasp, driving her chariot with golden reins, and everything else resplendent with gold, I would try to represent with colour rather than with gold this wealth of rays that strike the eyes of spectators from all angles.[4]

To ape the appearance of gleaming highlights, the painter should not use the whitest of white paints in depicting normal surfaces, such as white cloth, but keep it in reserve for special effects of shine.[5] This advice effectively dealt with reflected *splendore*, but it did not deal with rays of divine light traversing space. How could these rays be differentiated from normal light? How could the spectator be made aware of the kind of light described by Dante as essential for our vision of the divine as light and love? The gleam of light on shiny surfaces had already used the purest white and gold, leaving the painter with nothing in reserve. It required special talent and ingenuity to solve this dilemma.

Piero della Francesca, who inherited Alberti's mathematical and optical aspirations in full measure, remarkably devised a number of ways of signalling divine light. A good place to begin is with his *cause célèbre* of perspective, *The Flagellation of Christ* (fig.37). Within the limited dimensions of the painting, 58.4 × 81.5 cm (23 × 32.1 in), he has laid out a very detailed pictorial stage for the protagonists. Piero della Francesca has taken great care to construct the complex geometrical tiling pattern on the floor of the porch within which Christ is being scourged in front of the seated Pilate. To the right of the image, he describes a town square far behind the three standing men.

In this context, I do not want to become tangled in the elusive meaning of the composition, in particular the identity of those on the right who 'come together' to conspire against Christ – *convenerunt in unum*, as was once inscribed on the frame. Rather, in a picture that breathes an air of high rationality in its depiction of space and light, I would like to point out that a light, apparently from nowhere, floods the coffered ceiling compartment immediately above Christ. We may notice that the receding beam casts a diagonal shadow into the next compartment of the ceiling, and a short shadow is cast into the nearest coffered section. It also becomes apparent that the gilded statuette on top of the column glitters in the same stream of lateral light. We can work out that this light must be coming from the right of Christ (his left) at head height. It is located along the inside edge of the row of columns. We cannot explicitly see the light, nor can Pilate, the flagellators or the man in a turban. But Christ can and he turns to the light source.

Piero's strategy is similar to Dante's and comparably clever, demanding a lot from the viewer. Divine light is wilfully independent of earthly light. Seeing it is a special privilege, granted in this case to Christ – and to us if we are sharp enough to work it out. The light in Piero's painting can only signal the presence of God, unseen in person but visible through his acts. Piero is saying that if a light behaves outside natural law, it must be divine.

On a far larger scale, in the frescoes of the Bacci Chapel in the Basilica of San Francesco, Arezzo, which tell the story of the True Cross, Piero created a narrative that is explicitly about light. On the lowest tier to the right of the actual window, he tells the story of the dream of Constantine, who is sleeping in his military tent (fig.38) The next day he is to do battle with Maxentius, his rival to become Emperor of Rome. An angel precipitately dives into the space from the upper left with outpointed arm and finger. It looks as if Piero has oddly portrayed the angel's left hand on his right arm, as it seems unlikely that the angel is pointing with his little finger. His ambidextrous presence floods the main tent with light; the tents further away are dark. In the angel's hand is a small pale cross, as white as it could be painted. The dream-angel is announcing

38 Piero della Francesca, *The Dream of Constantine*, Arezzo, Basilica of San Francesco

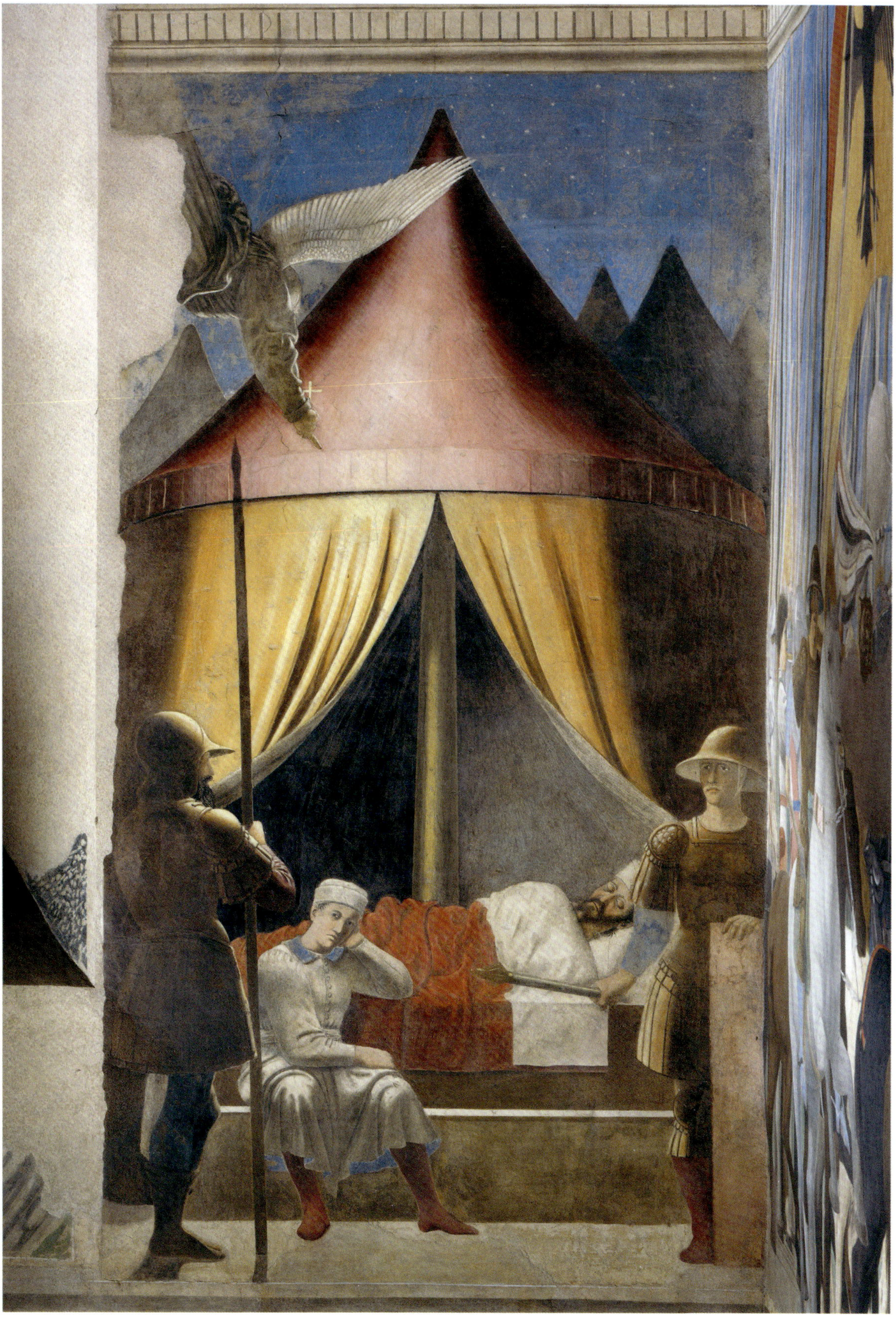

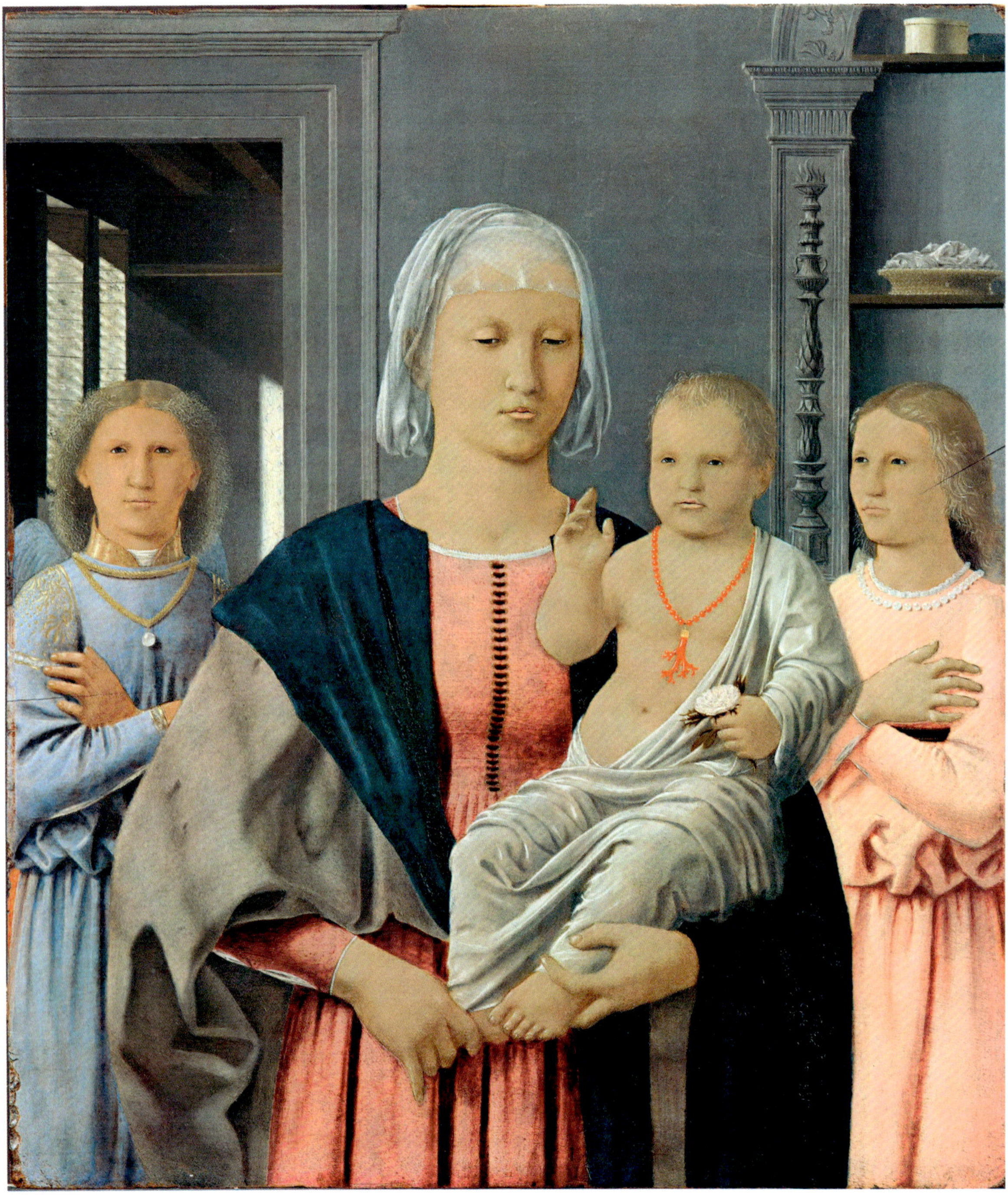

39 Piero della Francesca, *Senigallia Madonna,* Urbino, Galleria Nazionale delle Marche

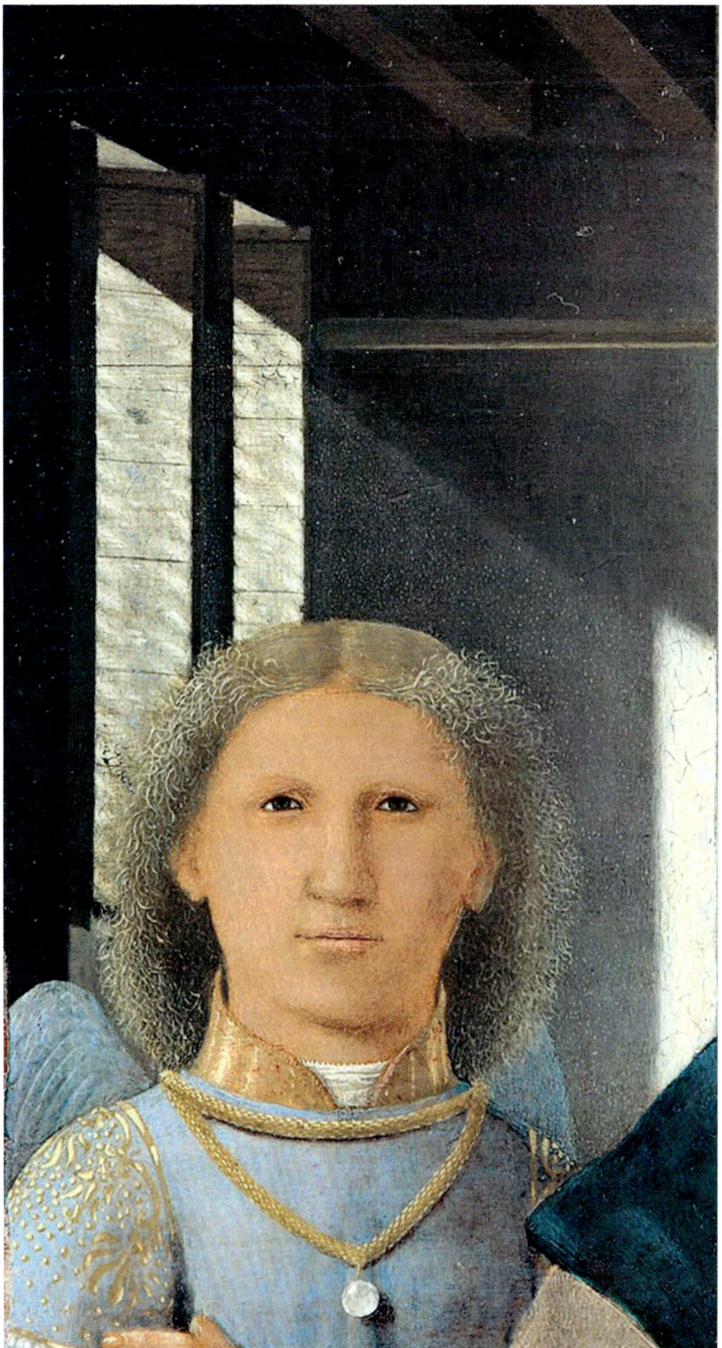

40 Piero della Francesca, *Senigallia Madonna* (detail), Urbino, Galleria Nazionale delle Marche

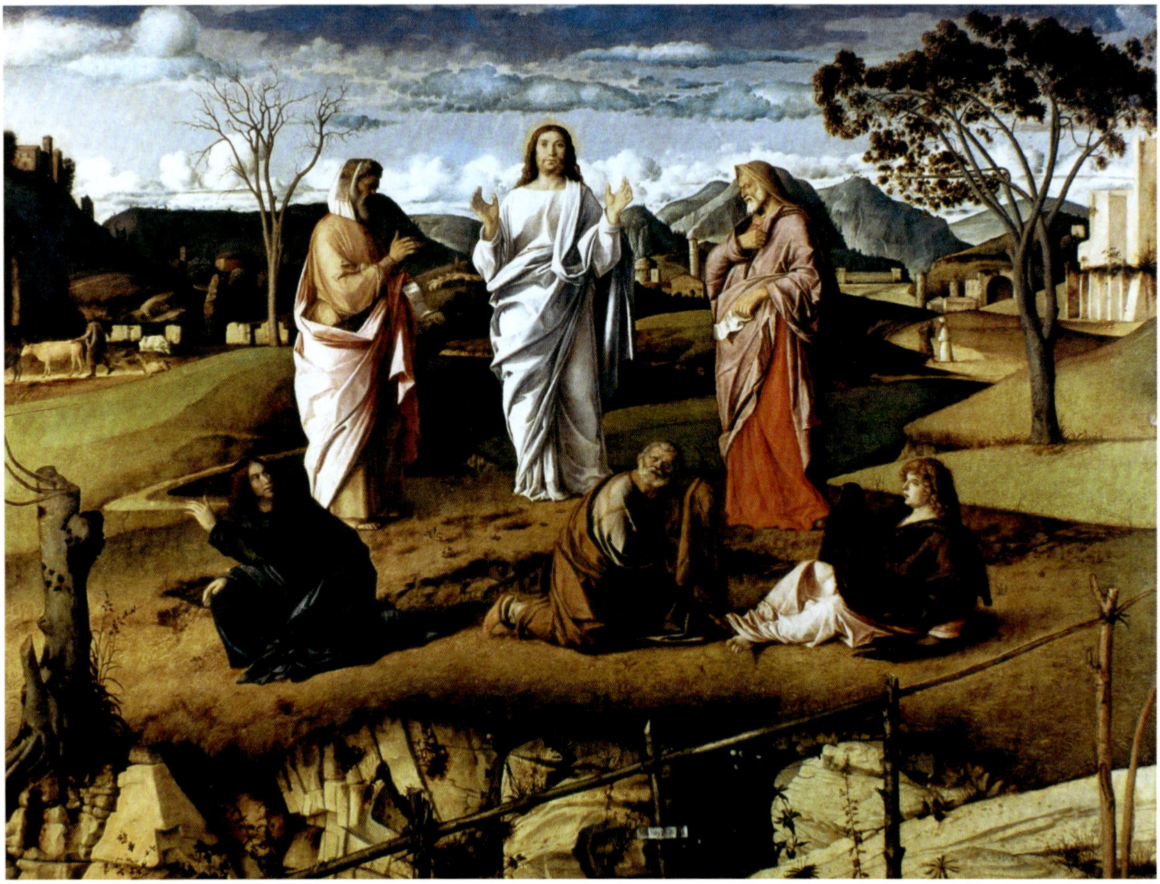

41 Giovanni Bellini, *The Transfiguration of Christ,* Naples, Museo di Capodimonte

the message that Constantine will triumph if he goes into battle under the sign of the cross, the cross of Christ. The two statuesque soldiers guarding Constantine are wholly unaware of what is happening, as is his servant, even though their eyes are open. The emperor's eyes are closed in slumber but his eyelids do not prevent him from seeing the vision. Again, complex Dantesque acts of seeing and non-seeing are involved, because the vision is both within Constantine's mind and in our eyes.

In one of Piero's paintings, a small *Madonna and Child*, formerly in Senigallia (and known as the *Senigallia Madonna*), he actually registers one of the optical phenomena adduced by the poet (fig.39). A monumentally calm Madonna with a resolute Christ is accompanied by two angels, one of whom draws us into the space with a direct glance. In the next room, depicting a handsome Renaissance interior, the sun streams through a two-light window, to strike the side wall (fig.40). Like Ibn al-Haytham's experiments with light through apertures, the image demonstrates that rays of light travel in straight lines. The penetration of the light through glass was taken as a symbol of the miraculous penetration of the immaculate Virgin at her Annunciation by the light of the Holy Spirit. Remarkably, the actual beam of light is visible as it passes from window to wall. Piero has distributed a myriad of little impasted spots of bright paint along the beam's slanted course. These spots are the 'bodies of minute dimensions, moving through the rays of light which sometimes streak across the shadow'; they composed the cross seen by Dante in the heaven of Mars.[6] We noted that there are a number of potential sources for this motif in ancient and Mediaeval writings.

Piero's intellect and learning cannot be in doubt. He was the author of a massively intricate treatise on perspective, *De prospectiva pingendi* (*On the Perspective of Painting*) and a geometrical treatise, *De quinque corporibus regularibus* (*On the Five Regular Polyhedra*). Both treatises are highly Euclidian in flavour. Whatever source or sources he used for geometry and optics, Piero was fully capable of understanding them and translating them into painted form in a unique manner. How different this approach was from Giovanni di Paolo's.

Not all the great masters of light and colour felt obliged to differentiate between the wonders of natural light and the nature of divine light. This is true above all for Giovanni Bellini in Venice. In his compelling painting *The Transfiguration of Christ*, the divine brilliance of Christ is rendered within an earthly register (fig.41). The biblical accounts tell how the disciples Peter, James and John go to a mountain to pray. Suddenly, Christ's face

> did shine as the sun, and his raiment was white as the light. And, behold, there appeared unto them Moses and Elias talking with him. Then answered Peter, and said unto Jesus, Lord, it is good for us to be here ... While he yet spake, behold, a bright cloud overshadowed them: and behold a voice out of the cloud, which said, This is my beloved Son, in whom I am well pleased; hear ye him.[7]

Bellini has rendered Christ's garment as brilliantly white, but not above the level of nature, and his face does not shine optically. Christ has a rather modest halo of gold rays. There may be a contrast of his raiment with the mildly threatening clouds, but it is not pronounced. Bellini has been quite free in his narrative: the mountain is at most a hillock that culminates in a rocky cleft. An odd feature of the set-up is that the three disciples are not positioned to see the vision. The disciple on the left (possibly St James) is looking over his shoulder but can at best glimpse Christ in the corner of his eye, while Peter looks generically upward and outward. St John (possibly on the right) seems to be falling backwards without seeing anything in particular. The only way to make sense of this scene is to think that the vision is occurring inside the minds of the collapsed disciples. Bellini's separation of the real and the visionary is thus conceptual rather than optical. With respect to the light, he is saying that the light of nature, as far as it can be captured in painting, testifies to its own ubiquitous divinity. As we will see, Raphael's approach to the Transfiguration was notably different.

However, Bellini's supreme demonstration of light in nature, the painting of St Francis in the Frick Collection, New York, does seem to have a reticently described source that is not quite the same as the natural light (fig.43). In what is one of the greatest of all renderings of nature, the saint stands outside his rather picturesque cave – definitely not in the 'desert' – with its rustic trellises, climbing vine and the basic reading desk with a holy book and ominous skull. Behind him is a pretty hill town with a grand fortification and a fertile plain with resident donkey and stork. Nature teems with vivacity, wonderfully observed. As often the case with Bellini, a tree barren of leaves sounds a sad note.

Francis himself stares upwards with rapt attention in the direction of a bent olive tree in the upper left corner. A special shaft of light seems to be catching its leaves as it passes. In the area behind it, at the very upper left, the blue sky fragments into jagged patches of golden light. Subtle and understated though it is, something is happening that lies beyond nature. Could this be the moment that the saint receives the stigmata, the marks of the nails, in his hands and feet? Only tiny marks in his hands are visible, and abraded traces of blood have been identified in his feet. The narrative as a whole does not correspond to traditional renderings of the Stigmatisation. My sense is that this depiction of St Francis is a new kind of painting for a smart younger patron. Its early history may be traced through Venetian private collections. The iconography does not fit into a narrative cycle and it is not a stock devotional image of the Stigmatisation. It may be regarded as a conversation piece and any insistence on a single definite narrative or subject excludes its intended flexibility.

Even if the Stigmatisation is the ostensible subject, the spirit of the picture draws prominently on the saint's famous *Canticle of the Sun*, written in 1224 and one of the earliest pieces of lyric poetry in Italian.

> Be praised, my Lord, with all your creatures,
> Especially through the honourable Brother Sun,
> Who is day, and you give light through him.
> And he is beautiful and radiant in all his splendour
> [*splendore*].
> Of you, Most High, he bears the sign.[8]

The picture is a wondrous hymn to the power of God's natural light and its life-giving properties, with a hint that something may even lie beyond this earthly register. Hints such as these are rare in Bellini's work.

APOCALYPTIC VISIONS

What seemed to be the progressive march of naturalism in Italian art at this time was diverted in Florence in a way that could not have been predicted. Apocalyptic events were responsible for this change. In 1494 the invading French, under Charles VIII, precipitated the expulsion of the Medici from Florence. Political and religious life in the city came to be dominated by the Dominican monk Girolamo Savonarola from his base in the monastery of San Marco, which had earlier been home to Fra Angelico. His fierce damning of pagan and secular culture in the city, epitomised in art by Botticelli's paintings of Venus and other lascivious Roman deities, led to 'bonfires of the vanities'. We do not know if any of Botticelli's mythologies were consigned to the flames. In any event, the climate had changed dramatically, and it seems that Botticelli harboured some sympathy for the monk's views. We know that his brother was a follower of Savonarola. In 1498, under pressure from the Pope, the tide turned against Savonarola, and he was hanged and burned with two companions in the Piazza della Signoria. In 1499, the new French king Louis XII invaded Italy, taking over Milan and Naples.

42 Sandro Botticelli, *Mystic Nativity*, London, National Gallery

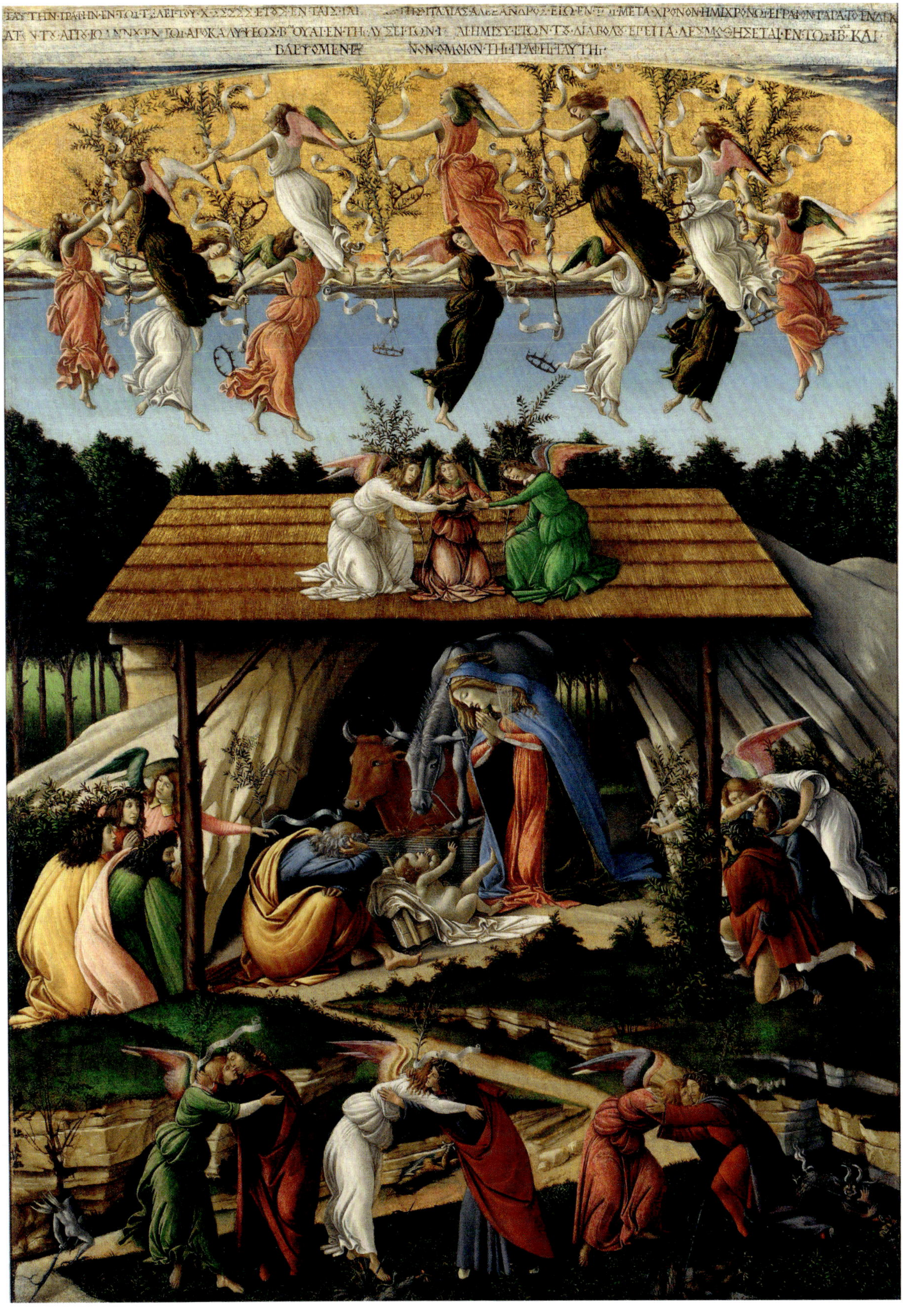

43 Giovanni Bellini, *St Francis in Ecstacy*, New York, Frick Collection

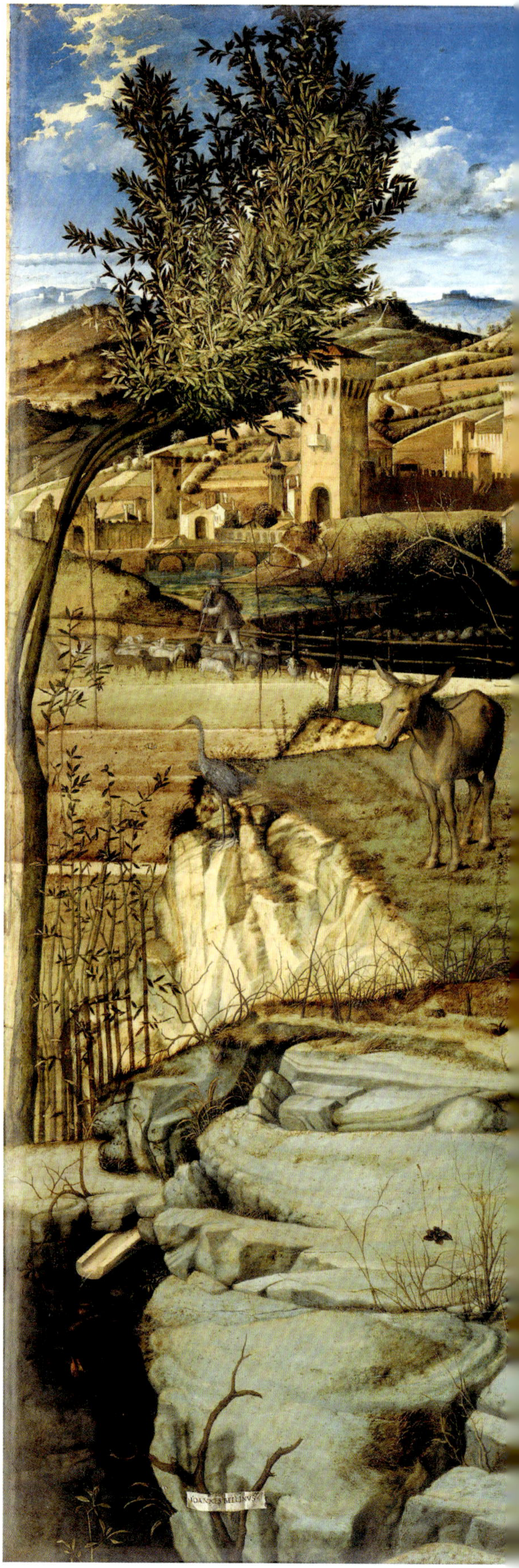

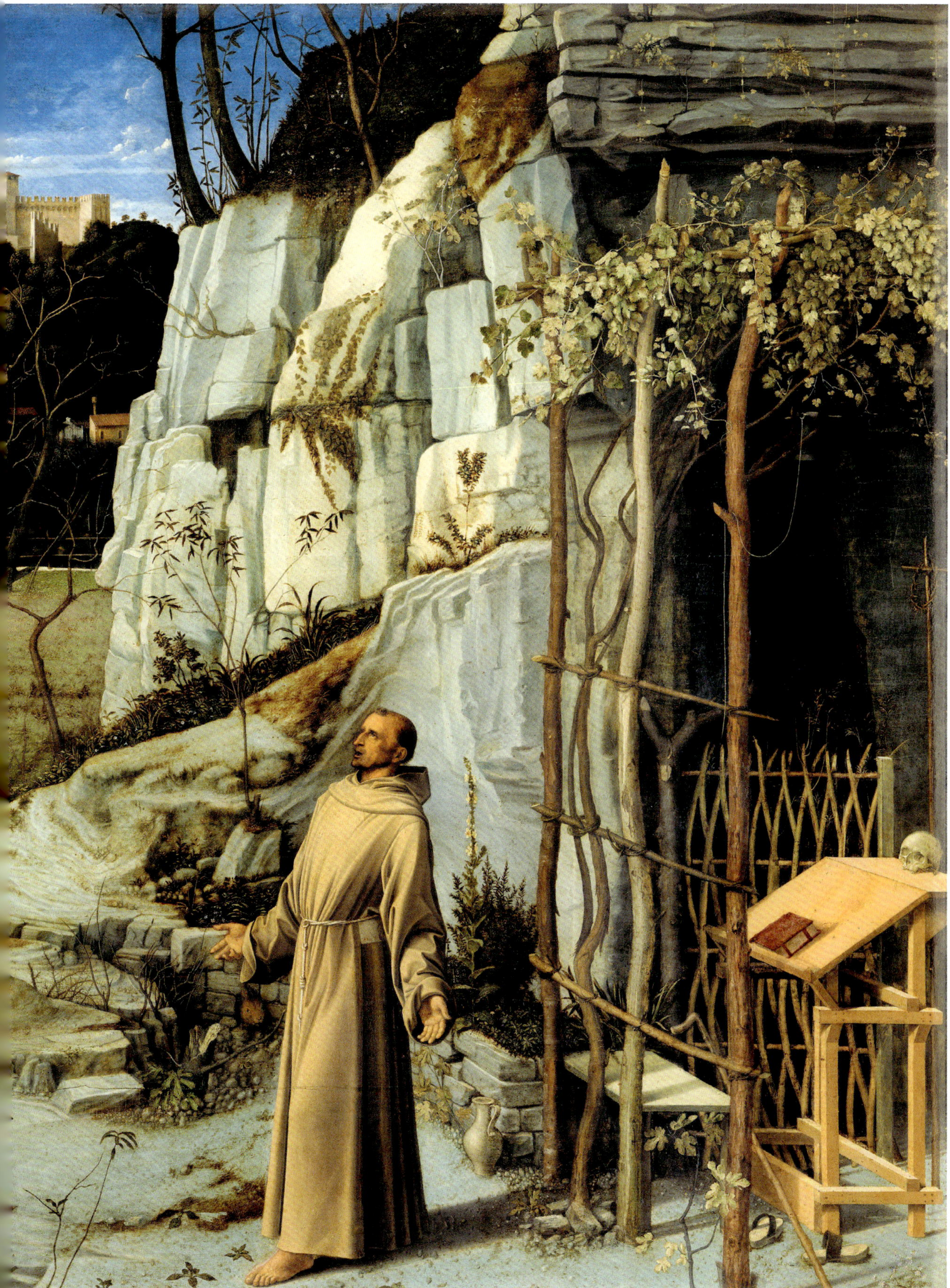

By 1500, the Italy of the cultured city-states seemed to be slipping into a disastrous condition. Could it be that the year marked the right time for the advent of the millennium, marked by the second coming of Christ? This idea became quite fashionable, or at least there might be a second coming in the hearts of Florentines. The year 1500 was when Botticelli painted what came to be called his *Mystic Nativity* (fig.42). The mode of presentation is a great surprise if we look at the Medicean allegories and his monumental altarpieces, but not if we look at his Dante.

The central group of the Holy Family, with attendant ox and ass, are rendered on a far larger scale than the adoring kings on the left (who are bereft of their normal kingly attributes) and the kneeling shepherds on the right. The angels on the roof are notably diminutive, as are three pairs of embracing angels and men at the base of the picture. The rhythmic rings of dancing angels, holding olive branches, orbit against the circle of a gold heaven, comparable to the Dante illustrations for *Paradiso*, but an anachronistic feature in a painting. Botticelli appears to have undergone a stylistic regression, moving away from perspectival logic and coherent naturalism.

Another old-fashioned element in the painting is the amount of text: the men in the foreground with the angels are given scrolls that declare biblically, 'peace on earth to men of goodwill'. The upper scrolls, held by the ring of dancing angels, read or originally read, 'Glory to God in the highest'. The inscriptions on the lower scrolls wrapped around the stems of the olive fronds held by angels are no longer readily visible, but scientific examination has confirmed that they are drawn from Savonarola's preaching about the 12 'privileges of the Virgin', including the Immaculate Conception, her role as Mother of God, her Perpetual Virginity and Assumption. The 12 crowns suspended from the fronds of olive reinforce the reference.

The most substantial inscription runs across the top of the picture. Surprisingly, it is in Greek (of a rather wobbly kind).

> This picture, at the end of the year 1500, in the troubles of Italy, I, Alessandro, in the half-time after the time, painted, according to the eleventh [chapter] of St John, in the second woe of the Apocalypse, during the release of the devil for three and a half years; then he shall be bound in the twelfth [chapter] and we shall see [...] as in this picture.

This is a cryptic reference to a cryptic source, the Book of Revelation in the Bible, also known as the Apocalypse of St John, which is saturated in visions of the violent battle between good and evil. In the 11th book we learn that the Holy City shall be trodden 'under foot for forty and two months', that is three-and-a-half years. At the bottom of the picture, a series of small but grotesque devils are being routed. The 'half-time', 21 months, takes us back to the era of Savonarola's death and the persecution of his followers (depending on the time in the year that it was painted). However we do the counting, we can be sure that the *Mystic Nativity* is a dangerously Savonarola-related image at a sensitive time.

Greek may have been used to conceal the Savonarolan basis of the inscription from all but learned readers of Greek. The reference can only be relevant to a private patron or organisation working closely with an artist who was in tune with the message of the picture. The compatibility did not just extend to its immediate content; it involved reversion to a style for a devotional picture that harkened back to earlier days. This is not to say that it looks exactly like an earlier picture, but it avoids following the prescriptions for a modern picture painted around 1500, just as Botticelli had avoided obvious narrative and spatial devices in his *Paradiso* illustrations. I suspect that without Botticelli's graphic experiments in the Dante illustrations, the *Nativity* would have looked rather different.

Exactly contemporary with Botticelli's late masterpiece is one of the most Dantesque of all

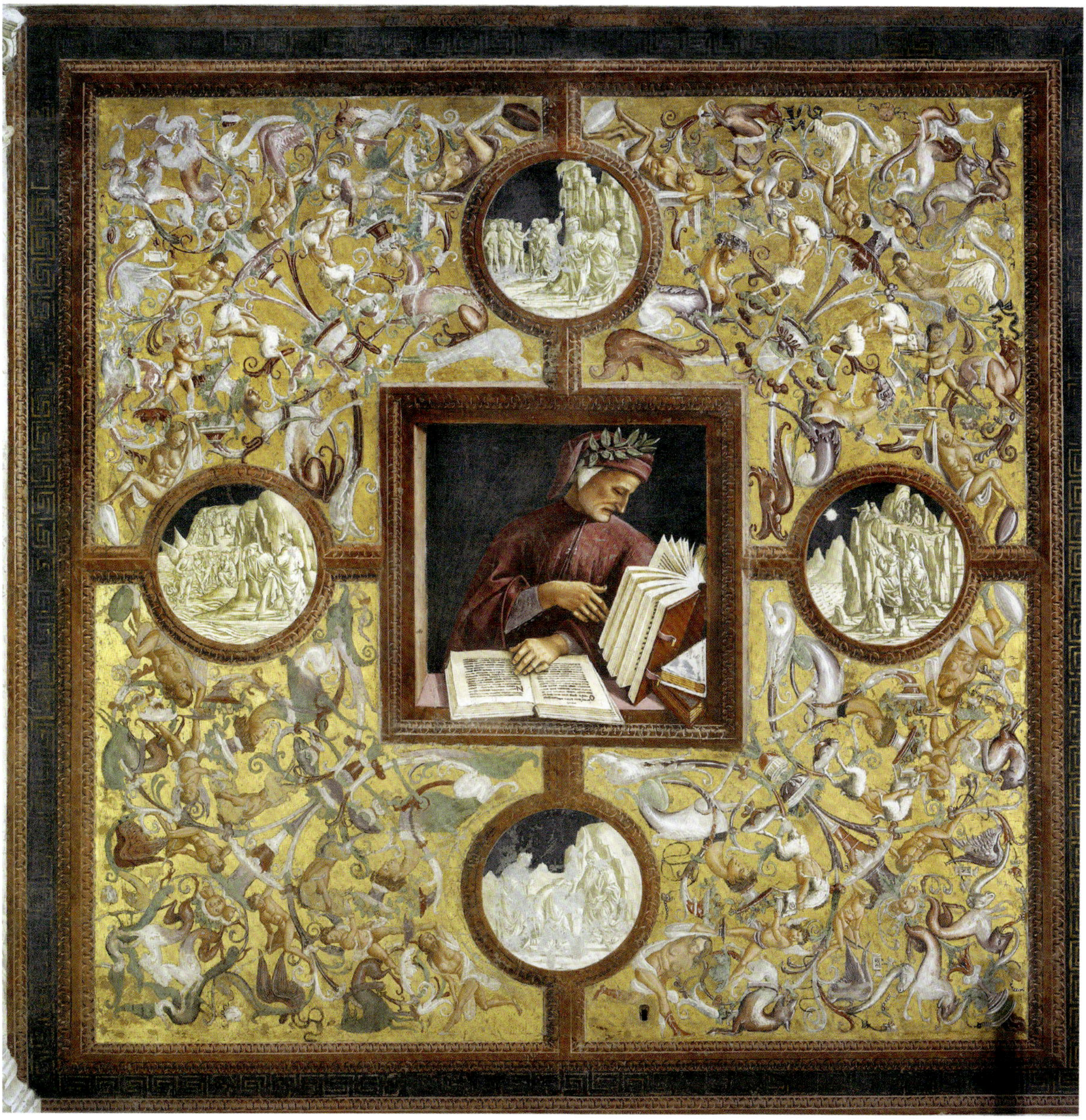

44 Luca Signorelli, *Portrait of Dante with Scenes from the Commedia*, Orvieto Cathedral, San Brizio Chapel

pictorial projects, Luca Signorelli's powerful fresco cycle in the Cappella Nuova in Orvieto Cathedral (now called the San Brizio Chapel). The commission had originally been assigned to Fra Angelico, and with his assistants he completed some sections of the vault in 1447, including a bright image of Christ as judge seated in a mandorla with a gold background. There things remained until the signing of a contract with Signorelli in 1499. By 1502 it seems that the complex series of paintings had been expeditiously finished. Signorelli and his assistants completed seven pictorial fields: the Actions of the Anti-Christ; the Destruction of the World; the Resurrection of the Flesh; the Damned; the Elect; the smaller fields of the Destruction of the World; Hell and Paradise. Below the narratives are ornamental panels containing portraits of writers and philosophers, with mini-narratives related to their texts. The portrait of Dante (fig.44), who is the only modern writer, includes painted reliefs from *Inferno* and *Purgatorio*.

Signorelli's way of telling stories, like Michelangelo whom he influenced, was to use the human body as the primary means of expression; the contexts tend to be secondary. The richest setting is in the scene of the Antichrist, in which a Christ-like figure on a podium is being prompted by Satan (fig.46). The sudden appearance of a fulminating angel with a sword (possibly St Michael) is accompanied by a burst of light, described with a modest amount of gold and a series of piercing rays that assault the plummeting figure and those on the ground. In the bottom left corner, the two men in contemporary dress are Signorelli and Fra Angelico, who do not participate as observers, but identify themselves as the self-conscious creators of the images.

In the adjoining field, we see the muscular elect, now resurrected in their flesh, welcomed by an angelic concert and by other angels who proffer crowns in a rather Botticellian manner (fig.45). The gold background, stippled with raised points that catch the light, comes as close to evoking the dazzling light of heaven as Signorelli will go. The clusters of naked figures turn their eyes towards the heavenly glare as described by Dante, unlike the sinful followers of the Antichrist. Signorelli's emphasis, as always, is on the physicality of what participants are doing. Signorelli's cycle of paintings in Orvieto confirms that the painting of figures *in extremis*, in keeping with the first two canticles in the *Commedia*, elicits a more creative response and more active engagement of viewers than the depiction of light and goodness in Paradise.

MICHELANGELO: LIGHT AS NARRATIVE

There is also a strong sense that for Signorelli light was the servant of form, sculpting bodies into three dimensions, rather than an active and independent force in its own right. This was an aesthetic choice, emphasising the direct expression of plastic form as the prime goal for the painter rather than diverting attention to optical complications of reflection, shine, atmospheric perspective and so on. This was very much the conviction of Michelangelo, for whom painting essentially acted as a surrogate for the values best embodied in sculpture. The only times that light plays an emphatic role in its own right on the Sistine Ceiling are in the first two compartments, where he portrays God's initial acts, the *Separation of Light from the Darkness* and the *Creation of the Sun and Moon and Plants* (figs 47 and 49).

The Separation is an event of dynamic spiritual action, bringing into being something that the Bible tells us is 'good'. As a keen student of Dante, Michelangelo would have readily recognised the identity of light with God, goodness and love. The surging sweeps of white paint applied on the damp plaster convey the essence of God's act. The shaded contours of God's foreshortened profile push the white towards enhanced brightness. Through the figure and the background, Michelangelo sets contours of enhanced darkness and exaggerated brightness against

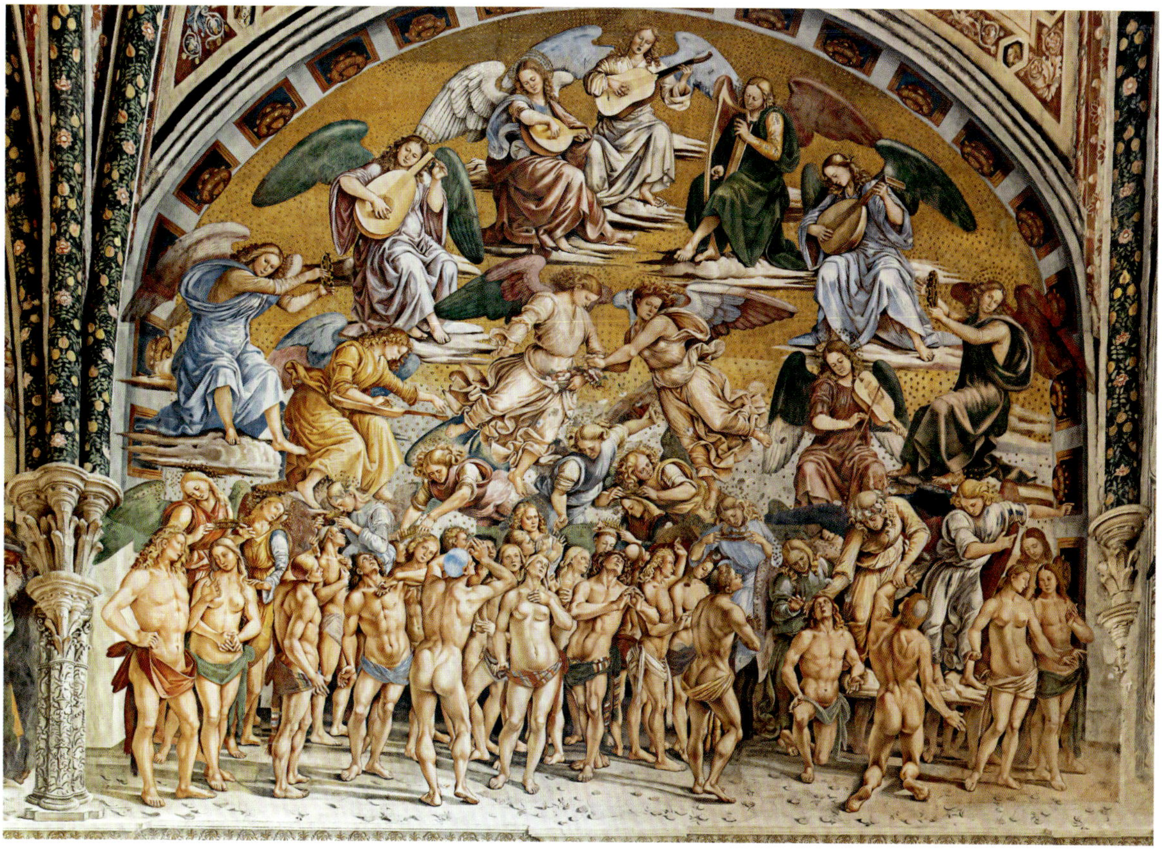

45 Luca Signorelli, *Resurrection of the Flesh and the Angels of Paradise,* Orvieto Cathedral, San Brizio Chapel

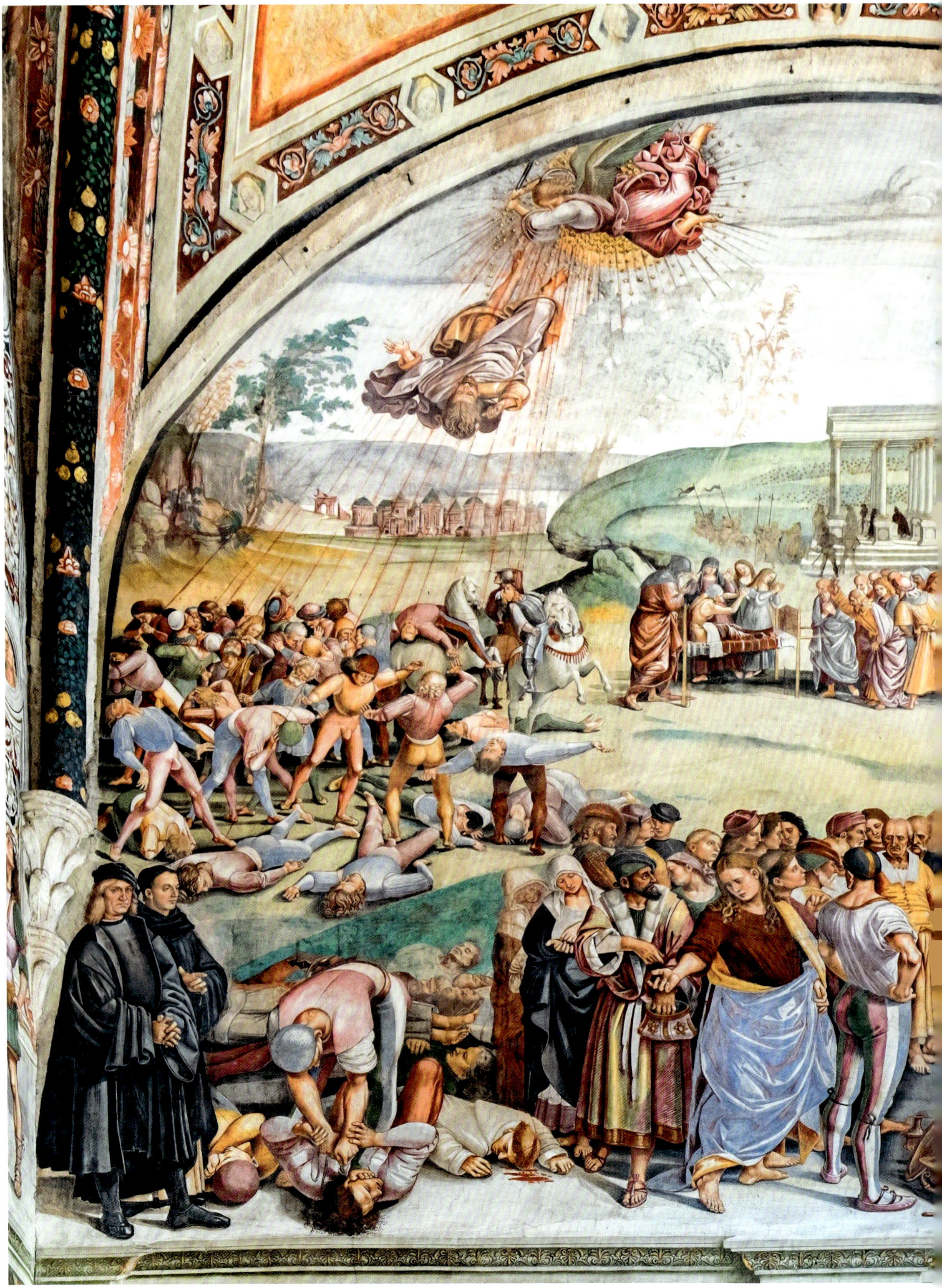

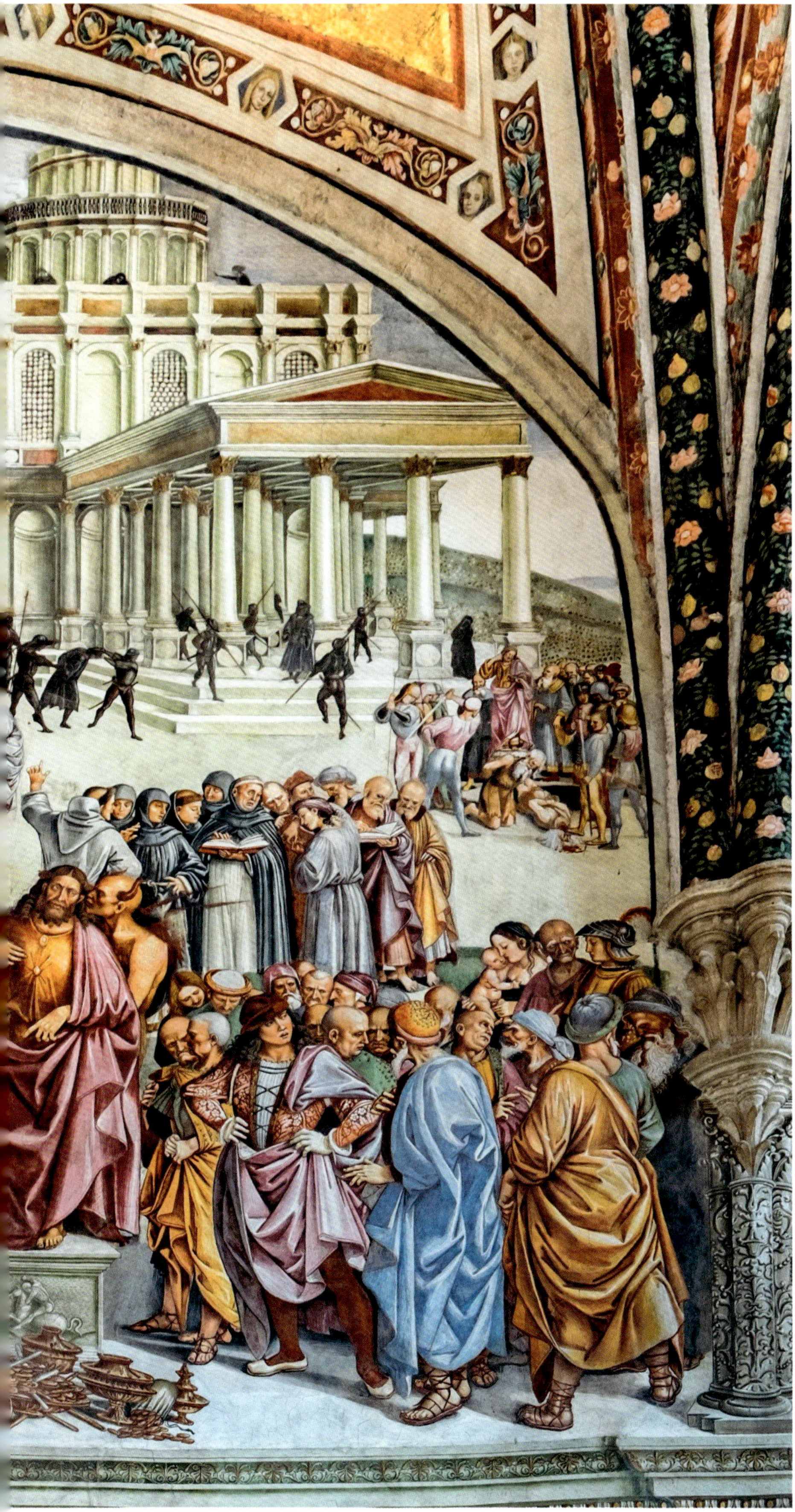

46 Luca Signorelli, *Acts of the Antichrist,* Orvieto Cathedral, San Brizio Chapel

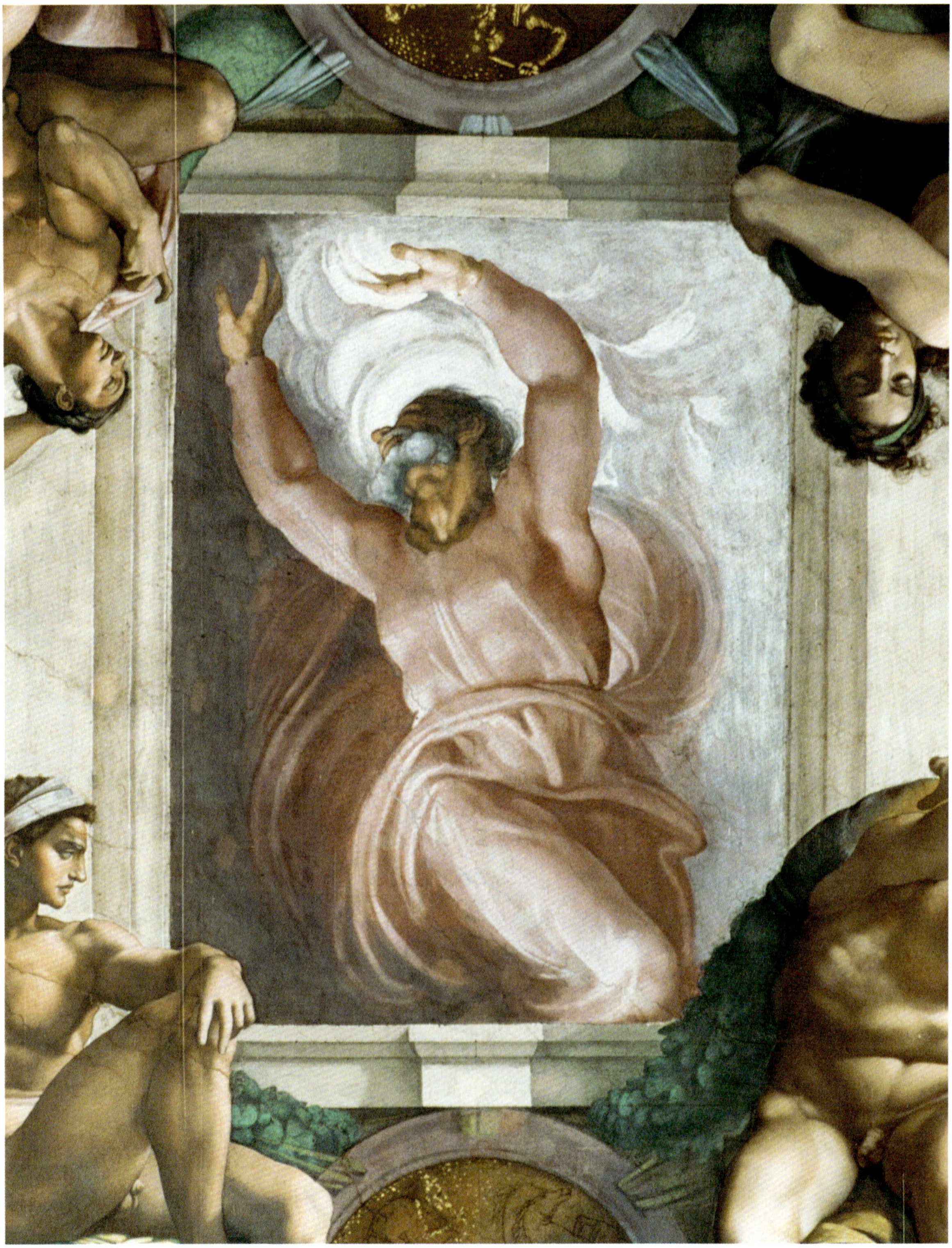

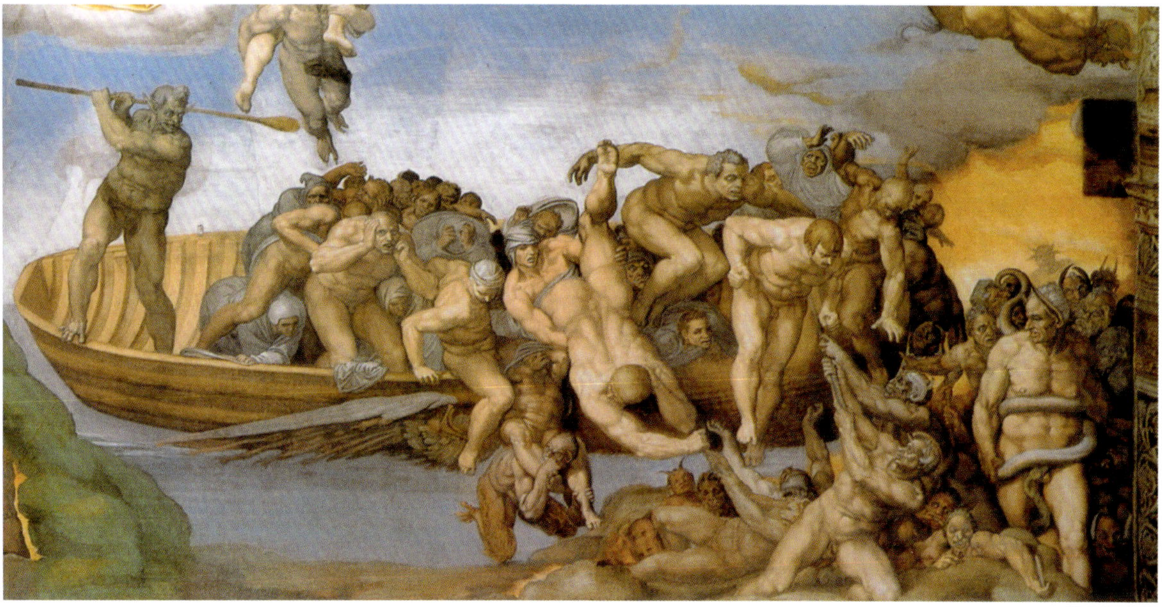

48 Michelangelo, *The Last Judgement*, detail of Charon, Minos and the damned, Rome, Vatican, Sistine Chapel

each other as edge-contrasts. These were placed in the service of formal definition and sculptural power rather than painted as optical subtleties observed in nature. The overall effect of the fresco is to suggest that the act of separation occurs as much in the mind of God, as a concept, as it does as a physical act in our world.

In the second compartment of the ceiling we witness the celestial creation of the sun and the moon, and the earthly plants (fig.49). It is a physical-cum-mental act of glowering command. The foreshortened figure of God is depicted twice, as occurs in some of Botticelli's illustrations. Also, like Botticelli is the celestial minimalism of the spheres of the golden sun and pearly moon. There are no rays of streaming light, no obvious description of the impact of the glaring sphere on the figures and no clear spatial definition of where the sun is placed. There is some suggestion in the sun – composed from densely packed circles of gold – that Michelangelo is actually thinking of the *Primum Mobile* as the radiant orb described by Dante. The moon itself seems to have a patchy surface, which we may recall became a bone of contention between the poet and Beatrice.

This engagement with light in its own right on the Sistine Ceiling is exceptional and occasioned by narrative necessity. Even in Michelangelo's much later *Last Judgement*, the magisterial figure of Christ is granted but a modest aureole of bright light. The figures remain the prime vehicle for Michelangelo's vision. Where Dante does impinge on *The Last Judgement* is in the lower right-hand corner of the mural, where the devilish figures of Charon, the gate-keeper and ferryman, and Minos, the king of hell, encircled by a horrible serpent, tumble the naked sinners into their deserved pits of torture (fig.48). The narrative is openly Dantesque. Again, it is *Inferno* that inspires pictorial representation rather than *Paradiso*. In thinking about the painter and the poet, we should remember that Michelangelo was himself a poet of great intensity and was steeped in Dante's vision.

47 (OPPOSITE) Michelangelo, *The Separation of Light from the Darkness*, Rome, Vatican, Sistine Chapel

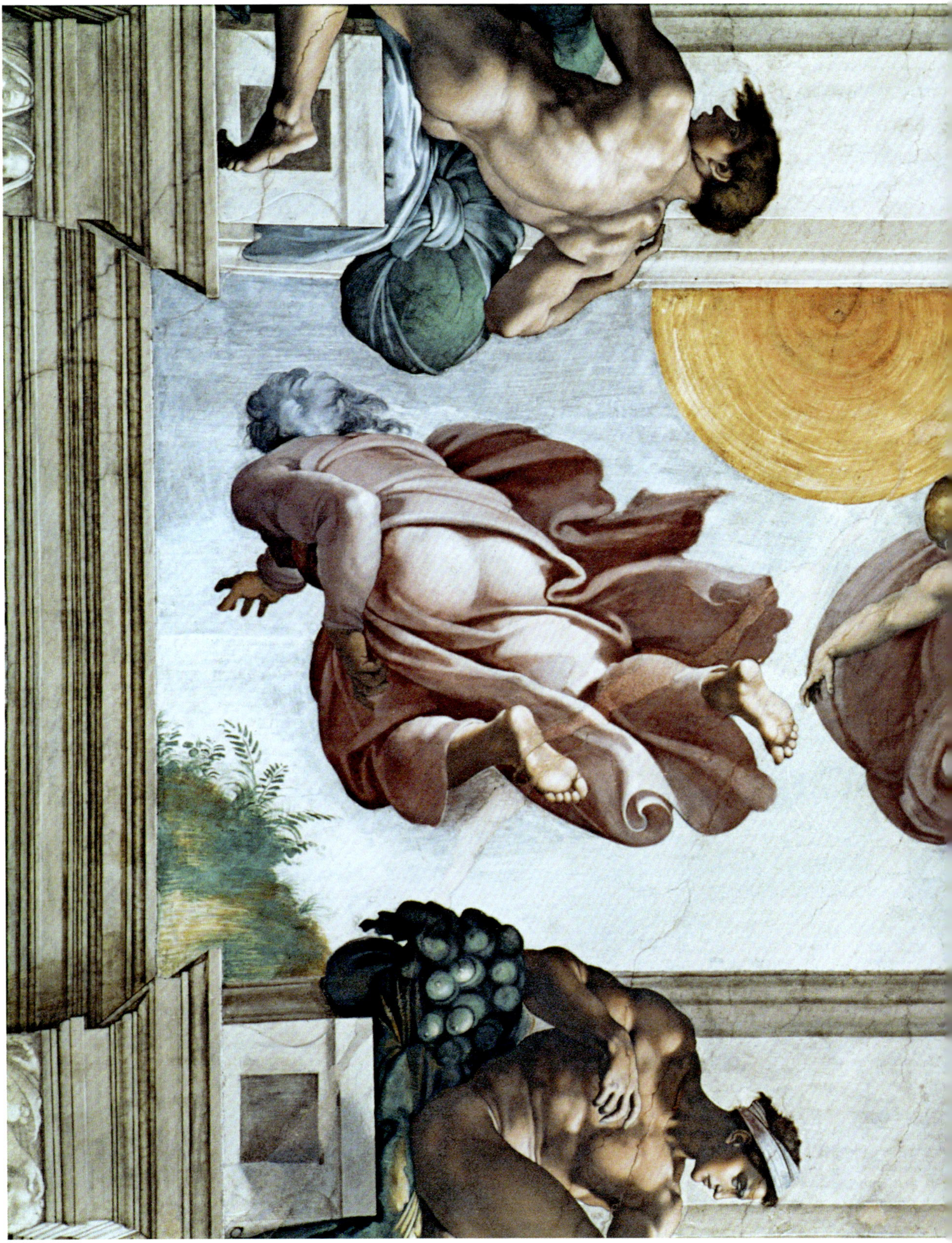

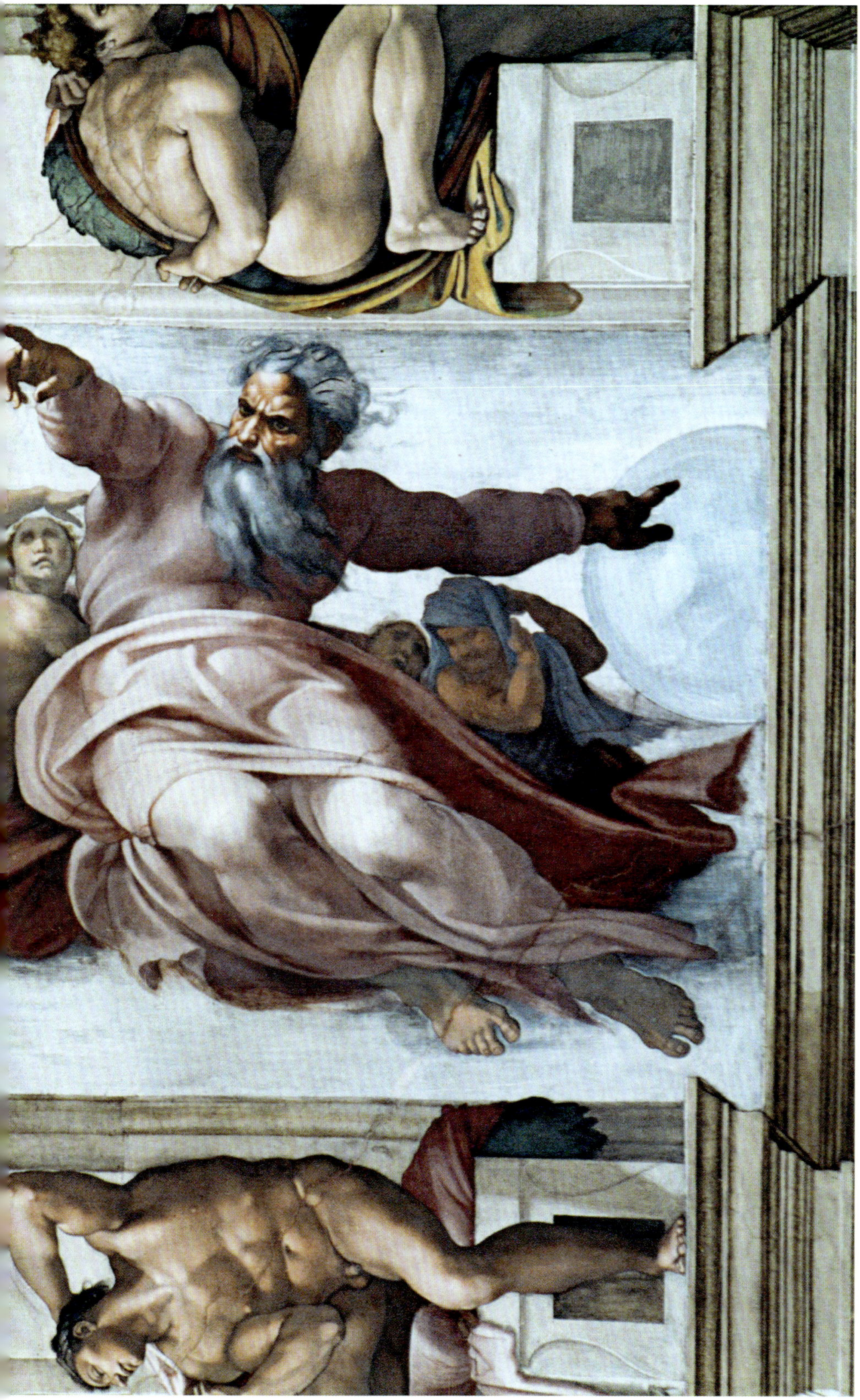

49 Michelangelo, *The Creation of the Sun, Moon and Plants*, Rome, Vatican, Sistine Chapel

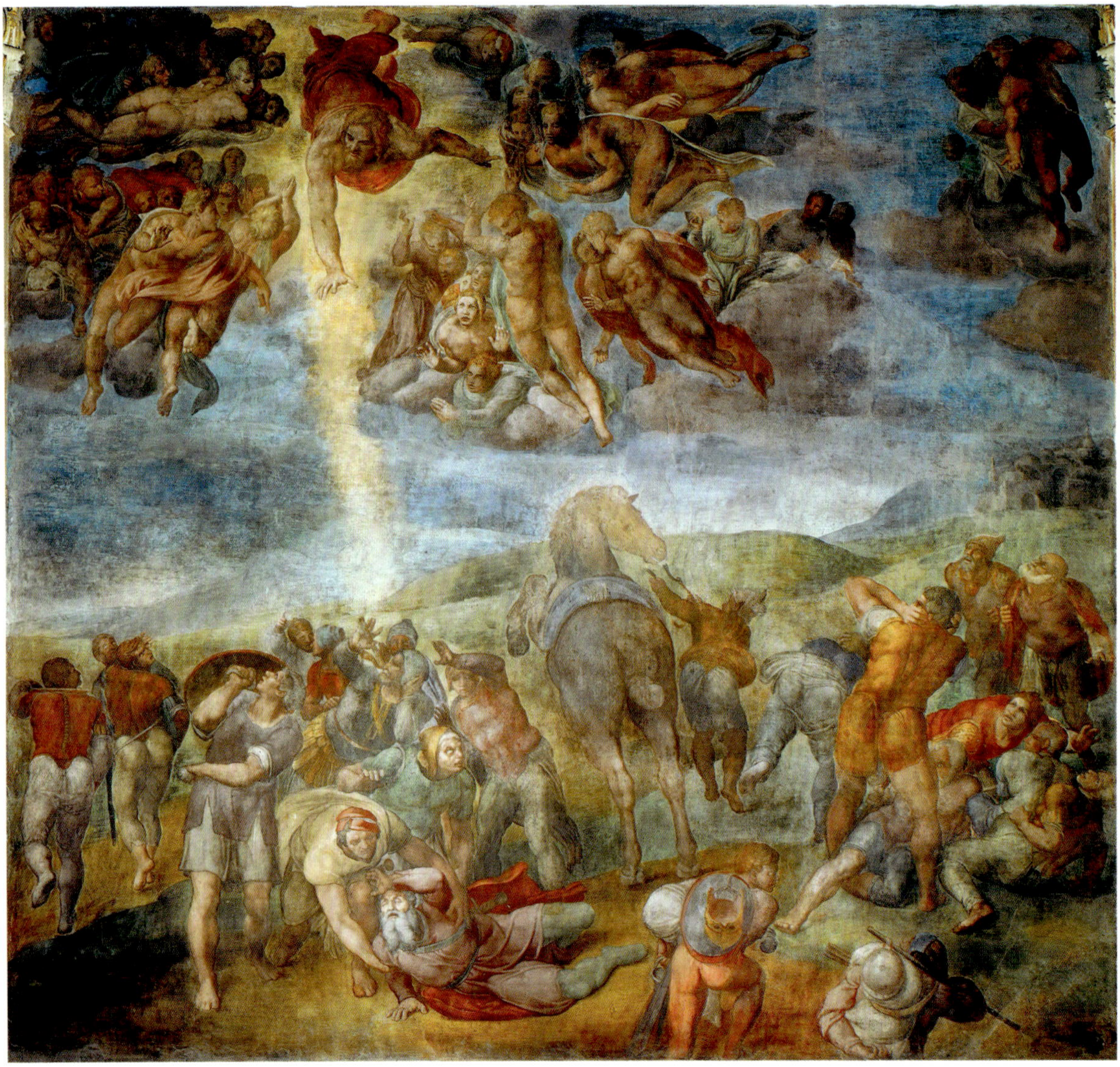

50 Michelangelo, *The Conversion of St Paul*, Rome, Vatican, Pauline Chapel

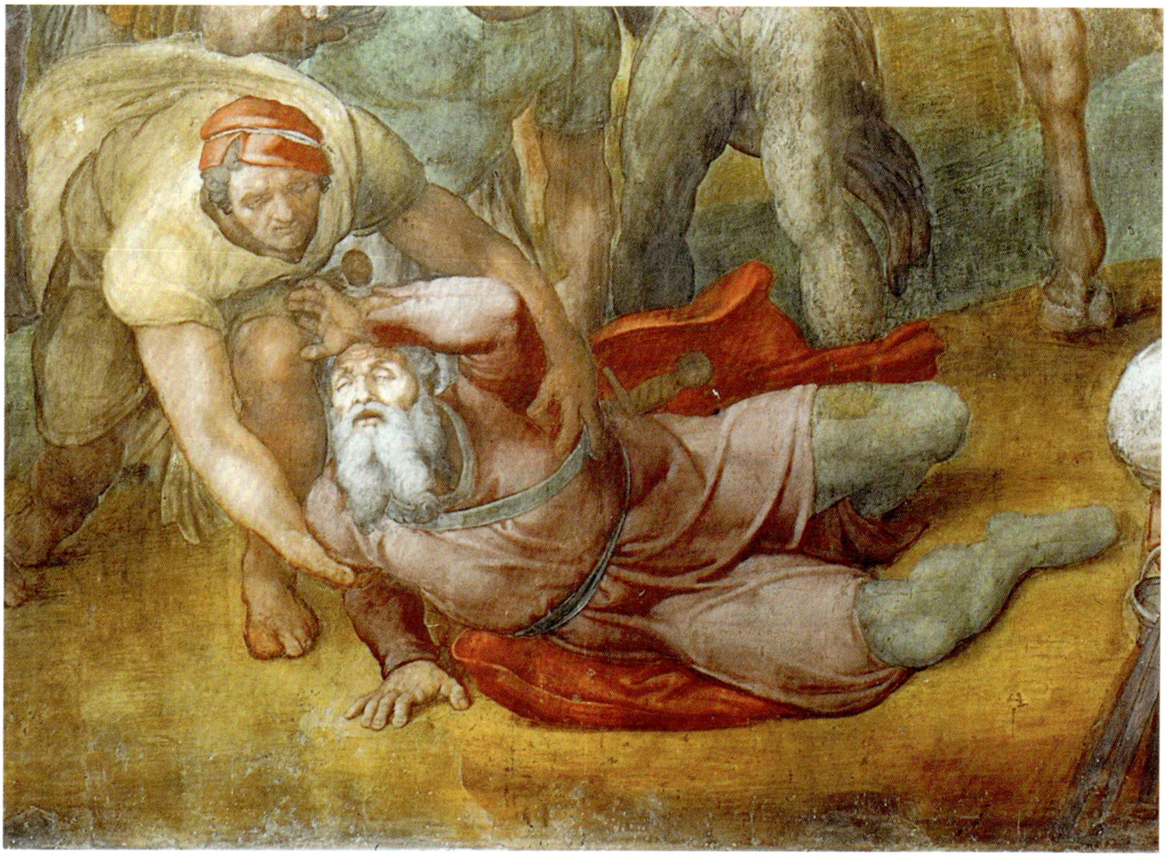

51 Michelangelo, *The Conversion of St Paul* (detail), Rome, Vatican, Pauline Chapel

There is one notable exception in Michelangelo's later art that portrays light as an integral part of the narrative content. The *Conversion of St Paul*, or the *Blinding of Saul*, is one of the great dramatic events in the Bible.

> And Saul, yet breathing out threatenings and slaughter against the disciples of the Lord ... came near Damascus: and suddenly there shined round about him a light from heaven: And he fell to the earth, and heard a voice saying unto him, Saul, Saul, why persecutest thou me? And he said, Who art thou, Lord? And the Lord said, I am Jesus whom thou persecutest ... And the men which journeyed with him, stood speechless, hearing a voice, but seeing no man. And Saul arose from the earth, and when his eyes were opened, he saw no man: but they led him by the hand, and brought him into Damascus.[9]

The blinding light in the painting is generated and forcefully projected downwards by Christ, visible in corporeal form, accompanied by angelic hosts (fig.50). The Bible makes it clear that Saul's astonished followers did not see Christ, nor presumably did Saul. Christ is shown to us for the sake of the narrative. Saul has been thrown to the ground, lying in a pool of light, while his horse rears in alarm. Propping himself up on one arm, Saul shuts his eyes and attempts to ward off the shaft of light. But his face remains bright, without a hint of a shadow cast by his arm and hand (fig.51). His attempt to protect his sight is futile. As Beatrice repeatedly reminds Dante, divine light does not obey the optical rules. It is three days before Saul's sight is restored.

LEONARDO: NATURAL AND DIVINE

In respect to divine light, the art of Leonardo da Vinci was very much about natural light as a potent agent in its own right. He was dedicated to understanding how light functions in the natural world: originating from sources of varied kinds; passing through space, either freely or filtered by the atmosphere; transmitted via translucent materials; diminishing with distance; percussing bodies of varied shape at different angles and with different intensities; creating gleaming highlights; passing through apertures; generating cast shadows; and rebounding from one surface to another, affecting the colour and tone of adjacent surfaces. This catalogue of visual effects lay at the heart of the challenge to poets and sculptors that Leonardo issued in his *paragone*. His victory over poetry was based rather spuriously on his identifying its prime task as the detailed description of things.

Leonardo da Vinci also needed to understand how the eye and perceptual apparatus deal with the complex optics of phenomena 'out there'. He increasingly realised, as he encountered Mediaeval optics in the succession of Ibn al-Haytham, that the faculty of sight acted in a complex and sometimes deceptive manner. His sources were close to those used by Dante. We have already seen that he recorded the rapturous preface of Pecham's *Perspectiva communis*. In marked contrast to Dante, Leonardo's concern did not extend into the irrationality of divine light, perspective was divine enough for him.

I think it is true to say that there is no direct attempt to differentiate natural and divine light in his paintings. There is a parallel with Bellini's approach to light. We may feel that the light that falls on the Virgin, Christ, St John and an angel in Leonardo's two versions of *The Virgin of the Rocks*, penetrating the shady cavern, is of divine origin, but it is entirely logical and comes from the same direction as the illumination of the rocks. The exception, at least an exception of a kind, is in his two late devotional images, the *Salvator Mundi* and the *St John the Baptist* (fig.52). They both have dark backgrounds, in keeping with the blackness of the 'void' that he defined in his astronomy. St John is picked up by a strong 'spotlight' that catches nothing else. The light behaves optically in defining the

52 Leonardo da Vinci, *St John the Baptist*, Paris, Louvre

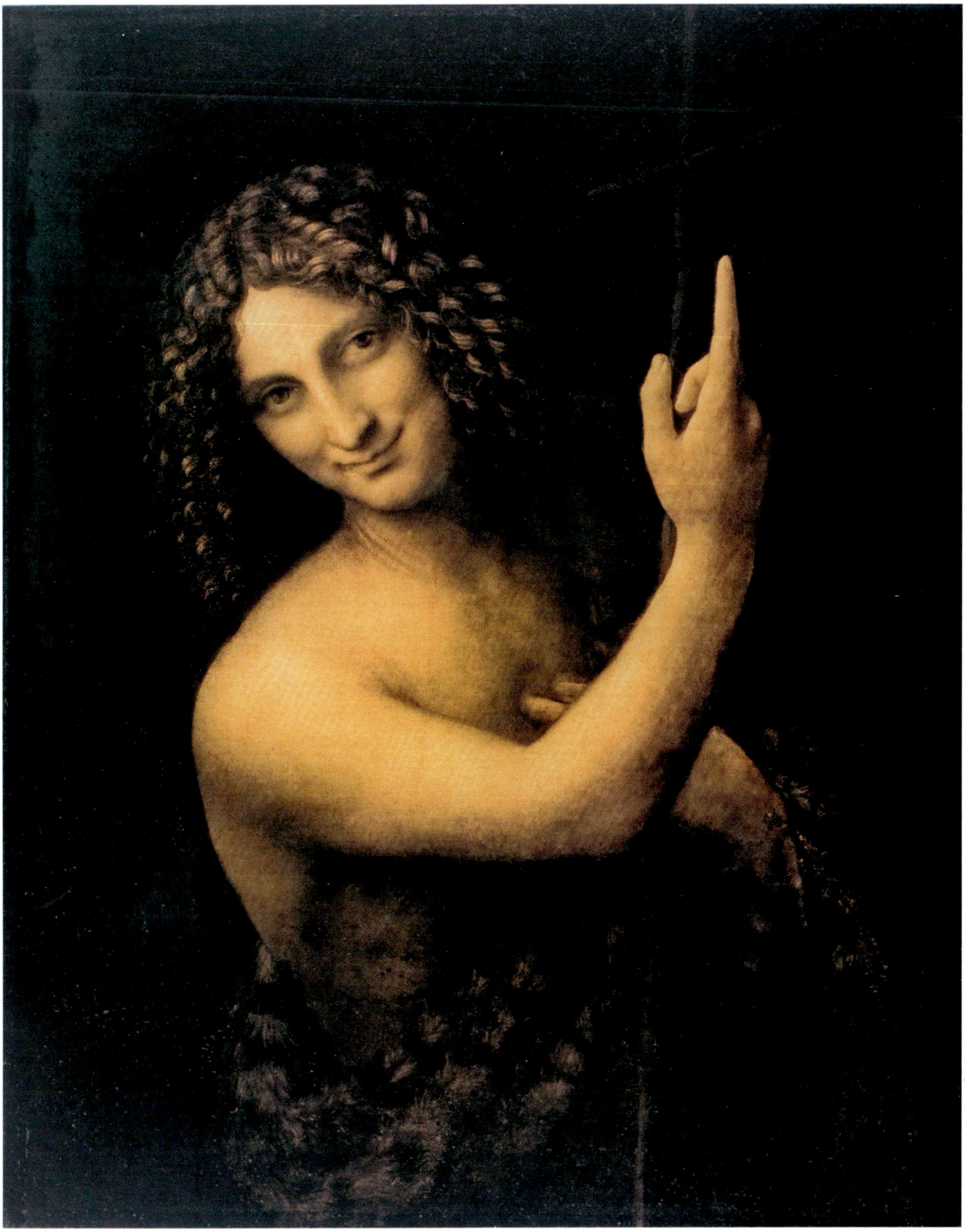

modelling of St John, and exhibits the soft ambiguity that Leonardo stressed in his late analyses of the eye's function.

If the light behaves naturally, its advent is exceptional and unnatural. There was no natural situation in which such a 'spotlight' could occur. If it were day, we could see some background; if it were deep night; there was no light source in the 16th century that could deliver such a selective shaft of intense illumination. Leonardo was not differentiating divine and natural light; he was making natural light behave in such a way that it can only originate from a divine source. These late paintings with dark backgrounds were much imitated by his followers, including Caravaggio; and at further remove by the many Caragavaggisti in Italy and elsewhere in Europe, including Rembrandt, who used extreme contrasts of light and shade to indicate divine presence and action. As explained in the introduction, this is a major book-length topic in its own right, and cannot be feasibly embraced in our present quest.

RAPHAEL, MASTER OF LIGHT

Of the great triumvirate of artists regarded as the stars in what used to be confidently called the High Renaissance, it was Raphael who made the most of Dante – which may come as something of a surprise, since we do not tend to think of the master from Urbino as an intellectual equal of Leonardo and Michelangelo. However, there is an important family connection that brings Dante into the forefront of Raphael's life. His father, Giovanni Santi, an underrated if not epoch-making painter, was also a poet and author. His chief composition was a *Rhyming Chronicle* in honour of Federico da Montefeltro, whom we have already encountered as the commissioner of a splendid manuscript of the *Divina Commedia.* A preamble to the *Chronicle* written by a colleague refers implausibly to the author of the *Chronicle* as a second Dante, which tells us a lot about Giovanni's aspirations. He uses the three-line unit (or *terza rima*) of the *Commedia* in his *Chronicle.* A substantial section of Giovanni's paean of praise for the Duke of Urbino is devoted to a notably well-informed account of Renaissance art and artists. He regards Andrea Mantegna as the supreme painter who:

> Glows and shines, expressing with great concepts
> So that I am left stupefied in my mind.
> In sum, what many high intelligences
> Have demonstrated in excellent painting,
> Shines out in him with all its terms perfected.[10]

Giovanni's admiration for Mantegna is rooted in Andrea's notable skills in perspective, involving geometrical foundations and optical veracities. Giovanni accords fulsome praise to perspective as the foundation of great art.

But there is further challenge to the painter who aspires to imitate all of nature's visual delights.

> Who will he be who has can ever counterfeit
> The ruby's shining bright transparent colour [*chiar colore lucido e trasparente*],
> And the beauty of its splendour [*splendore*]?
> Who is he who can ever paint the sun in the morning
> Or the mirror of the waters
> With the leaves and flowers at its margins?
> Who in the world was ever born so excellent
> As to form a white lily, or fresh rose
> With such purity as to please nature?[11]

These demands for scintillating light effects indicate that Giovanni had seen Netherlandish oil painting. Federico's brother owned a painting of a naked lady with her maid by Jan van Eyck, and the duke imported the artist Justus of Ghent, a master of the Netherlandish techniques, to become one of his court artists.

Giovanni Santi died in 1494, when Raphael was 11 years old. We cannot doubt that the young boy, who

53 Raphael, *Parnassus*, detail of Dante, Homer and Virgil (?), Rome, Vatican, Stanza della Sagnatura

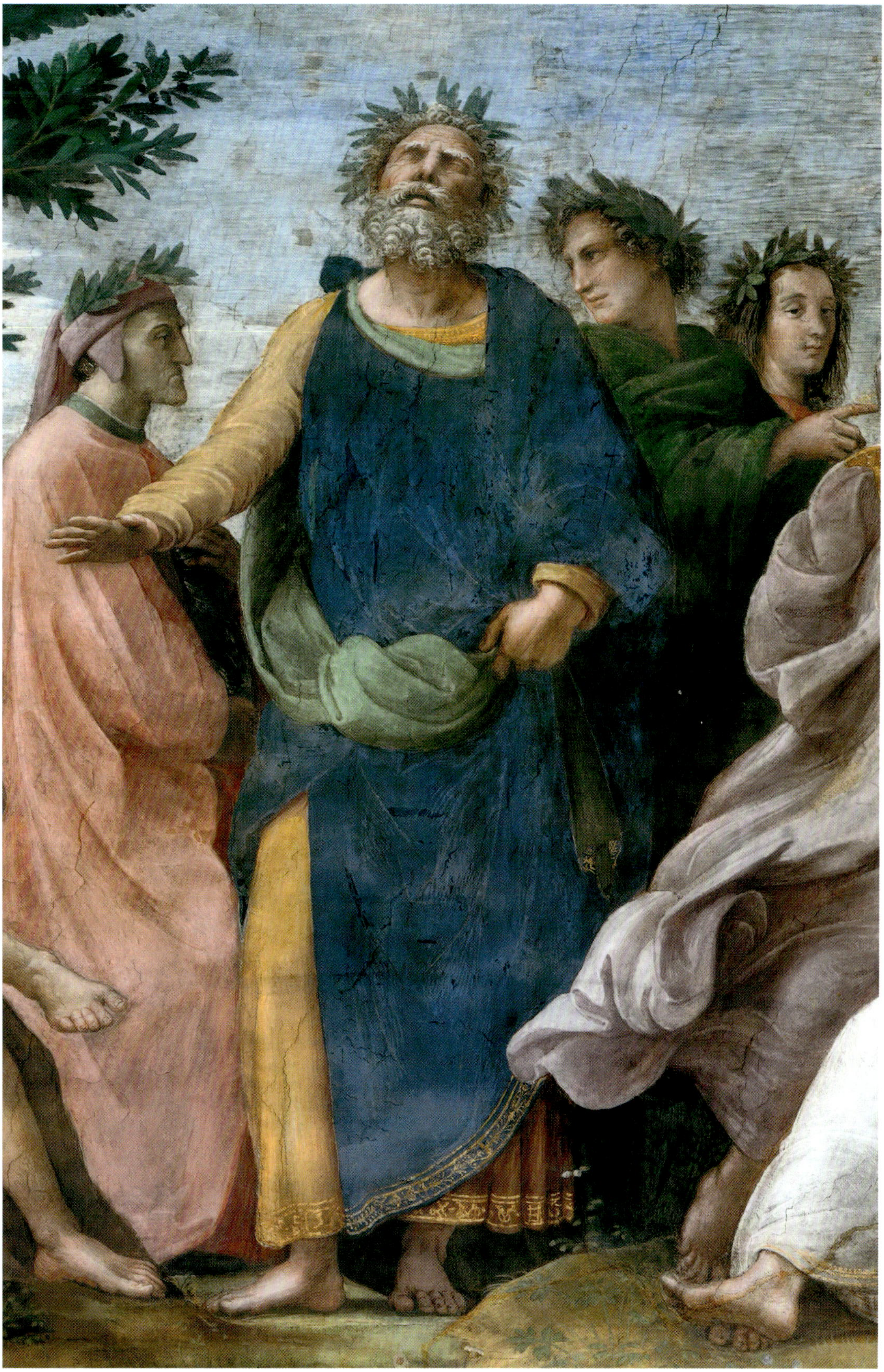

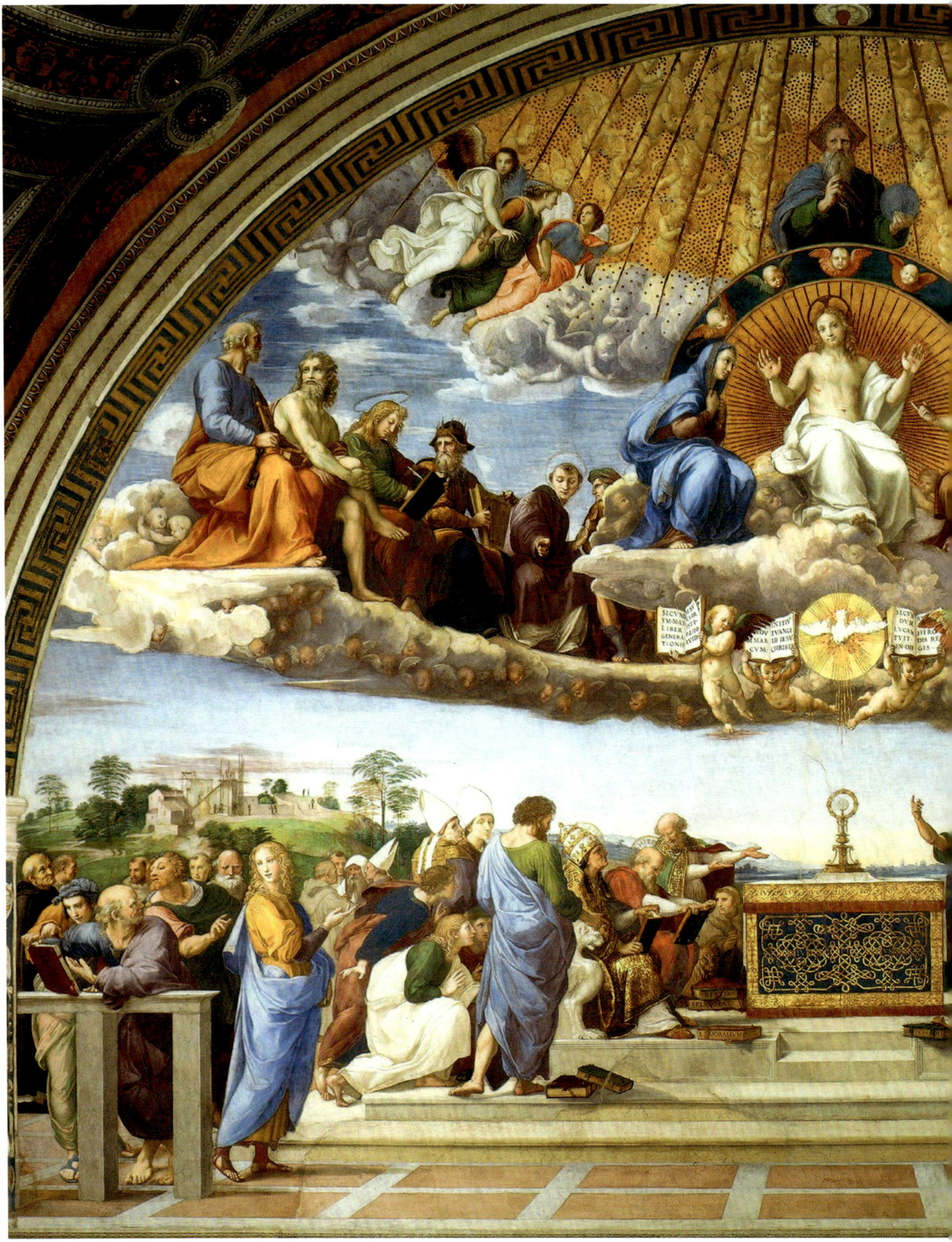

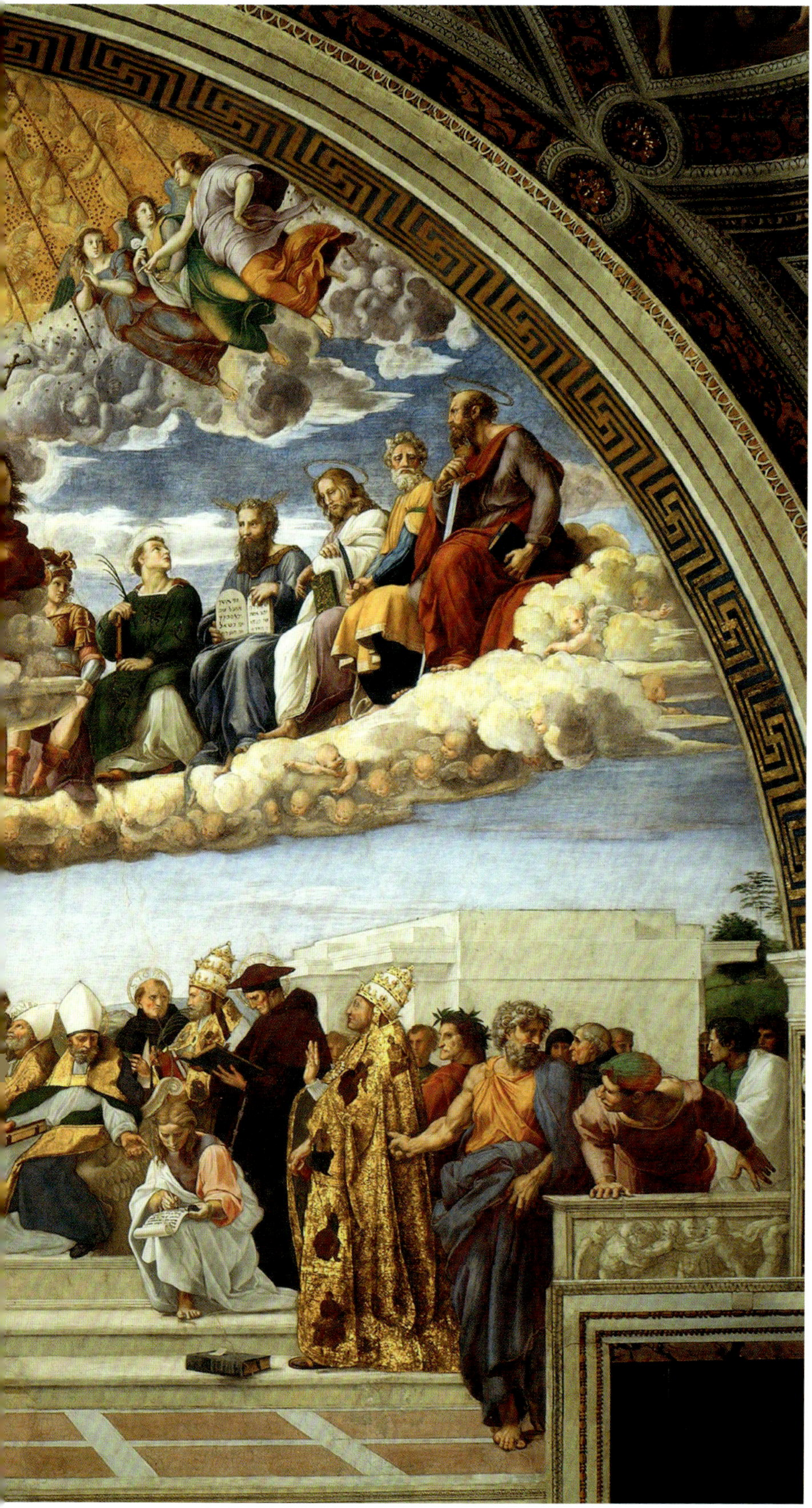

54 Raphael, *The Disputation on the Sacrament* (*La Disputa*), Rome, Vatican, Stanza della Segnatura

was a precocious talent, would have been introduced to Dante and was affected over the longer term by his father's literary ambitions. Raphael himself aspired to write poetry and there are six rough drafts for sonnets on his drawings, all connected with his frescoes in the Stanza della Segnatura in the Vatican, produced early in the second decade of the 16th century. One of the murals was devoted to poetry and portrayed great writers, ancient and modern, congregated on Mount Parnassus under Apollo's command, as described at the start of *Paradiso*. The stern-jawed Dante was of course present, beside the blind Homer, modelled on the head of Laocoon on the famous Hellenistic sculpture recently rediscovered in Rome (fig.53).

On a sheet of drawings that contains a drapery study for *La Disputa* in the Stanza della Segnatura, there is a draft, with much crossing out, part of which reads,

> Now I proclaim and declare that you [Love] are my master,
> From the centre to the heavens, more elevated than Jupiter and Mars,
> And that no defence of the mind has art
> Enough to contradict your power and your fury.

The adducing of the heavens is distinctly Dantesque within a poetic framework that draws special inspiration from the poetry of Petrarch. On the ceiling of the Stanza is an image of astronomy (or Urania) curating the transparent celestial sphere of the fixed stars.

Dante also features in the *Disputa*, devoted to theology, and is the only historical person to warrant two appearances (fig.54) in the Stanza. He can be seen rather inconspicuously behind the standing figure of Sixtus IV, builder of the Sistine Chapel, in the lower right of the painting. The two zones present an apparition of the heavens above and a prestigious earthly ensemble of those theologians who have valiantly sought to expound the eternal mysteries. To capture the full glory of the heavens, Raphael has resorted to a stippled, gold background, at the centre of which God the Father holds the crystalline sphere of heavens. A powerful set of expanding rays is incised into the gilded canopy, inhabited by ghostly, semi-seen *putti*. More nebulous little angels are elusively formed from the clouds below the rays, and more fade in and out of view in the cloud platforms supporting Christ, the Virgin, St John and the lower arc of saints. The way that this host of airborne infants stand on the edge of optical definition is deeply Dantesque.

There is a precedent for the cloud-angels. In 1509, Fra Bartolommeo completed a striking altarpiece in which God the Father is seated on a cloud-throne above the airborne St Mary Magdalene and St Catherine of Siena (fig.55). God is shown against a bright background of golden light in which a ring of cloud-angel heads is just discernible. The saints kneel on cushions of rather compressed cloud-angels. Did Raphael know about Fra Bartolommeo's invention before he left Florence for Rome in 1508? As we will see, the latter actually painted his picture in Venice. Was Fra Bartolommeo drawing upon Dante? Either way, we can be confident that Raphael was especially well placed to exploit the older artist's cloud-angels more fully as a Dantesque motif.

The dove representing the Holy Ghost is at the centre of *La Disputa*, and is accorded a gold orb, as is Christ himself. Somehow, this retrograde technique does not compete with the modernity of Raphael's figurative style and his assertive use of perspective. From the centre of the dove's orb a set of powerful rays passes downwards and into the monstrance on the altar. This signifies the transubstantiation of the Host, or bread or wafer, into the body of Christ, a key sacrament of the Church. The assembled theologians and churchmen are involved in explicating the nature of miraculous translation of bread into body that occurs every time the Eucharist is administered to the faithful.

But Raphael has performed an optical trick. We read the arch of saints as transforming the lunette-shaped field into a kind of semi-dome. Christ's cloud, which

55 Fra Bartolommeo, *God the Father with St Mary Magdalene and St Catherine of Siena*, Lucca, Galleria Nazionale

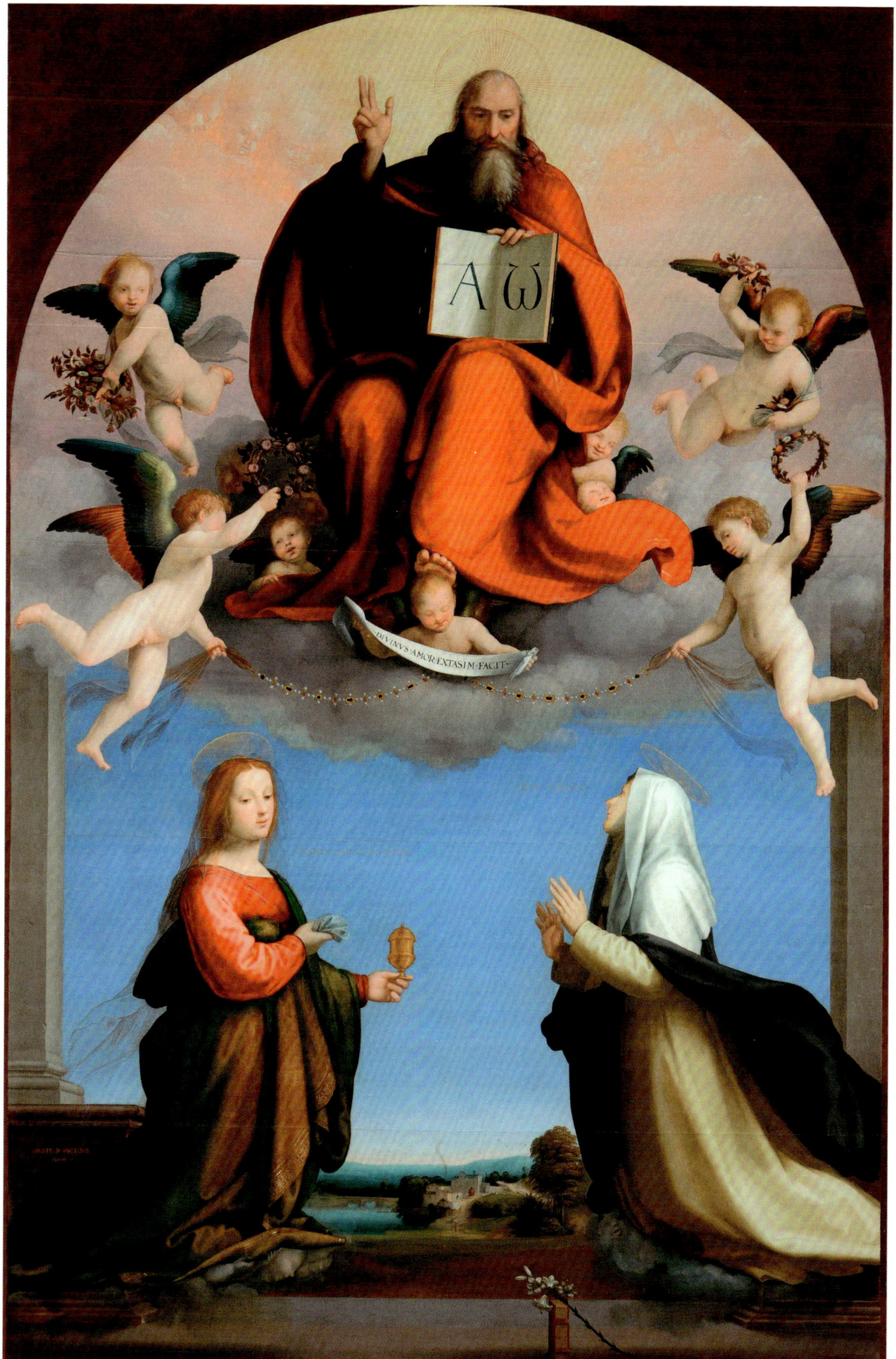
A Ω
DIVINVS·AMOR·EXTASIM·FACIT·

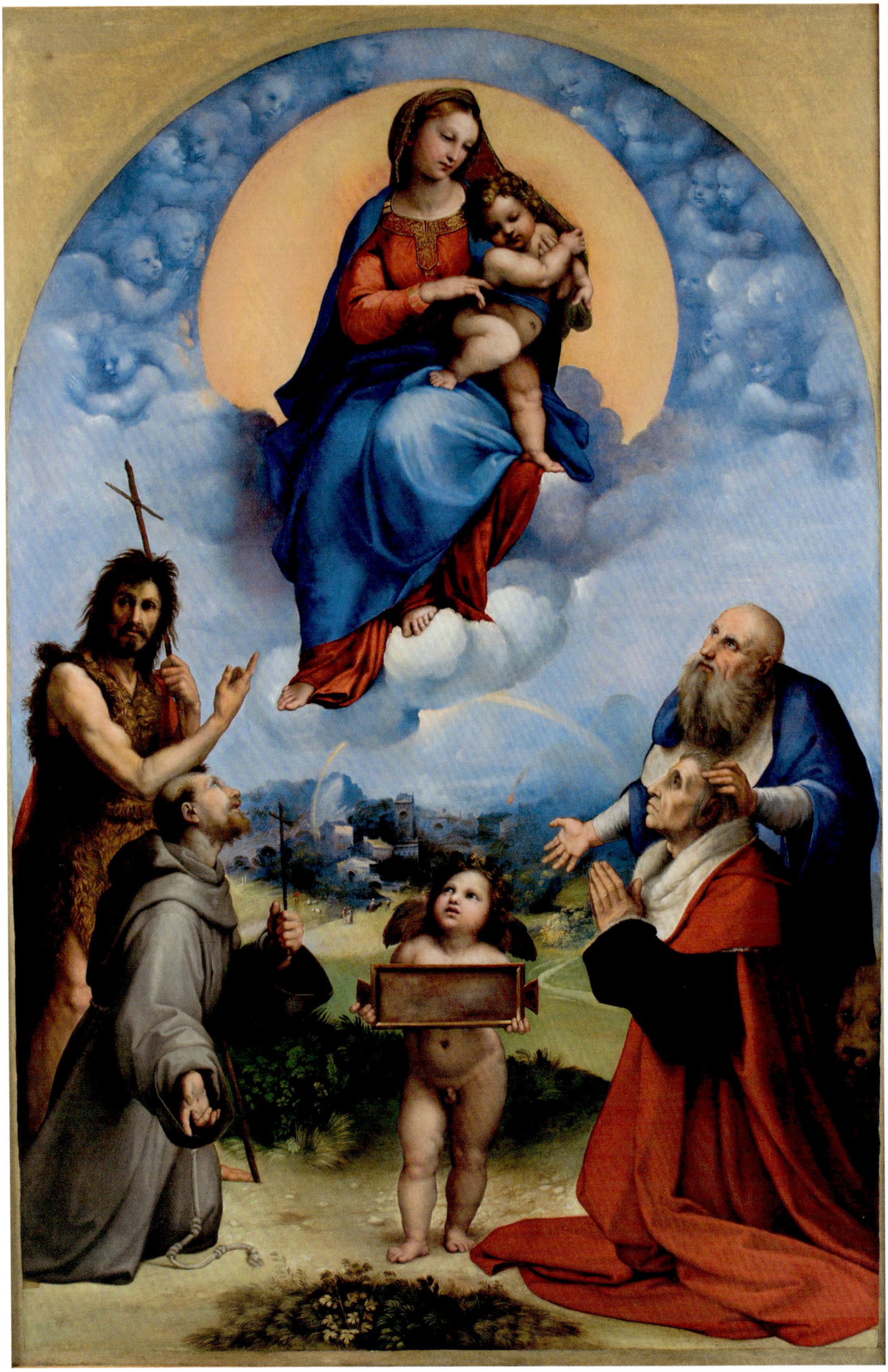

sits at the centre of the arc, is therefore notionally just behind the surface of the mural. But we also read the dove as vertically over the altar, which means that the curved array of saints must be set considerably deeper than the assembly of theologians. In this case, the figures in heaven are on a much larger scale than those on the ground. This, instinctively, is not the reading we make, but it has its own logic. The likely answer is that Raphael wants us to see the two figure groups as closely aligned, while we also see and understand the communication between the Holy Spirit and the Host. Only if we analyse what he has done do we become aware of the internal contradiction. Or is he relying, Dante-like, on the breakdown of optical rule in heaven? This is perhaps a bit too smart, but it is tempting to interpret the discrepancy in this way.

Dating from the same period, Raphael's *Foligno Madonna* effectively exploits the gold orb and cloud-angels in an altarpiece (fig.56). It was commissioned for the Church of Santa Maria in Aracoeli by Sigismondo dei Conti, poet and historian, who served as a state secretary to Pope Julius II from 1505 until his death in 1512. Sigismondo is being presented to the Virgin and Child by St Jerome in the presence of St John and St Francis. The visionary set-up corresponds to one of the legends in the popular, much cited and amplified text from the 12th century the *Mirabilia urbis Romae* (*Wonders of the City of Rome*).

> In order to reward Emperor Octavian [Augustus] for having established peace in the world, the Senate wished to pay him the honours of a god. But the wise Emperor, knowing that he was mortal, was unwilling to assume the title of immortal before he had asked the Tiburtine Sibyl whether the world would some day see the birth of a greater man than he. Now on the day of the Nativity the Sibyl was alone with the Emperor, when at high noon she saw a golden ring appear around the sun. In the middle of the circle stood a Virgin, of wondrous beauty, holding a Child upon her bosom. The Sibyl showed this wonder to Caesar; and a voice was heard which said: 'This woman is the Altar of Heaven (*Ara Coeli*)!' And the Sibyl said to him: 'This Child will be greater than thou' ... Where this miracle took place was consecrated to the holy Virgin; and upon the site the Church of Santa Maria in Ara Coeli stands today.[12]

The golden circle of the Sybil's vision is surrounded by bright blue cloud-angels who again stand on the edge of individual legibility. The Baptist performs the role that St Bernard assumed in the later stages of *Paradiso*, facilitating our ability to see the supreme vision.

Between the two groups of figures stand a flesh-and-blood angel holding a blank tablet. There is no sign that there ever was an inscription on the tablet, and the picture is evidently fully finished. It may be that the absence of words signals that the ultimate mystery can never be fully apparent to people on earth, as happens at the very end of *Paradiso*, where even Dante's words fail him. Again, this interpretation is tempting but not directly demonstrable.

The distant landscape of Foligno, the patron's home town, is painted with considerable bravura, predominantly in vibrant tones of blue. A rainbow arches upwards, behind the Virgin's cloud-platform. To the right, near the hand of Jerome, a fiery red ball with a trailing tail plunges towards a roof, which has been interpreted in a variety of ways. What is clear is that Foligno is subject to a dangerous threat from the skies. From the advent of the rainbow we may assume that the town or house was saved. It may be that the altarpiece was commissioned by Sigismondo to give thanks for a miraculous escape of some kind. In any event, if we imagine the painting in its original setting at the high altar in Santa Maria in Aracoeli, the vivid contrast of blue and gold would have given an extraordinary sense of the emperor's vision as reprised for Sigismondo.

A year or two later, the cloud-angels were taken to a new level in Raphael's *Sistine Madonna* (fig.57). The

56 Raphael, *The Foligno Madonna*, Rome, Vatican

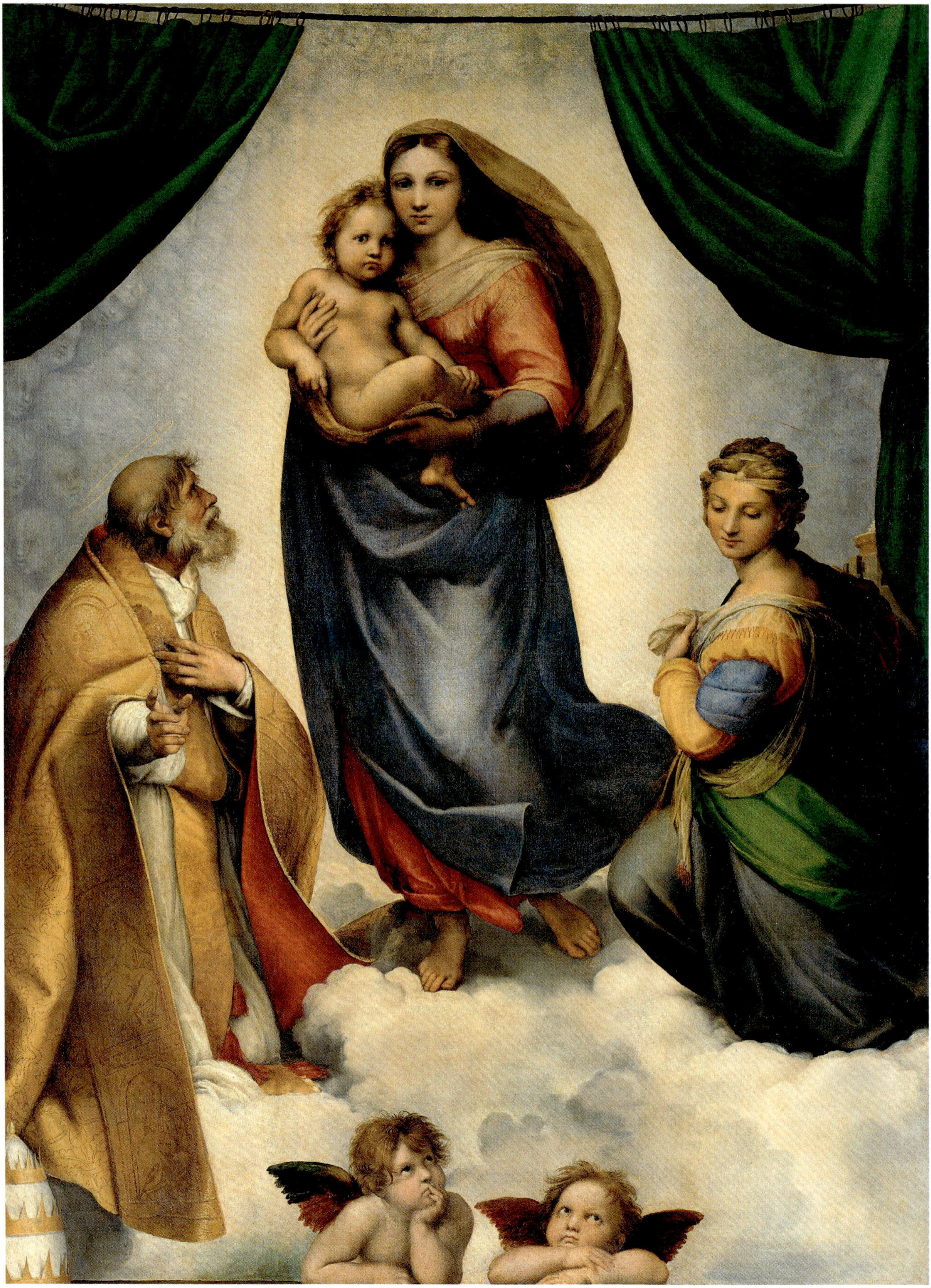

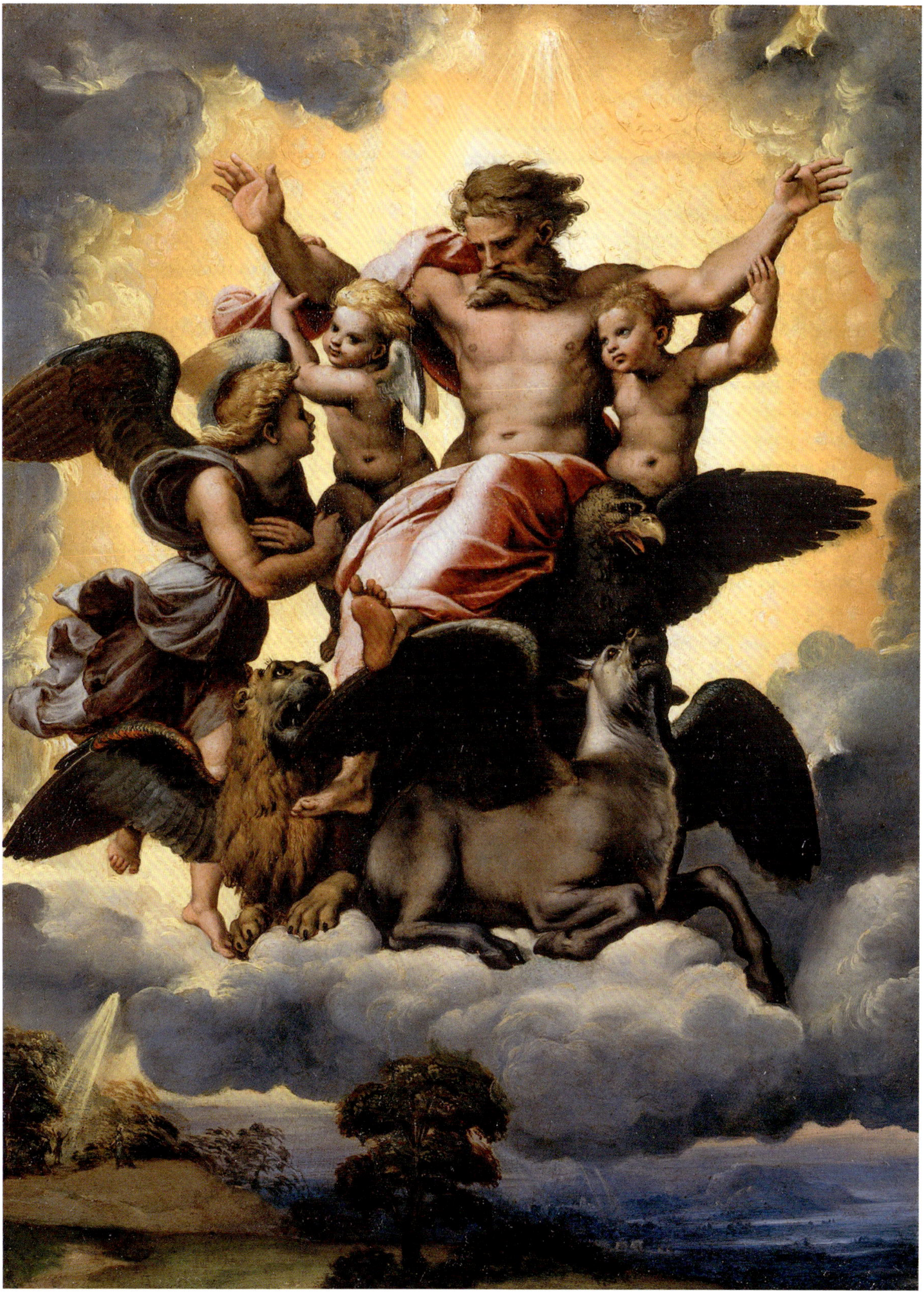

57 (OPPOSITE) Raphael, *The Sistine Madonna*, Dresden, Gemäldegalerie

58 Raphael, *The Vision of Ezekiel*, Florence, Palazzo Pitti

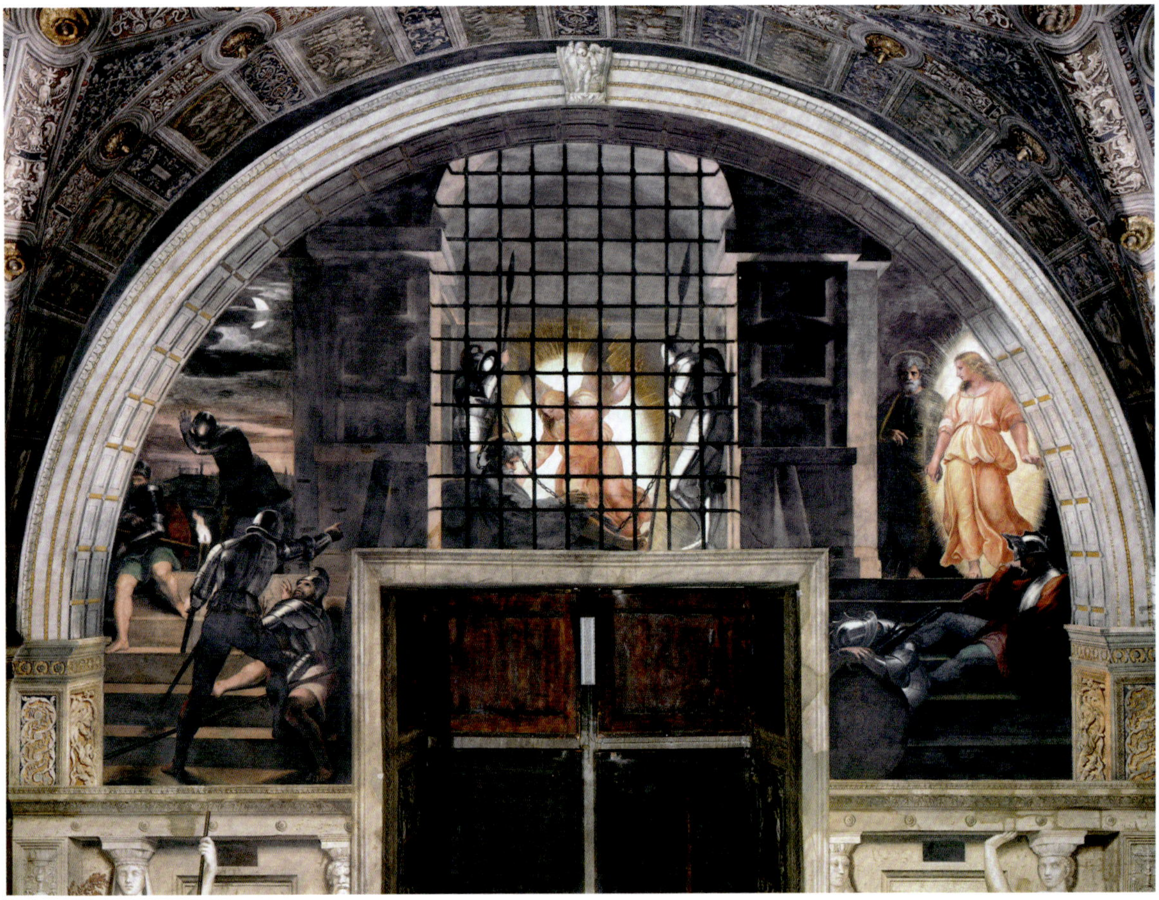

59 Raphael, *The Liberation of St Peter from Prison*, Rome, Vatican, Stanza d'Eliodoro

is relatively orthodox if notably brilliant in realisation. The story is illustrated with lyrical spirituality. He has held back the brightness of Christ's robe from the very highest white (as Alberti had recommended), so that he can create an aureole of light that is even brighter. The cloud of the biblical narrative is waiting to play its part: 'a bright cloud overshadowed them'. Moses and Elijah float weightlessly, as befits their blessed status, while the three earthly witnesses collapse physically and suffer visually in the face of Christ's blinding light. They might try to shade their eyes, but to no good effect. From this point on, the content of the image becomes more complex. To the left of Moses, who is holding his precious tablets of law, are two youthful witnesses, with whom we are invited to identify. They are likely to be St Justus and St Pastor, boy saints, to whom the cathedral at Narbonne was dedicated. The event in the lower section of the painting is saturated with the turbulent uncertainty that stymied the disciples' attempt to heal the possessed boy; nothing is comfortably resolved.

We can identify the violently afflicted boy, supported by his desperate father. But is he in the middle of a fit or does his open mouth signal the exit of the devil? We should remember that Christ still has to descend from the mountain to carry out the exorcism. Who is the extraordinarily beautiful kneeling woman who plays such a pivotal role in the composition? She does not quite look like the boy's mother. That role is better assigned to the woman just behind the ravaged boy. Is the woman in pink primarily a demonstration of Raphael's stylishness? The clustered disciples react in diverse ways, as they were to do at the Last Supper. The dramatic foreshortened and gesticulating disciple at the bottom left is a display of high artistic skill intended to rival one of Michelangelo's specialities. The disciple holds a voluminous book, perhaps to remind us to read our Bible to understand what is going on. Maybe he is St Matthew or St Mark?

The only direct link from the scene to the vision above is the figure in a yellow robe pointing to the boy, but he does not actually see the Transfiguration. He is saying to his companions and to us that Christ has ascended the mountain and we need him. The density of rather Leonardesque shadows at the foot of the mountain, cast by a light that comes from the front and left, is optically separate from the radiant drama above. The cacophonous failure of the disciples occurs in the shadows that characterise our earthly existence. Raphael ambitiously invites the viewer to participate in making sense of the action in the lower half of the altarpiece, and its relationship to the vision above.

TITIAN ABLAZE

In Venice at this time, Bellini's reticence with divine light is not matched by his greatest successor, Titian, whose majestic *Assumption*, the huge high altar in Venice for the Church of the Frari (Franciscan Friars), loses nothing in comparison to Raphael (fig.60). Did Titian know how the cloud-angels and radiant glare worked in *The Sistine Madonna*? It is unlikely that he knew it or Raphael's *Transfiguration*. More plausibly, he picked up the motif from Fra Bartolommeo, whose picture *God the Father with St Mary Magdalene and St Catherine of Siena* (fig.55) was actually painted in Venice in 1509 for the Church of St Peter Martyr in Murano – though the Dominicans failed to remunerate the painter and the altarpiece was donated to Lucca. Like Raphael, Titian has utilised the cloud-angels with a bravura that extended beyond Fra Bartolommeo's invention. God the Father, swooping like the Holy Eagle of Justice in Dante's *Paradiso*, provides a dark foil for the explosions of heavenly light towards which the Virgin rises, with the lively support of a chorus of angels. Some of the cloud-angels are defined, and others are not defined with great painterly brilliance. The frieze of awed disciples, partly shadowed by the Virgin's cloud, can react directly to the miraculous event in a way that Raphael's figures could not. The effect, as we walk through the arched opening in the choir screen in the Frari to witness the unfolding drama of the Virgin's ascent, is rapturous. The dedication of the church was to Santa Maria Gloriosa dei Frari.

That Titian's picture can stand beside Dante's vision of heaven is one thing, adducing his knowledge of Dante is another. Recently a volume of the *Commedia* owned by Titian's close colleague Giorgione has come to light; it was the Venetian edition of 1497. A copy owned by the University of Sydney contains an inscription recording the premature death of Giorgione on 17 September 1510, written above a subtle sketch in red chalk of a Madonna and Child. It seems likely to by Giorgione himself, or might we sentimentally think that it is by Titian, paying homage to his deceased companion?[15] Giorgione and Titian were linked to a circle of young *literati* and patrons, including the poet and author Pietro Bembo, who was responsible for the classic Aldine Press edition of the *Commedia* in 1502. Titian was later to paint two portraits of Bembo. The archetypal Giorgionesque painting for this group of connoisseurs was a secular picture, often on a small scale, of imaginative content that was overtly poetic in mood – later called a *poesia*, but at this early stage known as a *fantasia*. The young Titian was closely involved in the production of this new kind of painting. The *Assumption* shows that he was

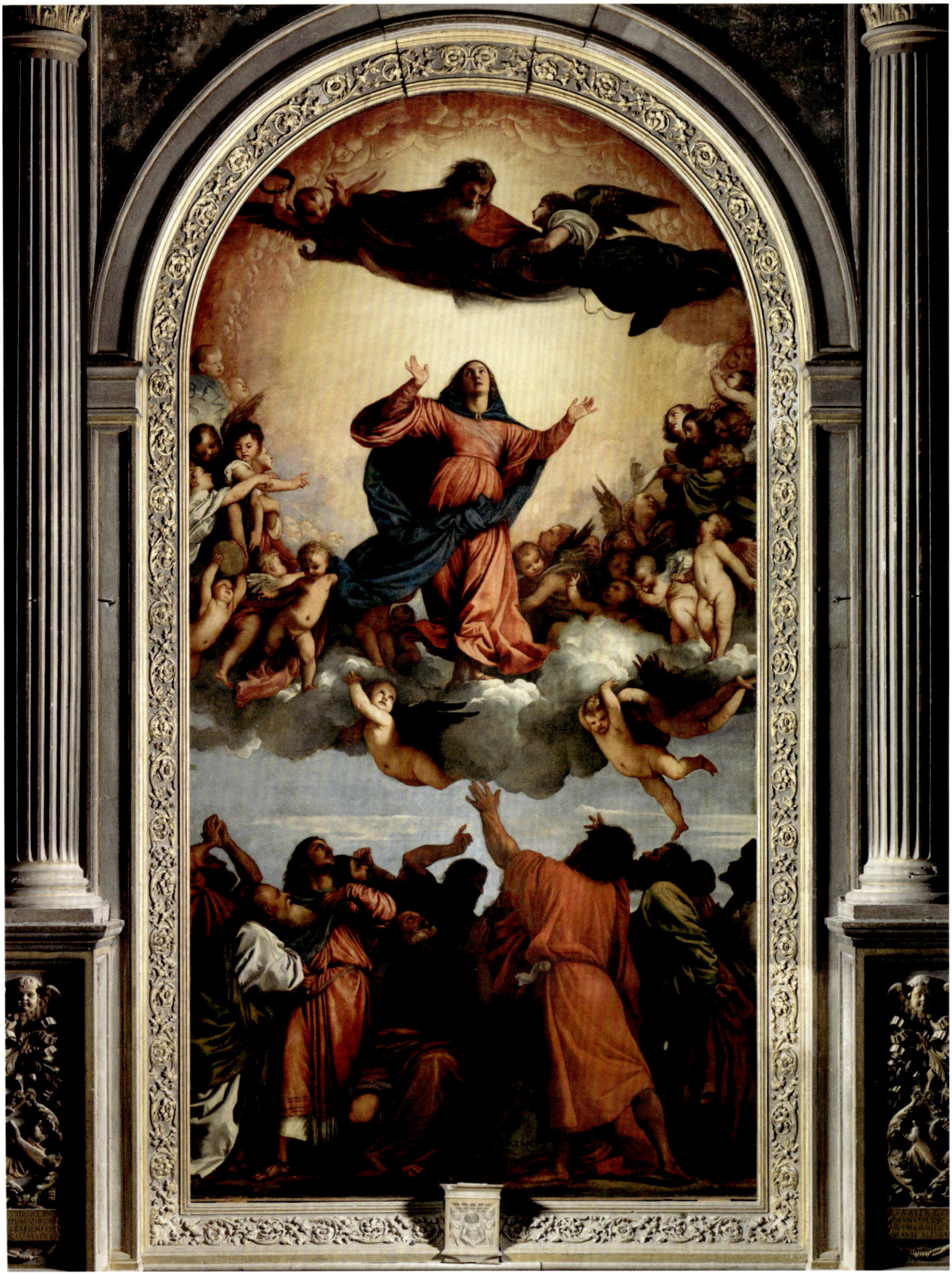

not restricted to poetic snippets but could emulate the grand narrative of a whole *canto.*

This artistic ability is certainly true of the great painting now called *La Gloria,* but more accurately described at an early date as *The Trinity* (fig.61). The patron, Charles V, the Holy Roman Emperor, called it the *Last Judgement* when he carried it with him towards the end of his life. But this title is only correct if we regard the painting as a specific vision of the elect, perhaps as in St Augustine's *City of God* in which the redeemed souls are resurrected in their bodies. Charles, who received the large picture 1554, kneels in supplication to the right of centre, with the shrouded figures of his wife Isabella, son Philip and other members of the family. The central motif of the Trinity, with very closely similar images of the Father and the Son, and a dove which is de-materialised in a cascade of light, is surrounded by freely sketched angel-heads. The Virgin walks towards the Trinity, at the same time looking down at the favoured figures below, who are much closer to the spectator. God and Christ hold comparable celestial globes topped with crosses. They sit on thrones tolerantly provided by angel-heads. The assembled company include what must have been a purposeful selection of characters, largely from the Old Testament. We can, for instance, recognise Moses with his horns of light and tablets, one of which he shares with St John the Evangelist. Noah holds aloft a model of his ark, with the dove holding the olive branch that announced the presence of dry land after the mighty flood. Does the brown skin of the maritime saviour indicate that he is of African origin?

The sharp beams of light that pierce the underside of the darkish cloud are very similar to those that Raphael invented for his *Vision of Ezekiel.* Indeed, the whole set-up, with an apparition, painted with a large but undefined sense of scale, over a vibrant landscape, is very Raphaelesque. In front of the coppice of trees and close to a wayside shrine, we can just see some tiny figures who serve as astonished witnesses. It is tempting to think that Titian knew of Raphael's little masterpiece, but it seems unlikely. It seems less than satisfactory to say that the two geniuses may have converged on the same conception.

By around 1560, when Titian painted his own light-filled image of the Transfiguration as the high altariece for the Church of San Salvador in Venice, he had been to Rome and would have seen Raphael's great altarpiece, which was never dispatched to Narbonne. Of Titian's three altarpieces commissioned for the church, the *Annunciation* and *Transfiguration* are still in place, while the *Crucifixion* is now in Ancona. The *Annunciation* is a great surprise (fig.62). Titian's earlier portrayals of this essentially domestic event had become more architecturally grand, but do little to prepare us for the angelic pyrotechnics of the San Salvador version. The grand archangel arrives with a beating of ample wings, to the understandable surprise of Mary. The impregnating dove surges forwards in a jagged burst of intense light from a conflagration of stomping angels. Apart from the two calm steps at the base of the picture, the sparkling carafe of lilies and the hint of a grand portico, the whole picture is activated by spiritual turbulence of the kind that regularly assailed Dante's mind as he strove to make sense of the visions with which he was presented in *Paradiso.* I am not adducing the direct impact of Dante on the *Annunciation* – though this is not impossible. Rather, it may be a shared matter of verbal and visual extremes in the service of religious wonder.

GRÜNEWALD: A TRIUMPHANT POSTSCRIPT

Finally, in this chapter – I am leaving Correggio for the next – let us look at a remarkable outlier. This is the spectacular compound altarpiece made for the Monastery of St Anthony in Isenheim, south of Colmar in the Alsace region, by the painter Matthias Grünewald and the sculptor Nikolaus Hagenauer, whose large carved and gilded images of St Anthony flanked by Augustine and Jerome would have been the most expensive components. Grünewald's paintings,

60 Titian, *Assumption of the Virgin,* Venice, Santa Maria Gloriosa dei Frari

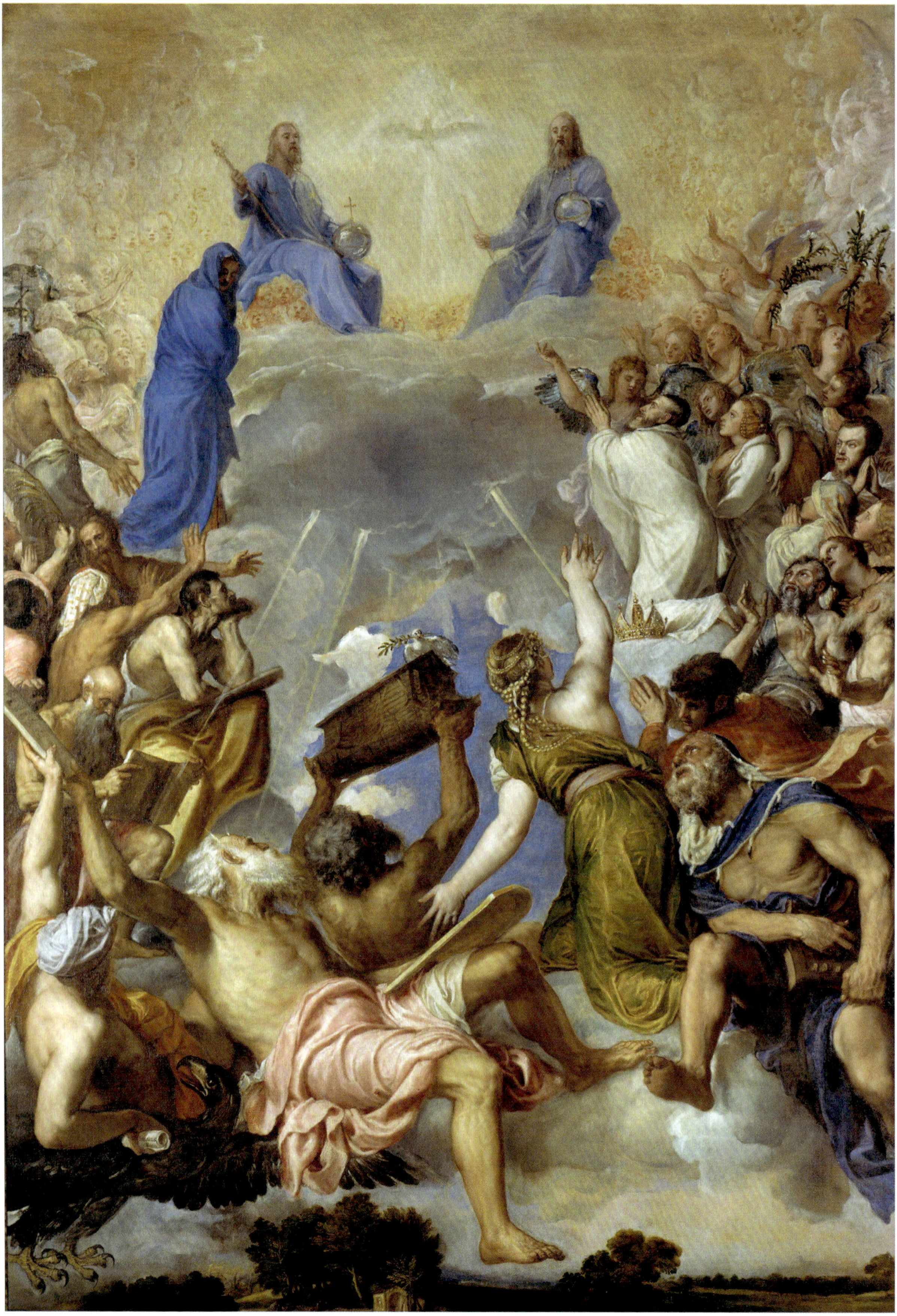

62 Titian, *Annunciation*, Venice, San Salvador

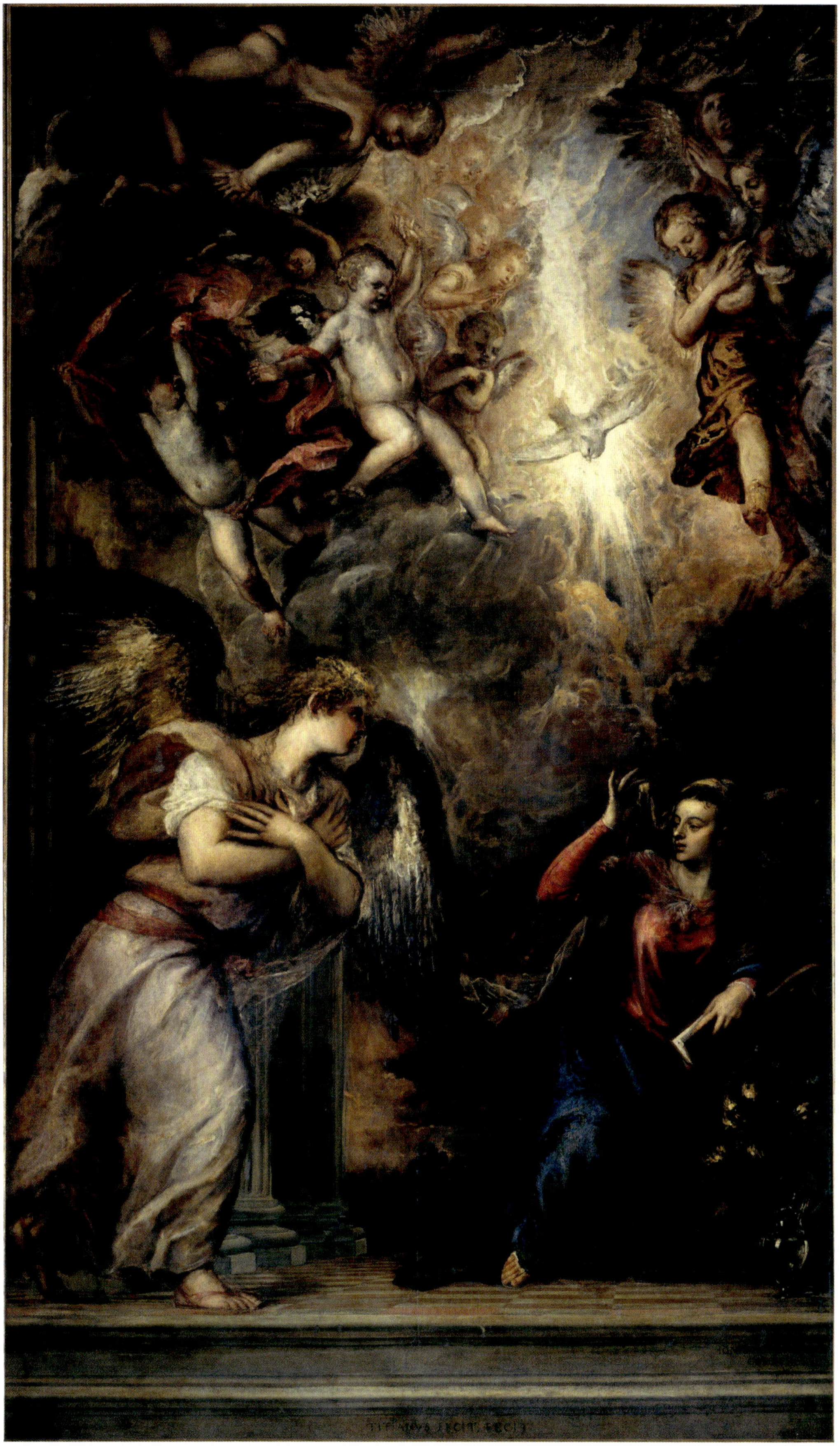

61 (OPPOSITE) Titian, *The Trinity ('La Gloria')*, Madrid, Prado

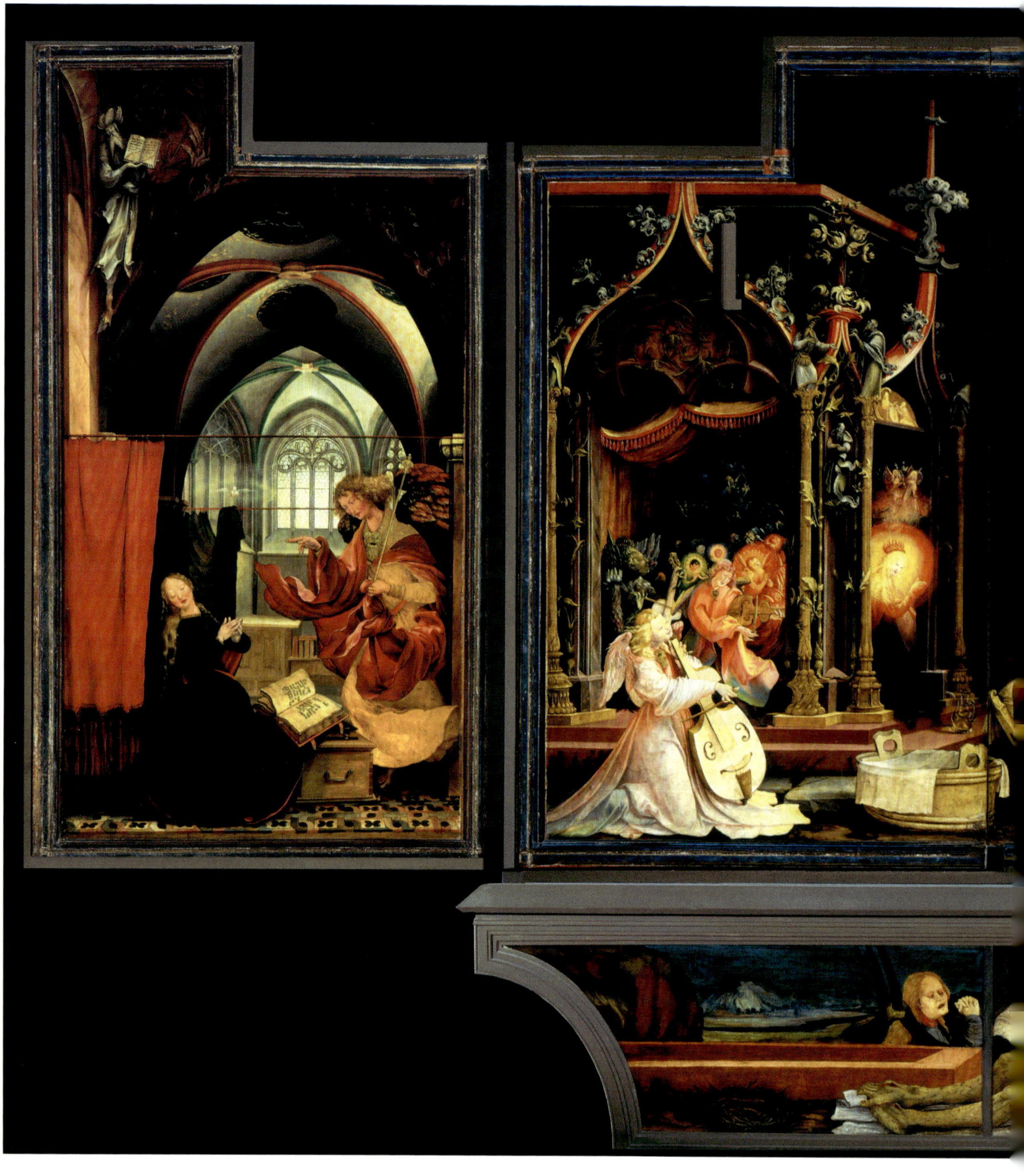

64 Matthias Grünewald, *The Isenheim Altarpiece: the Annunciation, the Nativity, the Resurrection and the Body of Christ*, Colmar, Musée Unterlinden

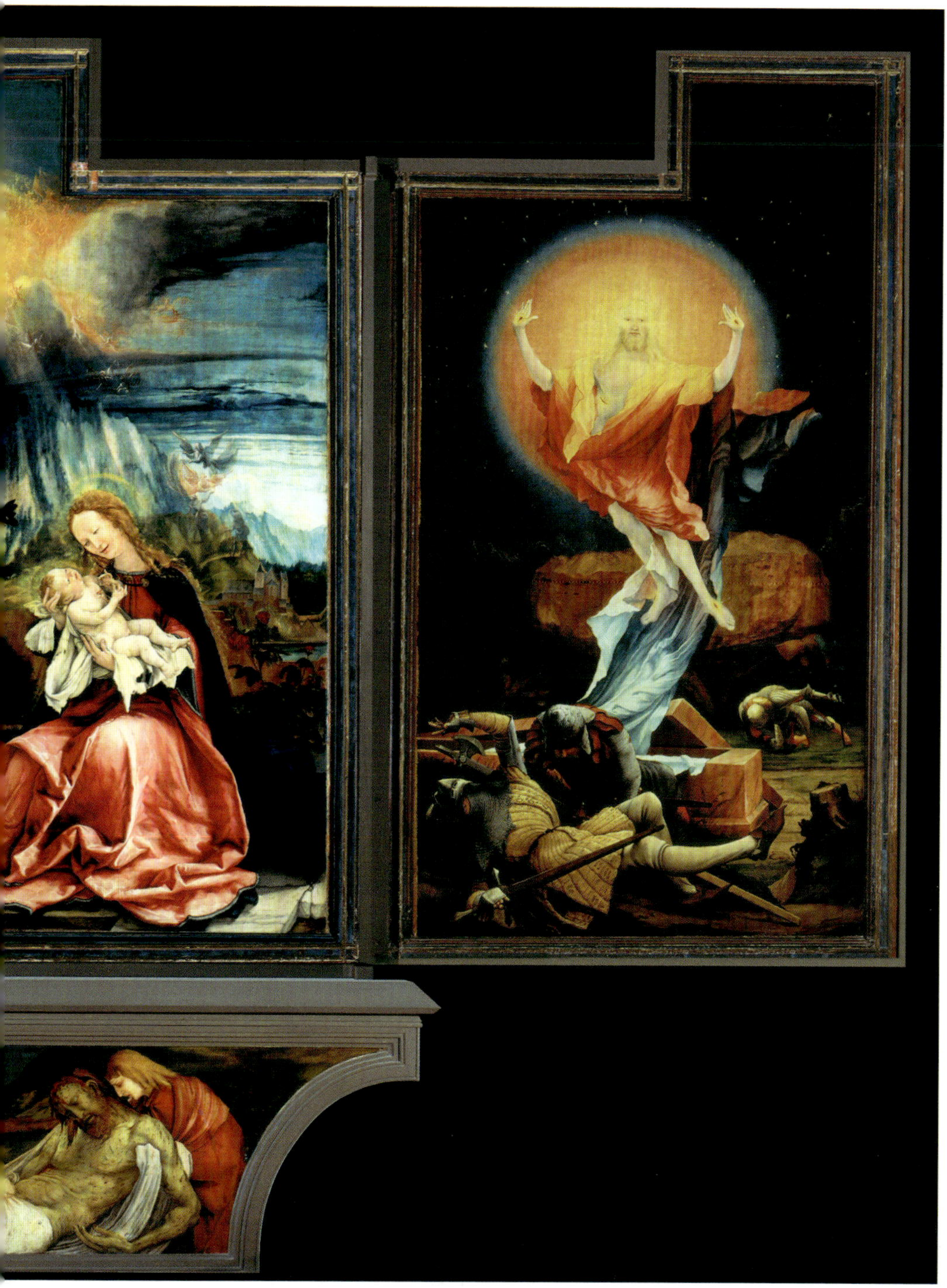

65 (NEXT SPREAD LEFT) Matthias Grünewald, *The Isenheim Altarpiece: the Nativity* (detail), Colmar, Musée Unterlinden

66 (NEXT SPREAD RIGHT) Matthias Grünewald, *The Isenheim Altarpiece: the Resurrection* (detail), Colmar, Musée Unterlinden

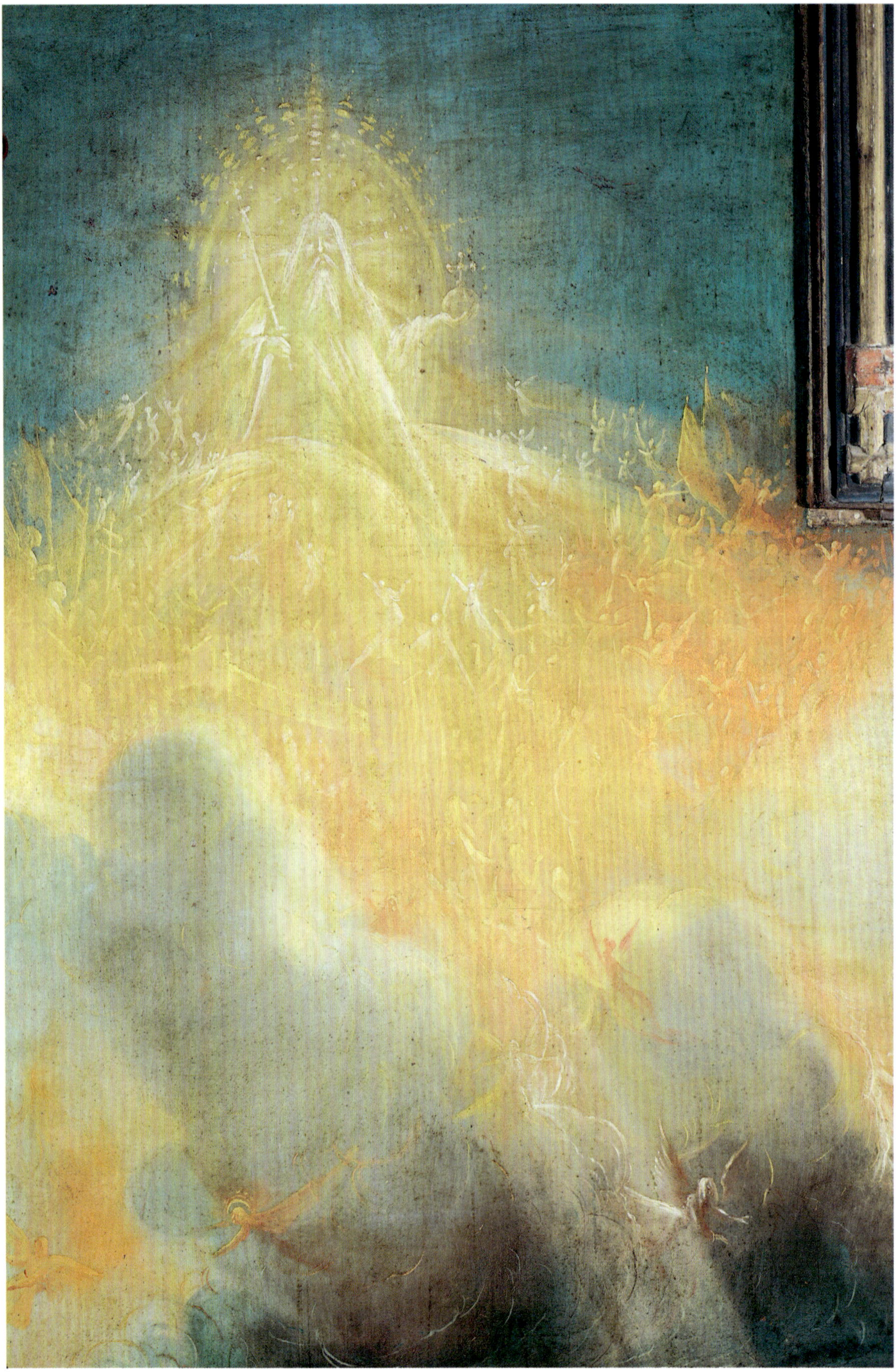

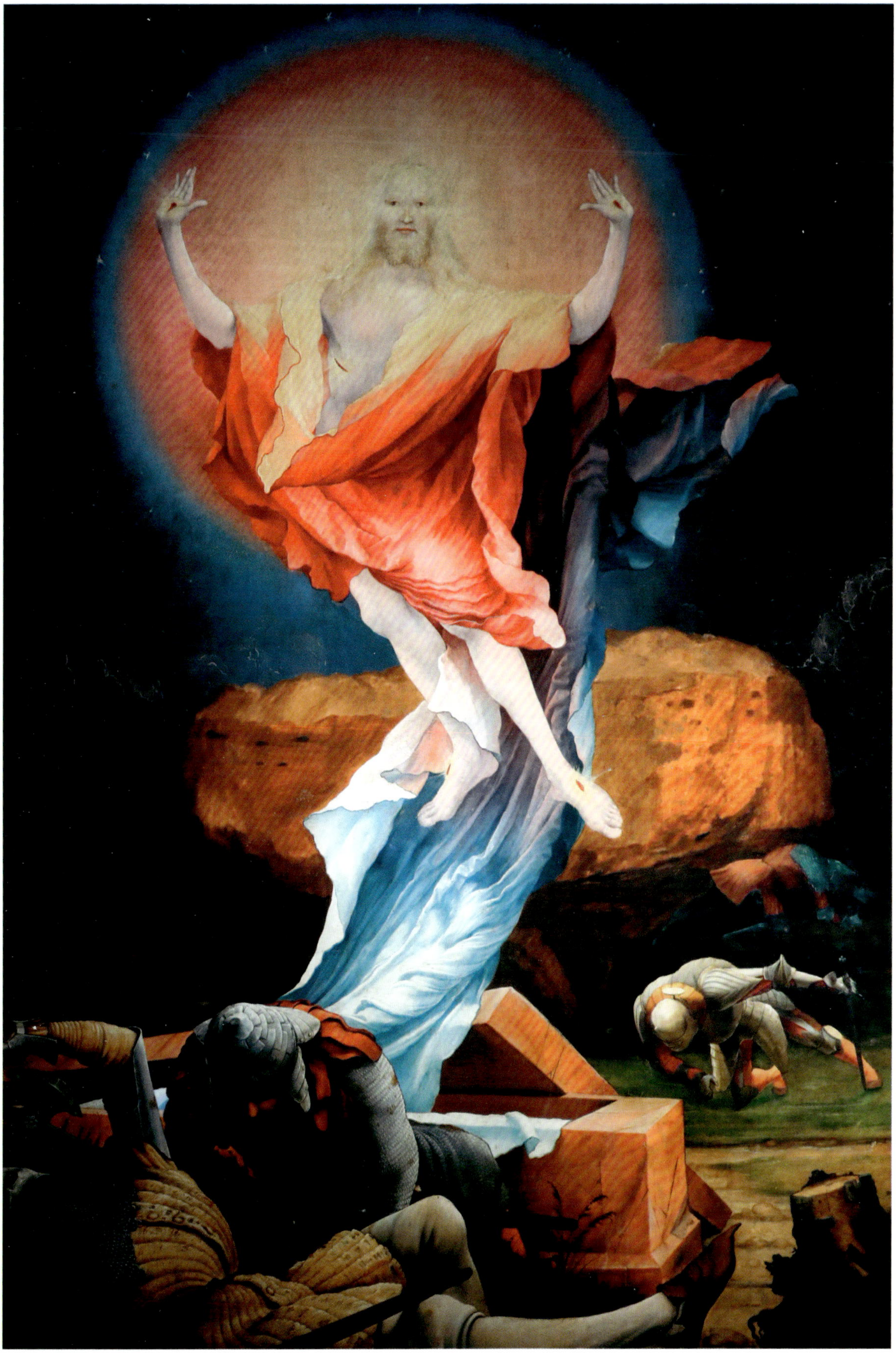

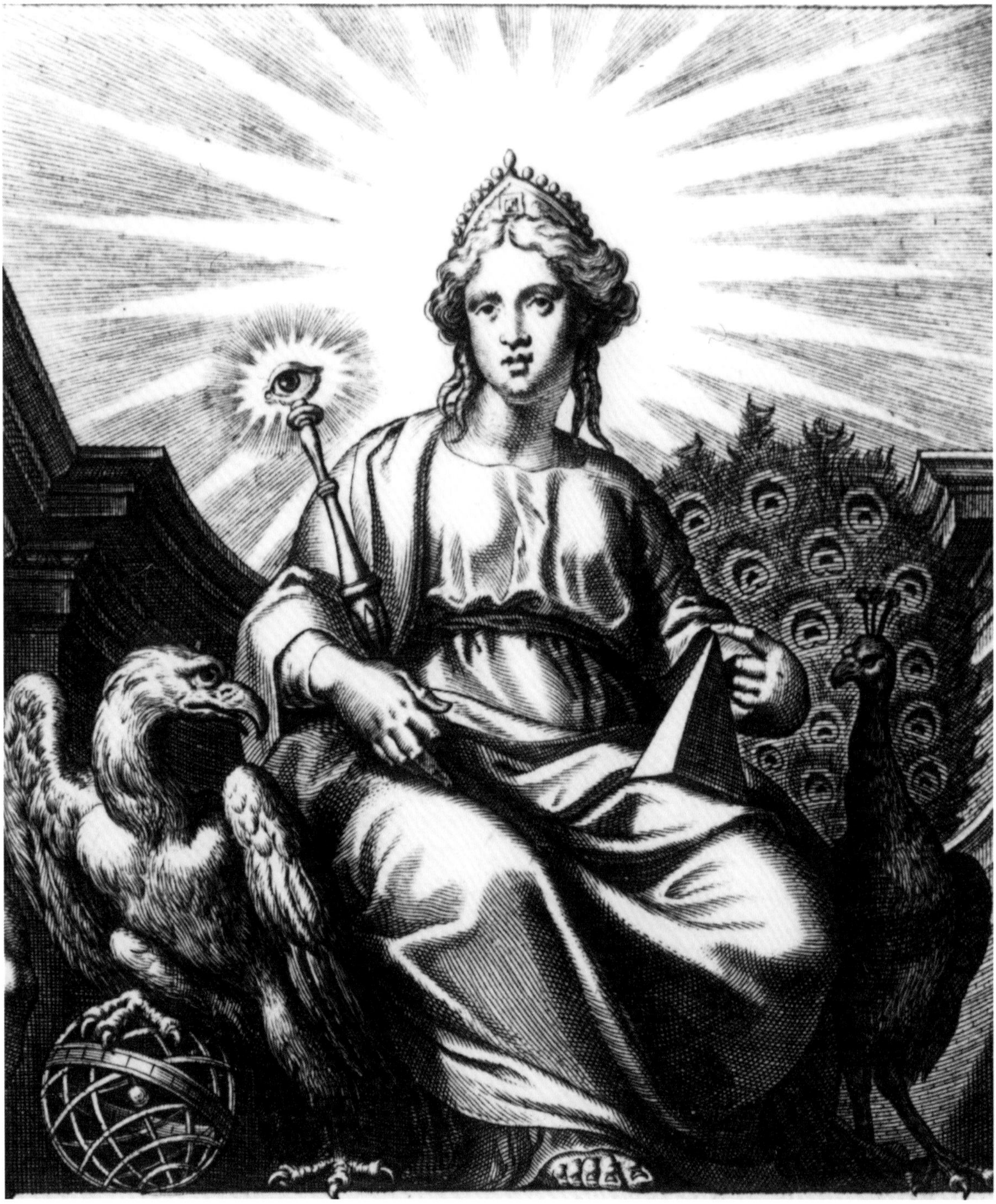

François de Aquilón (Aguilonius), *Opticorum libri sex,* Antwerp, 1613, title-page (detail) by Rubens, engraved by Theodoor Galle

5

Dantesque Dramas: from Correggio to Rubens

There is a paradox here: the sequence of Baroque vault and dome frescoes that follow in this chapter and the next present a series of dazzling heavenly visions in a truly Dantesque manner, yet Dante's own reputation was in decline after 1600.

In the Florence of Grand Duke Cosimo I in the middle years of the 16th century, Dante's great vernacular text was crucial in the promotion of Tuscan Italian as the true, learned vernacular. Two of the duke's academicians, Cosimo Bartoli and Benedetto Varchi, gave public readings in which they interpreted key Dante texts, including those that paraded his knowledge of optics. In 1588, Galileo delivered two lectures on the dimensions of the pit of Hell, as we will discover later in chapter 6. There was a continued clutch of printed editions of the *Divina Commedia* in the later 16th century. One edition contained the competing commentaries of Landino and Vellutello. It was dedicated in 1564 to Pope Pius IV in the pious context of the Counter-Reformation, and was reprinted in 1578 and 1596. The Florentine literary academy, the Accademia della Crusca, which refined and promoted the Tuscan language, published an edition in 1595. But after 1600, only three editions of the *Divina Commedia* were printed. After 1629, there were no further editions in the 17th century. The overarching answer to the paradox is that we are here concerned with something different from direct influence – something wider, more diffuse and more suggestive. The issue of direct influence exists within this wider remit. As we will see in the next chapter, when we look at cloud machinery in theatrical spectaculars, there is a strong continuity in the undoubtedly Dantesque imagery in sacred performances from the 15th century onwards. For the moment, it is best to tackle the possible impact of Dante, direct and indirect, on a case-by-case basis. Regardless of the more orthodox historical questions, the *paragone* between the *Paradiso* and the light-filled domes of the Baroque masters remains compelling in its own right.

The names of the painters responsible for the great Baroque illusions do not reside in popular consciousness to the same degree as the household names of the artists in the preceding chapter, but their achievements were no less substantial. Perhaps the biggest problem is that their major creations need to be seen in their actual locations to be fully appreciated. The great majority were designed to be seen from many positions, not from a single, central viewpoint. There may be one or more principal angles of sight for each heavenly assembly, from which the main protagonists are seen to best advantage, but the process of viewing is fluid as people walk within the spaces. Photographs make a limited contribution to the experience.

When we actually wander below the great domes or vaults, replete with foreshortened performers and divine radiance, we can more readily appreciate the levels of technical and artistic skill involved. Solid forms are apparently dissolved by miraculous bursts of irresistible light, taking over the real and painted spaces in a more extreme way than in any Renaissance decorative scheme. Looking at the blazing visions, we may again recall Dante's insistence that divine light does not follow the rules.

CORREGGIO, THE INSTIGATOR

The first two works in this chapter are both dome frescoes by Antonio da Correggio and we can sense powerful analogies with Dante. Chronologically Correggio belongs with the previous chapter; however, in terms of his place in art history, we may count him as an honorary member of the 17th century. His illusionistic dome decorations in Parma found their true following almost a century after their execution. Correggio knew something of the art of Leonardo and surely of Raphael. But he would have needed to travel to Rome to see a number of Raphael paintings that were relevant to his mature art – though the *Sistine Madonna* was relatively nearby in Piacenza at the time. I should like to think that he went to Rome in around 1517–18. Also, he lived at a high point in Dante's fortune.

Correggio's fine but rather provincial art suddenly moved into a different league in the dome fresco for the Church of San Giovanni Evangelista in Parma of 1520–21. The subject is the Vision of St John on Mount Patmos: in John's Book of Revelation, we are exhorted to 'Behold, he [Christ] cometh with clouds; and every eye shall see him'.[1] The incredibly complex sequence of St John's visions in the Bible have been condensed to a dominant image of Christ surrounded by disciples.

To gain a sense as to how Correggio's revelation works, let us progress in our minds along the nave of the church towards the dome. As we pass under the arch that marks the near edge of the dome, we see Christ on high, diagonally opposite (fig.67). He is the correct way up and presented lucidly to us on the floor below. As we move to a point directly under the centre of the dome, we see Christ brightly transfigured and suspended weightlessly within an aureole of light that radiates from white to gold. The surrounding ring of cloud is fringed by vaporous angel-heads. As we turn, our eyes scan the ring of disciples, modelled strongly in light and shade. They are powerfully posed like Michelangelo's *ignudi* on the Sistine Ceiling, which is another reason to assume that Correggio had visited Rome. It is only when we walk across to the far side of the dome, towards the high altar, that we turn to see St John cowering on the rim of the dome below a substantial cloud (fig.68). From his ragged appearance we can readily believe that he has been in long exile on Mount Patmos. The saint and the eagle, which is supporting his book, react with troubled astonishment. He is at least as alarmed as Dante by the extremely dramatic scene he sees. Only the monks in the choir would have been favoured with the sight of St John. The congregation would just have seen Christ ascending. Correggio's dome is both compelling in itself as an image and brilliantly orchestrated as a piece of sacred theatre in its architectural setting.

The cathedral dome was an even grander undertaking, Correggio began in 1522 and finished the work in 1530. Around the rim of the dome's octagonal base stand gesticulating disciples (fig.69). Their draperies flutter of their own accord, in concert with the urgent excitement of the Virgin's Assumption. The Apostles are interspersed with flaming torches and smiling angels. Moving inwards, we encounter a ring of bulbous clouds and then a cylindrical tangle of angels, supporting a dense melange of holy figures. One of the angels is provocatively foreshortened from below, exposing his naked buttocks; this suggests that Correggio had a sense of fun. As we move upwards, the heads of the blessed (not heads of angels in this case)

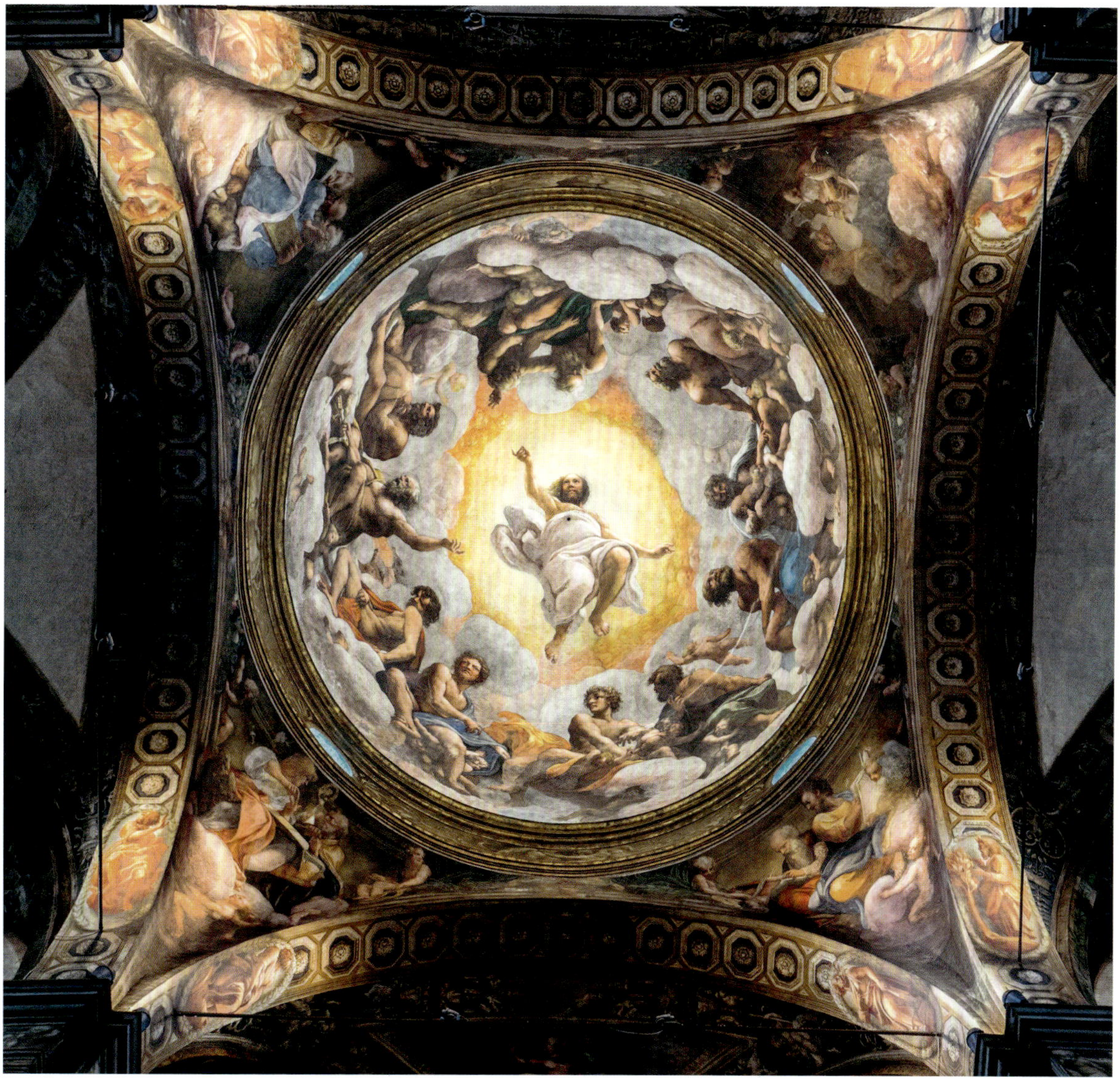

67 Antonio da Correggio, *The Vision of St John on Patmos*, Parma, San Giovanni Evangelista

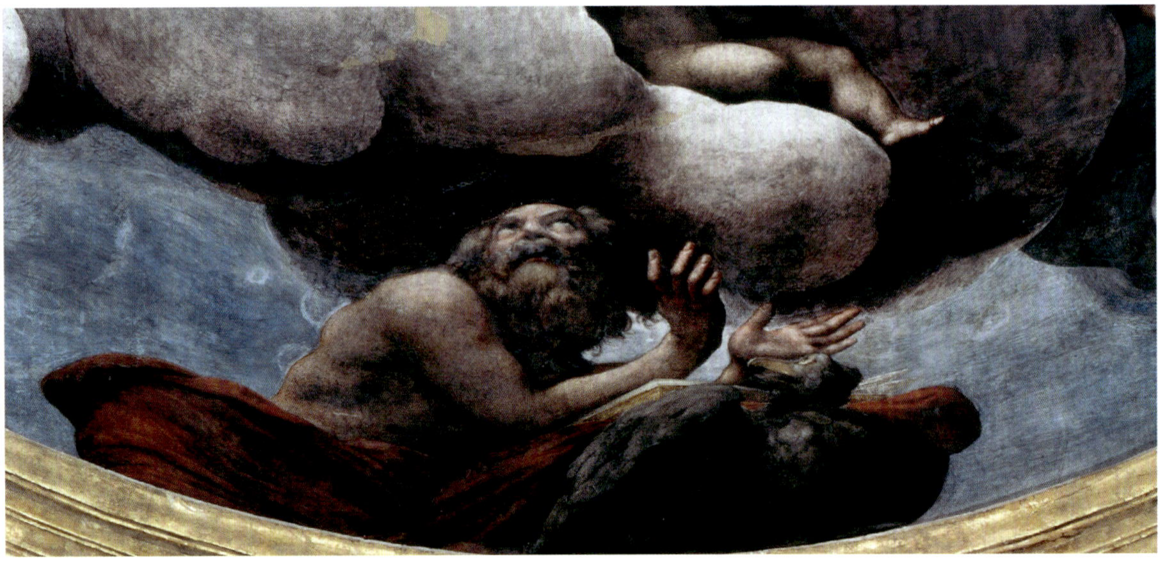

68 Antonio da Correggio, *The Vision of St John on Patmos*, detail of St John and the eagle, Parma, San Giovanni Evangelista

fade elusively into a golden glow with a vividly white centre. The semi-visible heads are just like those Dante took for faint mirror images in *Purgatorio*.[2] The clouded cylinder of figures is seen from off-centre as if we are viewing it as we enter the domed space of the nave, and before we reach the centre. The reason for this is so that we gain a better view of the inner side of the cylinder showing the majestic figure of the Virgin ascending, with arms spread wide. Her body, draperies and head are sharply foreshortened (fig.70). It takes a bit of time to tease her out of the background of clouds and angels, one of whom is visibly discomforted by being used as a leg-rest. The Virgin is flanked by Adam and Eve, whose original sin she is set to redeem, and she is looking up to greet her beardless son, who vertiginously spins in the air to catch her glance. He theatrically waves his arms like a master prestidigitator – in this case the magic is celestial.

In the curved triangular spaces of the spandrels, in which the four patron saints of Parma sit in grand shell niches, some draperies and clouds are painted on plaster that crosses the actual mouldings of the architecture. The dissolution of the painted and real spaces is taken to a new level.

The whole effect of the cathedral dome is truly extraordinary – and startlingly original. Although we can tease out its parts, not least Christ and the Virgin, the power of the dome comes from its overall effect of intricate unity under the diktat of heavenly light. Without in any sense being a direct visual realisation of Dante's culminating visions in *Paradiso*, it is a perfect pictorial equivalent.

In terms of vision and quality, it is not a surprise that Correggio's art should have gained an enthusiastic following; in terms of geography it is more unexpected. An important consideration is that the Farnese family provided successive dukes of Parma. The most notable was Alessandro Farnese, who became Pope Paul III in 1534, and was famed as a patron of Michelangelo and Titian. The Farnese circle in Rome were aficionados

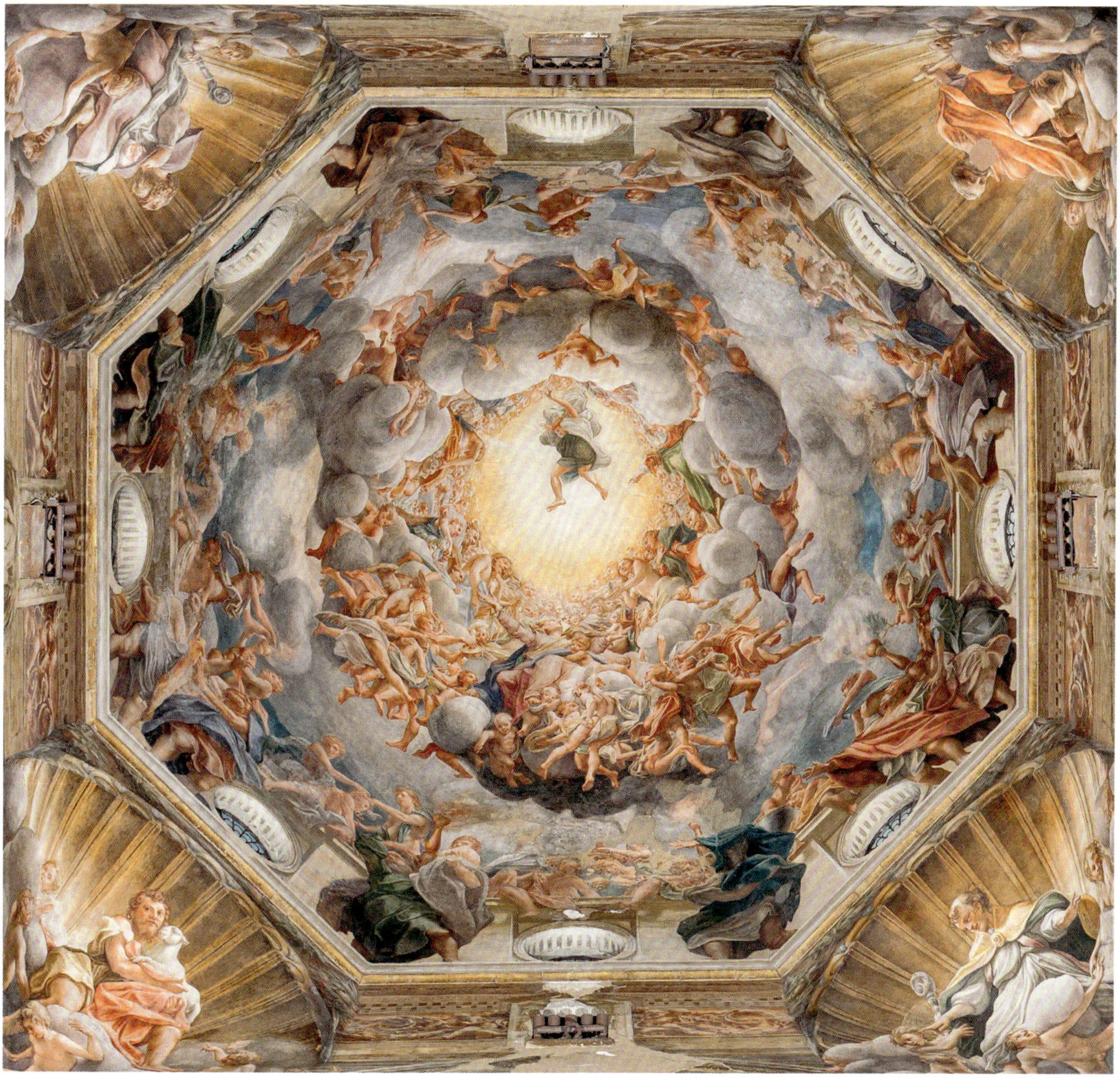

69 Antonio da Correggio, *The Assumption of the Virgin*, Parma Cathedral

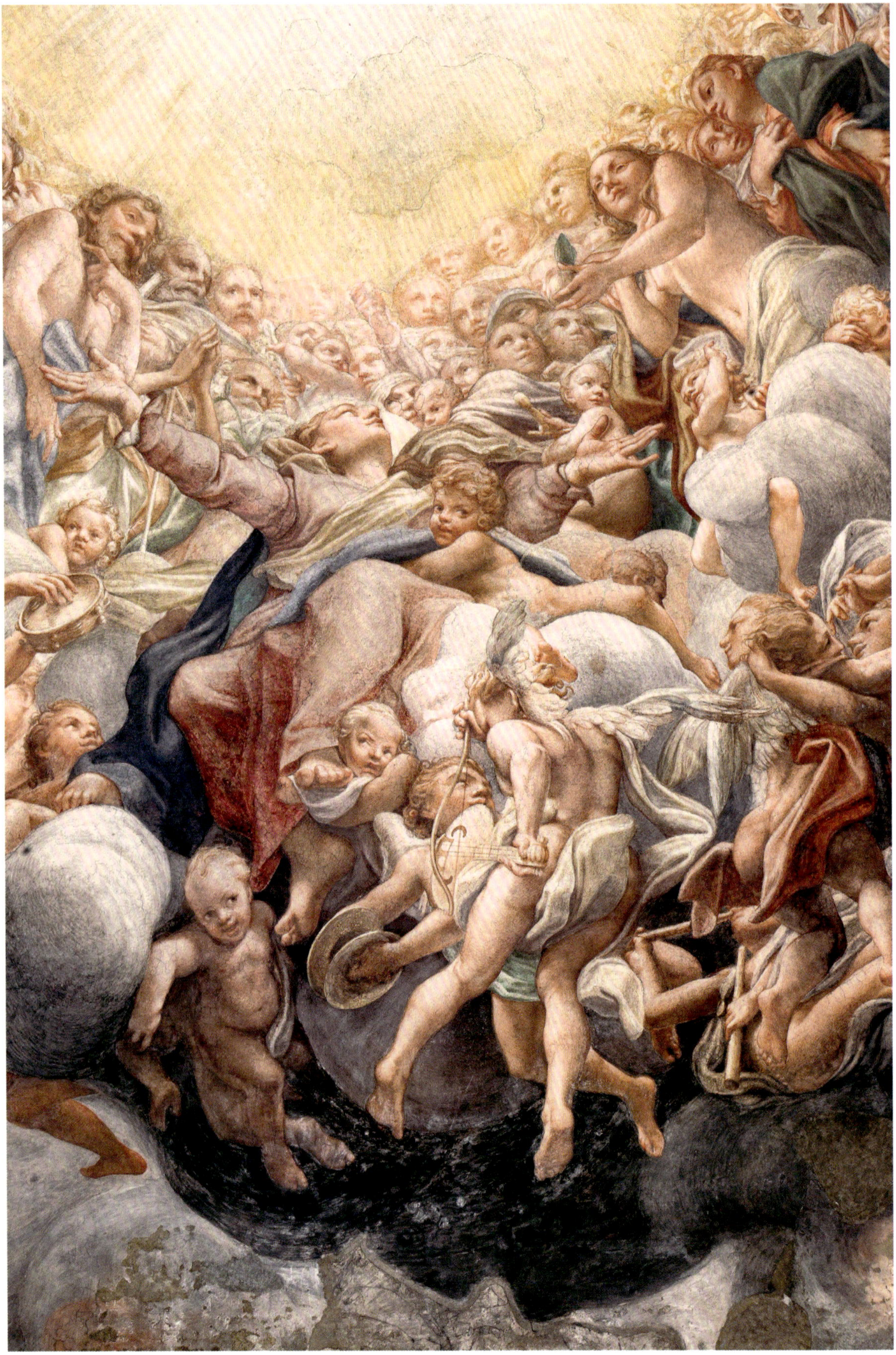

of Correggio's paintings; Cardinal Odoardo Farnese owned two copies of the dome and apse frescoes in San Giovanni Evangelista. The Parmese bishop in Rome, Gerolamo Garimberto, owned ten paintings by Correggio, including a copy of a section of the cathedral dome.[3] It is notable that successive popes and senior clerics in Rome typically gathered around themselves a home-town 'mafia'. Another crucial factor is that Giovanni Lanfranco, a key figure in the development of the Roman Baroque, came from Parma. It is with Lanfranco that we begin our selective look at the painting of celestial visions in the Holy City in the 17th century. It is the age of domes and vaults.

DYNAMIC DOMES, VAULTING AMBITIONS

A prolific painter of decorative schemes, Lanfranco's most important dome painting is in the Church of Sant' Andrea della Valle, Rome. Like Correggio's Parma Cathedral dome, to which it owes a good deal, it portrays the Assumption of the Virgin, but in a more overtly ordered way (fig.71). The Virgin, best viewed obliquely as we enter the space of the dome from the nave, is picked out more emphatically than Correggio had chosen to do. This helps her to be visible against the competing light from a ring of windows in the drum of the dome. She rises within the dome from a consolidated orbit of holy figures above which a band of sky is visible, except where Mary is enveloped by a golden light. A higher ring is reserved for entwined angels of various kinds, blending into gold towards the lantern. The central opening of the lantern is surrounded by a predominantly dark wreath or garland of plants, supported by shadowy angels, above which golden light radiates. Such a garland was first used by Ludovico Cigoli in Santa Maria Maggiore (fig.110). Lanfranco's garland is oddly asymmetrical; it looks as if it is still being finished! In the lantern itself is a drum of vertical windows, on top of which is a small secondary dome within which we can see Christ in a swirling robe of celestial blue (fig.72) awaiting his mother. The natural light from the two drums of windows sets up a good deal of optical conflict with the painting, a conflict that the human eye is better at resolving than a photographic image. Indeed, the eye is more accommodating in making sense of the painted spaces and figures when in the actual churches than even the most skilful photograph (or even video) can achieve.

If Lanfranco's dome brings Parma to Rome, its greatest rival in the middle years of the second decade of the 17th century directly imported Florentine ideas. Giovanni di San Giovanni (born in San Giovanni Val d'Arno, Masaccio's birthplace) worked for most of his shortish career as a well-patronised artist in Florence, but he is now rather underrated. His masterpiece is in Rome, the *Glory of Saints* in the Basilica of the Quattro Santi Coronati (fig.73). Finished in 1623, shortly before Lanfranco's dome, it may well have left its mark on the painter from Parma. In this case we are dealing not with a full dome, but with a very large semi-dome over the apse, which comprised a substantial addition to the revered fabric of the ancient church. Giovanni frescoed the walls of the apse with images and stories of the titular saints, who were early Christian martyrs.

The semi-dome is inevitably viewed at an oblique angle, but Giovanni suggests that we are looking at a fully domed space, almost one half of which is hidden from us by the arch high above our heads. The saints, the glory of whom gives the painting its title, are clustered on a populous and dense array at the lowest level, and are sitting and standing on a thin band of cloud above the curved ledge at the base of the semi-dome. Giovanni takes this somewhat unpromising crowd and endows the saints with marked degrees of individuality as a kind of group portrait (fig.74).

At the next tier is a less populated ring of high-ranking saints to the left and right, with evangelists, and a row of little winged angels across the centre of the ring. Above them a semi-circle of angels plays sweet music. Closer to us, and apparently a little lower, is a

70 Antonio da Correggio, *The Assumption of the Virgin*, detail of the Virgin with Adam and Eve, Parma Cathedral

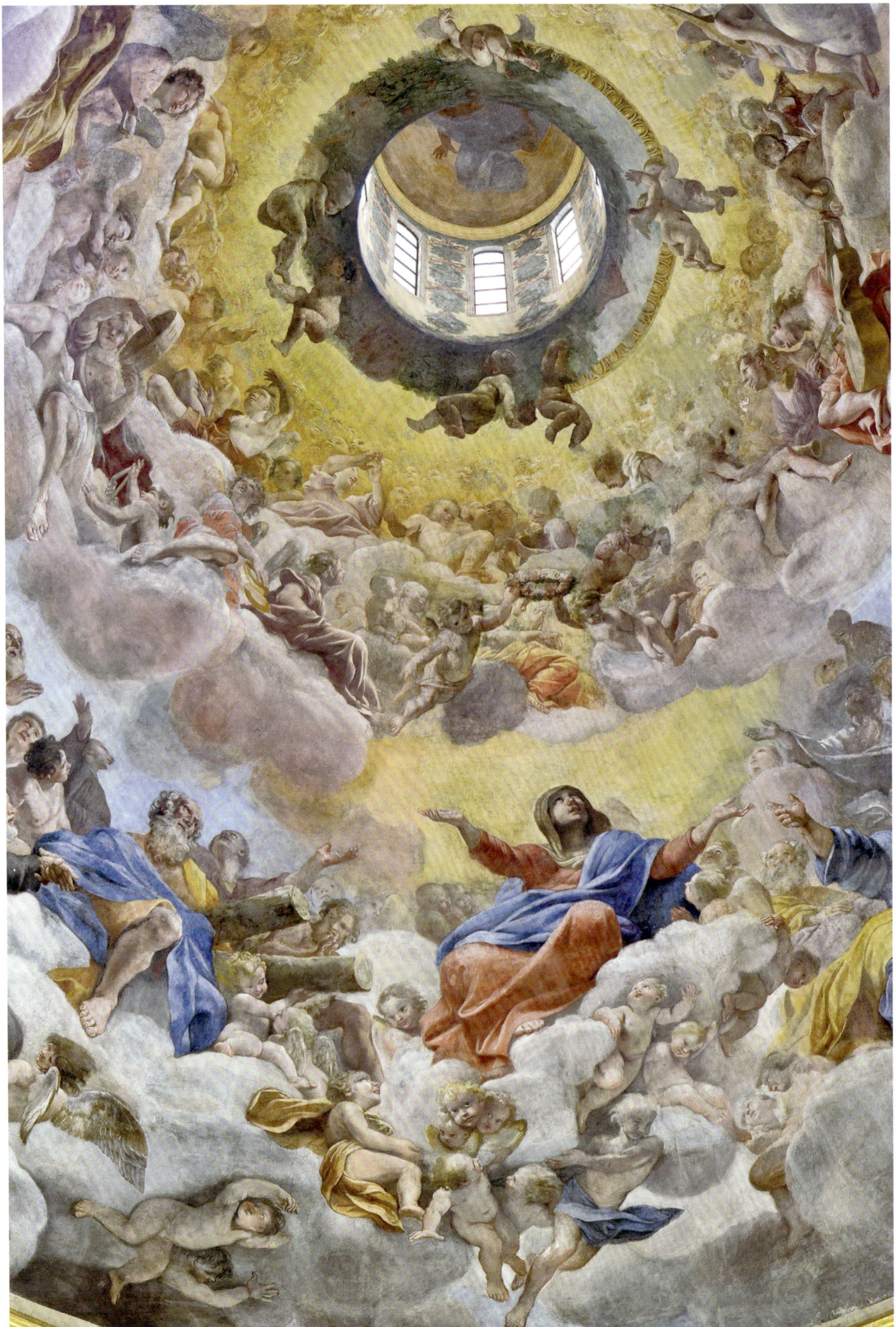

platform supporting three archangels, Gabriel, Michael and Raphael, with lesser angelic attendants and golden cloud-heads roughly sketched in. Other such heads appear more frequently elsewhere in the cloudscapes. A higher platform bears only the supplicating Virgin and John the Baptist, above whom the heavens open in an intense blaze of gold to disclose the Trinity. The white-robed God is defined with rather less assertive modelling than the other figures. There is still that Dantesque sense that the mystery of the supreme divinity should retain its ineffability, rather than appearing completely defined. Around this glowing vision are naked angels, dancing hand-in-hand, joyously celebrating the heavenly triumph. They, by implication, mark the upper margin of the unseen side of the dome. As we will see in the next chapter, Giovanni's work with Giulio Parigi, the great designer of theatrical *paradisi*, provides a demonstrable link with the tradition of Dante in Florence.

The grand – even grandiloquent – culmination of Baroque illusionism in succession to Giovanni di San Giovanni and Lanfranco comes in the next decade with Pietro da Cortona – though not in a church. His *Triumph of Divine Providence* was finished in 1639 on the large rectangular vault of the two-storey great hall built by Bernini in the Palazzo Barberini. Originating from Florence, the Barberini family's growing financial fortune peaked with the election of Maffeo Barberini as Pope Urban VIII in 1623, followed by the gift of senior posts to his Florentine relatives. He was a patron and collector on the grandest of scales. To paint the vault in the room that was the prime set-piece of his palace decorations, designed to awe visitors, he appointed the Florentine-trained Pietro da Cortona. Pietro's bombastically dynamic vault painting merged Maffeo's person with the supremacy of the Catholic Church – and even with the nature of the divine. It is an act of astonishing personal and spiritual bravado (fig.75).

The iconographical bravado is matched by the composition of the painting. Above a painted cornice that runs uninterruptedly around the rectangular opening at the top of the walls of the Salone, we are presented with painted images of figures (flesh-and-blood and sculpted), architecture, reliefs and decorative motifs that serve as the rhythmic frame for five compartments of allegorical narratives. It is unusual that landscapes and townscapes form backgrounds to the figures at the lowest level of the vault. Every element is subjugated to the surging energy of the tumultuous ensemble. The eye is not encouraged to remain static other than on the person of Divine Providence, regally commanding the central space with her sceptre, imperious gesture and aureole of dominant light, which bleaches her nearest attendants. The content has been worked out with huge elaboration and erudition, and would have been the subject of commentary by the intellectuals at the Pope's court. There was more than one contemporary publication designed to explicate the allegories.

A *Dichiaratione* (*Declaration*), written by Mattia Rosichino, was published in Rome in 1640, just one year after the vault's completion. Rosichino claimed

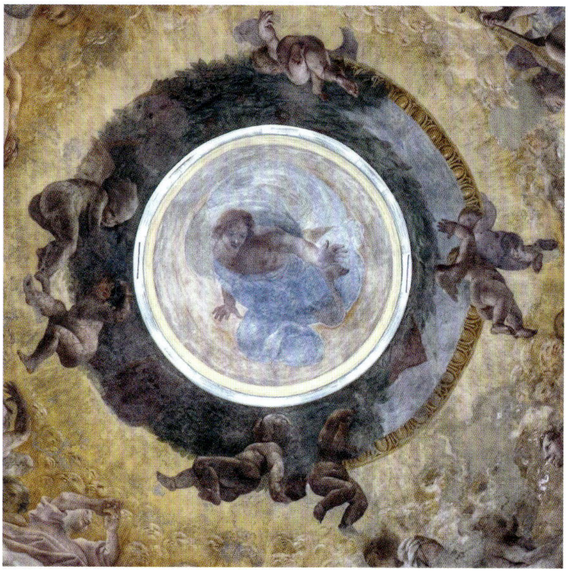

72 Giovanni Lanfranco, *The Assumption of the Virgin*, detail of Christ in the lantern, Rome, Sant'Andrea della Valle

71 Giovanni Lanfranco, *The Assumption of the Virgin*, oblique view, Rome, Sant'Andrea della Valle

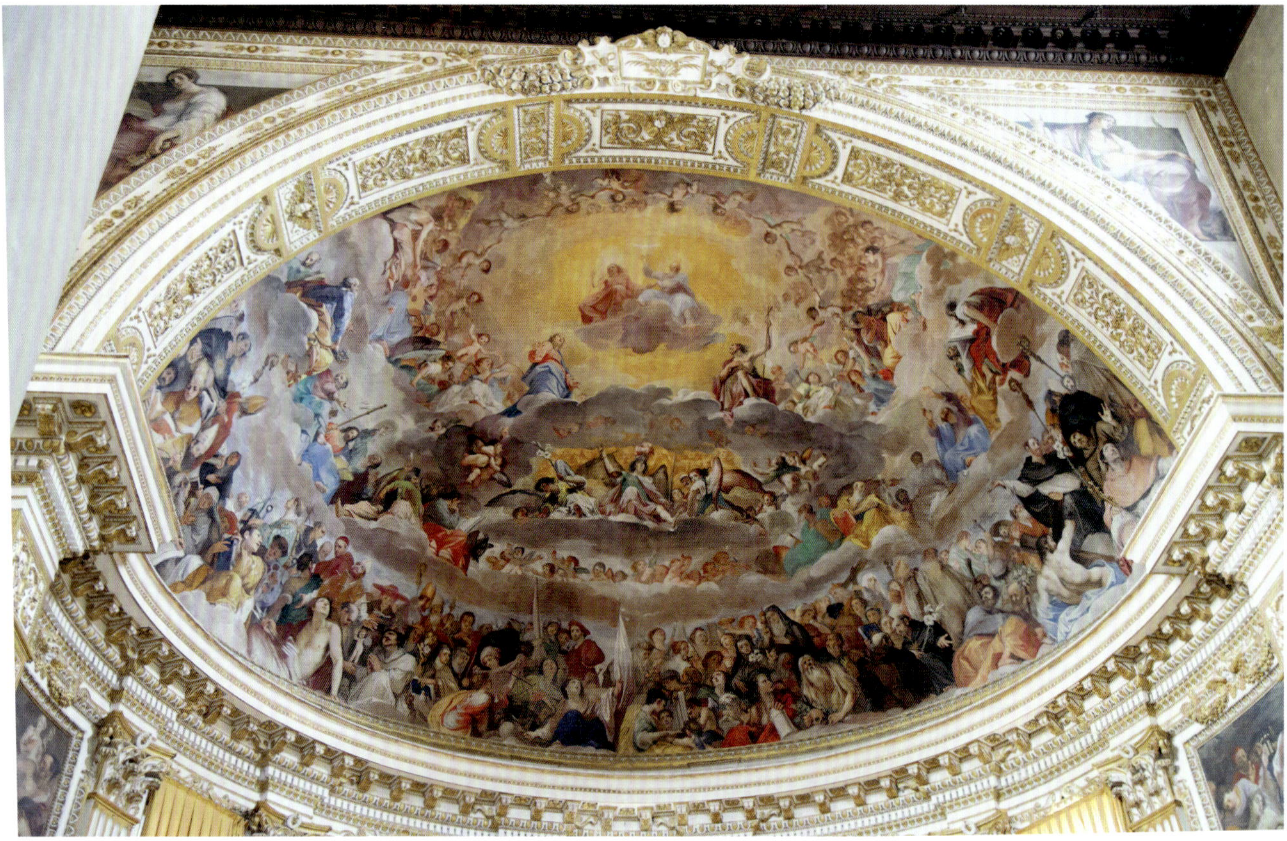

73 Giovanni di San Giovanni, *The Glory of the Saints*, Rome, Basilica of the Quattro Santi Coronati

74 Giovanni di San Giovanni, *The Glory of the Saints*, detail of the saints, Rome, Basilica of the Quattro Santi Coronati

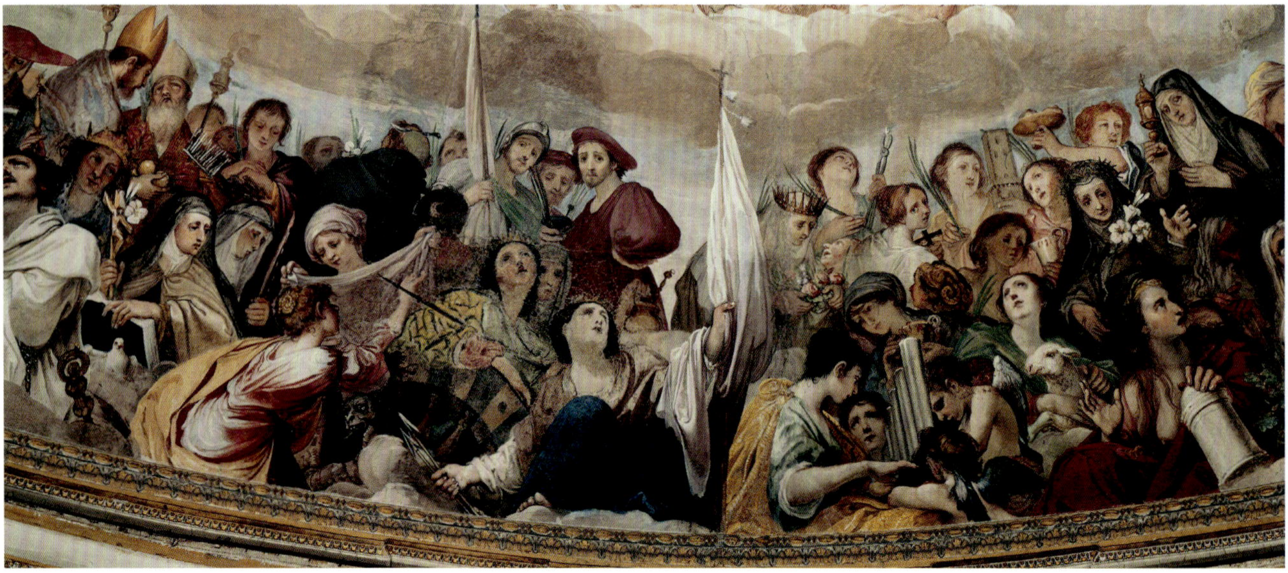

to be a kind of janitor/housekeeper who was quizzed by visitors when he was on duty. He tells how he researched the arcane content of the frescoes and decided to provide spectators with a compact explanation of what was going on above their heads. It may be that Rosichino 'the sweeper' is a pen name for one of the *literati* at the court. Given the inventive extravagance of the allegories, it will be worth some extravagance on our own part. We can read the account in full – it is quite a taxing read – or we can sample it.

Declaration of the Paintings
The vault of the great hall of the Barberini is divided and painted in five parts. In the centre part is Divine Providence, who sits on a cloud, ornamented with brilliant lights [*splendori*], with a sceptre, and in the act of commanding the present and the future. And therefore Time, who in the form of Saturn devours his own children, is held with the Fates under her. Around her are Justice, Mercy, Eternity, Truth, Purity, Beauty, and others who seem to want to obey her. But above all others Immortality appears to execute the commands, moving with the crown of stars to crown the arms of Urban VIII Supreme Pontiff. The papal arms are surrounded by two great branches of laurel, which rendered together create the image of a shield supported by Faith and Hope at the sides and by Charity at the bottom, with the three bees flying inside these. Above are Religion, with the keys and Rome with the Papal Tiara, and a child with a garland also of laurel – a sign of poetic excellence – is playing there nearby.

In the second part, that is, in the front of the hall toward the garden, is the image of Minerva, denoting Wisdom, who overthrows with her lance the Giants who are seen hurled down and weighed down by those mountains they themselves had amassed in order to challenge Heaven. Here is expressed the defence of ecclesiastical things.

Opposite, the third part represents the temporal government. Those two youths who seem to be coming from above signify, first, Authority with the consular fasces [a bundle of rods], and, second, Abundance with the cornucopia. Kneeling in front of these are all kinds of people, such as old men, children, and widows, and many others who expect gifts from them. There, by Hercules, who casts out the Harpies, is meant the chastisement of kings. Beneath this part, in the feigned bas-relief ornament is the club of this same Hercules, which sprouts – a device of the Barberini family.

On the right as you enter in the fourth part; here one sees Knowledge uplifted by Divine Assistance, which is denoted in the young man who is agile with his wings. Knowledge holds a book in one hand for the knowledge of things and, in the other, a flame to symbolize that it is her nature to uplift herself. She is also accompanied by Piety toward God, expressed in the modestly dressed and venerable woman who has a tripod with fire inside ready for the sacrifice. Beneath Knowledge are gluttony and lasciviousness. The first is represented by Silenus, for whom fauns and satyrs pour wine in the great cup he holds in his hand. Bacchantes, with young Bacchus in their lap avidly devouring a bunch of grapes, represent the bad upbringing of youths. Lasciviousness is embodied in a reclining woman next to whom are discerned some chaste and lewd cupids. But the chaste ones, urged on by Chastity, personified by the woman dressed in white with the lily in hand, drive away the lewd ones with torches so that she who is lying seems frightened by them. Not far from here there is painted a fountain with women around it, one of whom is adorning herself in order to denote the vanity of worldly pleasures. The device perceived here is the plough pulled by two [Barberini] bees with a third who steers it and is guiding them with a whip.

Opposite this, one sees the last section. In this, Dignity holds in the right hand the caduceus [herald's staff] and in the left a key. Prudence reverently holds up a mirror to her, and Power, delegated with a key and

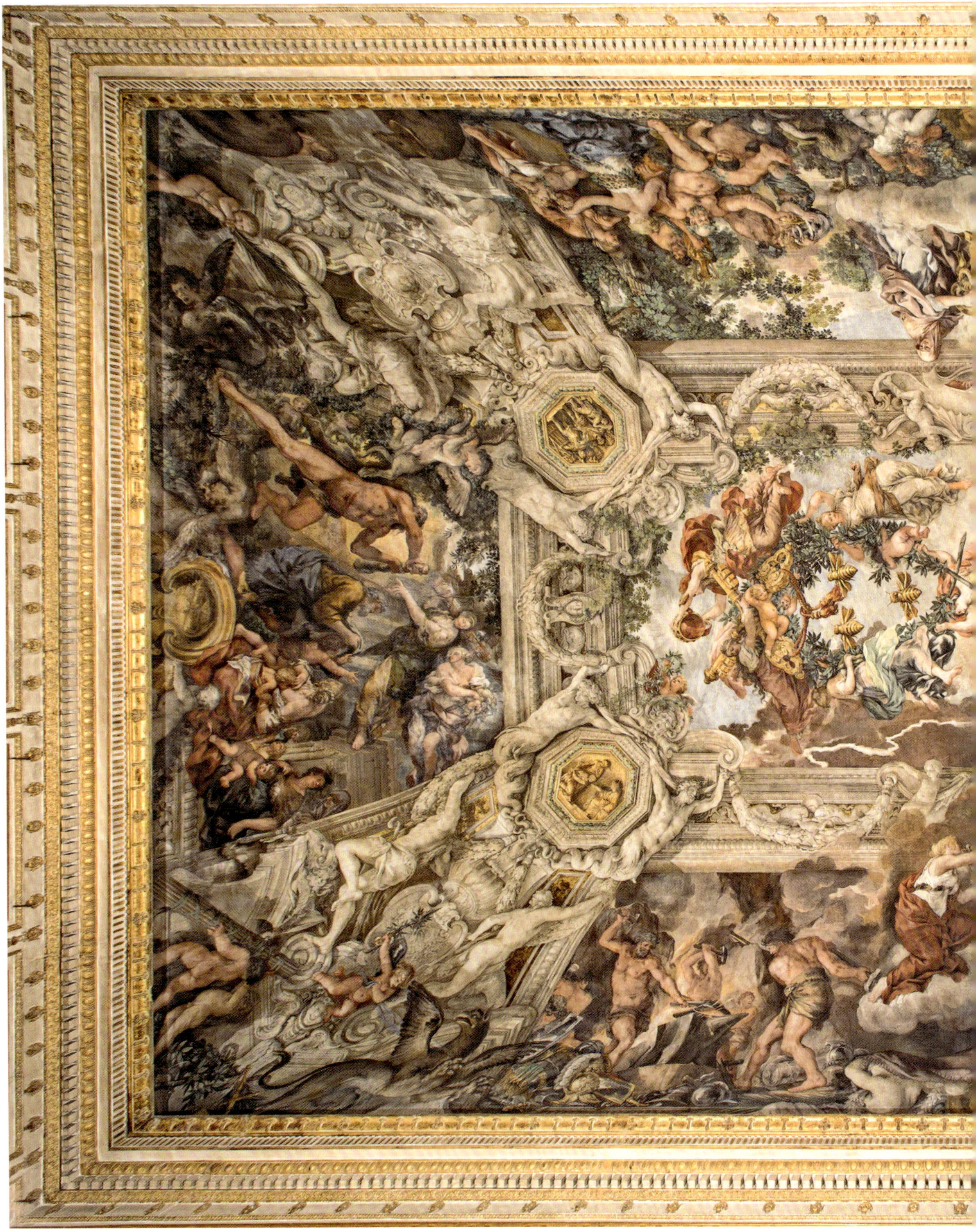

75 Pietro da Cortona, *The Triumph of Divine Providence*, Rome, Palazzo Barberini, Vault of the Salone

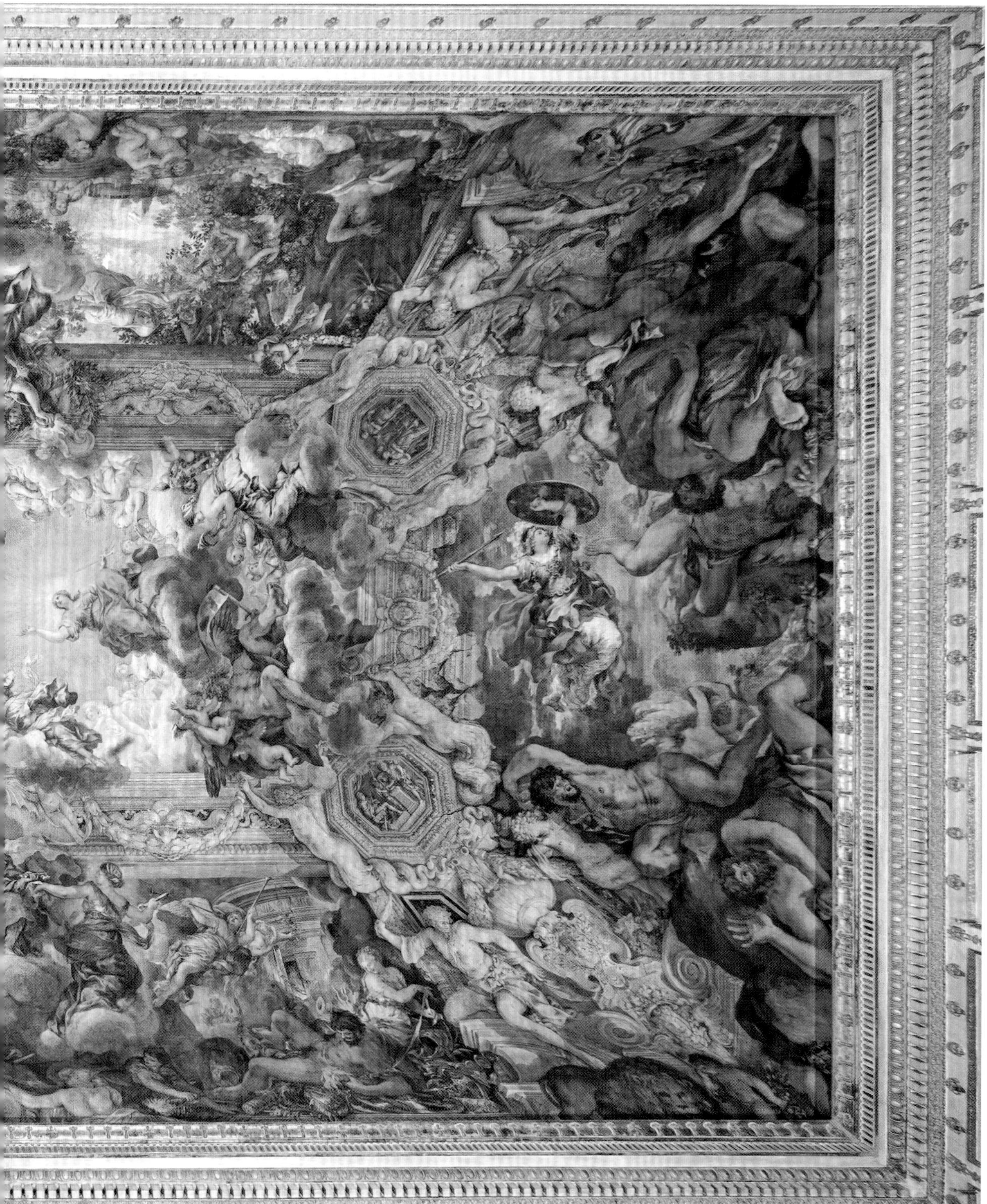

a written sheet, is nearby but in the act of departing. Then next is Fame. And Peace with the olive branch closes the door to the Temple of Janus, outside of which one sees Furor tied with his torches on top of many armaments. He seems in appearance to struggle, except that Gentleness holds him still with a noose. There is also Fury with her torch who, thrown down, appears deprived of strength. Not far away is the forge of Vulcan where several Cyclops exert themselves to make weapons, alluding to the preparedness which is necessary for the defence of the provinces even in peace time. Here the rising sun is the device.

Besides this there are four medallions in the four corners of this vault. In these there are expressed the four virtues – Temperance, Fortitude, Justice, and Prudence. Temperance: with Scipio the Younger sent back untarnished to her Saguntine spouse the young maid he had captured as his booty. Fortitude: with Mucius Scaevola when he burned his right hand, having erred killing a civilian instead of King Porsenna. Justice: with Titus Manlius when he even happily had beheaded his son who had violated his prohibition. Prudence: with Fabius Maximus when restraining himself in his quarters held Hannibal in check. Under the medallions one sees portrayed a unicorn to represent Temperance, a lion for Fortitude, a hippogriff for Justice, and some bears for Prudence because they develop their offspring slowly with time.[4]

We may well feel that working out the meaning of the whole and parts is heavy going. It is certainly not something for spectators in a hurry.

Pietro's vault decoration responds to the content with a riot of invention. Figures twist and turn, some with svelte grace, some with angular violence, some with fixed purpose, others to decorative effect. Every element is handled with great spatial and plastic conviction (fig.76). The papal tiara is ready to descend on Maffeo's proud head. The massive papal keys of St Peter, linked by a knotted rope belt, are worthy of Claes Oldenburg, the American pop sculptor. The three bees from the Barberini crest are prosperously well nourished, beneficiaries of the nepotism for which Urban was famed. In another of the narrative fields, Hercules carries out a thirteenth labour, the clubbing of evil harpies, with such violence that his lion's skin is falling off his loins. Justice, with her bundle of *fasces* (rods), supervises the rout, which allows the flourishing of Abundance with her rich cornucopia of provisions for the poor, who are seated on the ground, as Rosichino explains (fig.77). The adjoining narrative shows 'Vulcan where several Cyclops exert themselves to make weapons, alluding to the preparedness which is necessary for the defence of the provinces even in peace time'.

The learned use of mythological figures from antiquity in the service of moral concepts and high Christian virtue is very Dantesque. Can we say something more specific than this? As we noted, Pietro da Cortona was trained in Florence. His master, Andrea Commodi, worked for the Medici court as a stage designer and would have been well versed in the Florentine tradition of *paradisi*, with their Dantesque heritage. We will say more about the theatrical spectaculars in the next chapter.

Pietro da Cortona was on his own account a major contributor to a genre of ephemeral religious imagery that had grown to assume considerable importance. I am referring to the great displays that were devised to mark the *Quarantore* (or the *Quarant[a]ore*, the 'forty hours') of devotion to the Eucharist. Originating in the Middle Ages and much extended in the 16th century, the Forty Hours Oration or Devotion was held normatively, but not invariably, on the first Sunday in Advent. It developed into a major event, strongly promoted by the Catholic reformers. The display of the Sacrament was staged in such a way that the Oration became a kind of theatrical event. Within the churches the displays on and around the high altar of candles, flowers, textiles and precious items developed into great light-filled declamations of the spiritual glory of the Host, accompanied by impressive ceremonies and

76 Pietro da Cortona, *The Triumph of Divine Providence*, detail of the papal tiara, the keys of St Peter and the Barberini bees, Rome, Palazzo Barberini, Vault of the Salone

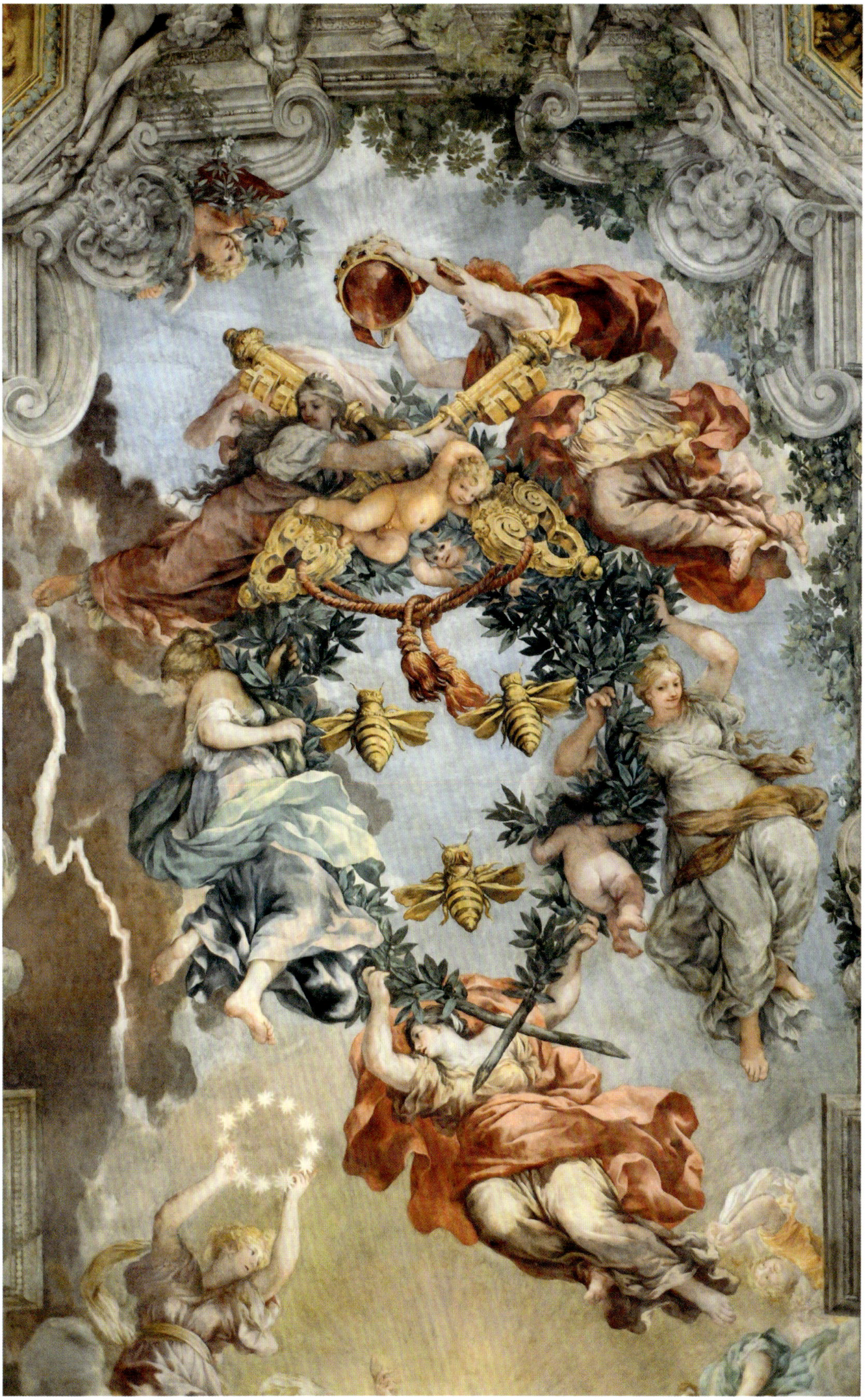

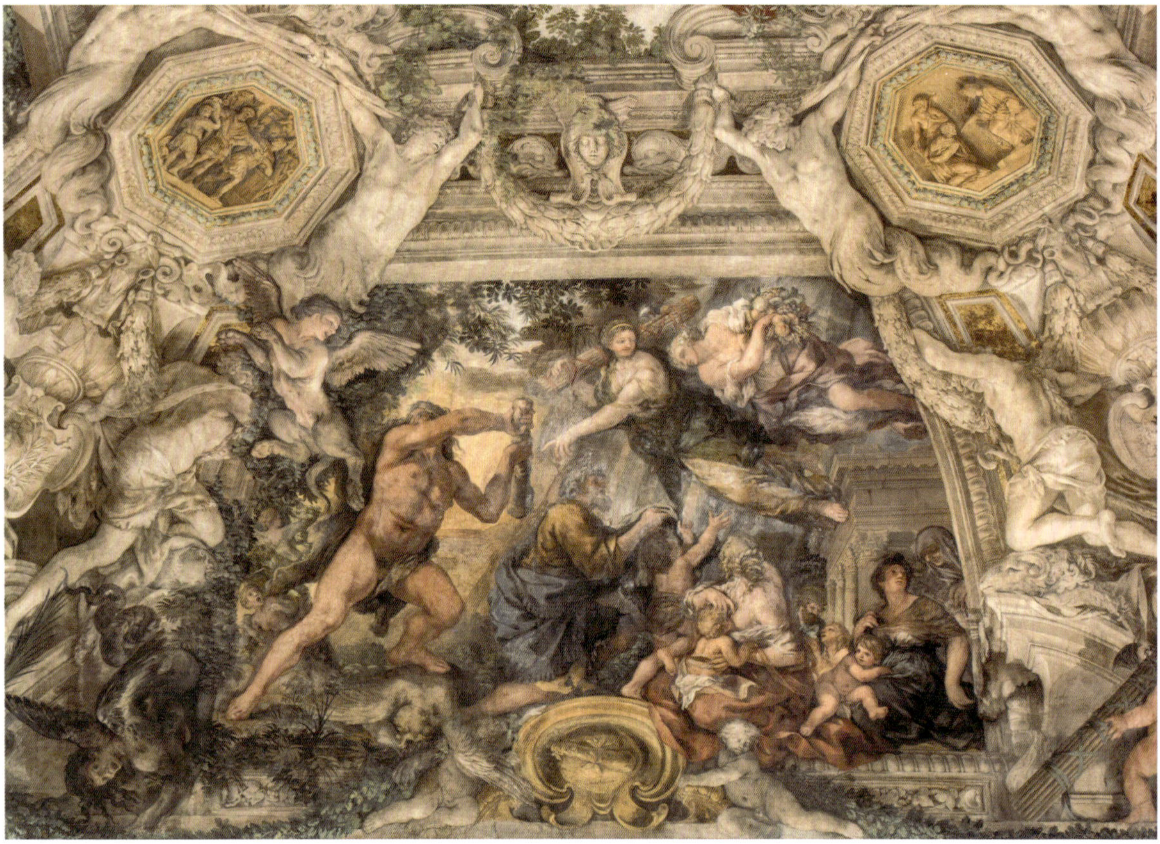

77 Pietro da Cortona, *The Triumph of Divine Providence*, detail of Hercules fighting the Harpies, with Justice, Abundance and recipients of Charity, Rome, Palazzo Barberini, Vault of the Salone

music. Large-scale temporary constructions (*apparati*) became an increasingly prominent feature of the celebrations. Outside the churches, grand processions passed from one site of worship to another. In 1595, Pope Clement VIII decreed that the Devotion should be held in the major Roman churches as a kind of relay, with prayers ending in one and beginning in the next. Clement also expressed concern about excessive decoration and theatricality, not least the use of excessive numbers of lamps and candles. His strictures seem to have exercised little effect.

Some major artists and architects were engaged in an escalation in the splendour of the apparatuses, in open competition with each other and on behalf of their patrons. In 1628, Gian Lorenzo Bernini devised an innovatory apparatus for the Pauline Chapel in the Vatican, which 'represented the Glory of Paradise with great radiance, without our being able to see any light except that which emanated from more than two thousand lamps hidden behind clouds'.[5] We do not have a visual record of Bernini's extravaganza. It is apparent that it dramatically exploited hidden light sources on a far larger scale than he was to use in the Cornaro Chapel (fig.87). In this case, hiding the number of lamps was both magical and prudent, given Pope Clement's rules. The central focus common to all the

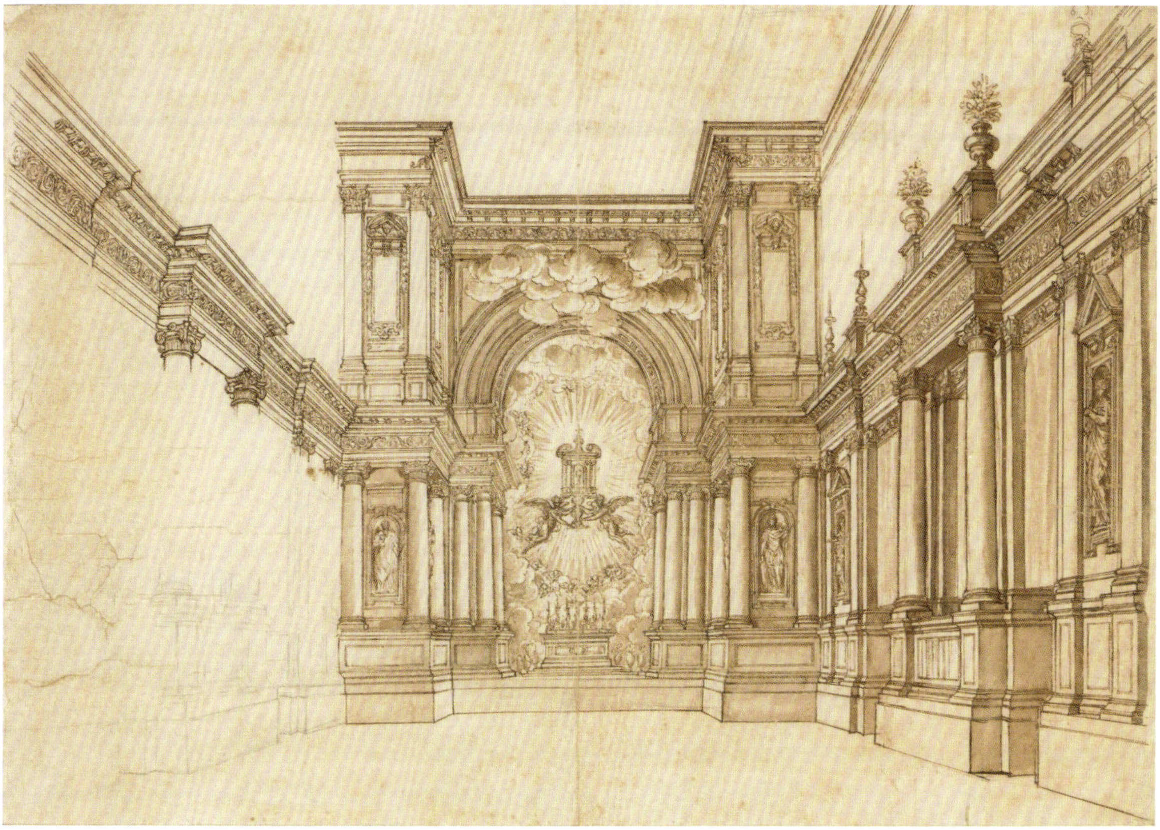

78 Pietro da Cortona, design for the 1633 *Quarantore* in the Church of San Lorenzo in Damaso, Windsor, Royal Library

displays was the small Host and its dazzling radiance, which bleached adjacent forms as do the blasts of light in the painted vaults and domes. There is a seamless relationship between the 40-hour displays and the permanent visions of heaven in Baroque churches. As a type of *Paradiso* they link back to the theatrical displays in the Renaissance, as we will see in the next chapter.

Again, one superb example will stand for the many; it is by Pietro da Cortona and we are fortunate to have a drawing for the whole set-up (fig.78). His great display was commissioned by Cardinal Francesco Barberini for the *Quarantore* in February 1633 in the Church of San Lorenzo in Damaso, Rome. Francesco was the powerful and privileged nephew of Pope Urban VIII, whose glorification in the Salone of the Palazzo Barberini we have already seen writ large. In addition to a hugely assertive display over the high altar, the interior of the church was remodelled by Pietro with temporary architecture to transform it into a reformist-style oratory like Il Gesù. Alongside the drawing, we have a nice description of the impact of this kind of devotional theatre.

> On Thursday the oration of the Quarantore took place in the Church of San Lorenzo in Damaso, the apparatus of which is considered the most

beautiful that has ever been seen in this city, in that the 'frontispiece' of the main altar remained covered with clouds, which, through the force of lights diffused so beautifully that, amongst them, we could see the hosts of angels and the large and small effigies of saints and the blessed, who enjoy the glory of Paradise, and all the time prayers were said there, with a countless number of people, and almost all the Confraternities of this city in procession, following the first sermon delivered by Monsignor Cesi, Bishop of Rimini.[6]

At the top of the triumphal arch that proudly surrounds the central vision is a substantial and luminous cloud of the kind that bore witness in the Old Testament and in the Transfiguration to God's presence. Such was the magnificence (and huge cost) of this grand temporary structure that it was carefully dismantled and re-used over the next 15 years.

Pietro da Cortona also contributed importantly to the genre of heavenly semi-domes and domes. From 1647 onwards, he decorated the apsidal semi-dome in the Chiesa Nuova (now usually known as Santa Maria in Vallicella) with an *Assumption of the Virgin*, while the crossing dome in the same church is devoted to a vision of the Trinity. In the semi-dome, the praying Virgin rises on a plump cloud into the now familiar open and asymmetrical funnel of evaporating angels, watched penitentially on the left by San Filippo Neri (fig.80). In 1575 a papal bull had confirmed his founding of the Oratory, a secular order of priests whose main church was the Chiesa Nuova. Filippo is watched by John the Baptist. There is some resemblance to Giovanni di San Giovanni's semi-dome, but is less obviously layered and more relaxed in composition.

In the full dome, Christ and God the Father are situated lower than we might expect, but this means that they are directly and effectively visible in an oblique view from the nave. Asymmetrical ranks of elusive angel-heads lead our eyes upwards. The spinning circle of gambolling angels holding the garland around the base of the lantern – recalling Cigoli and Lanfranco – provide a frame for an ethereal dove and just-visible angels painted on the small concave dome of the lantern ringed with windows (fig.79). If we approach the dome and semi-dome along the nave, we can read the two murals as closely coordinated (fig.81). The Virgin is ascending into the space above and beyond the arch over the altar. She is looking towards the crown that awaits her in heaven, beyond which lies the space of the dome. She is bound for the same heaven occupied by the Trinity. This explains the absence of Christ, God and the dove from the semi-dome; it is a clever and effective conception.

Pietro da Cortona was co-author in 1652 of *Trattato della pittura e scultura: uso et abuso loro* (*Treatise on Painting and Sculpture: their Use and Abuse*).[7] Both he and his co-author, the Jesuit Giovanni Domenico Ottonelli, hid their identities behind anagrams. Ottonelli was a militant and roving voice against licentiousness in life and the arts, not least in the theatre, where he opposed the use of women actors. In the treatise he sets out to transfer his moralising precepts to the visual arts. He prescribes the kind of spiritually uplifting subjects that should be placed before the eyes of the Christian viewer. The book pursues these arguments at wearying length with torrents of learned references. The pious Cortona contributed some considerable and well-informed accounts of art and artists from ancient Greece onwards. These accounts promote the worth of the visual arts. The impression is that the painter was concerned to soften Ottonelli's more intolerant views.

The authors considered unremarkably that the artist should cultivate worthy concepts and learn how to convey feelings when telling stories. Variety was to be praised but not at the expense of clarity. The chief protagonist or protagonists in a composition should be readily apparent, and not subject to such extreme foreshortening that prevents us from seeing them clearly. Above all, pious devotion should be promoted and anything that was lascivious and licentious should be banned.

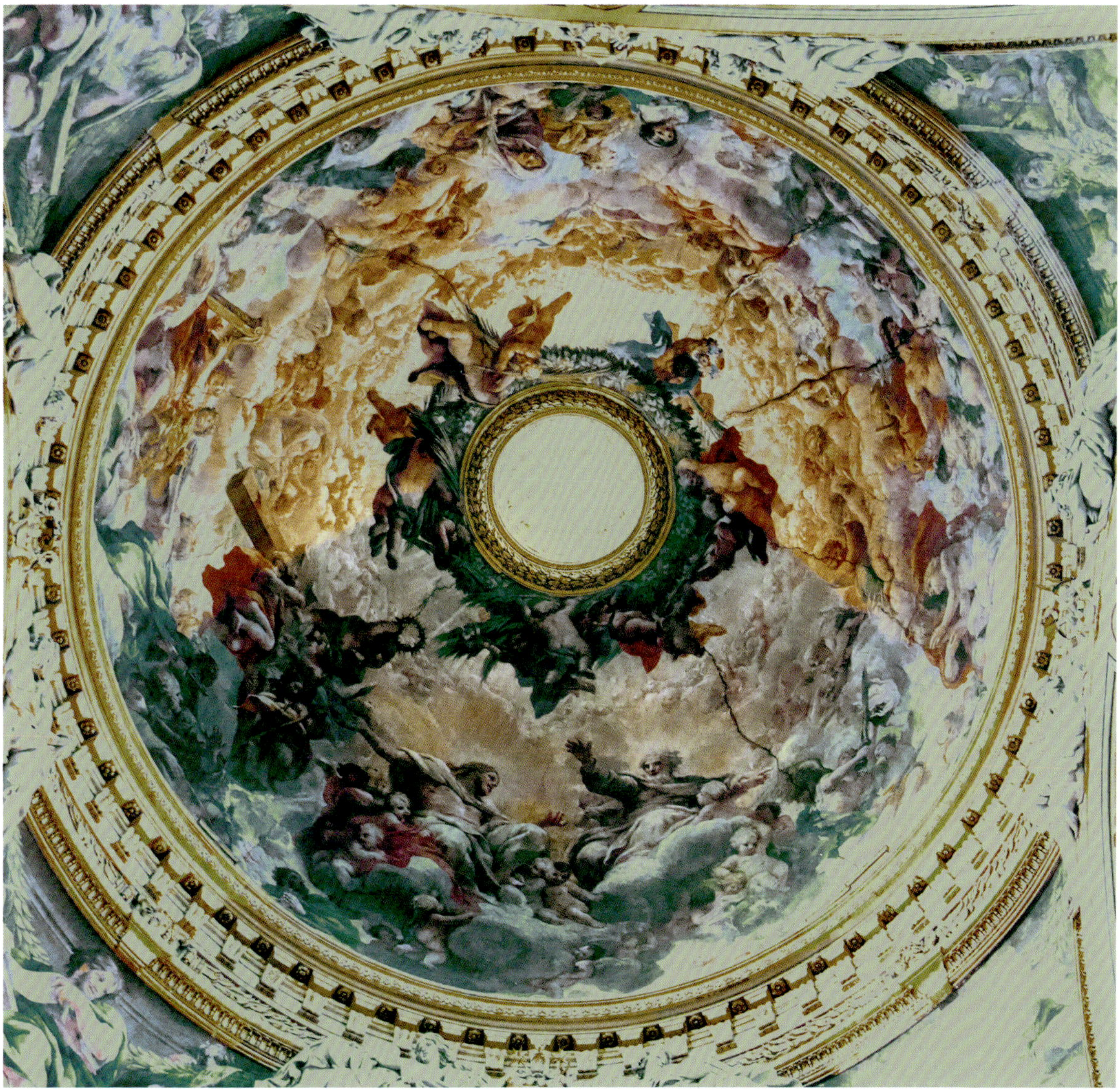

79 Pietro da Cortona, *The Trinity*, Rome, Chiesa Nuova

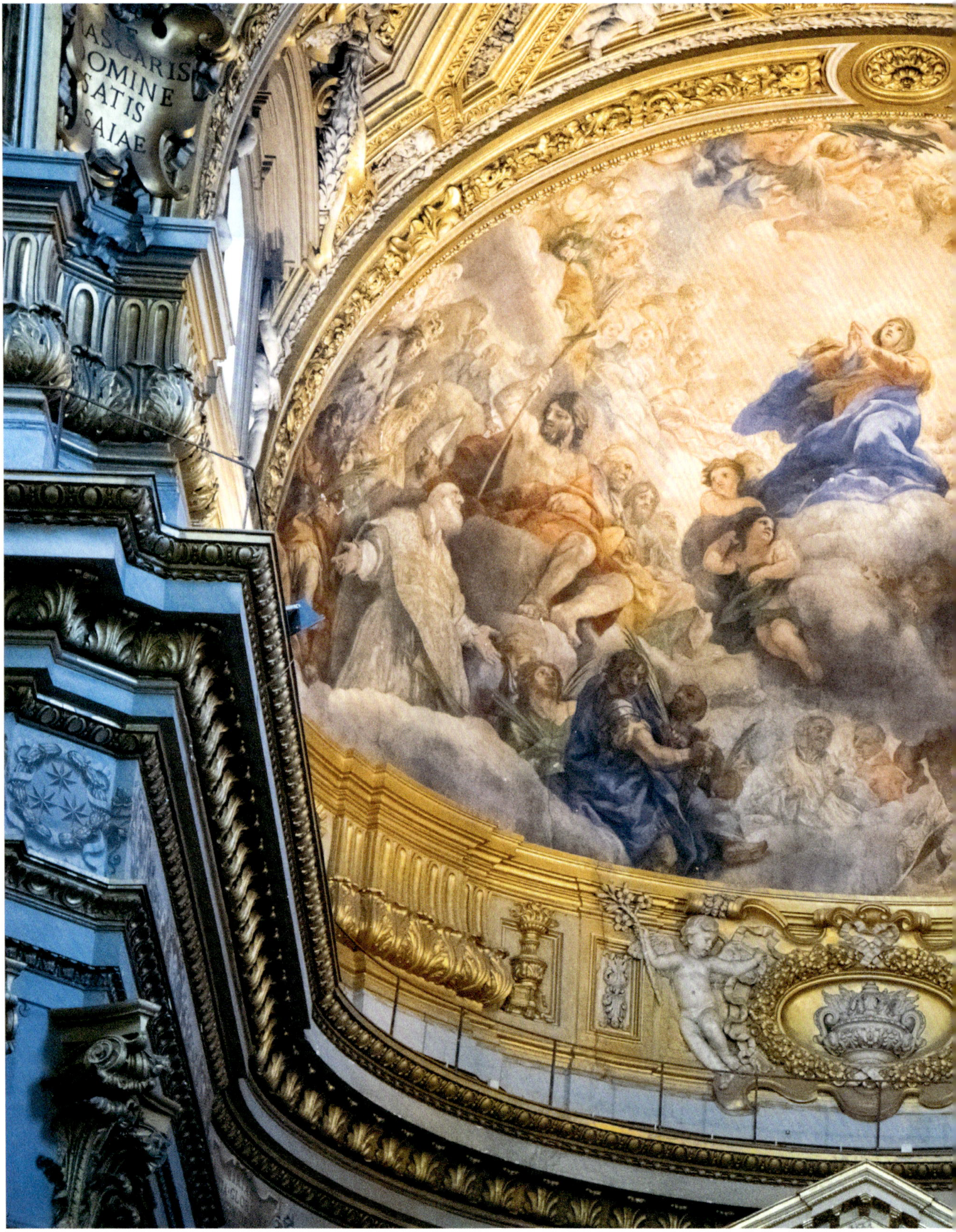
ASCARIS
OMINE
SATIS
SAIAE

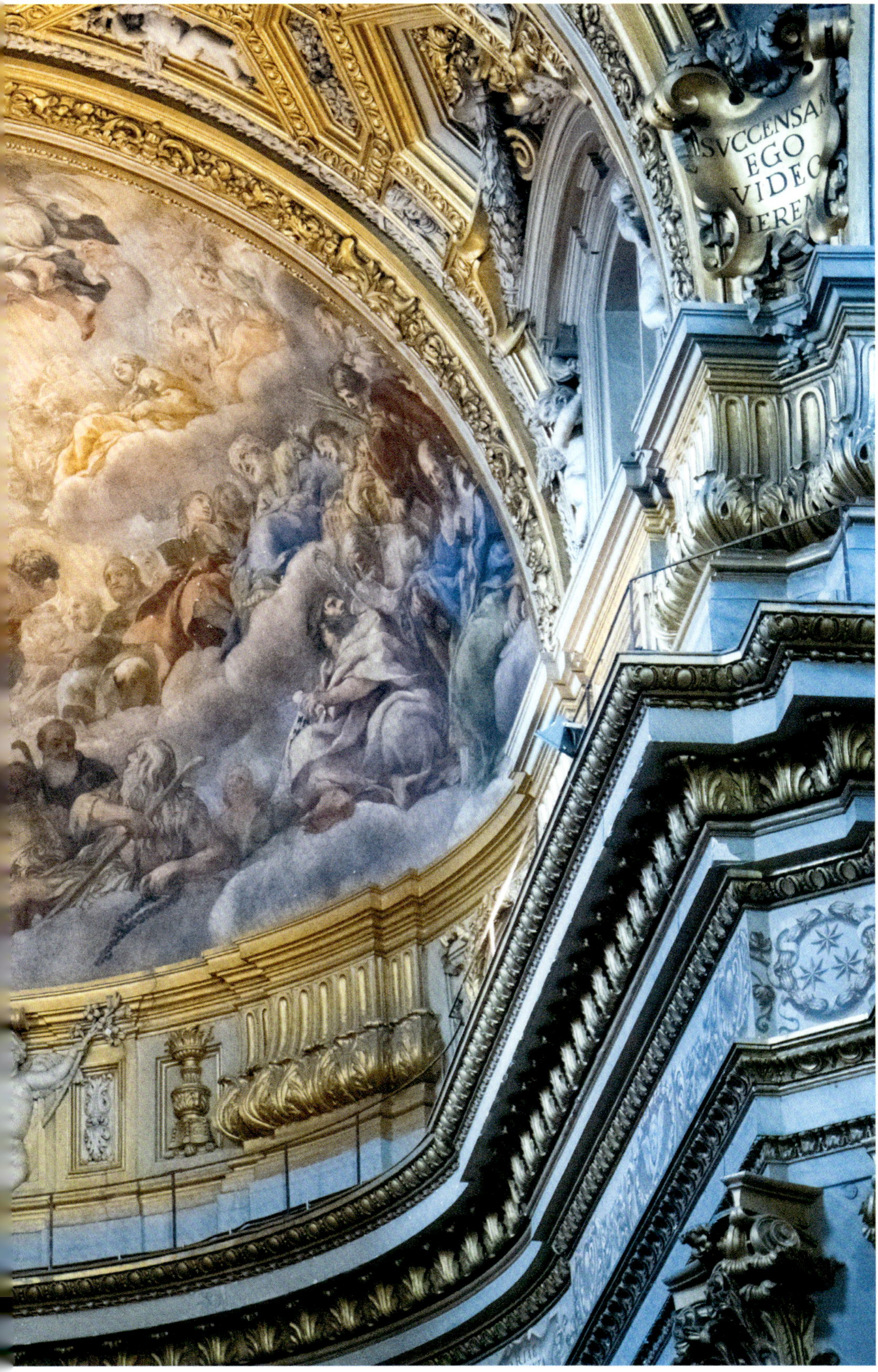

80 Pietro da Cortona, *Assumption of the Virgin*, Rome, Chiesa Nuova

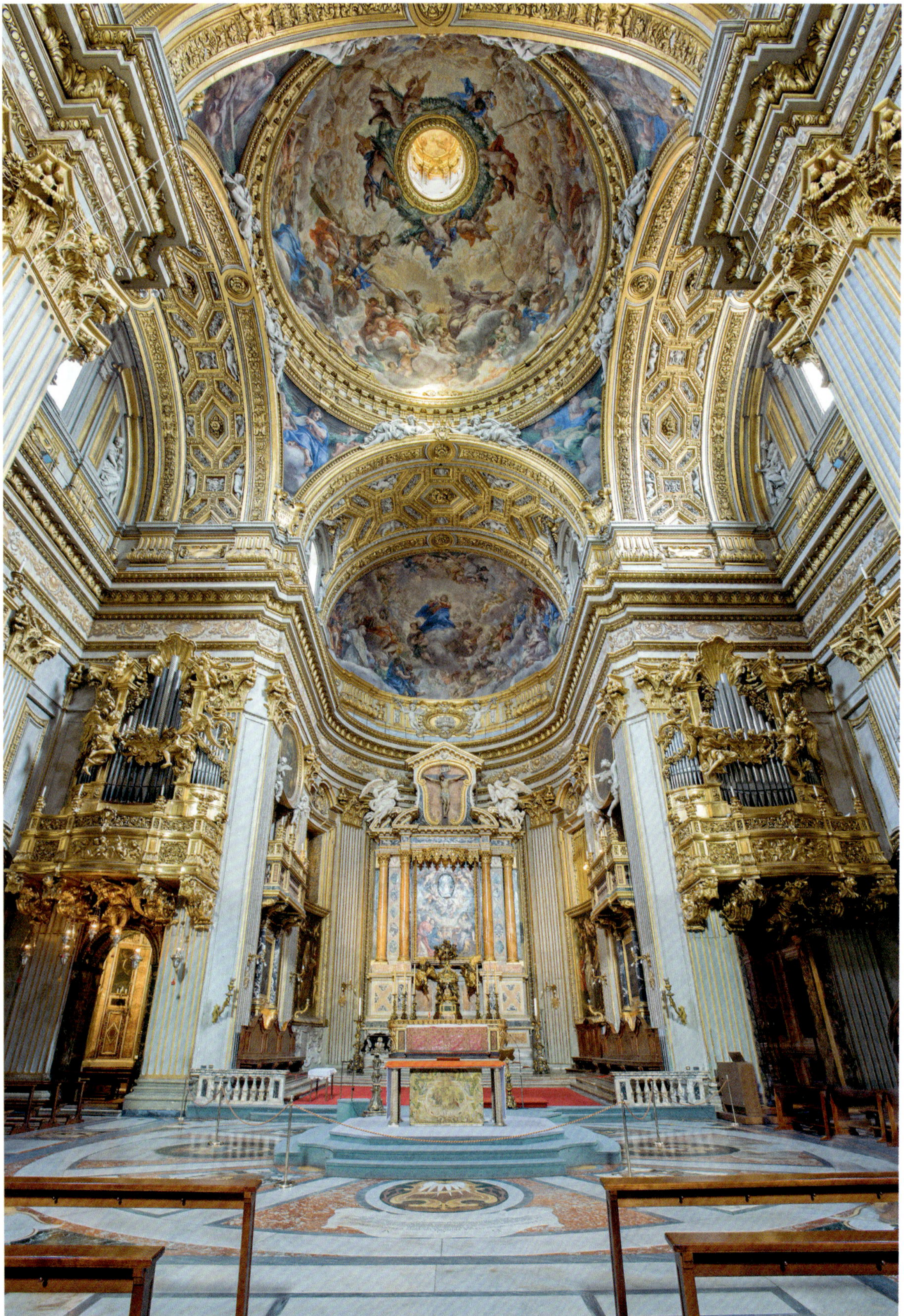

Amongst Pietro's predecessors none was praised more than the 'most excellent' Correggio. His illusionism in Parma was so convincing that one would need to touch the painted surfaces with a rod to know what was real and what was not.[8] Leonardo was lauded for his *Treatise on Painting* but not for his erratic practice. Raphael was a much admired exemplar, as was the less famous Baldassare Peruzzi. It is noted that writers have accorded Michelangelo the epithet '*divinino*', from which the authors do not dissent.[9] The sober Andrea del Sarto was respected for his virtue. The Venetians Giorgione, Tintoretto and Veronese were also recognised as important painters. Of more modern masters, Annibale Carracci was accorded special praise for the vault he painted in the Palazzo Farnese. The range of reference is notable, and Pietro obviously knew the published writings on art and artists, but a good number of his remarks testify that he looked and travelled extensively.

If we place the *Trattato* in the context of the Chiesa Nuova paintings, it is not difficult to see how they fit with what the authors were saying. The identities and actions of the chief figures – the Virgin, God and Christ – are emphasised with clarity, and serve to express the content. Their foreshortening is not extreme and the two frescoes have a powerfully spiritual air. It is less clear that the Barberini vault quite matches the authors' pronouncements.

GAULLI AND BERNINI: LIGHT TRIUMPHANT

Matching Pietro da Cortona's Barberini vault for sheer inventive bravado and introducing a new phase in Baroque illusionistic painting is the *Triumph of the Name of Jesus* painted by Giovanni Battista Gaulli (also known as Baciccio) on the nave vault of the Church of Il Gesù in Rome. Before looking at the vault, it would make sense to see where Gaulli came from. In the literal sense he had come to Rome from Genoa and was quickly picked up as a protégée by Gian Lorenzo Bernini, who occupied a mighty position as a sculptor and architect. Gaulli became in effect Bernini's arm and hand in painting, or at least he was seen as such by contemporaries. We can best tell the story of Gaulli at Il Gesù by looking at his preceding painting *The Church Triumphant in Heaven* in the dome of the same church. Il Gesù was the home church of the Jesuit order, which rose to high ecclesiastical power during the course of the 16th century, not least in combating the Protestant Reformation. In 1661 a new Superior General of the Society of Jesus, Gian Paolo Oliva, was appointed. Along with his reforming agenda for the world church, he determined that the decorations of the interior of the society's mother church should become an unrivalled expression of Jesuit ambitions. The names of a number of painters were mooted, but Bernini successfully lobbied for his young Genoese friend. That Oliva also came from Genoa probably helped. The contract was signed on 21 August 1672. Gaulli was to paint the vault of the nave, the dome, the pendentives and the vaults of the transepts: a huge task. He was to start with the unusually large dome.

There is no doubt that Bernini played an active role in the conception and design of Gaulli's composition. Five Bernini drawings survive for the motif of Christ, the Virgin and the cross – a particularly tricky part of the composition. But other designs and painted *modelli* (small-scale prototypes for the frescoes) show that Gaulli played the determining role in the dome as a whole. To ensure that the young painter was up to the challenge, Bernini arranged for him to visit Parma to inspect Correggio's miracles of spiritual illusion.

By the time of its execution in 1672–5, there was nothing particularly novel in the basic conception of how to paint a dome. The general idea is akin to Pietro da Cortona's Chiesa Nuova composition (fig.80). And the consequences of Gaulli's visit to Parma are apparent. There are the expected rings of saints and angels, some of whom make music, with glowing cloud-heads and brilliant golden light (fig.82). The central subject, best viewed obliquely from the nave, is the conjoined supplication to God the Father by

81 View of the Dome and Apse of the Chiesa Nuova, Rome

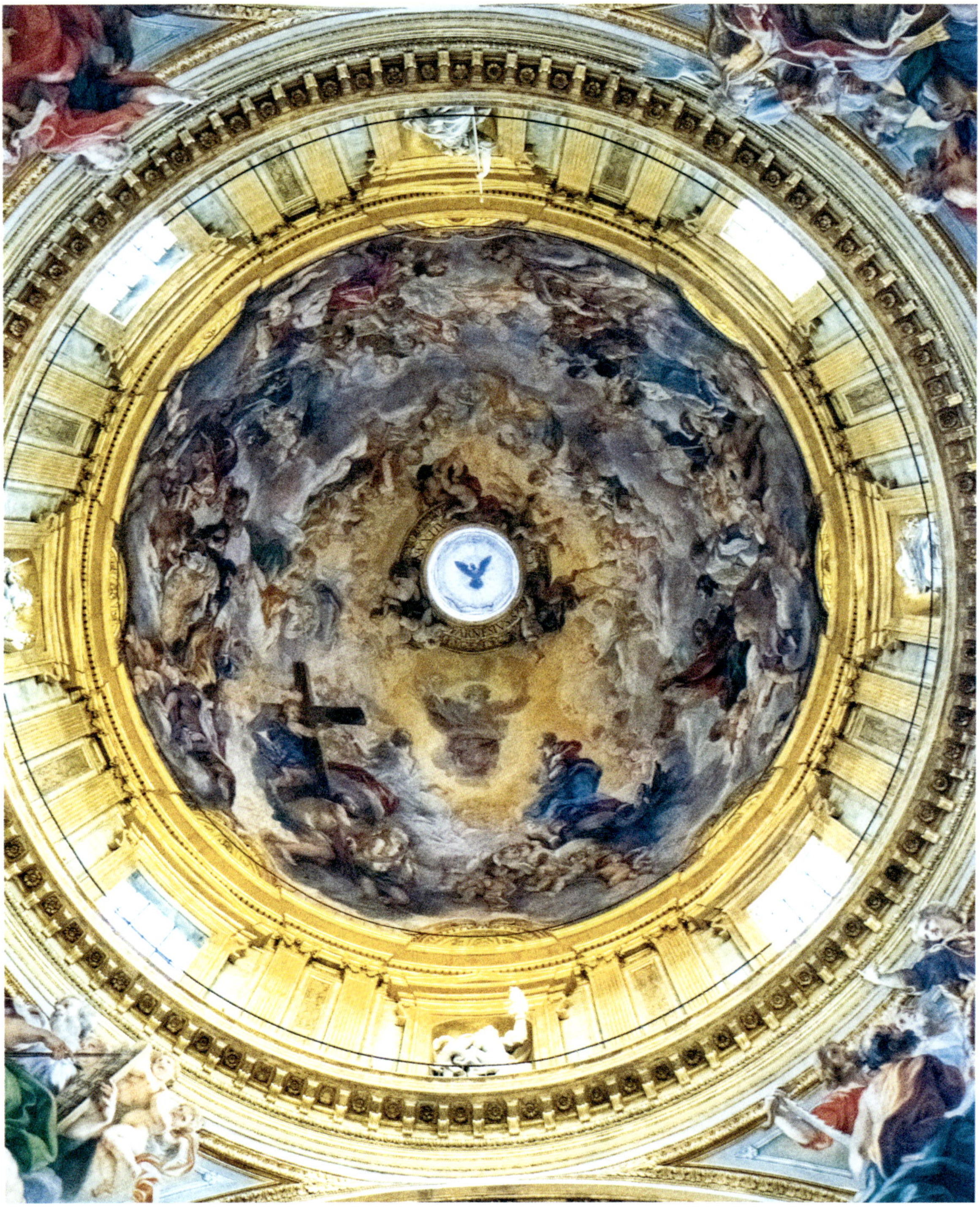

82 Giovanni Battista Gaulli (Baciccio), *The Church Triumphant in Heaven*, Rome, Il Gesù, dome

an adoring Christ and a rather ravaged Virgin. God is usually adjacent and accessible. Bernini's drawings had envisaged an even closer relationship. The foreshortened cross, at the base of which are a cowering Adam and praying Eve, is a masterly piece of illusionistic painting. God spreads his arms in welcome, with an oddly truncated body, just about rationalised by his having bent his legs. The gesture of his arms is echoed by the spread wings of the silhouetted dove high on the secondary dome of the lantern. All this is, for the most part, carried out ingeniously and with skill. But it does not prepare us for what comes next in 1678–9 on the nave vault of Il Gesù (fig.83).

Gaulli's illusion broke new bounds in both the metaphorical and literal sense. It is in its own way as innovatory as Michelangelo's Sistine Ceiling, though very much less famous. It all starts with the Christogram, the monogram of Christ's holy name, IHS, *Jesus Hominum Salvator*, that served as the assertive logo of the Jesuits. It is only just discernible, slanting in space as a bright golden glare against an explosion of white light (fig.84). The subject is taken from one of St Paul's letters to the to the Philippians.

> God also hath highly exalted him and given him a name which is above every name: That at the name of Jesus every knee should bow, of *things* in heaven, and *things* in earth, and *things* under the earth; And *that* every tongue should confess that Jesus Christ *is* Lord, to the glory of God the Father.[10]

A key portion of the text is inscribed on the furling ribbon borne by angels in the oval compartment located next to the top of the open heavens.

The spiritual luminance seems to have been fed down a widening funnel from veiling clouds at the top of the arched margin of the open heavens. The bodies and faces of the adoring angels are modelled in delicate tints of white; they wriggle and squirm in a starburst of luminous ecstasy. All the figures who have transitioned from the space of the church to the zone of heavenly radiance share something of the ethereal paleness of the angels. Those below them, who are making their weightless way upwards, are sumptuously portrayed in glorious colour in their material form with gorgeous draperies and even with gleaming armour. Helpful angels support the clouds that bear the figures aloft. Two clusters of colourful figures arrive on their mobile clouds from outside the confines of the oval-cum-rectangular frame that Gaulli has located in the centre of the vault. The plaster of the figures and clouds radically cross the confines of the frame and actual architecture as they rise from our space towards the divine apparition of Jesus's name. From ground level, it is difficult to work out what is real and what is painted. The painted space, painted light, painted figures, painted sculpture and painted architecture merges with actual space, actual light, actual sculpture in plaster and actual architectural features in a way that is still magical in our age of digital illusions.

Those represented in full colour and modelled in light and shade are not yet spirits – to make the same differentiation as when Dante cast a shadow but Virgil did not. The question arises as to who the figures are. It is tempting to try to identify them as known holy persons, but they are not accorded standard attributes or costumes. They appear to be representatives of the saved – albeit ones of a distinctly aristocratic kind. The exception is the robed ecclesiastic who crosses the frame and whose right hand is not far from the group of women who ride on a darkish cloud (fig.85). He cranes his head backwards to stare fixedly at the Christogram. He is surely St Ignatius, the Spanish theologian who was the co-founder of the Jesuits.

We have left to last the protagonists who are closest to us. Below the heaven-bound elect, a disorderly rabble of naked and near-naked muscle-men and fleshy women tumble precipitously from the lower margins of the frame and into our space (fig.86). They have been ejected by a series of bright, broad light rays that have sped through gaps in the clouds; they inhabit a world of shades. One 'woman'

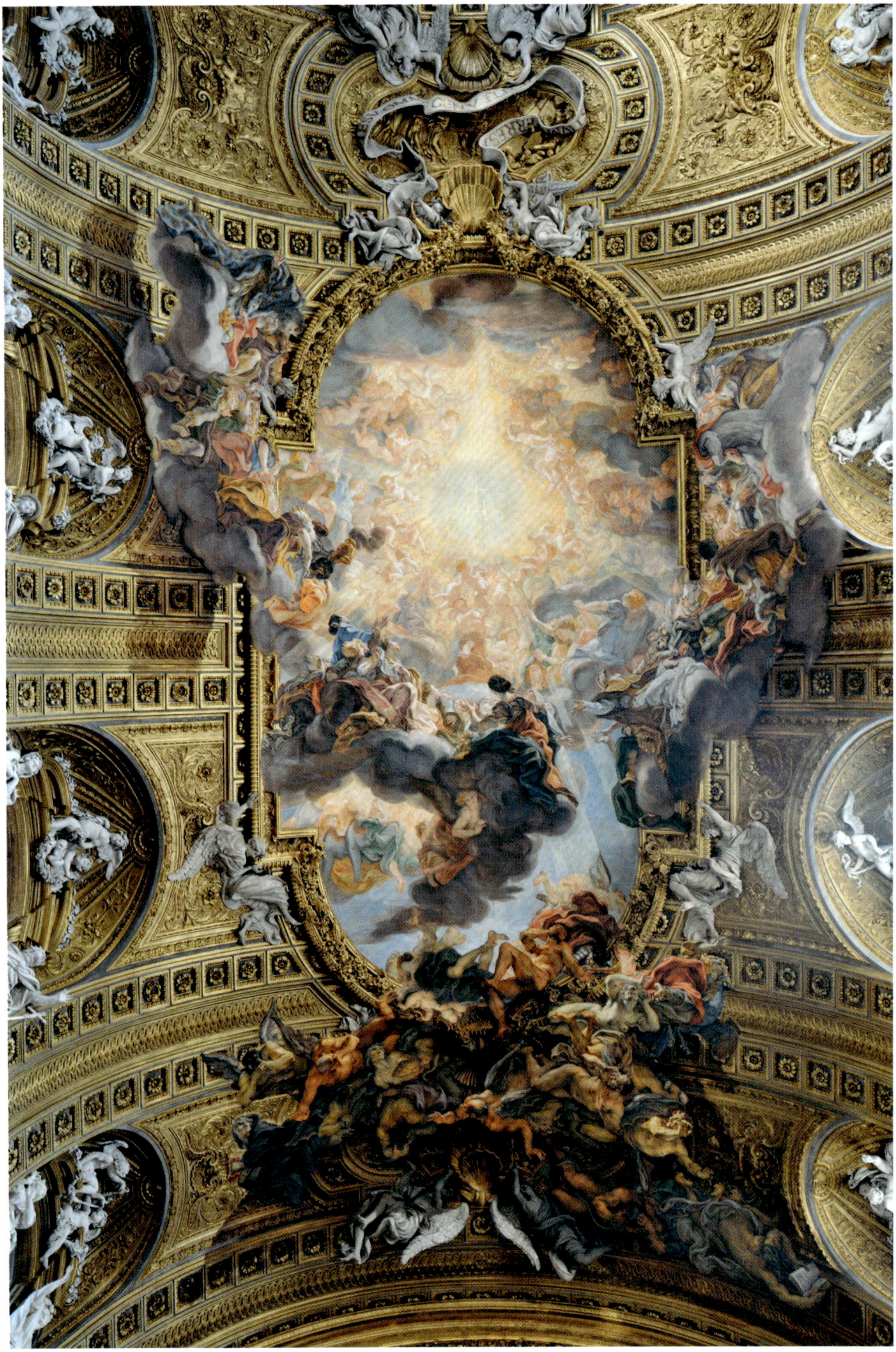

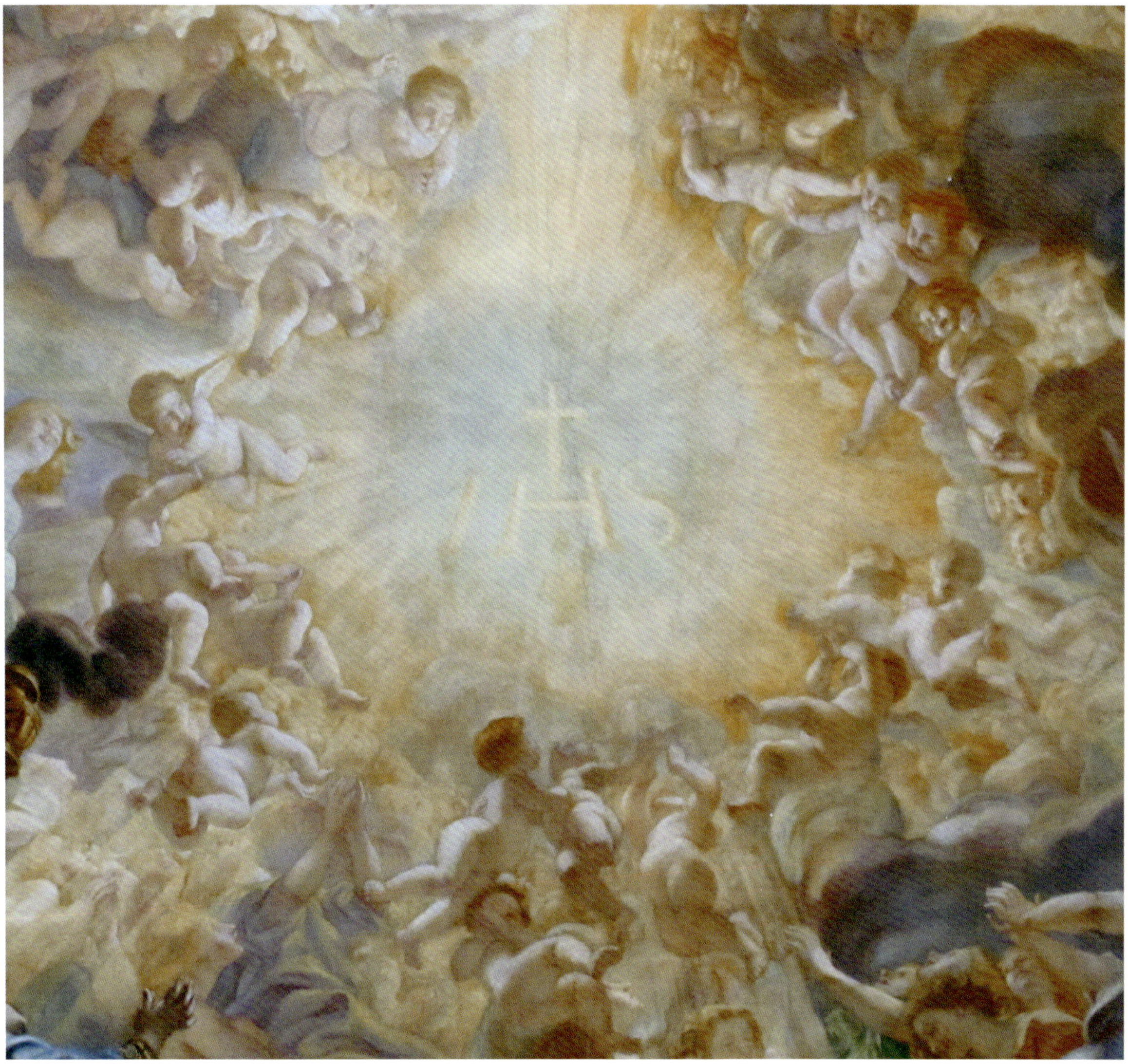

84 Giovanni Battista Gaulli (Baciccio), *The Triumph of the Holy Name of Jesus*, detail of the Christogram and angels, Rome, Il Gesù

83 (OPPOSITE) Giovanni Battista Gaulli (Baciccio), *The Triumph of the Holy Name of Jesus*, Rome, Il Gesù, nave vault

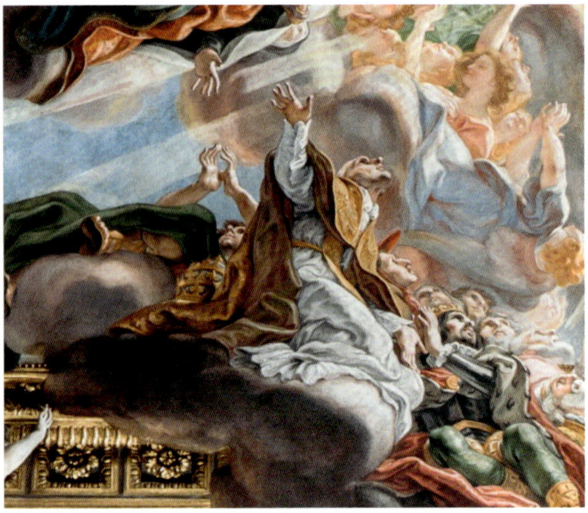

85 Giovanni Battista Gaulli (Baciccio), *The Triumph of the Holy Name of Jesus*, detail of Saint Ignatius of Loyola, Rome, Il Gesù

is a snarling harpy, as on the Barberini vault. There are fallen angels, reconfigured as winged demons. In the upper right a proud peacock struts for the last time, and the monstrous dog's head next to him is probably one of the three possessed by the infernal Cerberus. The inventions and the foreshortenings of the figures are superb.

The conception and execution of the vault are on a quite different plane from Gaulli's dome. Do we attribute this to Bernini's radical vision, in which the margins of the real and artificial are dissolved? We can best attempt to answer this by looking at the supreme example of Bernini's transgressive illusions, his *Ecstasy of St Theresa*, finished in 1652 for the Cornaro Chapel. Although in this book we are concentrating on painting – and Bernini is a sculptor and architect – the Cornaro Chapel in the Church of Santa Maria della Vittoria in Rome refuses to be categorised as just sculpture and architecture. Not only does it contain key painted elements (often overlooked), the whole ensemble is a sacred theatre of light and colour, in a genuinely pictorial manner (fig.87). Like Gaulli's vault, it was produced in what we would now call mixed media.

The chapel was built, at stupendous expense, for Cardinal Federico Cornaro, the son and brother of doges of Venice, who became a powerful figure in the Roman hierarchy. The convent and church were the Roman base of the Discalced (barefoot) Carmelites, co-founded by St Teresa of Ávila, and the chapel is dedicated to her. It is not large, with just enough room between the balustrade and the altar to accommodate a priest and communicant. The best viewpoint is at the entrance in the low balustrade. The chapel was designed to be Federico's mortuary. Accounts almost inevitably begin with Bernini's visionary sculpture of Teresa with an angel, but this is because we are confronted by a great work of art. Let us, by contrast, deal first with the overall design and then the vault.

It is said that there are 17 different types of marble in the chapel. The extraordinary colouristic richness presents us with a feast for our eyes and serves as an advertisement of the patron's conspicuous splendour. He would argue, no doubt, that Teresa (and God) deserves nothing but the best. The densely assembled components of the chapel are powerfully sculptural, and the 'portico' containing the sculpture bulges towards us in a pregnant curve. Above the cornice is an arch lined by an arc of vivacious angels, one of whom holds a ribbon proclaiming, 'If I had not created heaven I would create it for you alone', derived from one of the saint's visionary conversations with God (fig.88).[11] The vault dissolves into a spaceless glare of light, at the centre of which the dove of the Holy Spirit spreads its wings, surrounded by cloud-heads and celebratory angels of varied kinds. The plaster on which they and their clouds are painted straddles the cornice of the window and pours down the sides of the vault, in such a way that the architectural structure becomes implicit rather than dominant. The painted forms realise in a small compass what

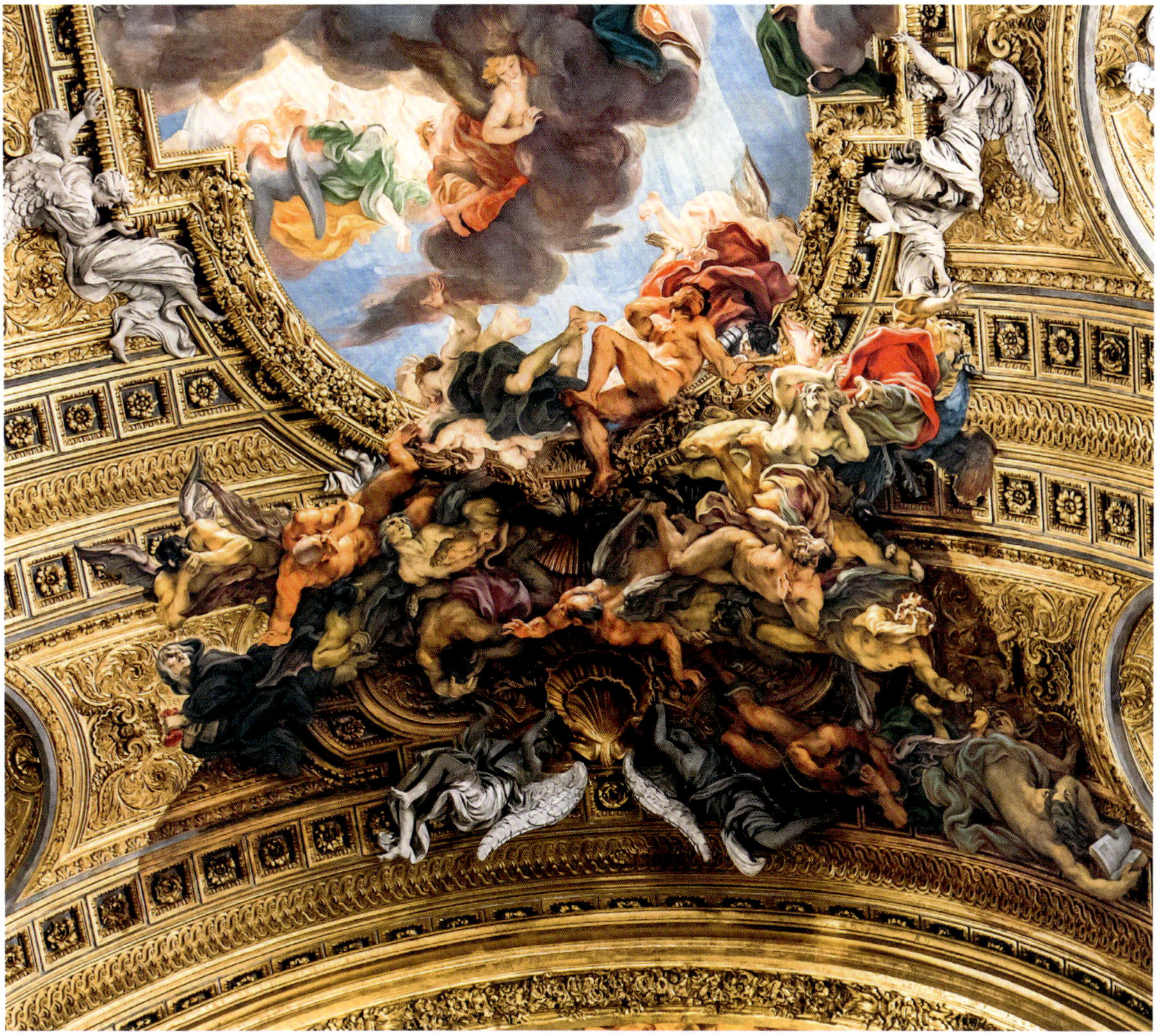

86 Giovanni Battista Gaulli (Baciccio), *The Triumph of the Holy Name of Jesus*, detail of the fall of the damned, Rome, Il Gesù,

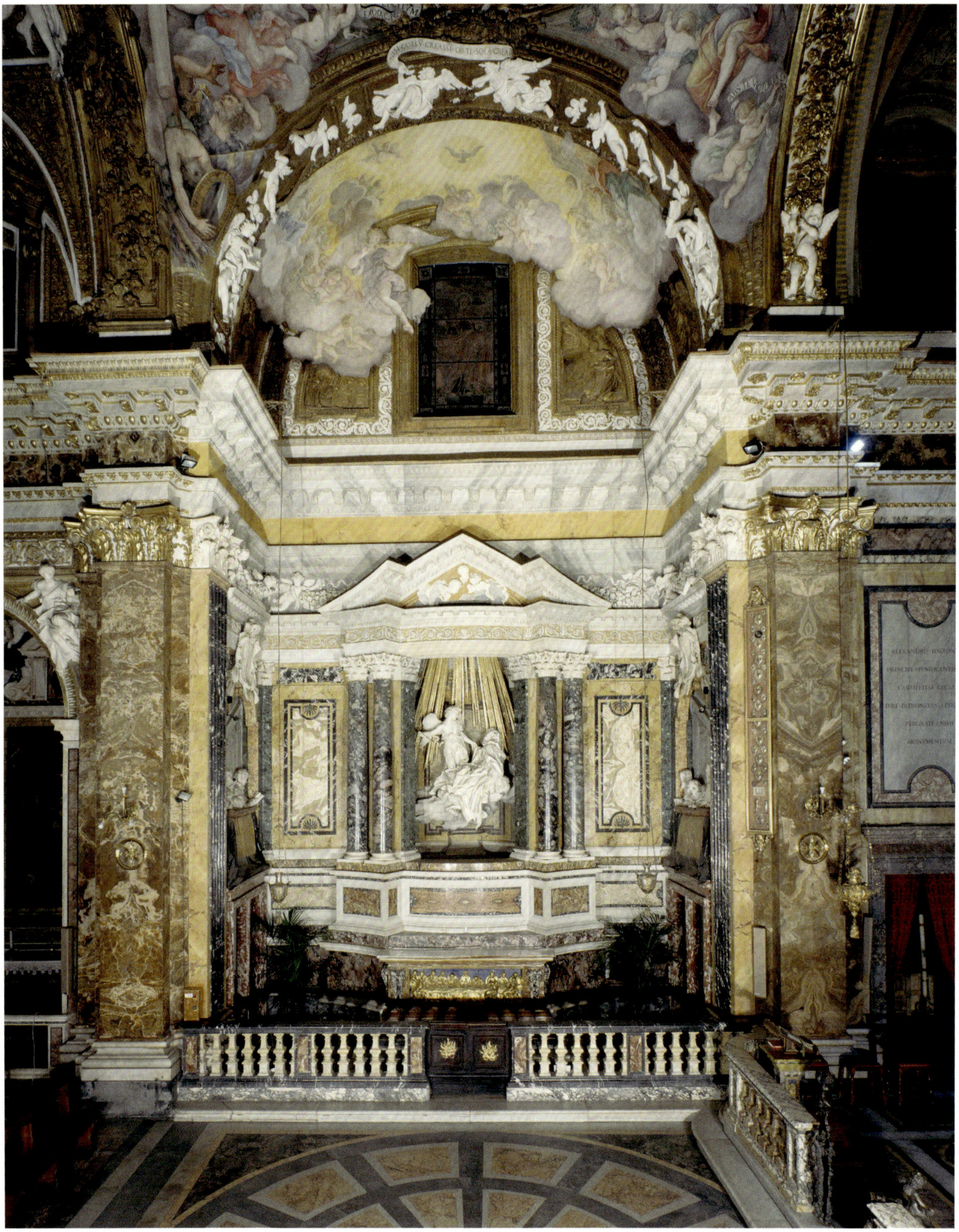

87 Gian Lorenzo Bernini, the Cornaro Chapel, Rome, Santa Maria della Vittoria

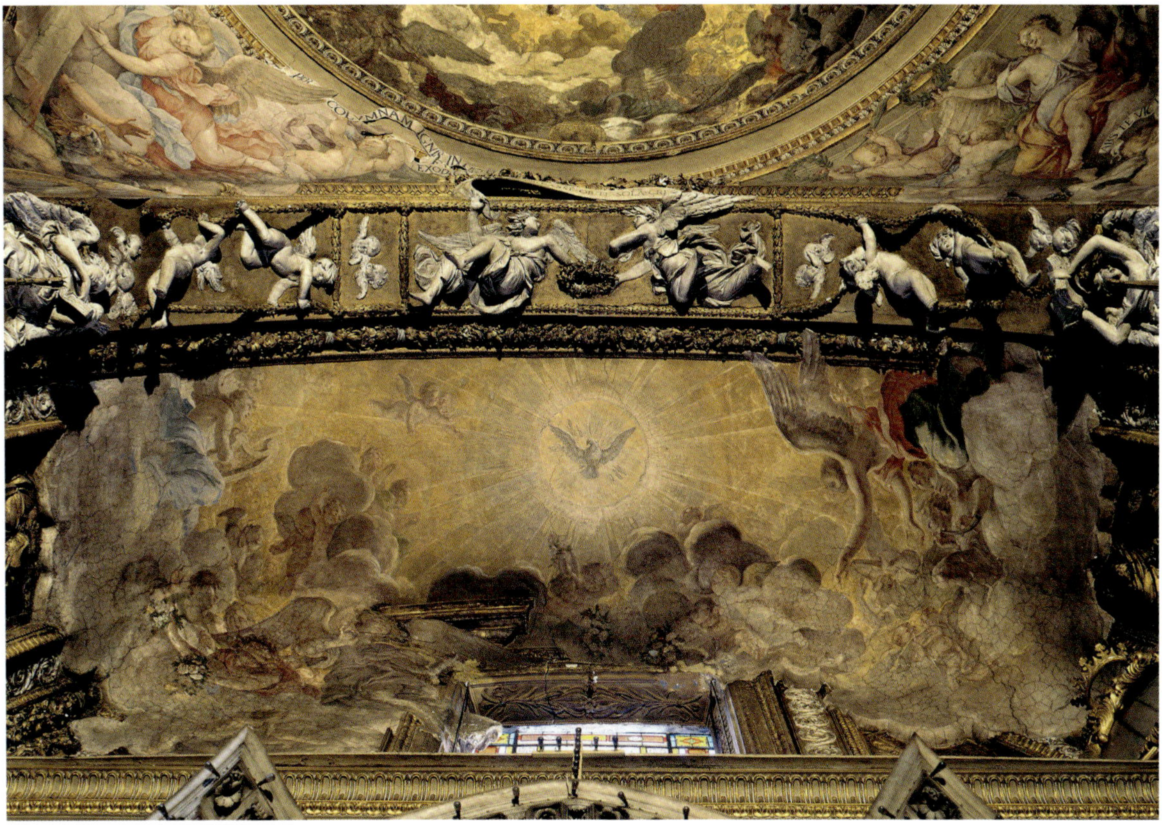

88 Gian Lorenzo Bernini, the Cornaro Chapel, detail of the vault, Rome, Santa Maria della Vittoria

the dome painters had worked to achieve. Who painted it? Maybe Gaulli, though we know that Bernini could also paint.

The breathtaking set-piece is of course the marble sculpture the *Ecstasy of St Teresa* (fig.89). Concurrently with her reforming activities in and then outside the main Carmelite order, she was one of the most extraordinary visionaries of all, recounting her fervent encounters in a substantial body of writings. Her reformist zeal and unrestrained spirituality disturbed more conservative elements in the Church. The prime text for the vision that we are privileged to witness is drawn from her account of her life. It is highly charged in every respect.

It pleased the Lord that I should sometimes see the following vision. I would see beside me, on my left hand, an angel in bodily form – a type of vision which I am not in the habit of seeing, except very rarely … It pleased the Lord that I should see this angel in the following way. He was not tall, but short, and very beautiful, his face so aflame that he appeared to be one of the highest types of angel who seem to be all afire. They must be those who are called cherubim: they do not tell me their names but I am well aware that there is a great difference between certain angels and others, and between these and others still, of a kind that I could not possibly explain. In his hands I saw a long golden spear

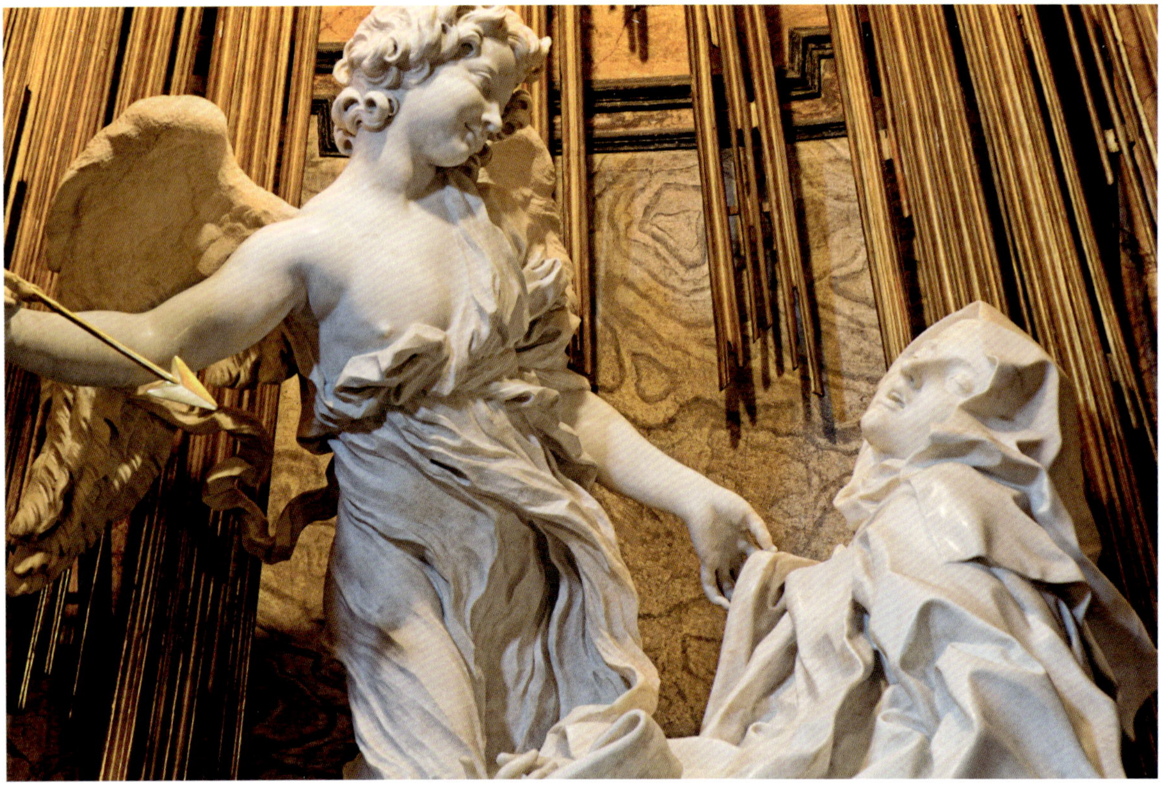

89 Gian Lorenzo Bernini, *The Ecstasy of St Theresa*, Rome, Santa Maria della Vittoria, Cornaro Chapel

and at the end of the iron tip I seemed to see a point of fire. With this he seemed to pierce my heart several times so that it penetrated to my entrails. When he drew it out, I thought he was drawing them out with it and he left me completely afire with a great love for God. The pain was so sharp that it made me utter several moans; and so excessive was the sweetness caused me by this intense pain that one can never wish to lose it, nor will one's soul be content with anything less than God. It is not bodily pain, but spiritual, though the body has a share in it – indeed, a great share. So sweet are the colloquies of love which pass between the soul and God that if anyone thinks I am lying I beseech God, in His goodness, to give him the same experience.[12]

Bernini has captured the deepest moment of the saint's spiritual intercourse with God's messenger. God transforms the supreme discomfort of her flesh into the divine delight of her soul. Such is her overwhelming ecstasy that she has collapsed, insensible yet enraptured, her open mouth emitting the 'moans' of which she wrote. Her limp and slight body, devoid of entrails, is swathed in an expressive excess of piled cloth, markedly coarse compared to the angel's delicate folds. The angel himself, smiling angelically, performs his penetrative duties with sweet delight. The sense of spiritual ascent, of elevated *afflatus*, is underscored by their being borne aloft on a floating cloud, akin to the painted clouds of Baroque domes. A ton of marble has been transfigured into something weightless.

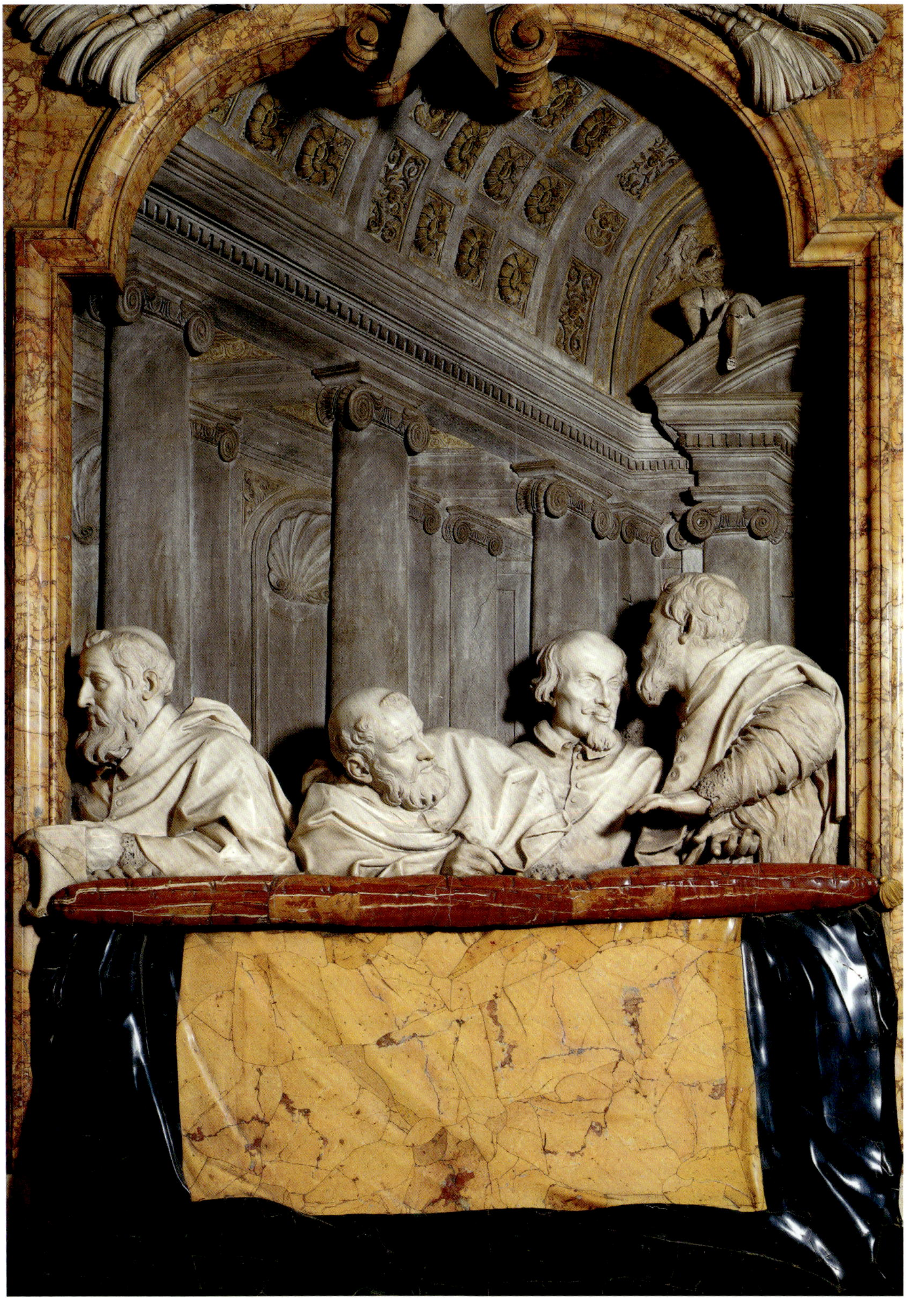

90 Gian Lorenzo Bernini, the Cornaro Chapel, detail of men from the Cornaro family (including Federico, second from right), Rome, Santa Maria della Vittoria

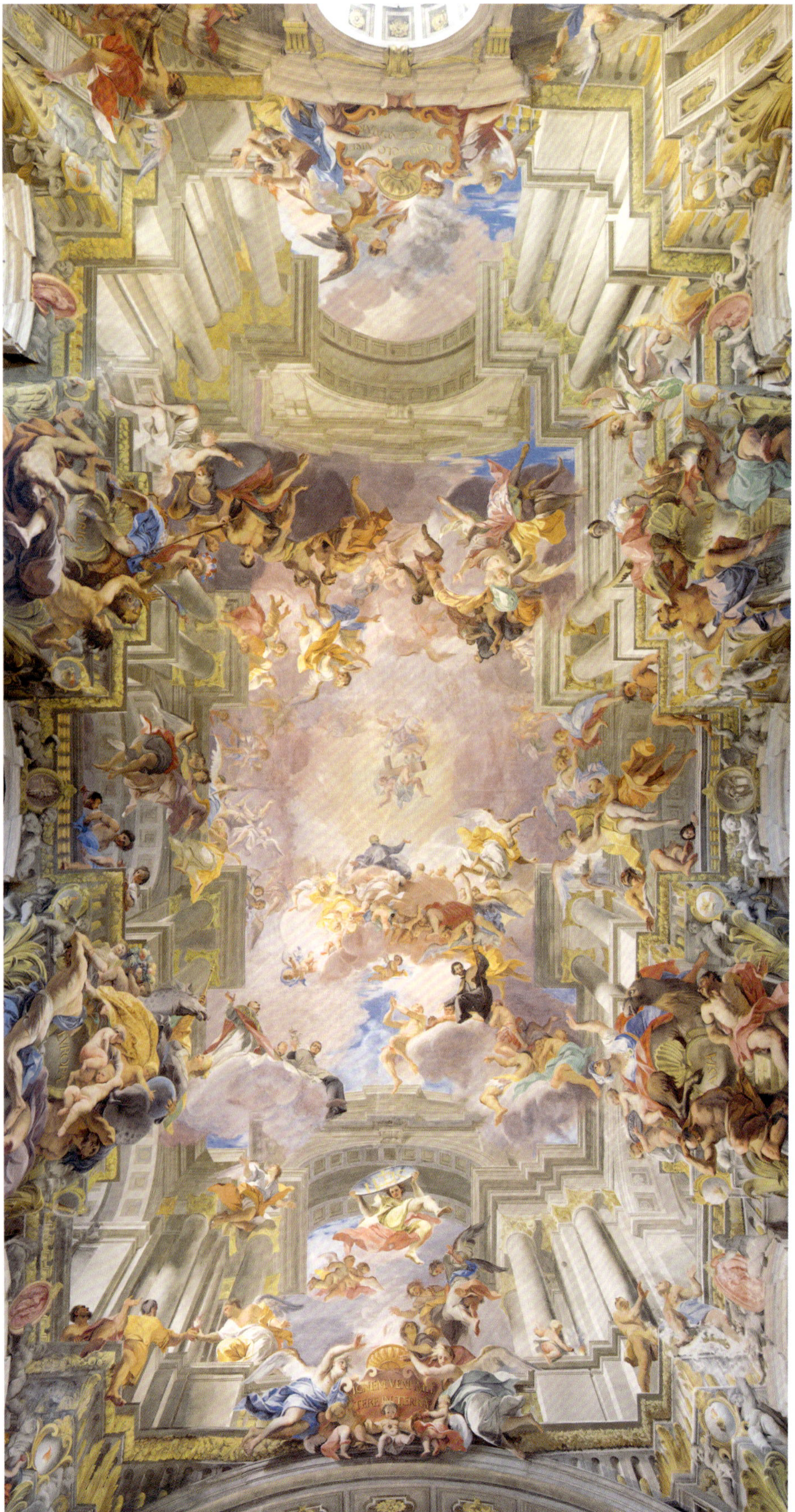

92 Andrea Pozzo, *The Apotheosis of St Ignatius*, Rome, Sant'Ignazio

93 (OPPOSITE) Andrea Pozzo, *The Apotheosis of Saint Ignatius*, detail of the centre of the vault, Rome, Sant'Ignazio

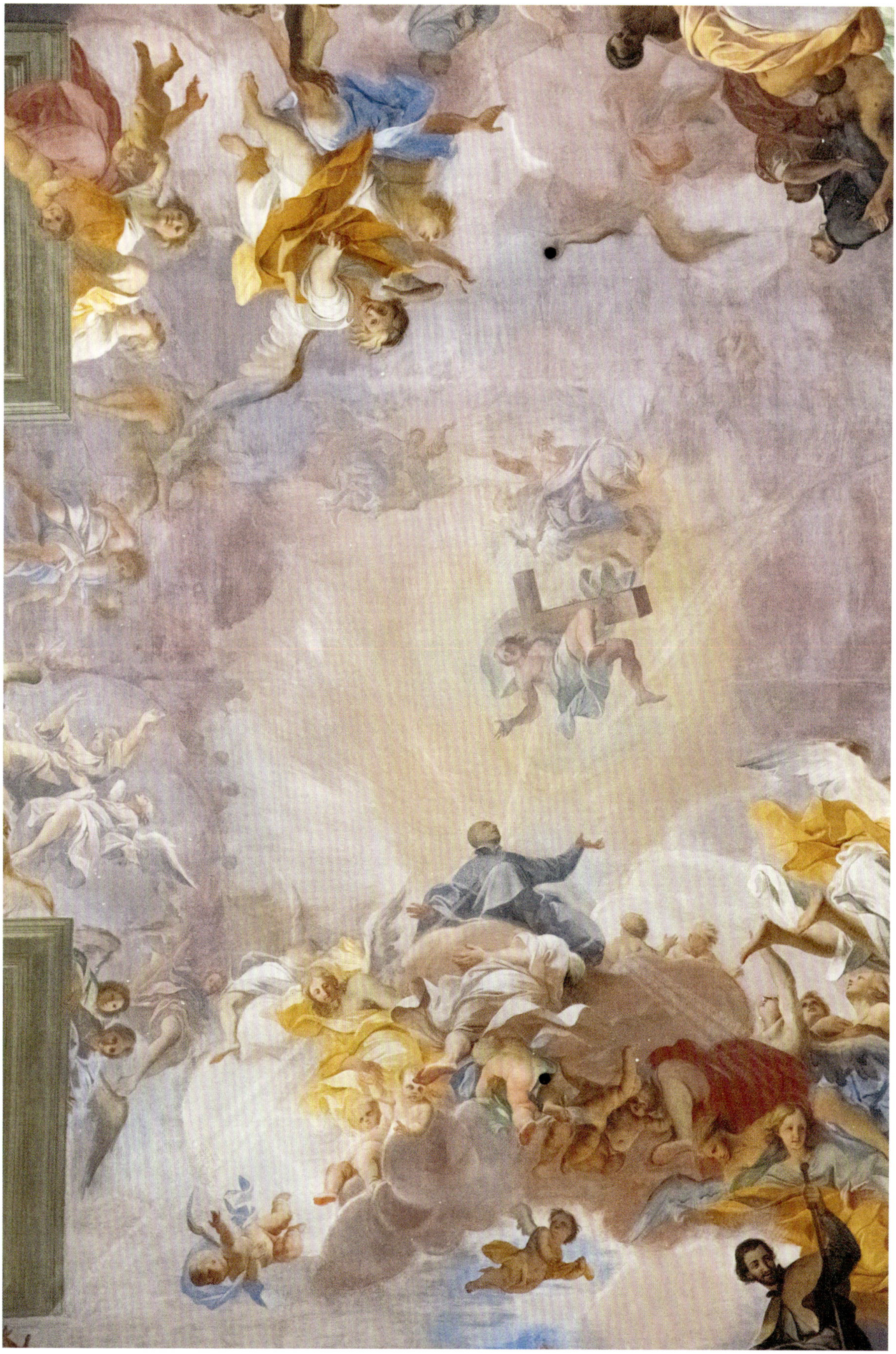

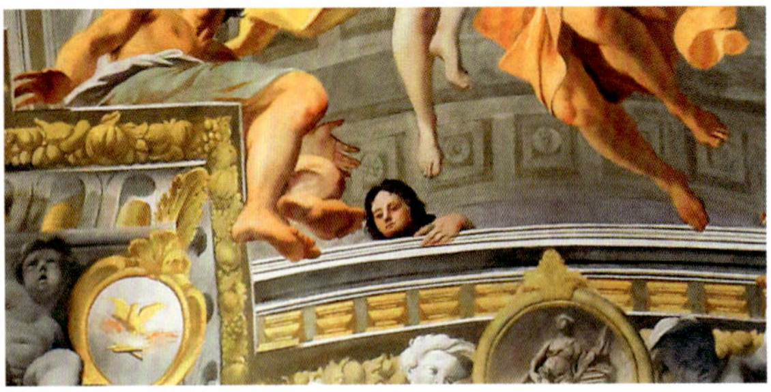

94 Andrea Pozzo, *The Apotheosis of Saint Ignatius*, detail of Pozzo's self-portrait, Rome, Sant'Ignazio

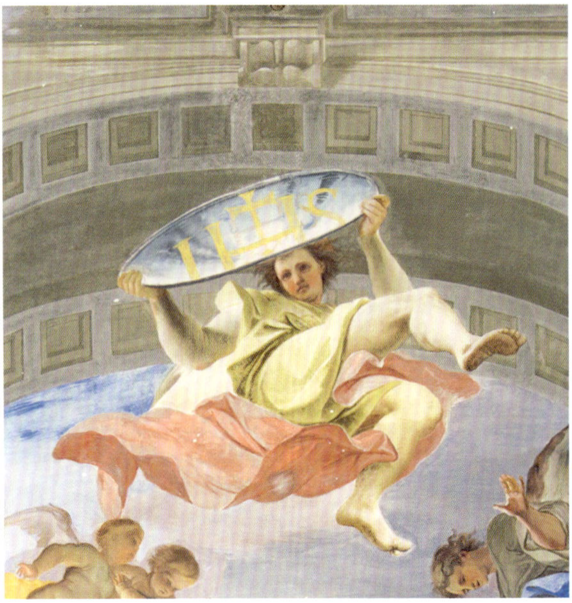

95 Andrea Pozzo, *The Apotheosis of Saint Ignatius*, detail of the angel with a concave mirror, Rome, Sant'Ignazio

This array of continents signals the Jesuits' global aspirations. As Pozzo said, the Son of God 'sends forth a ray of light into the heart of Ignatius, which is then transmitted by him to the most distant regions of the four parts of the world'.[13]

The figures twisting and turning within the zone of the architecture are markedly larger than those in the more distant heavens and tend to be more assertively modelled and coloured than those who occupy the upper regions. The level of skill in figure painting and foreshortening yields nothing to Gaulli. A small youthful head rendered in natural colours appears twice, just visible above the cornice at the middle of each of the lateral sides of the vault (fig.94). This is Andrea himself, still firmly anchored to the real structure, physically and optically.

One beam of light shoots downwards through Ignatius's cloud and passes under the arch on the end wall. There it meets a concave mirror held by a smiling angel who looks down directly at us (fig.95) In the glare of concentrated light in the mirror we can just see a golden Christogram. Given the properties of concave mirrors – used at the time as burning mirrors to generate focused heat – we are being treated to an intensely directed and personal light that has passed from Christ via St Ignatius before being reflected into our eyes. It was known that concave mirrors could also be used for projecting images; in this case the reflection forms the name of Jesus. Fittingly, the inscription on the cartouche held by two angels below the mirror-bearer records Christ's pronouncement 'I am come to send fire on the earth'.[14]

The use of dogmatic perspective at this time was unusual. Generally Baroque illusions had become increasingly fluid. Pozzo even placed a disc inset in the pavement to mark the exact position from which the construction should ideally be seen. Criticised for the anachronistic inflexibility of his scheme, he argued that the more fluid systems did not look right from anywhere and that the distorted views from unfavourable viewpoints demonstrated the legitimacy of his optical system. Finally, in his *Breve descrizione del disegno della Capella di Sant'Ignazio* (*Brief Description of the Design of the Chapel of St Ignazio*) in 1697, Pozzo deployed his clinching argument that he had resolved to 'draw all the lines thereof to that true POINT, the glory of GOD'. This was a rather different solution to the Dante problem of how optics behave in the heavens – or rather misbehave. The heavens in Pozzo's scheme use Euclidian geometry to extend space into the

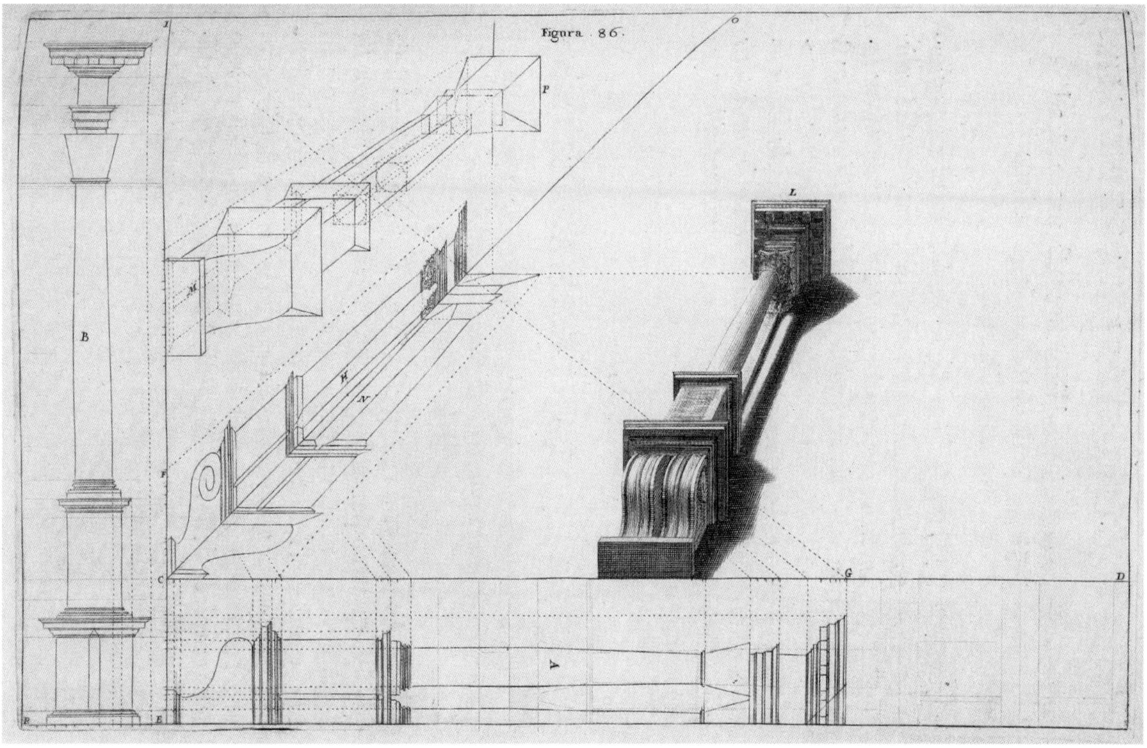

96 Andrea Pozzo, *Projection of a Column*, in *Perspectiva pictorum et architectorum*, Rome, 2 vols., 1693, I, fig.87

infinite, beyond measure. The 'vanishing point' thus marks the infinite mystery of God's realm.

In 1693, Pozzo published one of the most accomplished books on artistic perspective in two very handsome volumes, his *Perspectiva pictorum et architectorum* (*Perspective for Painters and Architects*). He uses the two recognised systems of perspective, the convenient 'distant point' method and a full system of projection. This is not the place to enter into a technical explanation of the two methods, but suffice it to say that the former is explained from its basic principles and then applied to a series of specific designs, including the projection of a column on to a ceiling, as would have been used at Sant'Ignazio (fig.96).

It is one thing to accomplish this already tough task on a flat surface. It is altogether another to transfer the design to a concave vault. Over the years, various systems had been used to accomplish this, including a perspective machine, as we will see when we encounter Cigoli in the next chapter. Pozzo used a squared grid. A complete drawing of the foreshortened architecture was drawn on a large scale. The drawing was then squared with ruled lines. Next, a series of strings were tightly suspended from the actual ceiling at cornice level (fig.97). From the key point on the ground (marked 'o' in his diagrams), the network of squares was projected laboriously, with the help of assistants, on to the vault, where it only appeared as squares from the key point on the ground. The design was then transferred square by square to the warped grid on the vault, using the intersections of the strings as key markers of position. The resulting design on the vault worked against its actual shape to create the necessary illusion. This was not an easy task, requiring knowledge, skill,

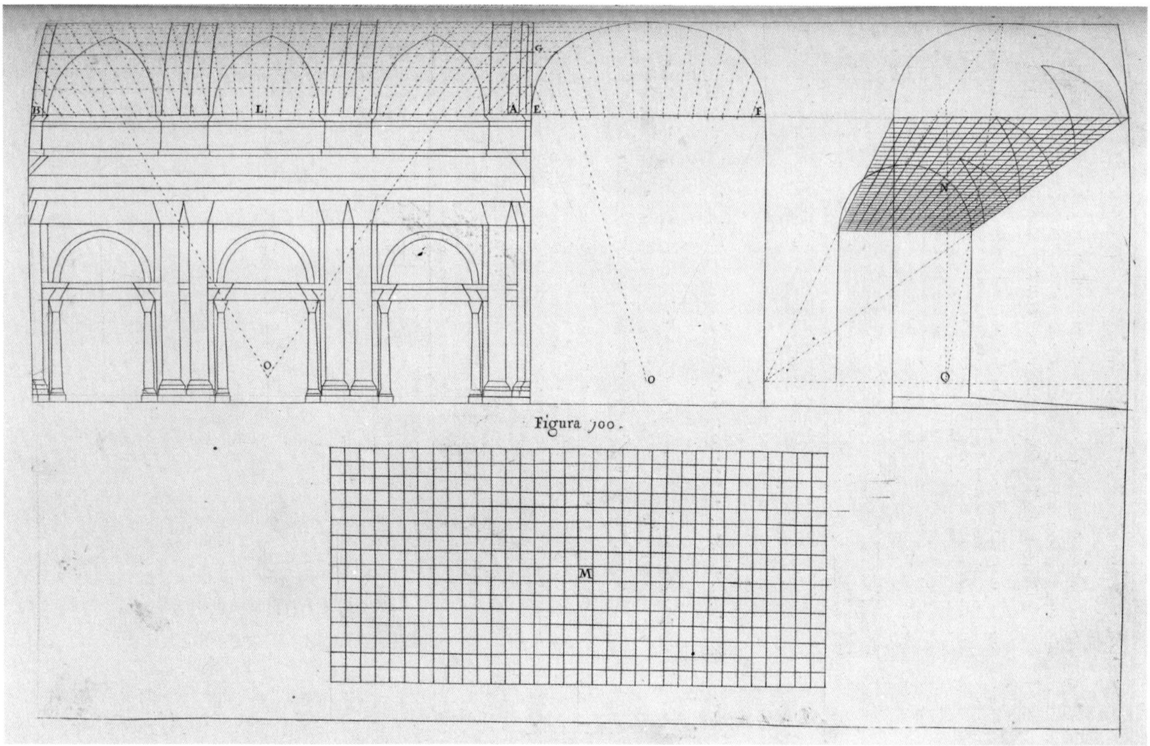

97 Andrea Pozzo, *Grid Method for the Projection of the Design on to the Vault of Sant'Ignazio*, in *Perspectiva pictorum et architectorum*, Rome, 2 vols., 1693, I, fig.100

patience and experience. Well might Pozzo argue that mathematical optics of this high order was serving transcendental ends.

Of his other major contributions to Sant'Ignazio, I will limit my comments to the very prestigious chapel dedicated specifically to the saint, which is a visual feast of form, space and light. Capturing its complexity and verticality in a single photograph is impossible and I am illustrating the chapel with a fine engraving from 1697 by Vincenzo Mariotti, who was a protégée of Pozzo and provided the excellent plates for his *Perspectiva* (fig.98). The rich ensemble of painting, sculpture and architecture was conceived in emulation of Bernini's Cornaro Chapel, though on a much larger scale. The already costly marble of the architecture is further enriched by intensely blue lapis lazuli, which was as expensive as gold. Pozzo specifically referred to such decorations as *teatri*.

The most effective sculptures were provided by the very accomplished French artist Pierre le Gros (the Younger), who won a competition in 1685 for the intricate marble group at the lower right of the chapel. It dynamically represents Religion Overthrowing Heresy and Hatred. A graceful lady brandishing a cross and thunderbolt casts down a vitriolic hag and a man wrestling with a serpent. They are accompanied by books authored by Luther and Calvin, while a *putto* rips pages from a volume by Zwingli, the Swiss Reformist. Then in 1697 le Gros won a further competition for a silver statue of St Ignatius, which glitters with a profusion of jewels and gilded ornaments (fig.99). As in Pozzo's ceiling, Ignatius is

98 (OPPOSITE) Vincenzo Mariotti, *Chapel of Sant'Ignazio*, Rome, Sant'Ignazio, engraving (reverse of subject), London, British Museum

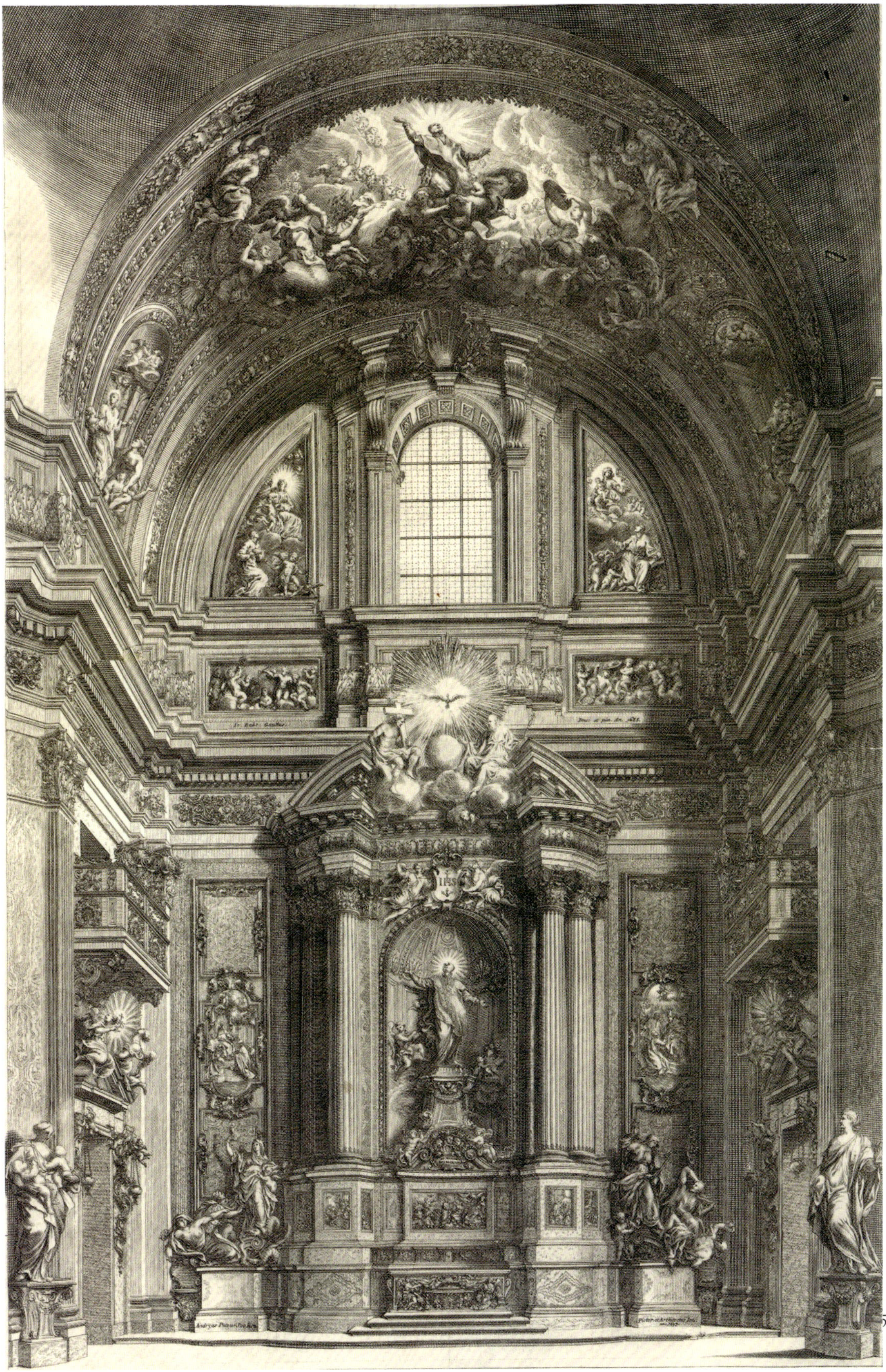

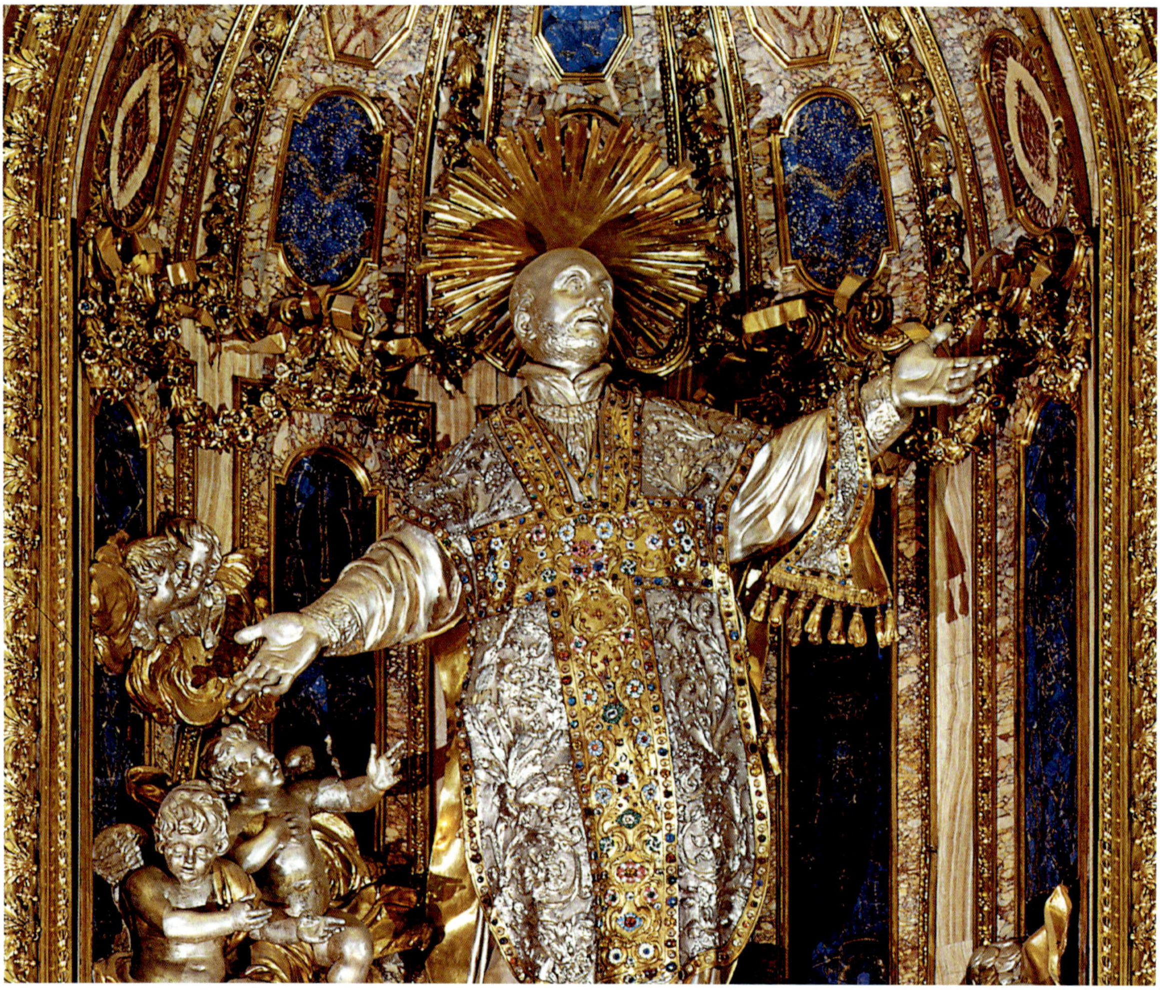

99 Pierre Le Gros (the Younger), detail of the silver statue of Sant'Ignazio from the Chapel of Sant'Ignazio, Rome, Sant'Ignazio

transmitting the reflected light of Christ. The statue stands within a Bernini-like altar frame, with a broken pediment occupied by the Trinity, at a lower level than we might expect. On either side of the high window are two visionary events from the saint's life, and, should we doubt who is the dedicatee of all this fervent devotion, another figure of Ignatius is borne by angels into the heavens, up, across and beyond the arch of the vault, his head haloed by a starburst of divine light. There are least nine such sources of painted or sculpted light in the chapel.

The dominant forces behind sequences of domes and vaults in the 17th century have been the vigorous and ambitious religious orders that arose in response to the Protestant Reformation: the Oratorians of San Filippo Neri, St Ignatius's Jesuits and the Discalced Carmelites of Saint Teresa. Against the personalised austerities of Calvin, not least his condemnation of idolatrous images, the visions of heaven offered to Catholic worshippers had become more immersively dramatic in their pictorial, sculptural and architectural realisations. They had, in a generic sense, become more sublimely Dantesque. The question of how far we can associate (if we need to) the light-filled effusions of the Baroque decorative schemes with acts of seeing in Dante's *Paradiso*, we take up again in the next chapter.

RUBENS AND JESUIT ILLUMINATION

To end this chapter we will return to northern Europe, not to look at an outlier in the manner of Grünewald, but to witness the early transfer of Italian reformist modes into Catholic Southern Netherlands (Belgium). Our focus will be on the Church of the Jesuits in Antwerp, first dedicated to the Virgin and then to St Ignatius. Before looking at Rubens's large-scale involvement with paintings for the interior, it is worth exploring the design and conception of the church and its very sophisticated orchestration of light.

The designers of the new church, which was constructed between 1615 and 1621, were François de Aguilón and Pieter Huyssens. Aguilón was the learned rector of the Jesuit 'Professed House' at Antwerp, with a special interest in mathematics, and he had already been involved in architectural design. Huyssens was an experienced architect and lay brother. The former is of special interest to us since he wrote an important textbook on optics, published in 1613, *Opticorum libri sex* (*Six Books on Optics*) for which Rubens provided the title-page (fig.100) and introductory illustrations for each of the six sections of the treatise. The frontispiece shows an enthroned Juno with her peacock, the tail of which is replete with the eyes that Juno had harvested from the decapitated Argos. She also holds a pyramid, referring to the rays that enter the eye pyramidally, and she is accompanied by an eagle (who as we learnt can look directly at the sun). The eagle, who grasps the sphere of heavens, may also pun on Aguilón's name – *aquila* in Latin means 'eagle'. The eye on Juno's sceptre radiates brightly, as she does herself, on a much larger scale.

Aguilón's treatise, which is described on the title-page as 'useful for philosophers and mathematicians alike', is a masterly and comprehensive exposition of the science of direct sight as understood at the time, although he did not know about Johannes Kepler's recent demonstration of the crystalline humour as a focusing 'lens'. He was also little affected by some of the latest ideas about the anatomy of the eye, preferring to concentrate on the geometry of light. His *Six Books on Optics* are laid out in a very systematic manner. Unsurprisingly, he insists on the divine dimension of light. Optics is a mathematical science visible on earth that leads to a spiritually directed ascent to the realms of the sun, God and the Trinity. Some of the contents of the treatise are familiar from the classical and Mediaeval authorities, in the succession of Ibn al-Haytham, but Aguilón also embraces the more mathematical approaches to projection developed in the 16th century by Federico Commandino and Guidobaldo del Monte. He was also much interested in optical and mathematical instruments, and in the role of two-eyed vision. His theory of sight relies fundamentally on intromission, but, like Pecham, he grants a discriminating power to light from the eye, which can be profitably exercised on worthy objects.

Rubens's chapter openers, which demonstrate a keen understanding of the text, show a bearded philosopher investigating key phenomena under instruction from knowing *putti*. A good example is the engraving for book five which deals with the problem of the relationship between the brightness of a light and its distance from a receptive surface (fig.101). We might expect that if a single light is placed at half the distance of a double light, they would produce matching luminance. This proved not to be the case. The conundrum is much the same as that in Beatrice's three-mirror experiment, though Aguilón does not resort to theological metaphysics as a way around the problem.

Aguilón's awareness of the effects of light of varied intensities were brought to bear on the manipulation of light within the church, although he died in 1617 before his work was completely finished. The illumination

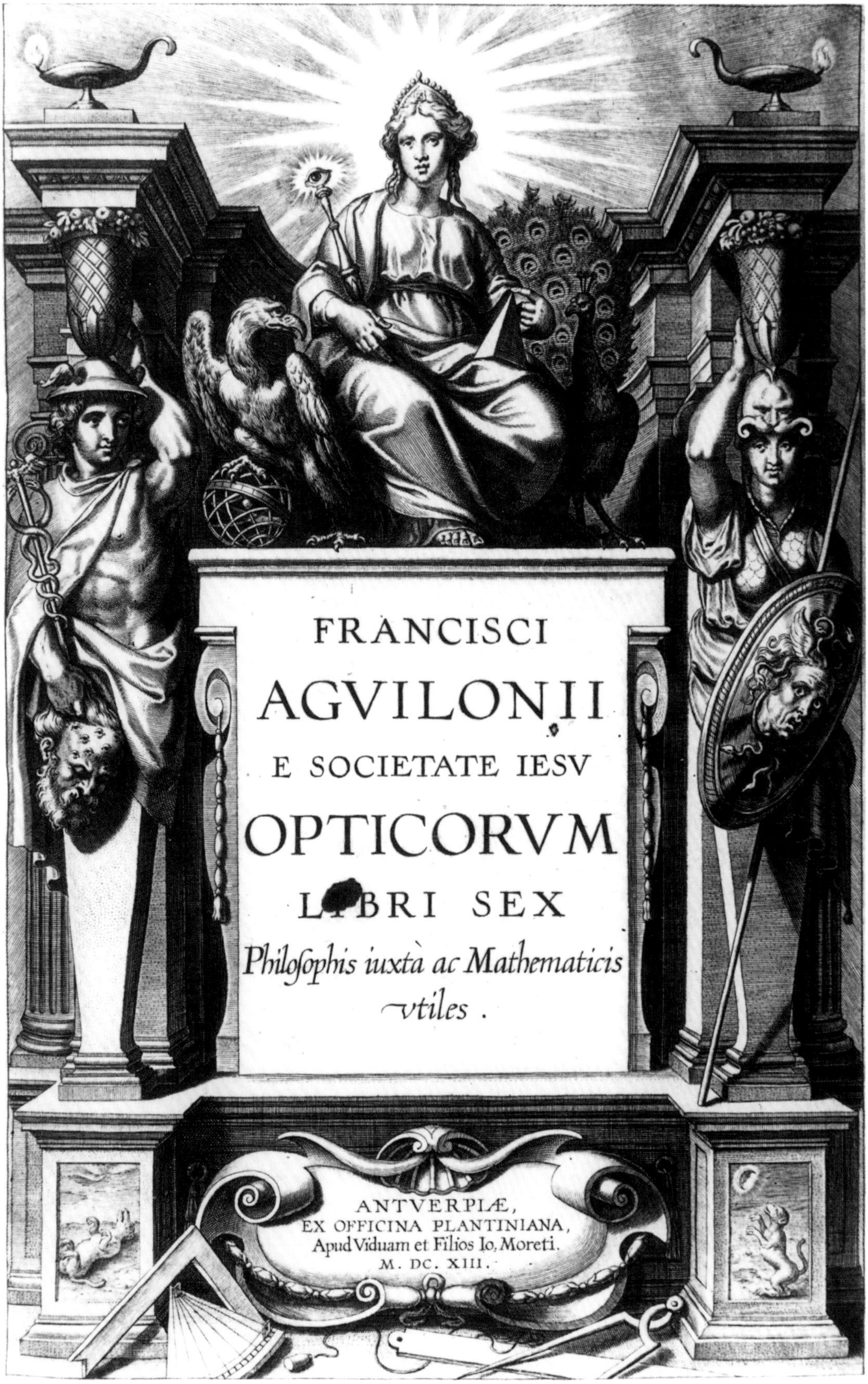
FRANCISCI
AGVILONII
E SOCIETATE IESV
OPTICORVM
LIBRI SEX
Philosophis iuxtà ac Mathematicis
vtiles.
ANTVERPIÆ,
EX OFFICINA PLANTINIANA,
Apud Viduam et Filios Io. Moreti.
M. DC. XIII.

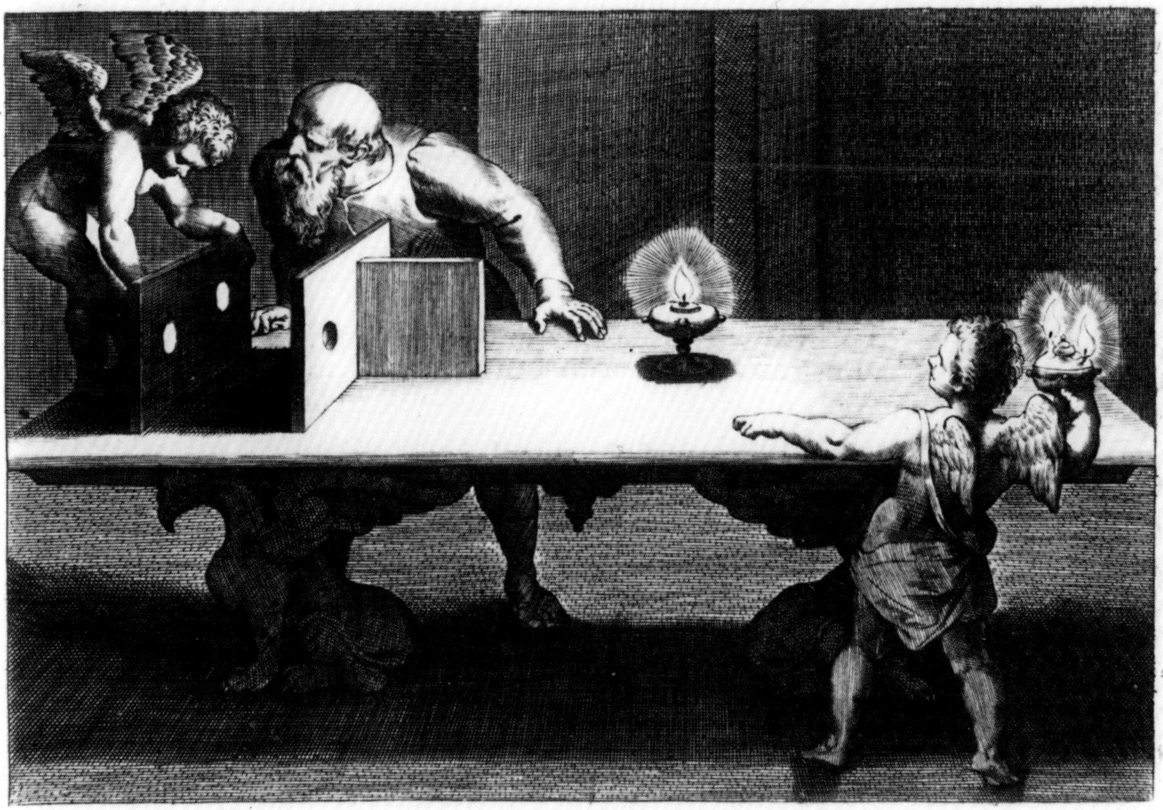

101 François de Aquilón (Aguilonius), *Opticorum libri sex,* Antwerp, 1613, illustration to book v by Rubens, engraved by Theodoor Galle

of the sculpture within the church has been contrived with remarkable care and ingenuity. This is most vividly apparent in the Lady Chapel, in which a concealed dormer window has been specially constructed to illuminate God the Father on the cornice above the altarpiece (fig.102). In normal circumstances, God would have been rather inconspicuous in the shade of the vault, even with his gold corona. As it is, he is picked out by the light in such way that he becomes radiant, and our gaze is drawn upwards to meet his downward stare and gesture. St Paul, in the same Lady Chapel, is also strongly illuminated directly from a window on his left side, and his face seems to radiate light. As argued in the optical treatises, a strong light overwhelms that from less brilliant sources. The light is natural, but in the Lady Chapel it is admitted directionally in such a way as to endow it with a force that becomes spiritual in effect. Other of the statues within the church and on the high altar receive shafts of natural light at particular times, so that the interior acts as a kind of theatre of illumination across the days and seasons.

Aguilón's illustrator may well have played an active part in the planning of the church and its exterior and interior decorations. As a painter, Rubens was awarded major contracts for the Jesuit Church. Rubens was commissioned in 1617 to paint two large altarpieces and in 1620 to supply no less than 39 paintings of the life of St Ignatius for compartments on the ceilings of the aisles. He was awarded the princely sum of 10,000

100 François de Aquilón (Aguilonius), *Opticorum libri sex,* Antwerp, 1613, title-page by Rubens, engraved by Theodoor Galle

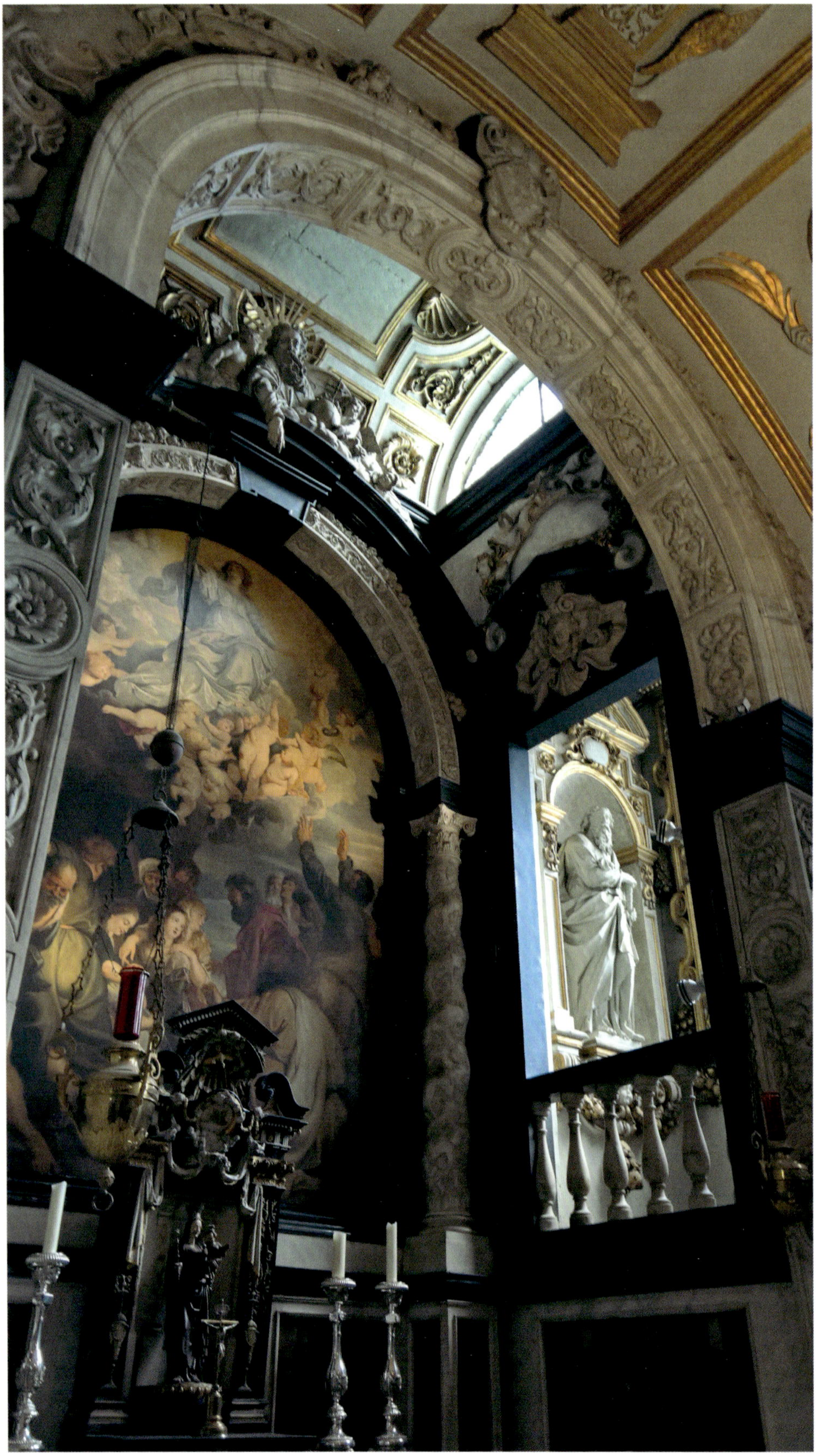

102 The Houtappel or Lady Chapel and view into the Burial Chapel in the Church of St Ingatius in Antwerp

florins. The aisle paintings were destroyed by fire, but Rubens's sketches, copies and engravings show that there were plentiful bursts of divine light to accompany the saint's numerous visions. The altarpieces depicted St Ignatius and St Francis Xavier in miraculous action, and were to be displayed in alternation on the high altar. Francis Xavier was a founding member of the Society of Jesus and an important missionary.

Of the two, the altarpiece of St Francis makes the more telling use of divine light as the saint is seen as if simultaneously performing various miracles during his missions in Asia, and most notably in Goa (fig.103). Accompanied by an acolyte, the saint on his raised platform calmly and confidently points to the heavenly source for his powers and reaches out to cure those in need. There are multiple narratives; the most violent involves the destruction of a Hindu idol, which necessitates the direct involvement of heaven. The figures in the crowded pyramid to the left are subject to acts of resuscitation, including the story of an Indian mother whose drowned baby was to be drained of water and given renewed life. The man at the bottom left, whose shroud is being removed, is a victim of the plague, which was taken as a metaphor for heresy. His grave is being prematurely dug by a bald man with a spade, while a merciful woman is inspecting his armpit for signs of infection. Above the plague victim, a man with an exotic hairstyle is being raised from the dead. The men in voluminous robes and unusual hats near the shoulder of the soldier in armour are Koreans, who initially refused to acknowledge the saint's healing powers. Just below Francis a blind merchant is feeling his way into space. He will have his sight restored in due course. The altarpiece presents a catalogue of the saint's curative abilities. For his part, Rubens's marked interest in foreign costumes and exotic 'types' serve the content very effectively. Powerful stories powerfully told cumulatively add up to an expressive allegory of the saint's life and of the Jesuit mission. Rubens's mastery of light, shade and colour produce a compelling effect in its whole and in details.

The ultimate source for the saint's powers, and the direct agent for the shattering of the idol, is signalled by the light that streams through the heavenly apparition. A foreshortened 'Jesuit' cross is borne by angels, one of whom directly engages the spectator's vision. They are accompanying a figure symbolic of the Catholic faith, with a chalice and globe. The main stream of directional light comes from an unseen source beyond the upper frame of the painting. We may imagine that source to be the Trinity.

Related to Rubens's altarpieces for the church is a portrait-style image of St Ignatius from about the same time (fig.104). A shaft of swift and purposeful light breaks through the clouds of doubt, to convey a vision that is seen and by implication heard. The saint's brocaded chasuble, the gilded thread of which is notably raised, is painted with breathtaking observational acuity and painterly virtuosity, adding impact to the saint's already monumental presence as seen from a low viewpoint. He holds open the notably legible book, the *Institutum Societatis Jesu* (*The Institution of the Society of Jesus*), which opens with Ignatius's motto, *Ad maiorem Dei gloriam* (To the greater glory of God). The saint's head is fringed by an aura of delicately rendered rays of light, indicating that he is a source of divine illumination on his own account.

What Rubens's image of the saint shows is that a masterly ability to transform oil paint into illusions of light, colour and texture can be used to portray divine light with both subtlety and clarity. In this he shares as much with Bellini as he does with the painters of the great Baroque vaults. His *St Ignatius* provides a quiet conclusion to a chapter that has been predominantly clamorous. The relationship of that clamour to theatrical performances follows in the next chapter.

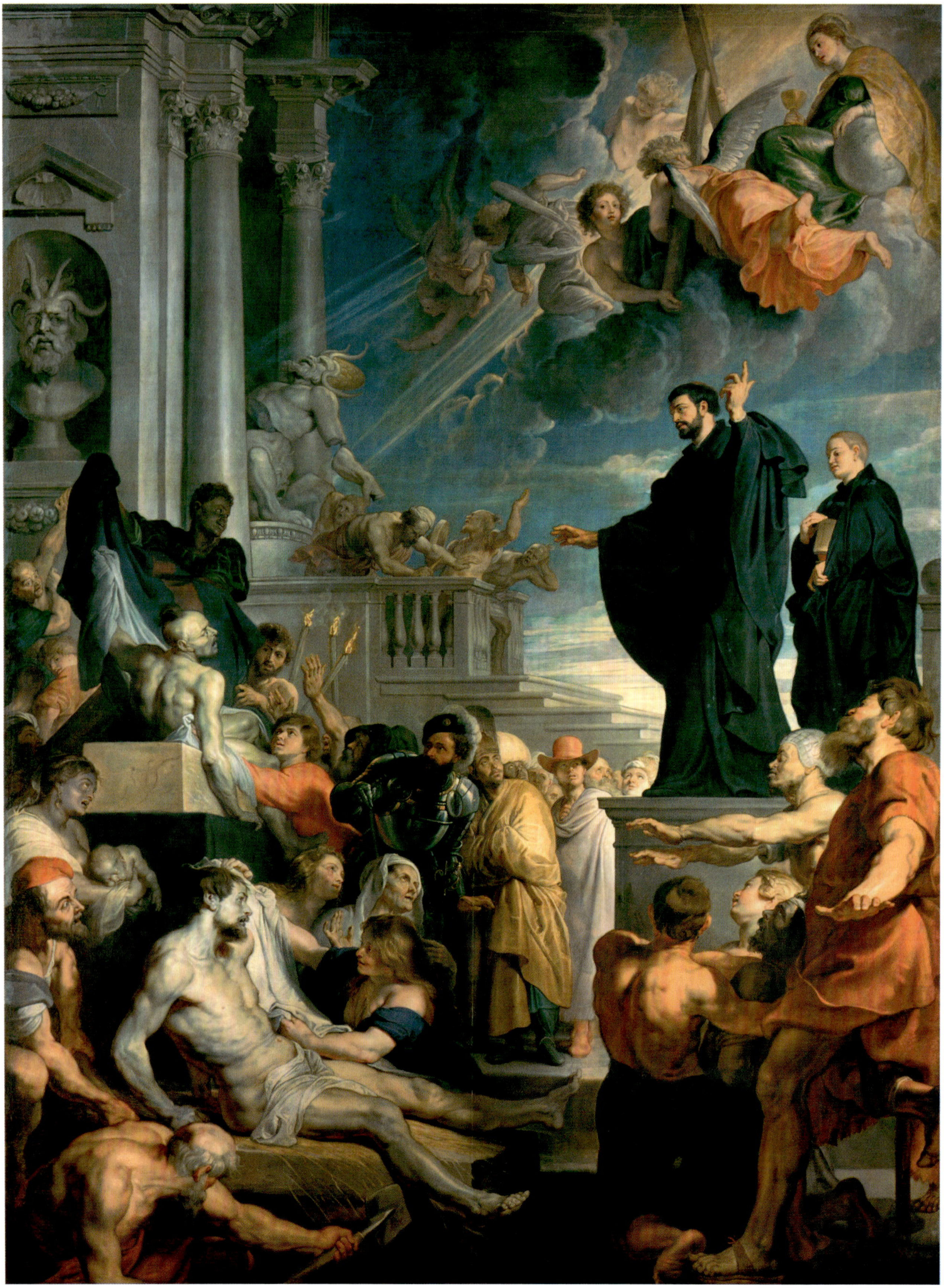

103 (OPPOSITE) Peter Paul Rubens, *A Sacred Allegory of St Francis Xavier*, Vienna, Kunsthistorisches Museum

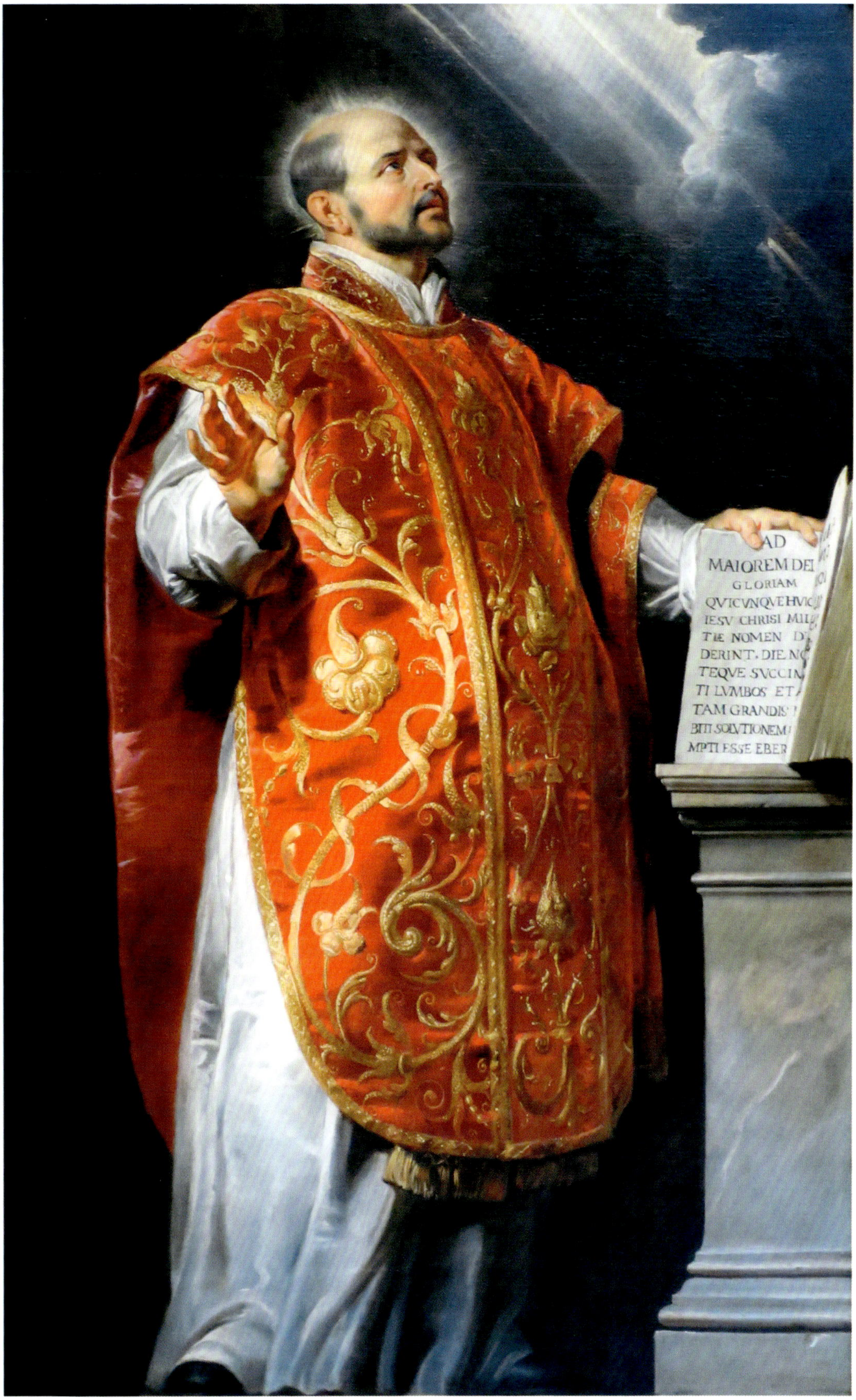

104 Peter Paul Rubens, *St Ignatius*, Pasadena, Norton Simon Museum

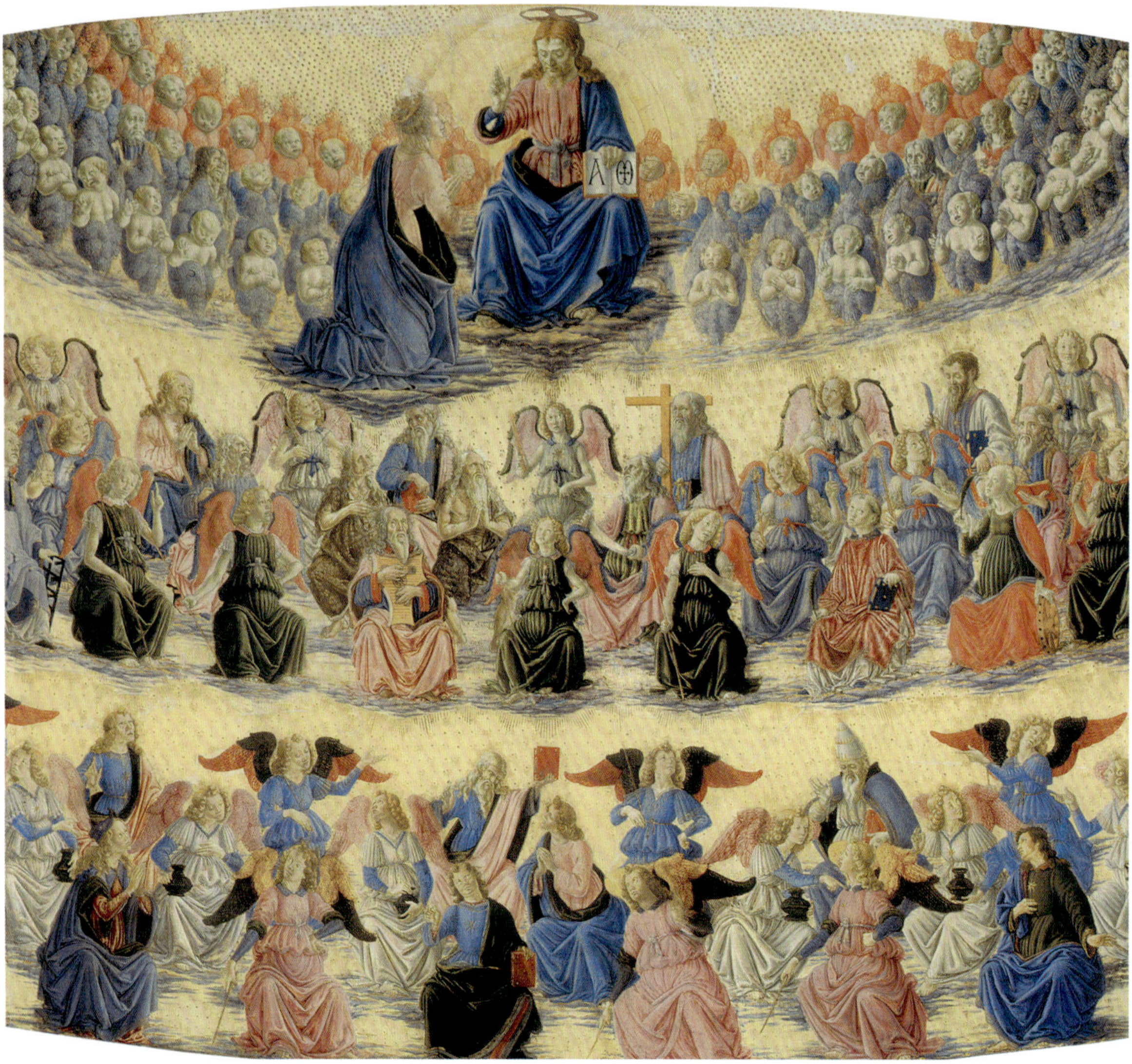

Francesco Botticini, *Assumption of the Virgin* (detail), London, National Gallery

6

Paradise Performed: from the Renaissance to the Baroque

If we look at the range of sacred representations in the public domain, the most striking, popular, dramatic, dynamic, engaging, impressive, exciting and accessible – and the *most costly* – were the theatrical spectaculars staged in streets, squares and churches. They were generally scheduled for important annual feast days. For many people, images of popular saints and the key biblical stories may well have been engraved on their memories by theatrical performances.

Centuries later these remarkable manifestations have left disproportionately meagre visual records, and few adequate written accounts survive, although matters were beginning to improve by 1600. Performances have accordingly received patchy attention from historians of Renaissance painting, sculpture and architecture. In our present quest for visions of heaven, the spectacles are not only of interest in themselves, but they also provide one of the keys to the actual transmission of images of heaven across the centuries from the age of Dante onwards. Chronologically, they effectively span all the preceding chapters. My tactic here is to rely upon some extensive quotations from the few descriptions that survive. The eyewitnesses impart the flavour and impact of the events even if a precise reconstruction of what they saw is not always possible.

Florence was famed for its innovatory spectaculars. They took the form of floats outdoors in the city, and fixed installations in churches. Typically, they were organised by proud and competitive confraternities and staged by specialists in festivals. In his *Lives of the Most Excellent Painters* Giorgio Vasari describes floats designed for the major Florentine feast day of St John the Baptist. The mastermind was the architect, military engineer, inventor and designer Il Cecca (Francesco d'Angelo), who was a specialist in such things (which has not helped his posthumous reputation). He was born in 1447 and killed in battle in 1488. Vasari was writing long after the events, but he was a designer of theatrical spectacles on his own account and he had tried to restore some of the earlier machinery.

Il Cecca began by covering the large piazza in front of the cathedral and around the baptistery with a vast blue cloth embroidered with Florentine lilies and other heraldic motifs. This mighty covering was suspended 14 m (almost 46 ft) above ground. The displays on the floats typically involved aerial assemblies of figures borne aloft on clouds made from planks and cotton-wool. Each confraternity created the 'cloud machines' in their own way, but the standard structure consisted of a framework on which

> two panels were laid crosswise, each one *braccio* wide [a little less than 58 cm (23 in)], with a hole in the middle half a *braccio* in diameter, in which was fixed

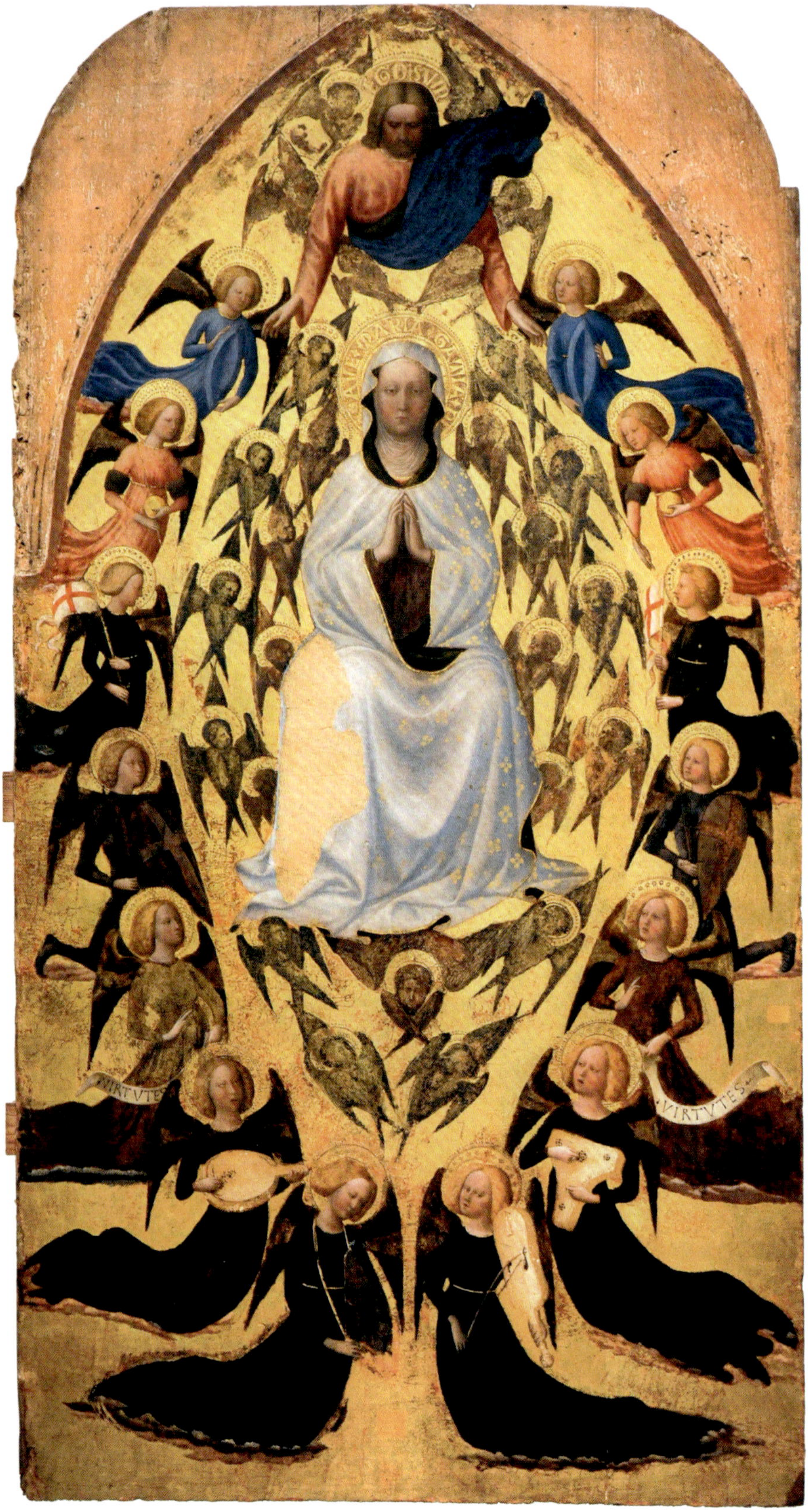

105 Masolino, *Assumption of the Virgin*, Naples, Museo di Capodimonte

> a high pole, whereon there was placed a mandorla all covered with cotton-wool, cherubim, lights, and other ornaments, and within this, on a horizontal bar of iron, there sat or stood, according as might be desired, a person representing that Saint whom the particular Confraternity principally honoured as their peculiar patron and protector – to be exact, a Christ, or a Madonna, or a Saint John, or some other – and the draperies of this figure covered the iron bar in such a manner that it could not be seen. Round the same pole, lower down, below the mandorla, there radiated four or more or fewer iron branches in the manner of a tree, and at the end of each, attached likewise with irons, stood a little boy dressed like an angel. These boys could move round and round as they liked on the iron brackets on which their feet rested, for the brackets were hinged. And with similar branches there were sometimes made two or three tiers of angels or of saints, according to the nature of what was to be represented. The whole of this machinery with the pole and the iron bars, which sometimes represented a lily, sometimes a tree, and often a cloud or some other similar thing, was covered with cotton-wool, and as has been said, with cherubim, seraphim, golden stars, and other suchlike ornaments. Within were porters or peasants, who carried it on their shoulders ... All the machinery, steps, and other things were covered, as has been said above, with cotton-wool, which made a beautiful effect. And all these machines were called Clouds.[1]

It is not hard to set this account beside paintings of the Virgin and other holy figures in mandorlas accompanied by angels. Unusually, we have a document that helps substantiate this impression. It concerns Masolino, a colleague of Masaccio, and records expenses for a Feast of the Ascension in 1425.

> To Masolino the ... painter ... for painting the cloud and for applying the azure and fine gold, lire 2 soldi and 4. To the same ... for painting the angels who turn around the cloud, lire 4 soldi 19 ... To Lionardo da Rigo ironmonger for making the iron screw fixed behind the cloud, lire 4 soldi 10. To the same for having the lights below and to the side of the cloud made, lire 4 soldi 10. To Antonio di Bartolo ... for sheets to make the angels of the cloud, lire 3 ... For 4 pairs of red stockings for 4 boys who went up by the ropes ...[2]

We can accompany this description with Masolino's image of the Virgin in a mandorla for an altarpiece in Santa Maria Maggiore in Rome in 1428 (fig.105). If we then add a drawing by the engineer Bonaccorso Ghiberti, grandson of the famous sculptor, we can complete the picture (fig.106). It shows an engineered mandorla with a pair of pulleys and a light that can be moved up and down, as Ghiberti explains in his *Zibaldone* or notebook. Lights that inexplicably appeared and disappeared were features of the theatrical designs within the churches, and were described in Vasari's account of the Annunciation apparatus.

The major performances in churches in Florence were concentrated each year to the south of the River Arno. San Felice in Piazza staged the Annunciation; the Assumption of the Virgin and the Ascension of Christ were mounted in Santa Maria del Carmine (where Masaccio and Masolino painted the Brancacci Chapel); and the Pentecost in Santo Spirito, which was to be rebuilt by Brunelleschi. For the Annunciation and Ascension, we are fortunate to have enthusiastic and detailed descriptions by Abraham of Suzdal, a Russian bishop who was visiting Florence for the Church Council in 1439. He praised the Annunciation as a 'marvellous spectacle'.[3] He does not specifically name the designer, who was 'a certain clever man, Italian by birth'.

> The scaffold was meant to represent the heavenly spheres from where the Archangel Gabriel is sent down to the Virgin by God the Father; on the top

Suzdal describes the mechanisms in some detail:

> High above [the Mount of Olives] is a wooden structure about 4 sagenes[10] square [6.1 sq m (65 sq ft)] and 8 sagenes high [12.2 m (40 ft)], beautifully painted underneath and on the sides. In the middle of the upper part of this structure is a large round opening, 2 sagenes in diameter [3 m (10 ft)], draped with a blue curtain, on which the sun, the moon and the surrounding stars are painted: a representation of the first celestial sphere. At the appointed time this drape is lifted, that is, the doors of Heaven are opened, and above is seen a man with a crown on his head, just like God the Father; he is supported in such a wondrous fashion over the doors of Heaven lowering his gaze down over the Mount of Olives, where his divine Son, the Holy Virgin, and the Apostles are gathered, and blessing them with his hand. He seems, as he hovers in the air, not to be supported by anything. Around him is a throng of little children who represent angels with pipes and lutes and lots of tiny bells, and in their midst numerous tiny candles. And beside the Heavenly Father and the children is fixed, against the opening which represents Heaven, a paper disc, whose lower edge touches that of the opening: on it are painted life-size angels. From the opening of Heaven down to the Mount of Olives run seven fine strong cords with ingenious iron pulleys. From these a young man, representing Christ in the act of ascending to the Father, is pulled up.[11]

Christ then undergoes Transfiguration and ascends to heaven, in elaboration of the biblical narratives.

> A peal of thunder is heard, Christ appears on the Mount, and all turn their eyes upwards to see Heaven open and God the Father floating above, suspended in the air in wondrous fashion, in a great light, which comes from innumerable lamps; the little boys, who represent the heavenly Powers, move around him to the sounds of deafening music and sweet singing; the big painted angels on the discs move in the shape of a circle so that they seem to be alive. From Heaven where God the Father is there descends on the seven ropes an exceedingly beautiful and cleverly constructed cloud: it is round and surrounded by swiftly turning discs. To the right and to the left are two children dressed as angels, with golden wings. When the cloud is half-way down ... he [Jesus] goes up with the help of the seven ropes in the direction of the cloud, blessing Mary and the Apostles with his hand ... When he approaches the cloud, this envelops him from head to foot, the two angels bow before him on the left and the right, and in the same instant the cloud is lit up by a multitude of lights which shed their splendour everywhere ... Jesus goes higher and higher, accompanied by the two Angels, and soon he steps out next to the God the Father, the music ceases and it grows dark.[12]

If we reconstruct, as best we can, what would have been seen in the two *feste* described by the bishop, the time-based narrative, the actual motion of the figures in space, the circling heavens and the dramatic light effects add crucial dimensions to our *paragone* with Dante.

Again, we can readily look to 15th-century paintings for comparable visions of radiant heavens; Fra Angelico and Botticelli come to mind. But there is one remarkable painting that seems to transcribe the theatrical set-up in a more direct way than any other. The *Assumption of the Virgin* by Francesco Botticini in the National Gallery, London, offers the most concrete link between Dante, the cloud machinery and paintings of the layered orbits of the heavens – indeed it serves as a kind of missing link (fig.107). It is distinctly idiosyncratic – perhaps all missing links are. Its horizontal format is remarkable. The painting measures 3.75 m (over 12 ft) wide. It originally occupied much of the end wall of the south transept of the now demolished Church of San Pier Maggiore in Florence, where the donor, Matteo Palmieri, was buried. He kneels to left, in front of a skilfully presented view of Florence, with his wife, Niccolosa, to the right. It must have created quite an immersive experience, and still looks unexpected in an art gallery alongside other Renaissance paintings. It is worth looking at in some detail.

Palmieri was a notable figure, prominent in the Medici circle and serving the city in major political roles. He is famed for his treatise *Della vita civile* (*On Civic Life*), which is a key statement of civic humanism, in which he stresses that a man of learning (above all a scholar with a knowledge of the classics) should actively engage with the affairs of his city. That he wrote it in Tuscan not Latin was itself an important statement. The commission for the painting in 1475 came at the end of his life and was seen to its conclusion by his widow in 1477. Kneeling on the right, Niccolosa is dressed in the Benedictine habit of the nuns of San Pier Maggiore, which indicates that she entered into a special arrangement with the convent after her husband's death. Understanding the altarpiece involves another posthumous dimension.

In the middle years of the century, Palmieri had written an extraordinary sacred poem, *La città di vita* (*The City of Life*), in close emulation of Dante's *Commedia* in three books, 100 chapters and written in rhyming sections of three lines.[13] But it is a Dante for a new century, and advocates novel theological views that he knew were sensitive. His friend Leonardo Dati, head of the Dominicans in Florence, wrote a laudatory Latin preface. However, Palmieri stipulated that *La città* should not be made public until after his death. When it did gain some exposure, it was quite widely censured and it is not hard to see why.

Palmieri adapted the views of Origen from the third century to the effect that God created a huge but finite number of souls or 'intelligences', all of whom were devoted to God. In time the souls separated into three kinds: those who retained their devotion; those whose love had cooled but was still present; and those who had become remote from God and were transformed into demons. Those souls in the middle rank were in due course to be united with their earthly bodies where they pursued their human life with greater or lesser degrees of virtue. Palmieri adapted this basic scheme, and granted the souls who were undecided the option to join either the fallen or heavenly angels. These intermediate souls waited to pass into the material world, and passed downwards through the planetary spheres, picking up characteristics along the way. They were given the generous chance of three lives to make the right choice.

Palmieri's three books trace the journey of the soul, guided by the Cumaean Sibyl and then by an angel, but the narrative differs significantly from Dante's. Book one is devoted to the nature of God, the angels and the souls and their descending voyage of incarnation. The journey of the second book deals with the hierarchies of sinners. The entry to the third book, now under the guidance of a good angel, is marked by the intense sun of the summer solstice. The climax comes in Dantesque fashion with a heavenly vision of the Virgin and Christ, and ultimately of God, accompanied by ranks of adoring angels. The vision portrayed by Botticini blends the penultimate image with the Virgin's reception by Christ after her Assumption (fig.107). There is a stark separation between the gilded heaven on a grandly expansive scale and the landscape of the natural world, within which the disciples react with bewilderment at the sight of the open tomb, now full of lilies.

If we look in detail at the three rings of angels, sitting and standing on rather uncloud-like banks of clouds, we find that they are interspersed with ordinary mortals (fig.108). Some, towards the front of the lowest rank, look distinctly undivine, while others have small nimbuses of rays, like the angels. In the second rank, the earthly figures are recognisable as saints or prophets, such as David with his harp below the Virgin. Amongst the cherubim and seraphim in the upper realm are just four 'humans', identifiable on the left as St Peter

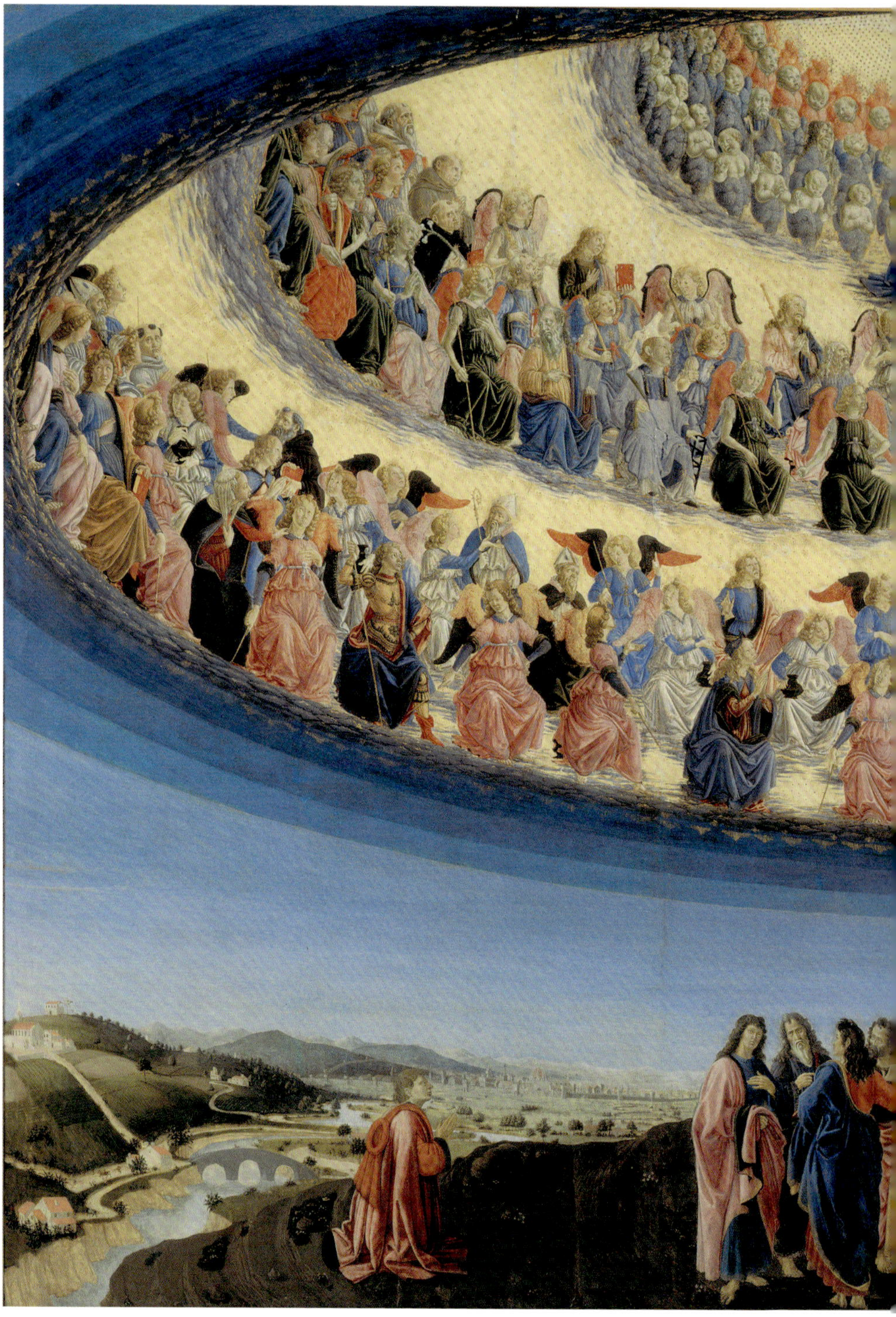

107 Francesco Botticini, *Assumption of the Virgin*, London, National Gallery

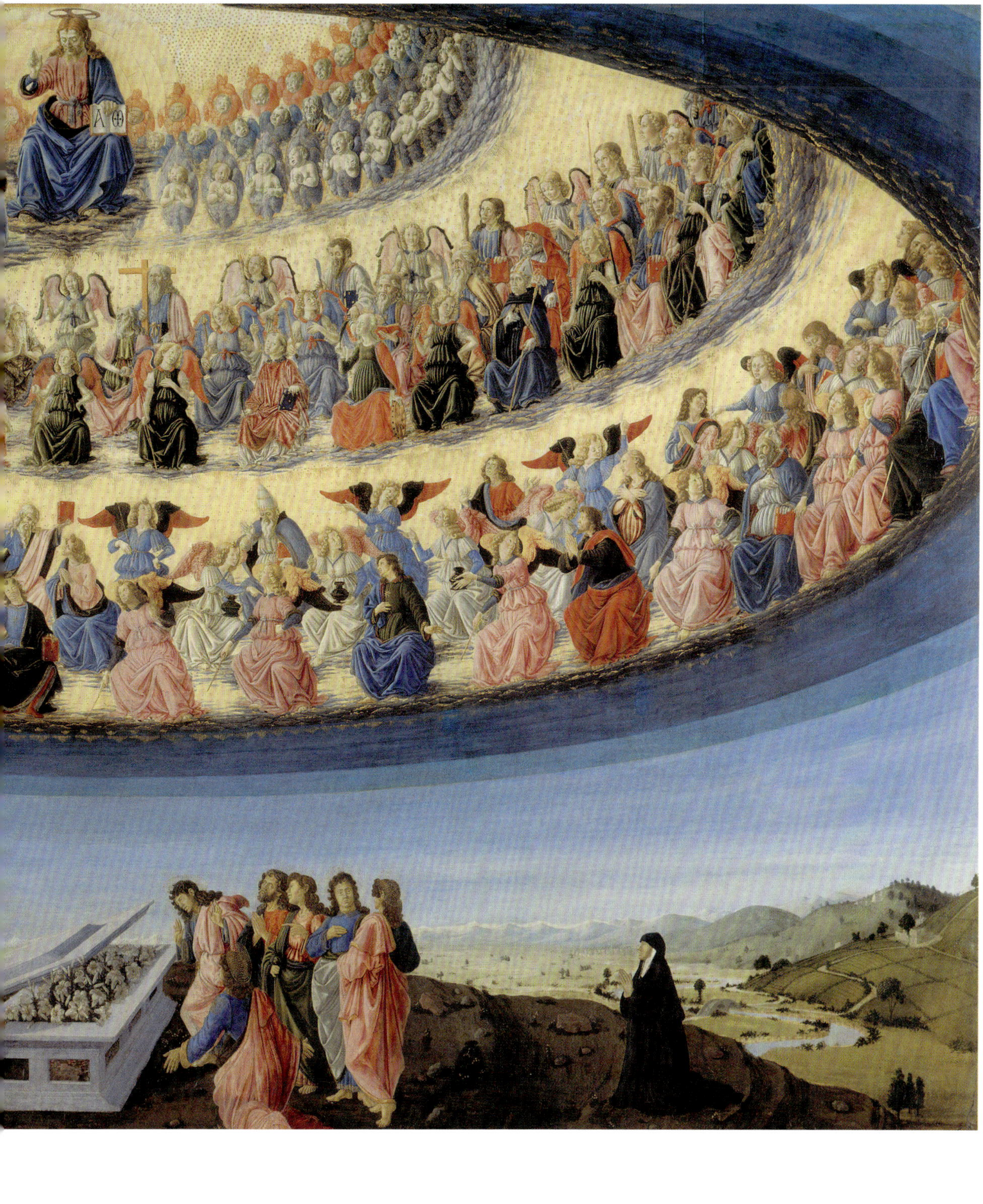

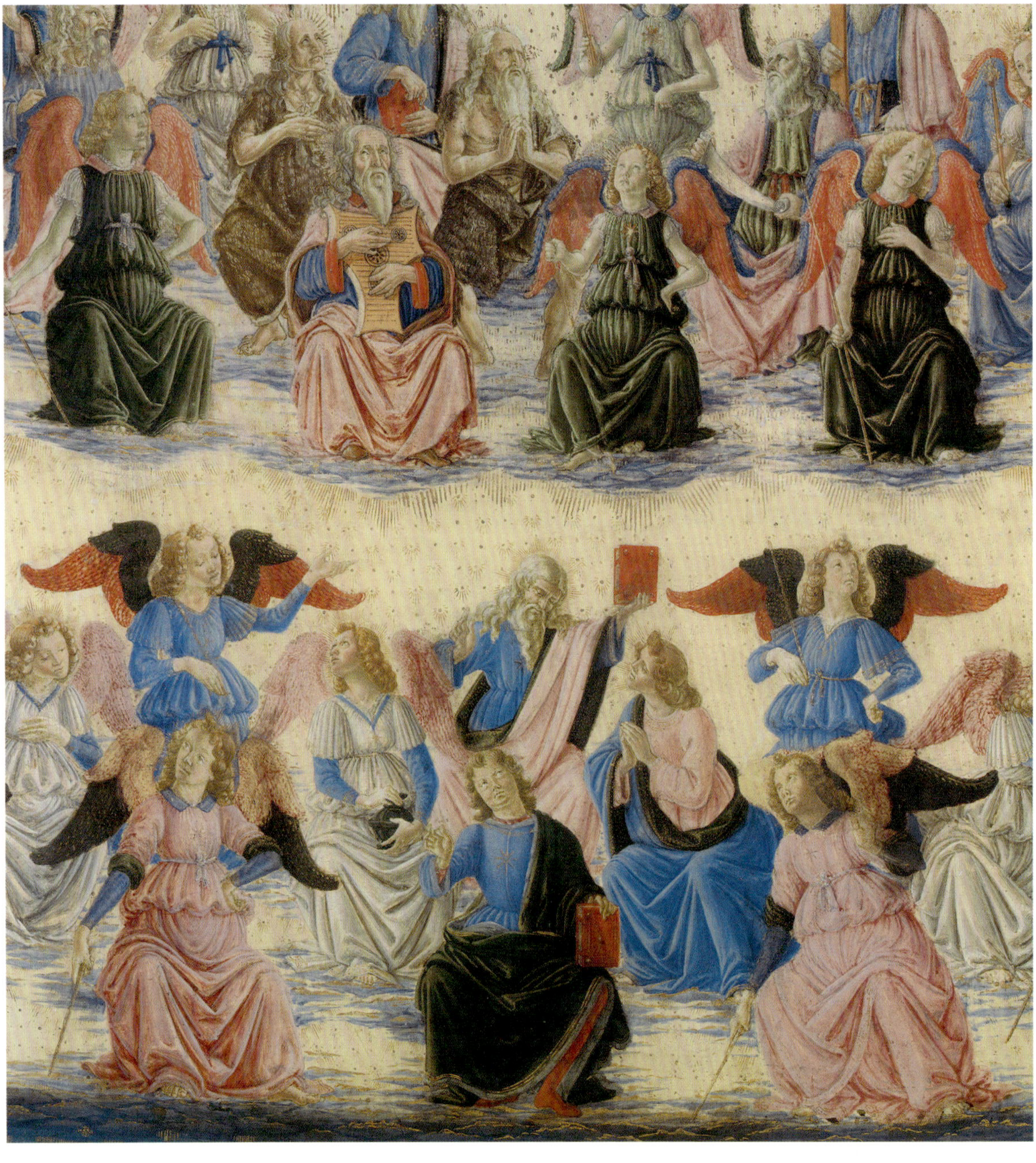

108 Francesco Botticini, *Assumption of the Virgin*, detail of the two lower rings, London, National Gallery

and St John the Baptist, and on the right as St Paul (probably) and Mary Magdalene with a jar of ointment. The hierarchical intermingling of people and angels corresponds closely to Palmieri's ideas of incarnated intelligences who are striving for salvation. Palmieri must have exercised quite strict control over the form and content of his painting.

The importance of Palmieri's altarpiece is not just that it represents a notable episode in how Dante's *Commedia* was reworked in the later 15th century, but it also brings together a Dantesque vision of heaven, the theatrical *paradisi* and painted imagery. Botticini's portrayal of the layered cloud platforms could hardly be more evident. The large painting must have been something of a sensation, if not stylistically (it is quite laboured in draughtsmanship), then in terms of its overall set-up. As we will see, it is an obvious ancestor of some key later schemes.

During the course of the 15th century, the Florentine spectaculars were taken up by rulers in the enterprising northern courts and converted to perform dynastic functions. Most famous is the Milanese *Festa del Paradiso* staged in 1490 for the marriage of Gian Galeazzo Sforza (the young and nominal Duke of Milan) to Isabella of Aragon. The libretto was written by the poet Bernardo Bellincioni and the design was by his fellow Tuscan Leonardo da Vinci, who was maestro of visual effects at the Sforza court. Bellincioni acknowledged that the setting was 'made with great brilliance and skill by Maestro Leonardo Vinci, the Florentine'. It showed 'all the seven planets, which turned, and the planets were represented by men'.[14] The *paradiso* in this case was that of the ancient gods rather than the Trinity, with Jupiter playing the role of God the Father. A later stage design by Leonardo for a performance of *Orpheus* also used the term *paradiso* for the underground realm of Pluto. The term clearly made reference to the theatrical set-up rather than the content.

Fortunately, there is an eyewitness account of the 1490 *festa*:

> The Paradise was made to resemble half an egg [displayed hollow side forward] which from the edge inwards was completely covered with gold, with a very great number of lights representing stars, with certain gaps where the seven planets were situated, according to their high or low ranks. Around the upper edge of the aforesaid hemisphere were the twelve signs [of the Zodiac] . . . All of which made a fine and beautiful sight. In the Paradise were many singers, accompanied by many sweet and refined sounds.[15]

The reflected lights sparkling in the golden orb and the rotating planets must have created a ravishing effect. This is the first certain account we have of a solid half-dome of the heavens suspended above the spectators' heads.

Such spectaculars were taken up in other north Italian courts – at least by those who could afford them. A *paradiso* was staged in Ferrara with a mechanised Annunciation to mark the marriage of Duke Alfonso d'Este and Lucrezia Borgia in 1503. Isabella d'Este wrote a letter in which she describes the machine as a 'very expensive and luxurious apparatus made of wood'.

> Suddenly a sky was opened where one could see a person resembling God the Father, and it was impossible to discern what he rested upon. Around him there were angels rotating slowly, and it was hard to see where their feet rested. There were also six angels hovering in the air hooked to iron bars. In the middle was the Angel Gabriel, supported by another iron bar. God spoke to him. After having received the divine order, by means of an admirable trick, Gabriel went down on to the top of the organ . . . Gabriel descended thanks to invisible iron bars in such a way that it appeared that his feet were resting on a cloud. After he delivered his message, he returned to the sky with the other angels and one could hear songs and music all around. One could also hear these spirits reading some passages

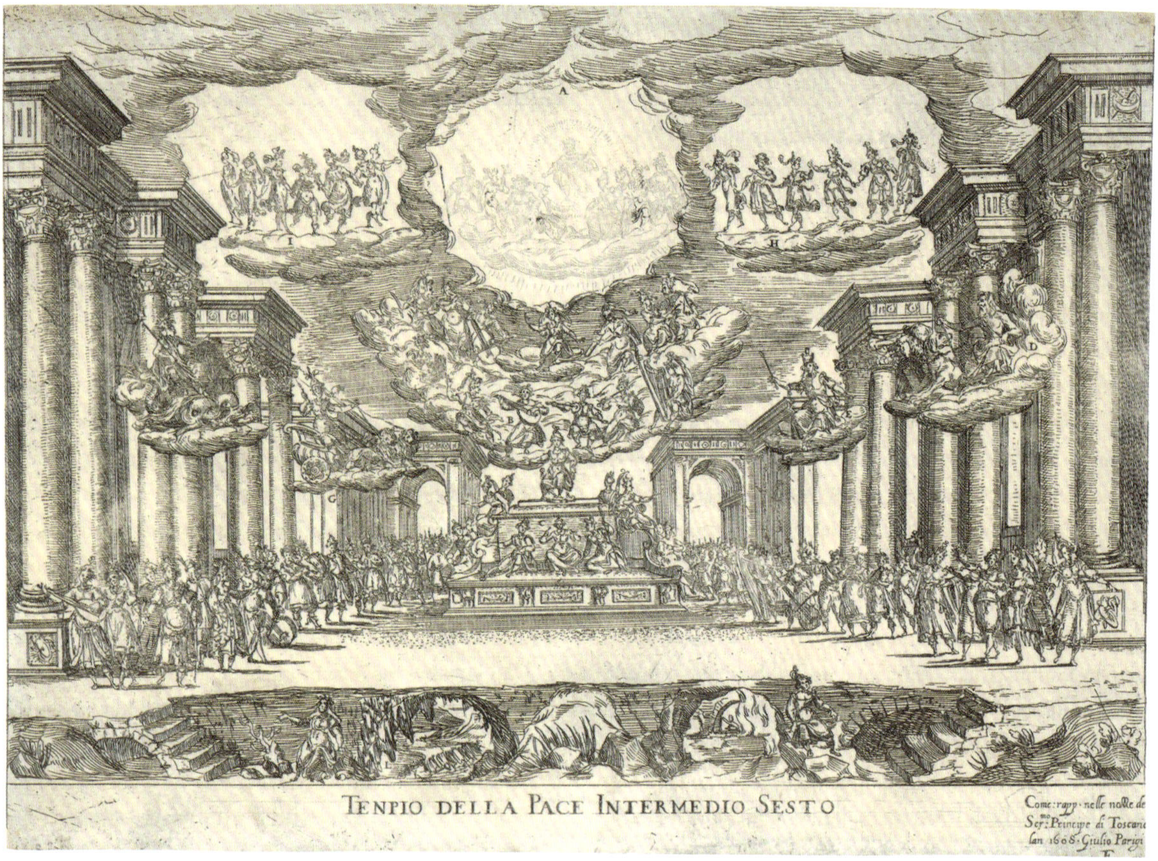

109 Giulio Parigi, *The Temple of Peace from the Sixth Intermedio for Il Giudizio di Paride*, etched by Remigo Catagallina, New York, Metropolitan Museum

If we think back to the Bishop of Suzdal's account of the Annunciation in San Felice, we can only conclude that they were describing different events. It seems likely that Vasari's account of Brunelleschi's *festa* is an imaginative reconstruction that conflates it with his own later design. We are better thinking that the Bishop of Sudzal's account is our best record of what the 1439 performance actually looked like. Brunelleschi might well have been responsible for it, but even this is not absolutely certain.

The Florentine court of the Medici Grand Dukes also developed the *paradisi* as a secular genre. From the 1550s, Giorgio Vasari was in charge of much of the court theatre staged in the great hall of the Palazzo Vecchio, the former government palace where the Medici had transferred their domestic and governmental activities. A permanent theatre was constructed in the Uffizi by Bernardo Buontalenti, whose career had been fostered by Vasari. Bernardo was a highly inventive architect, engineer and designer of all kinds of courtly delights, who was in turn succeeded by Giulio Parigi, who ran his own academy of design. Their schemes for various kinds of *paradisi* paid clear homage to their historical antecedents, but also introduced innovations of form and scale. The Medicean secular spectacles were now staged as *intermedi* or *intermezzi* (intermissions) in stage plays, which came to attract more attention and expense than the plays themselves. They were characterised by remarkable machinery, special effects, brilliant white and coloured lights, dance and delightful music. The subject matter of the court *feste* was secular.

We are increasingly well informed about later *paradisi*, not least with the publication of the first specialised treatise on scene design by Niccolò Sabbatini in 1638. His *Pratica di fabricar scene e machine ne' teatri* (*Practice of Making Scenery and Machinery for Theatres*) synthesises what had been happening over the course of a century or so. He describes an important development, perhaps dating back to Vasari, in which a large aperture high in a backcloth, initially covered over with a painted sky, opened to reveal a luminous vision of the heavens populated by divinities. We may recall the central vision of Giovanni di San Giovanni's Roman dome (figs 73–4). The motions of the cloud platforms were orchestrated in ever more surprising and fluent ways. Large numbers of elaborately costumed performers were involved. Official descriptions and prints began to be published to ensure that the magnificence of the ephemeral spectacles, with their financial extravagance, should not be lost to posterity.

One example will stand for many: an etching from 1608 documents the sixth *intermedio*, the 'Temple of Peace', that Parigi designed for a performance of *Il Giudizio di Paride* (*The Judgement of Paris*) (fig.109). This was staged to celebrate the marriage of the frail but intellectual Grand Duke Cosimo II to the Archduchess Maria Maddalena of Austria. The libretto was written by Michelangelo Buonarotti the Younger (the artist's grandnephew).[20] The composer was the madrigalist, Giovanni Battista Strozzi the Younger. The subject matter – the beauty competition in which Paris judges between Venus, Pallas, Athena and Juno – sets the tone for a dazzling display of visual delights. The print shows a massive perspectival stage set, teaming with musicians and allegorical figures. Within the two high lateral openings in the sky, men and women dance with elegance, while in the centre we begin to see the heavenly apparition that was previously concealed. The print cleverly implies the radiant glare as the central figure-group moves forwards through the opened aperture in the backdrop. The libretto indicates that cast of leading soloists was accompanied by a chorus of nymphs and shepherds. The print confirms that large numbers of instrumentalists were involved. We can well believe that the spectators in the Uffizi theatre, numbering about 3000 people, were royally entertained.

There is no great problem in linking the Florentine innovations in religious and secular spectacles to the Roman vaults and domes. We have already seen that the Florentine Giovanni di San Giovanni, who played a key role in Rome, had worked in the Parigi organisation. Pietro da Cortona was trained in Florence by Andrea Commodi, who was involved in theatrical design and painted an illusionist semi-dome in Rome. Commodi was a pupil of Ludovico Cigoli. They were both involved with stage and festival design, working with Buontalenti. Cigoli included a section on the geometry of perspectival stage sets in his erudite technical treatise *Prospettiva pratica*. On moving to Rome, Cigoli undertook a key experiment in illusionist dome design in his *Assumption of the Virgin* in the Pauline Chapel in Santa Maria Maggiore in Rome (fig.110). For once, Correggio does not appear to be the obvious source of inspiration.

Supervised by a seated God the Father in the small dome of the lantern, the Virgin is encircled by foreshortened angels of various kinds, some of whom occupy platform-clouds while others fly freely against a background of nine celestial rings. Small *putti* cling to the garland around the base of the lantern, a motif that was followed in other domes. The Apostles stand rather inconspicuously on a ledge around the base of the dome. The Virgin herself is emphatically present, as the woman of Apocalypse, crowned with 12 stars, standing on the moon and over a coiled snake lurking in a shadow. We can imagine her being cranked upwards to heaven by cloud machinery.

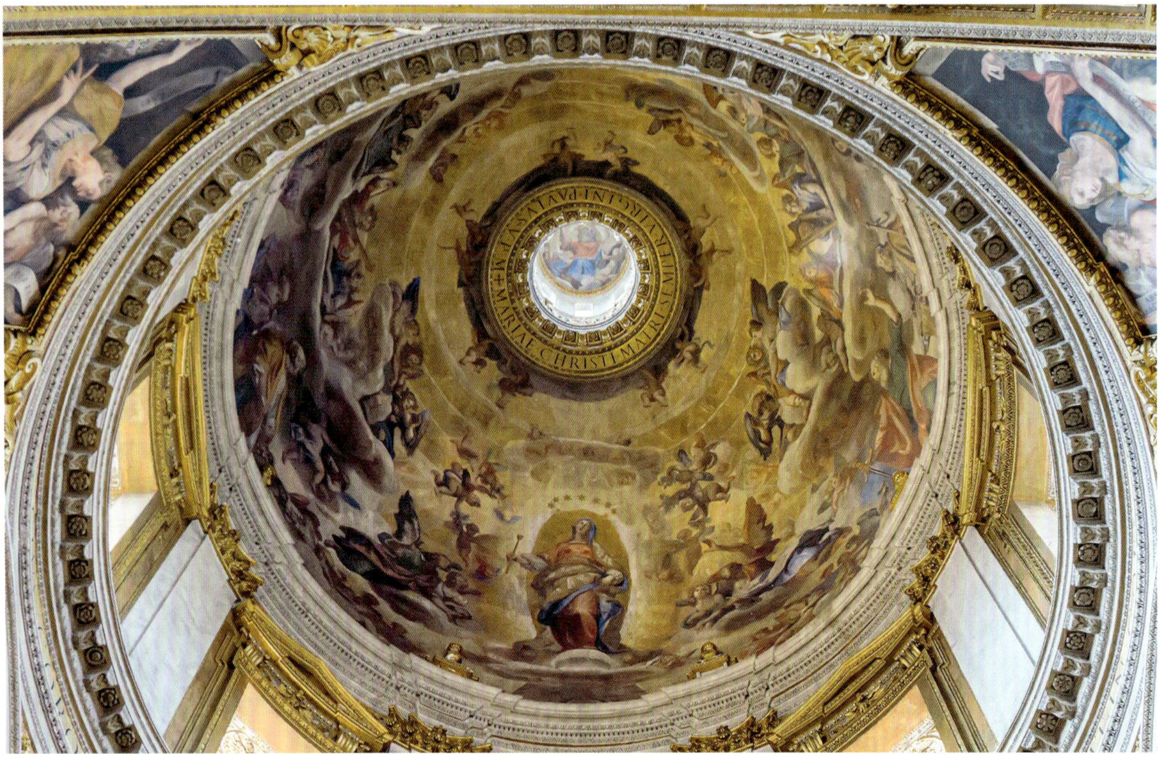

110 Ludovico Cigoli, *Assumption of the Virgin*, oblique view, Rome, Santa Maria Maggiore, Pauline Chapel

Her moon, remarkably, is pitted with craters in keeping with the revolutionary telescopic observations published in 1510 by Cigoli's friend Galileo, whose treaty the *Sidereus nuncius* (*Starry Messenger*) was dedicated to Grand Duke Cosimo II de' Medici. We have seen that Cosimo's marriage was celebrated with Parigi's designs. Cigoli was one of the artists involved in designs of temporary architecture for the wedding; it was a small world. Mary is portrayed within a kind of frameless gold mandorla set off against a blue fringe. She is seen from below but not sharply foreshortened and seems rather detached from the angelic throng. She only makes spatial sense when seen from a pronouncedly oblique view. It is an uneasy solution, and the artist himself was said to have been deeply unhappy with it once the scaffold and the platform for painting had been taken down.

Cigoli may well have exploited his perspectival drawing instrument, which was the most automated device of its kind (fig.111). The draughtsman looks through an adjustable eye-hole at the object to be represented, in this case a cube. With his left hand he pulls a looped string that moves the upright axis laterally across a horizontal rod. With his other hand, holding a rounded block with a sharp 'beak', he pulls a string that passes under the horizontal frame, up the vertical rod and over a pulley from where it terminates in a hanging weight. A sighting bead is located on the

111 Ludovico Cigoli, *Prospettiva practica*, frontispiece (and detail), Florence, Uffizi, Gabinetto Disegni e Stampe, Codice 2660A

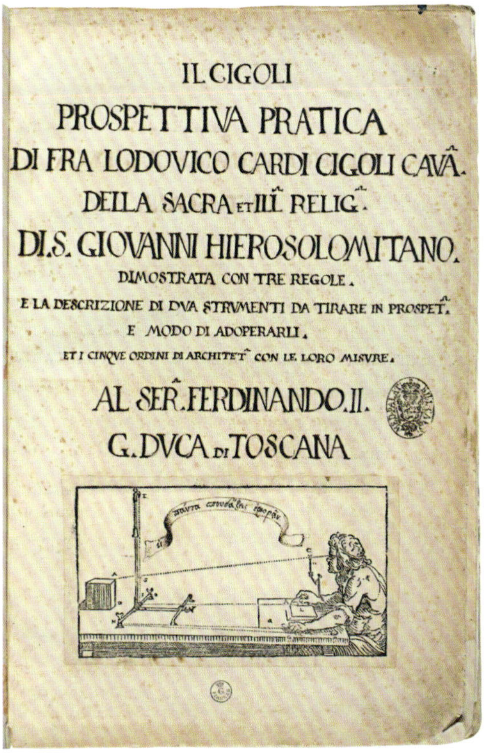

IL CIGOLI
PROSPETTIVA PRATICA
DI FRA LODOVICO CARDI CIGOLI CAVÂ.
DELLA SACRA ET ILLE RELIG.^NE
DI.S. GIOVANNI HIEROSOLOMITANO.
DIMOSTRATA CON TRE REGOLE.
E LA DESCRIZIONE DI DVA STRVMENTI DA TIRARE IN PROSPET.^A
E MODO DI ADOPERARLI.
ET I CINQVE ORDINI DI ARCHITET.^A CON LE LORO MISVRE.
AL SER.^MO FERDINANDO.II.
G. DVCA DI TOSCANA

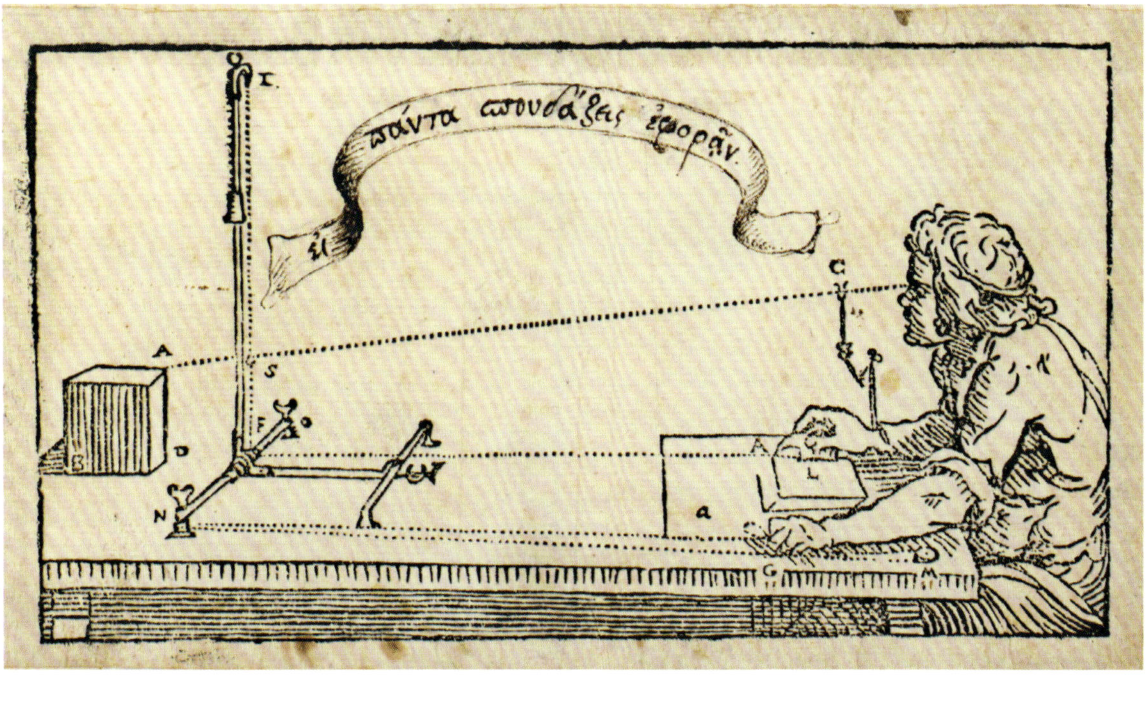

upright section of the string. Coordinating the motions of both hands, which requires some practice, the bead can be aligned by eye with key points of the object, and those points marked on a drawing surface with the sharp 'beak', held in the draughtsman's right hand. The resultant marks will provide the key markers for a perspectival projection of the object, in this case a cube.

Cigoli also shows how the perspectograph can be used in reverse, working from an existing drawing and projecting it onto a wall (fig.112). Used in this mode, a second pair of hands is needed. He also explains that the system of projection can be used on curved surfaces. He shows the instrument tilted in such a way that he can inst ruct his assistant – perched precariously on a stool placed on a beam fixed through a post-hole – to transfer the drawing on to a dome or vault. Using it for this purpose seems rather ponderous. I wonder if he reserved it for the figure of the Virgin, before the painting platform was in place, which would have obscured the surface of the dome from ground level. Or maybe he made a scaled drawing on a curved surface for transfer to the vault. Even if the result was not wholly successful, the design of the dome fresco is a very Florentine-style enterprise.

How does Dante relate to this story, if at all? An important link is through Cigoli's close friend Galileo Galilei. In 1588, the year in which he was granted the post of lecturer in mathematics at Pisa, the 24-year-old Galileo had been invited by the Florentine Academy to deliver two lectures 'On the Shape, Location and Size of Dante's *Inferno*.' His task involved studying the alternative schemes of Alessandro Vellutello, the writer and editor of Dante, and Antonio Manetti, the architect and biographer of Brunelleschi. He concluded decisively in favour of Manetti's earlier solution – though he later admitted that he needed to revise his calculations. Given Cigoli's expertise in architecture and things spatial, it is virtually certain that the two men discussed the matter. There are two fine drawings in the Uffizi of a Dantesque Lucifer by Cigoli from the later 1590s, one of which is highly finished and provided the basis for an engraving by Cornelis Galle, incorporating texts by Manetti on the dimensions of *Inferno*.[21] A monstrous Lucifer, ingesting and egesting a succession of sinners, had featured in the fourth *intermezzo* for a performance of *La pellegrina* (*The Pilgrim*) by Girolamo Bargagli, staged for the wedding of Ferdinando de' Medici to Christina of Lorraine in 1589, a year after Galileo's lecture.[22] Galileo calculated the height of Lucifer at a massive 1180 m (3871 ft). Given these conjunctions, it is difficult to imagine that Dante's vision of the Virgin in the final canto of *Paradiso* was not in Cigoli's mind as he pondered the imagery of his dome.

Whatever the success or failure of Cigoli's *Assumption*, it and its author were active players in what was a crucial period of experiments with dome illusions in Rome at the end of the 16th century and beginning of the next. There was no shortage of participants in the visual debate in a remarkable burst of dome and ceiling painting. They included Andrea Commodi, who was the teacher of Pietro da Cortona; the Alberti brothers, Cherubino and Giovanni, who specialised in perspectival effects; Matteo Zaccolini, a Leonardesque theorist of the science of art; Cristoforo Roncalli, whose great dome in the Basilica of the Santa Casa at Loreto no longer exists, Niccolò Circignani, who was associated with the Jesuits; Giovanni di San Giovanni and Giovanni Lanfranco. Nowadays, these once high-ranking painters are of little renown outside specialist circles.

Central to the experiments was Federico Zuccari, an internationally prominent painter and theorist. In 1595, he became the founding president of the Accademia di San Luca in Rome (the painters' academy) and in 1607 he published his erudite *L'idea de' pittori, scultori ed architetti* (*The Idea of the Painters, Sculptors and Architects*). His first experience of dome painting could hardly have been in a more prestigious location. He completed the massive *Last Judgement* in the dome of Florence Cathedral, a project that had been planned and begun by Vasari in 1572. The iconographic programme was devised by

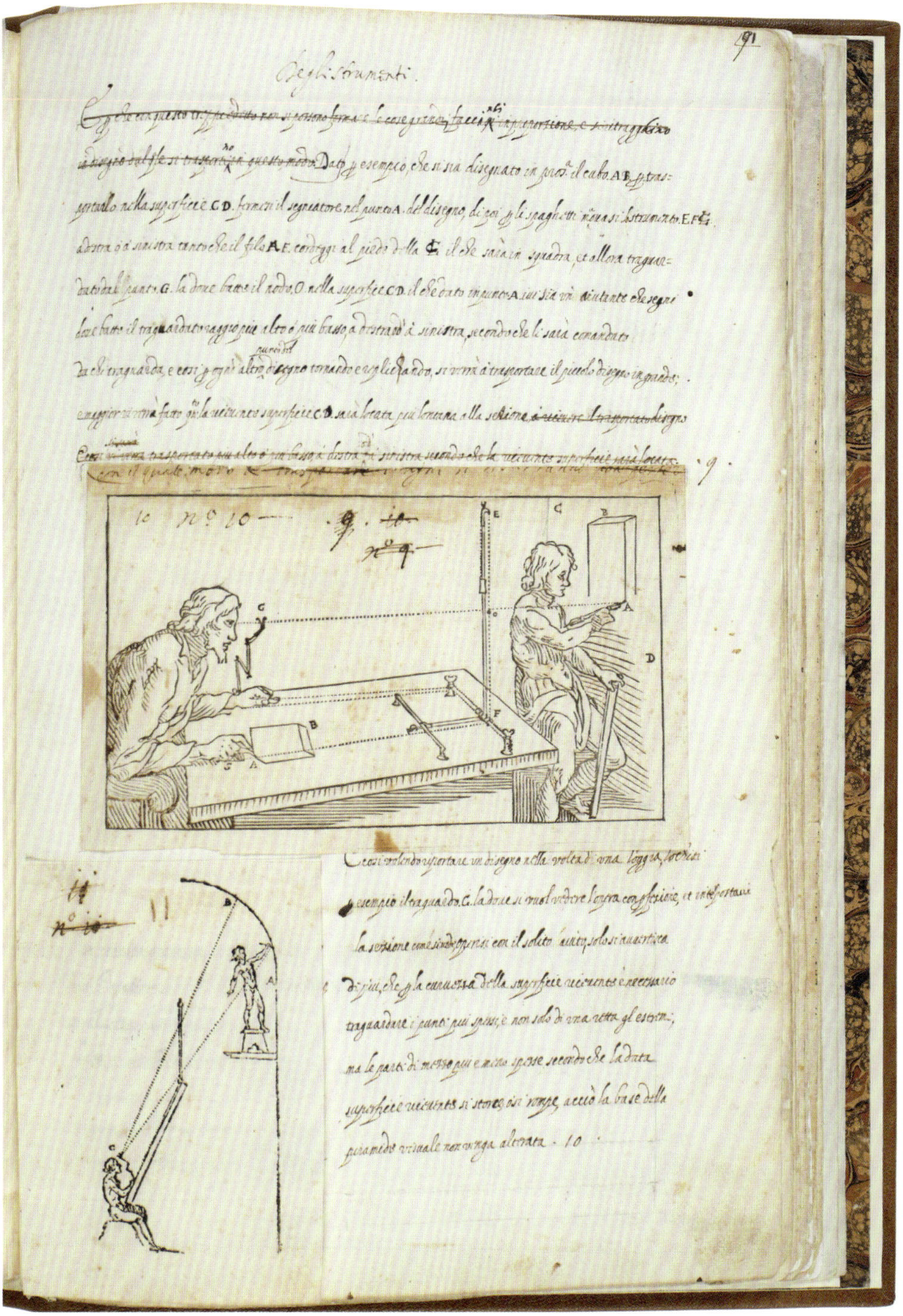

112 Ludovico Cigoli, *Prospettiva practica*, perspectograph used to project a drawing on to flat and curved surfaces, Florence, Uffizi, Gabinetto Disegni e Stampe, Codice 2660A, fol. 91r

113 (NEXT SPREAD) Cappella degli Angeli with paintings by Federico Zuccari, Rome, Il Gesù

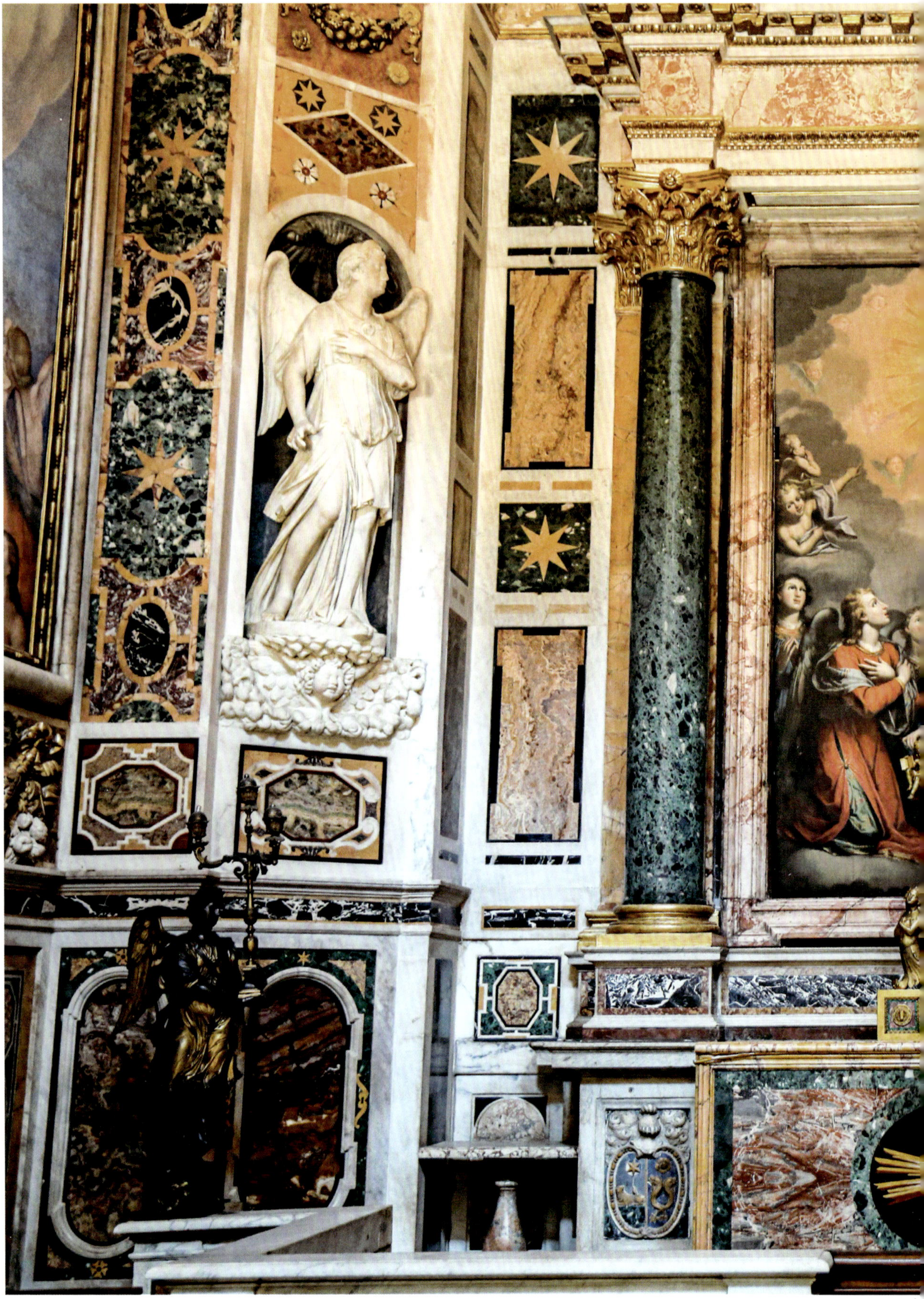

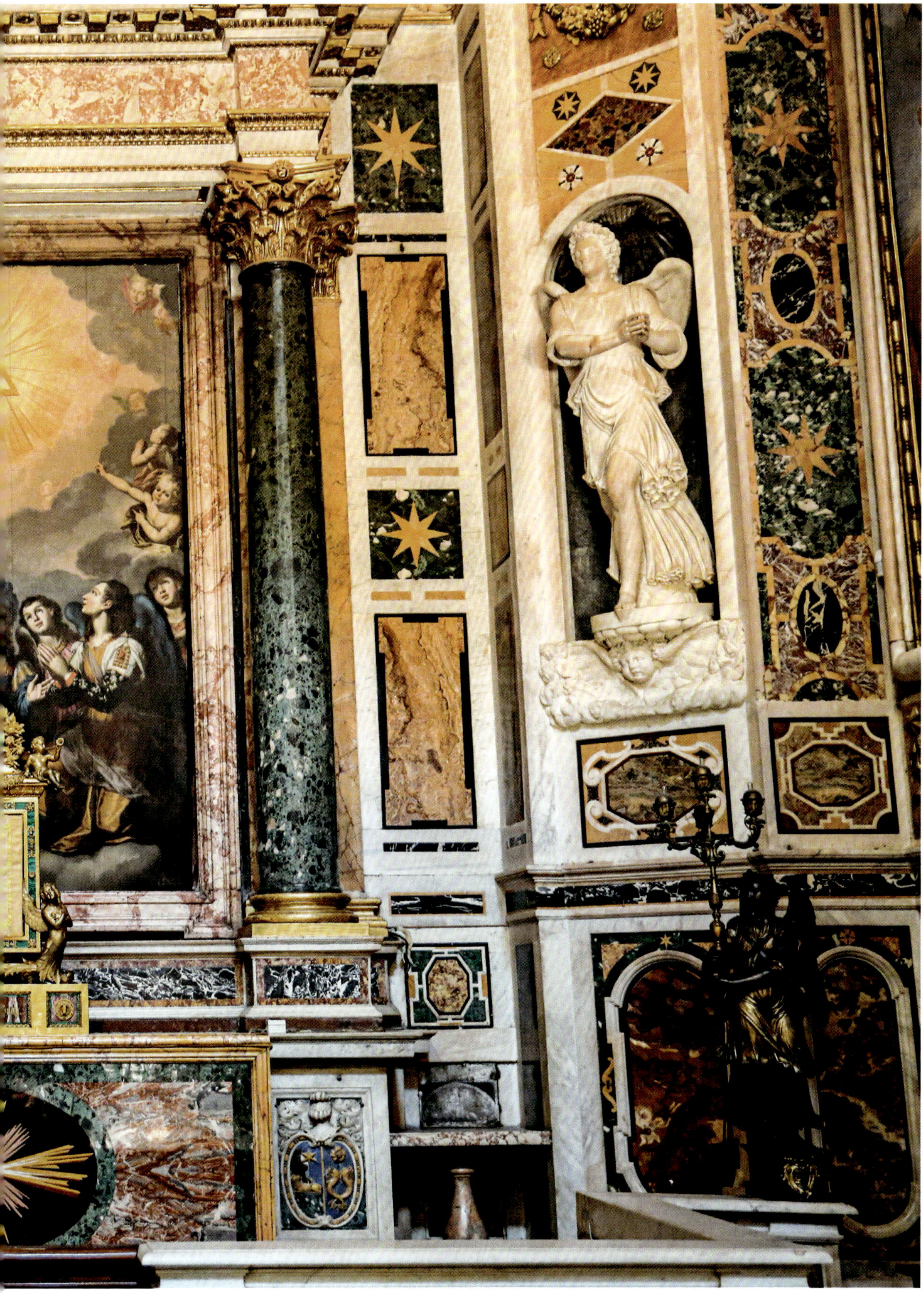

Vincenzo Borghini, a Florentine intellectual and chief officer of the Accademia del Disegno in Florence, the first ever artists' academy, which had been founded in 1563 by Vasari. The portrayal of sinners banished to hell is unsurprisingly Dantesque. Vasari died in 1574 to be succeeded by Zuccari. The result in 1579 is full of noble striving but looks as if it was designed by committee.

Zuccari's major contribution to the Roman domes was a notably coherent and dramatic scheme for the Chapel of the Angels in Il Gesù of 1594–9 (fig.113). It warrants particular attention in our present context, since it exhibits strongly Dantesque qualities. As we approach the balustrade at the entrance to the chapel, we become aware of the altarpiece *Seven Archangels Worshipping the Trinity*. The status and agency of angels was of much concern to the Jesuits. St Michael in the centre and his companions look adoringly at a brilliant triangle of the Trinity displaying the Alpha and Omega of Christ – 'I am the beginning and the end' – from the Book of Revelation. The blaze of light bursts through a corona of soft clouds and cherubim. The presentation is simple and direct. The vision of the Trinity witnessed by the major angels has an abstraction and luminosity that matches Dante's final vision – in type if not in artistic quality. If Zuccari needed to learn about divine light, he certainly could have done so when he painted a close variation on Raphael's *Liberation of St Peter* for the Pauline Chapel in the Vatican, which contained Michelangelo's *Conversion of St Paul* (figs 50 and 51) and *Crucifixion of St Peter*. Zuccari emulated Raphael's remarkable use of light very knowingly.

Looking at the right wall of the Chapel of the Angels we see the *Fall of the Rebel Angels*, in which St Michael presides over an angular tangle of tumbling nudes. The left wall is devoted to *Angels Delivering Souls from Purgatory*, where Christ and the Virgin await the redeemed in a ring of clouds and angel-heads illuminated by the bright golden glow of heaven (fig.114). The emphasis, here as elsewhere in the chapel, is on the role of the angels, who are accorded iridescent draperies. Those on the left and right usher the redeemed from the flames of hell to the radiant heavens, while two at the centre tenderly convey diminutive soul-bodies into the realm of Christ and the Virgin. We may recall that angels were indeed present and active in Dante's *Purgatorio*.

The dome, well populated by evanescent angels, is devoted to the Assumption of the Virgin, which is portrayed with notable lucidity (fig.115). She has been granted her own substantial cloud and is not overly foreshortened. The individually characterised angels are positioned against the seven rings of heaven at the centre of which is positioned a light-filled Trinity. Jesus and God hold the glorious crown that awaits Mary. The composition strongly recalls the Florentine spectacles of the Assumption, as well as carrying obvious echoes of Dante. We cannot doubt Zuccari's detailed knowledge of the *Commedia.* While he was in Spain in 1586–8, he made a set of 88 spirited and ingenious drawings for Philip II, which reflect a careful and intelligent reading of Dante's text and the commentaries. The drawings for *Paradiso* exploit a striking range of celestial geometry and radiant light. It is good to have such direct evidence of a painter's engagement with Dante at this date. Zuccari and Cigoli share their roles as Dantisti in Rome.

As we pass into the 1620s, we can also adduce theatrical references for the domes by Lanfranco and Giovanni di San Giovanni (figs 71–4). By the time we reach Pietro da Cortona and Gaulli (figs 75–86) the basic conventions of tiered cloud platforms and central glare were well established for dome illusions, even if their vaults used different principles of organisation. We have seen Pietro's brilliant light effects in his design for one of the overtly theatrical *Quarantore* (fig.78), which belongs as much in this chapter as the preceding one. Equally, the compact theatre of Zuccari's chapel could well have featured in the preceding chapter. Large-scale painting and theatre were parts of the same devotional whole. What applies to the theatrical allusions also applies to our central quest to discern

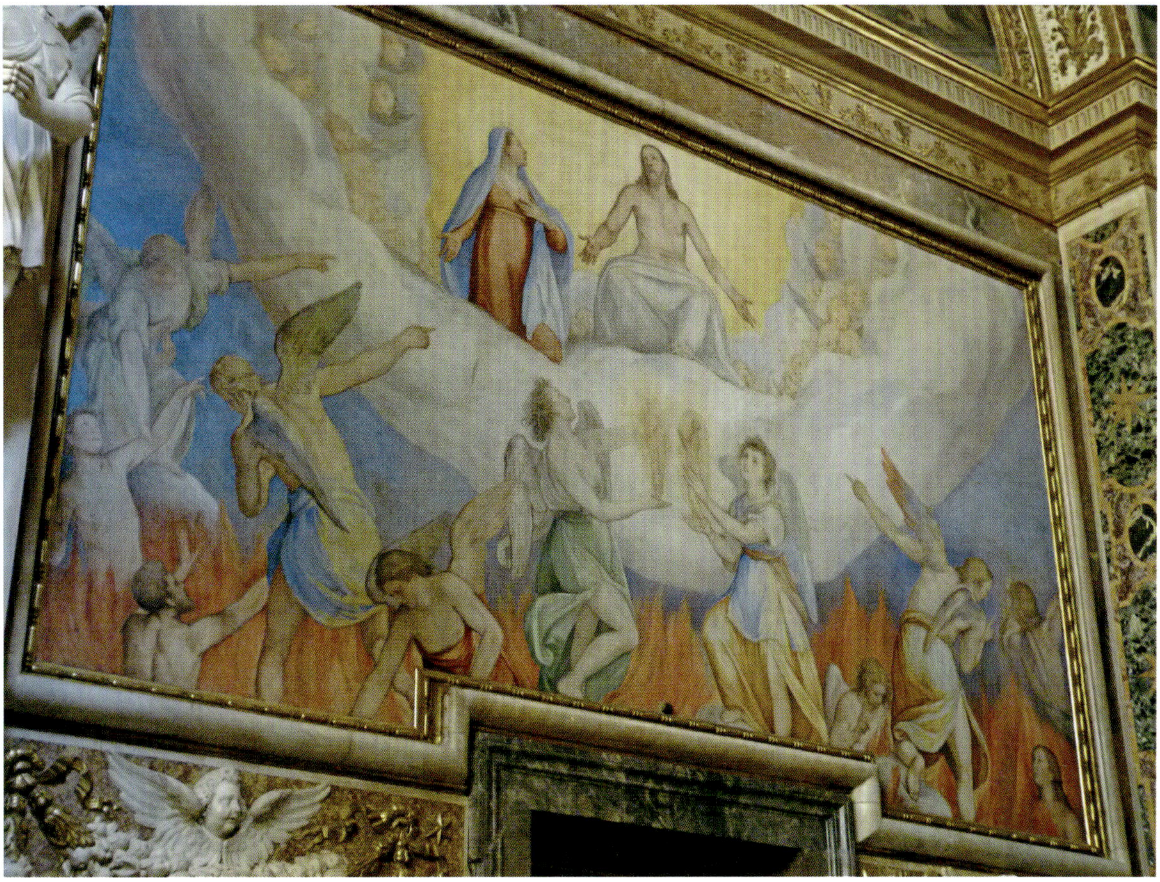

114 Federico Zuccari, *Angels Delivering Souls from Purgatory*, Rome, Il Gesù, Cappella degli Angeli

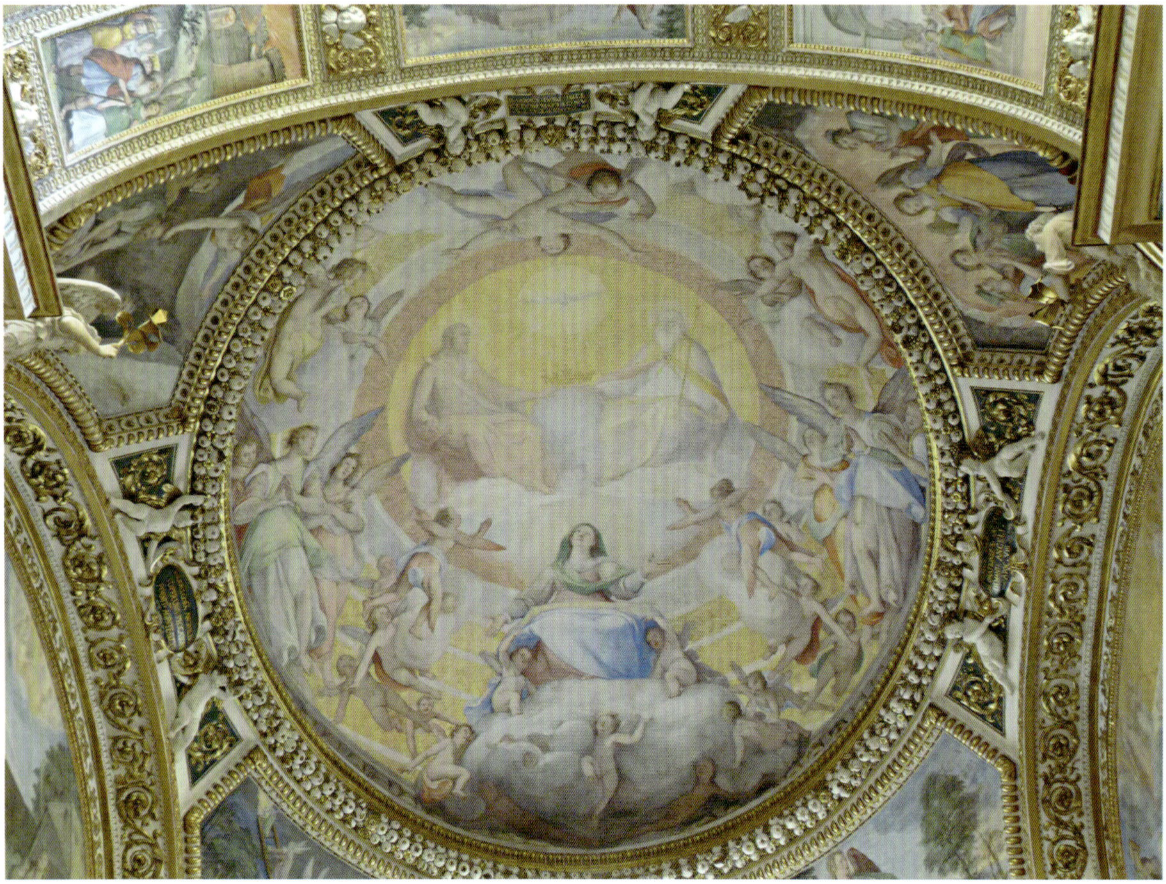

115 Federico Zuccari, *Assumption of the Virgin*, Rome, Il Gesù, Capella degli Angeli

Dantesque elements. There are two dimensions to this quest in relation to the Renaissance and Baroque masters. A compact review of these will provide a way of looking back on the main chapters.

The first dimension is the obvious one of the historical divine visions and accompanying light from Dante's *Paradiso* disseminated either directly or by more general and unspecific diffusion. In the majority of dome and vault paintings there is no way of documenting the direct impact even if it was in operation, although we have just seen two notable exceptions. The more general and less definable diaspora is something that can be sensed as a common factor as we pass from one scheme of decoration to another. This is not a matter of firm historical demonstration so much as the deployment of visual and poetic instinct.

The second dimension is one of mutually conceived or compatible goals within art forms that have very different ways of functioning. Dante's great aspiration was to find a verbal way of evoking a vision of the indescribable and the invisible, something that was ineffable and transcendent. He accomplished this through his accounts of light, not least the many incidents of sensory overload by a radiance that lay outside the range of 'moderateness'. This mode was not directly available to a painter who was limited to the material brightness of white lead on his palette. Yet by control of the ratios of light and shade within a picture and the descriptions of forms that were smothered, corroded or otherwise transformed by light, the painters successfully cheated their limitations. The mutual goal was glare, or what was called *splendore*. Dante got there in the early 14th century. Successive artists got there in incremental and often individualistic steps. A few, like Raphael, took more than one step on their own account. Looking at the bigger picture, we might say that painting only got to the point reached by Dante in the late 1670s with Gaulli's vault in Il Gesù. Dante set the bar dauntingly high, even if the painters did not consciously know that the bar existed. At the end of the day, we need not prioritise the question: did the painters know the *Divina Commedia*? Understanding their mutual quest to transcend the act of seeing and representing in words or images sheds a sharply focused light on both poetry and painting, and on their *paragone*. There was a famous Latin tag, *Ut pictura poesis* (as is painting, so is poetry), recorded by the Roman author Horace in his *Ars poetica*. Faced with Dante's visionary poetry, we might wonder if Horace's equation was ever completely solved by the painters when they strove to portray divine light. That they got so close is remarkable.

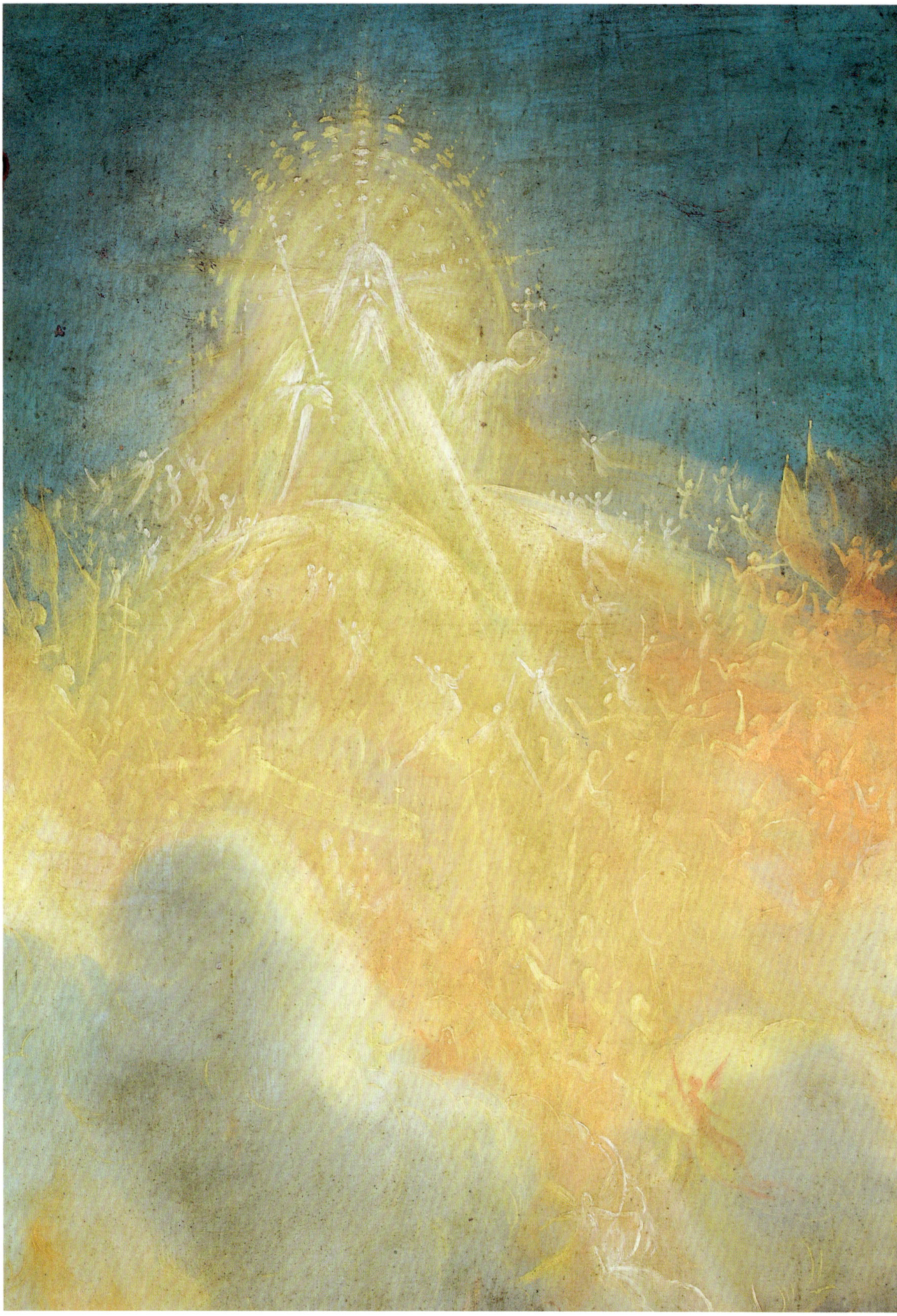

7

Limits of the Knowable

This is not so much a conclusion to the book as a concluding essay that offers some thoughts on the implications of Dante's vision for more than one of the really big, enduring questions. It looks at four of the more demanding authorities in the Mediaeval and Renaissance periods and in the modern philosophy of science, not so much to propose solutions as to say that the old dilemmas remain current and continue to fuel creative imaginations.

There are obvious limits to what we know at any one time. But are there absolute limits to what we can ever hope to know? Is it outside these limits of the knowable that we can accommodate the realm of the divine? Before tackling these questions head on, I would like to begin by looking at light as a parallel enquiry in the Middle Ages and today, which will lead us conveniently on to the big questions. I will not be claiming to have answers, but will conduct a historical dialogue with the present, in the context of what we have explored in the preceding pages.

Light is now regarded as a (or even *the*) fundamental property of the universe. Its speed serves as the one constant in the malleable dimensions of time and space. In its broadest sense, as electromagnetic radiation, light extends to waves whose length lies outside our visible spectrum. It is comprised of photons, elementary particles that are discrete bundles of dynamic energy (*quanta*). A photon is defined as having no mass or electric charge. In empty space it moves with the speed of light and is seen to do so regardless of the motion of the observer. Light insistently travels unfathomable distances from distant galaxies but is bent by humble water. This much is the territory of the sciences of physics and cosmology.

In broad historical terms, the fundamental nature and necessity of light (and resultant warmth) have been apparent to every human culture and the subject of sophisticated thinking and intense religious devotion. If we choose to look outside the framework of this book at light within human culture as a whole, we would be essaying the near-impossible.

Let us begin this excursus with an amazingly precocious statement of the primacy of light from the early 13th century. It introduces a great Mediaeval philosopher, whose name we did no more than drop in the first chapter. I am referring to Robert Grosseteste, Bishop of Lincoln, in the 13th century. I should say I am not going to adduce his influence on modern physics or to claim that he 'anticipated' current notions of light. Rather I will be looking at

Matthias Grünewald, *The Isenheim Altarpiece: the Nativity*, detail of God the Father and angels, Colmar, Musée Unterlinden

analogous reactions to age-old concerns – another kind of *paragone*.

Grosseteste played a foundational role in Mediaeval optics, particularly in Britain, though his knowledge of preceding optical science was limited compared to Bacon and Pecham. Yet, compared to them, and indeed compared to almost all the philosophers of light from antiquity onwards, he assigned an absolutely primary role to light as the first substance of the cosmos. This is advocated in his brief and difficult treatise *De luce* (*On Light*). Its opening words announce his high ambition in unequivocal terms. It warrants extended quotation, and makes demands on the reader as on myself. Everything in the orbs of the universe stems from a primal point of light, the *forma prima*, created by God.

> The first corporeal form … is in my opinion light [*lux*]. For light of its very nature diffuses itself in every direction in such a way that a point of light will produce instantaneously a sphere of light [*lumen*] of any size whatsoever, unless some opaque object stands in the way. Now the extension of matter in three dimensions necessarily attends the nature of a body, and this despite the fact that both shape and matter are in themselves simple substances lacking all dimension. But a form that is in itself simple and without dimension could not introduce dimension in every direction into matter, which is likewise simple and without dimension, except by multiplying itself and diffusing itself instantaneously in every direction and thus extending matter in its own diffusion … I have proposed that it is light which possesses of its very nature the function of multiplying itself and diffusing itself instantaneously in all directions. Whatever performs this operation is either light or some other agent that acts in virtue of its participation in light to which this operation belongs essentially. Being a body, therefore, is either an act of light itself or of the agent that performs the aforementioned operation and introduces dimensions into matter in virtue of its participation in light, and acts through the power of this same light. But the first form cannot introduce dimensions into matter through the power of a later form. Therefore, light is not a form subsequent to being a body, but it is embodiment itself…
>
> When the first body, which is the firmament, has in this way been completely actualised, it diffuses its light [*lumen*] from every part of itself to the centre of the universe. For since light [*lux*] is the perfection of the first body and naturally multiplies itself from the first body, it is necessarily diffused to the centre of the universe …
>
> Just as the light generated from the first body completed the realisation of the second sphere and left a denser mass below this second sphere, so the light generated by the second sphere completed the realisation of the third sphere, and through its gathering left below this third sphere a mass of even greater density. This process of simultaneously gathering together and separating continued in this way until the nine heavenly spheres gathered together below the ninth and lowest sphere the dense mass which constitutes the matter of the four elements.[1]

None of this is easy, but it is very remarkable. Even if those who followed Grosseteste did not adopt his radical philosophy of light as the *prima forma*, the notion that it radiates in all directions, diffused throughout space, is present in the almost universal idea of the 'multiplication of species'. We have seen that the anatomy of the eye was arranged so that intelligible and selective order could be extracted from the diffuse array. There was also the general sense amongst the Mediaeval philosophers that the mathematics of light was a supreme manifestation of God in nature and that its heavenly essence comprised the highest spiritual value. None of those we have encountered, from Dante to Andrea Pozzo, would have dissented from this basic stance.

Grosseteste's is a heroic theory, and involves rethinking the standard ideas of form and matter. There is an obvious temptation to align Grosseteste's fundamental form with particle physics in its modern guise, and he makes approving reference to the ancient atomic theory of Epicurus and Lucretius. However, this would be to manipulate the past so that it seems to be part of the present. What modern physics and *De luce* do have in common is a vision of all forms – tangible, visible or detectable – as expressions of energy rather than mute materiality waiting to be shaped by form.

The big difference involves the role of the creator and of the position of human beings in the system. Grosseteste, like his Mediaeval colleagues, equates light with theological truth and mental enlightenment. The order of things is not solely discernible to humans but they are the designated recipients of the system. To quote the ancient tag attributed to the Greek philosopher Protagoras, 'man is the measure of all things'. However, what we can measure and understand with our mind is limited in scope. Grosseteste compares the supreme truth to the brightest light, which we mortals cannot regard directly but only by dint of its reflection by bodies. We have seen that light in *Paradiso* confounds Dante's established powers of sight and reason. Repeatedly, he has to learn that the optics of terrestrial phenomena do not apply in the realm of the divine. The visual miracle of *Paradiso* is that Beatrice permits him to transcend the limitations of his terrestrial sense – at least until the very last vision of the ultimate realm of light.

In historical terms, what lies outside our discernment of scientific phenomena in our material is the realm of the ineffable. I am thinking in the broadest sense of the term ineffable, not just as the indescribable (which could simply be the fault of our descriptive apparatus), but as the profoundly unknowable in some kind of absolute way. In Dante's time the unknowable was characterised according to the doctrine of the 'double truth', the truth of the human intellect and divine truth – or reason and revelation. The basic idea, explored in detail by Albertus Magnus and Thomas Aquinas – theologians much studied by Dante and both located by him in the heaven of the sun – is that the truth of which the human mind is capable is ultimately mutable and finite, while divine truth is immutable and infinite. For Albertus, as master of various scientific disciplines, these two truths were distinct but not hostile, even when they offered different versions of truth. Each had its own zone of competence, though ultimately divine truth overarched everything.

Where do the visual arts stand in this? For the Mediaeval artist, real gold was explicitly or implicitly analogous to divine light, generating its own radiance and resisting spatial definition. In the Renaissance new challenges arose. I think it is not going too far as to see Renaissance and Baroque painters operating with a kind of double truth, even though the concept might well have been unknown or inaccessible to them. They became masters of the logic of perspective and light and shade. They knew the rules of light on earth and how to apply them to the job of representation. But we have also seen how painters needed to exploit light of a licentious kind to signal divine presence. The light in Constantine's dream and of the angel who liberates St Peter, and the explosive light that emanates from the Jesuit logo, belong to a different world of optical phenomena. That world is heaven.

In modern physics, the divine is for the most part not assigned a magisterial rule, and the place for any kind of divinity has been increasingly restricted to philosophically generalised areas of the ultimate design of the cosmos. But even for the atheists, amongst whom I count myself, there are vast swathes of the unknown beyond the present reach of science and understanding. The central question remains: are there unknowns that are unknowable? There is a double sense of unknowable: the first involves testability by some kind of experimental or observational process. We may recall Dante's three-mirror experiment, which worked validly to demolish Dante's own theory, but left the final answer not to physics but to metaphysics. The second sense of the question involves what may be the inherent limits to the operation of the human mind.

To deal with these issues in science – as a historian – I will look very briefly at two of the great 20th-century warhorses who tackled the limits of knowledge: the revered theoretical physicist Werner Heisenberg and the magisterial logician of mathematics Kurt Gödel. I will in no sense be making judgements as to their correctness – though I find their ideas appealing – but will be observing that these two of the most remarkable thinkers in modern science have argued for limits, for a kind of double truth. There is no reason why there should not be limits. We may reasonably assume that humans have developed in such a way that their bodily, sensory and mental apparatus is adapted to the very particular set-up of earth as a planet. Over the centuries we have learnt how to use the complexities of our mind specifically to handle the complexities of our environment – not always well. We have remarkably learnt to model phenomena that lie outside our optical and functional reach. But there is no automatic reason to assume that the complexities of our mind are well matched to the more remote complexities of the cosmos, or even the material realm of extreme minuteness. The two theories are Heisenberg's uncertainty principle and Gödel's incompleteness theorems. After that, I will touch briefly on the limits of experimental observation (with Beatrice's approval). The brief accounts that follow make no claims for certainty or completeness on their own account.

In 1927 Werner Heisenberg introduced his uncertainty principle. It states that the more precisely the position of a given particle is determined, at a given instant, the less precisely its momentum at the same instant can be predicted from initial conditions, and vice versa.[2]

He initially used the term 'indeterminacy' (*Ungenauigkeit*), rather than 'uncertainty' (*Unsicherheit*). The former seems rather better, since it indicates that something cannot be determined, whereas uncertainty suggests an implicit human dimension that might be attributed to our mental apparatus rather than the phenomena and the tools of measurement. As a historian, the uncertainty principle is appealing, because it suggests a level of humility not always apparent in science.

Kurt Gödel's theorems belong to the same era, but reside in the sphere of mathematical logic. He formulated two theorems of incompleteness. They were published in his 1931 paper 'On formally undecidable propositions of *Principia Mathematica* and related systems'. The first theorem states that any consistent formal system, within which a certain amount of elementary arithmetic can be carried out, is incomplete. That is to say that there are statements which can neither be proved nor disproved by the formal system itself. There are statements about natural numbers that are true, but that are unprovable within the system. The second, closely related theorem states that a formal system cannot prove that the system itself is consistent, even though we assume this to be the case. Although these theorems are those of mathematics, applicable for instance to Euclidian geometry in a rather basic manner, they carry broad implications for the kinds of sciences we have been dealing with, since they challenge the ultimate demonstrability of the revered axioms on which optics has relied from the time of Euclid. Far from fading away, the logical paradoxes to which Gödel drew attention seem to be encountered in new areas, most recently in machine learning.[3]

Alongside Gödel's abstract conception of incompleteness run other more practical and operational limits in physics – of the Heisenberg kind. There is no shortage of them. If we consider observation of the heavens, we encounter limits at the upper range, where the passage of light over vast distances and intervals of time only takes us back so far. We may be able to theorise back to the first second before the Big Bang, but what lies beyond this seems intractable. What lies at very beginning or even beyond it? Is there a beyond it? And, coming down to the very smallest scales, we are dealing with systems that are minutely sensitive to acts of observation, with all the hazards that go with that.

Even within the extraordinary range of our detectors, there is much that we cannot detect other than by inferring its presence. I am thinking most obviously of 'dark matter', which is believed to comprise 80 per cent or so of the mass of the universe, but is so unreactive that it cannot be directly 'seen' in action – or rather inaction. Overarching all this there is the standard model of physics that sees photons acting as both particles and waves depending on the act of observation and the choice of the context of demonstration. If this long-standing duality is in the course of being resolved, it is likely to lead on to other profound questions. As with much acquisition of knowledge, one solution throws out a range of other possibilities. My sense is that there are ultimate limits, but that within those limits we can forge endless lines of enquiry. The detectable complexity that lies 'out there' is in practice inexhaustible.

These lines of enquiry will be necessarily limited by what our mental equipment can achieve. As someone who finds quantum mechanics a real struggle, I am not prepared to speculate as to where these limits might lie. I suspect that we are dealing with the endless perfectibility of our theories, but that the going will get tougher and tougher. We recall that at the very end of *Paradiso* Dante's vision is permitted to discern effects beyond the eye's assigned limits, but ultimately his words fail and his conceptual apparatus, his *alta fantasia*, fails. Instruments have allowed us to go far beyond the limits of our eyes, but a Dantesque final barrier may remain.

I will let the Renaissance have the last word on knowability and unknowability – and I suspect the unknowability of the answer. The word is by Cusanus (Nicholas of Kues or Cusa), as great a philosopher as the 15th century produced. Like Grosseteste, he offers a radical rethinking of the nature of the universe that carries its resonance from the Renaissance into our time.

Cusanus was a prolific and subtle author, and a patron of artists, who donated a painting. the *Salvator Mundi*, to his home monastery in Germany. He accompanied the iconic image, probably painted by Jan van Eyck, with a discourse on the universal and unfathomable vision of God.[4] The German cardinal was a major figure in the institutions of the Church, rising in 1459 to become its Vicar General. His doctrine of 'learned ignorance' is fruitful beyond the immediate theological and philosophical intentions of his treatise *De docta ignorantia* (*On Learned Ignorance*) in 1440. To put it crudely, the more we really know, the better we are equipped to realise our ignorance. In more specific terms, Cusanus offers a highly refined concept of the infinity of the divine and the nature of human understanding in a way that does not follow the standard Mediaeval manoeuvres. He draws more on Plato than Aristotle. Cusanus's 'exemplars' owe much to Plato's notion of divine ideas that we can only discern in shadowy form.

Cusanus defined God as the unfathomable 'maximum', of which the world that is observable and describable is a 'contraction' such that the 'maximum' is of a different order: 'Now, I give the name "Maximum" to that than which there cannot be anything greater. But fullness befits what is one. Thus, oneness – which is also being – coincides with

Maximality.'[5] At the other end of the scale, as an omega to the alpha, is the 'minimum' of zero, which is also the realm of the divine, as a negative version of infinity. Between these two unknowable extremes, which are not separate extremes for God, we have to make do with images that are approximations. We can only deal with 'contractions' of the absolute reality and truth of God.

> Since what is caused derives altogether from its cause and not at all from itself and since it conforms as closely as it can to the Fount and Form [*ratio*] from which it is that which it is: clearly, the nature of contraction is difficult to attain if the Absolute Exemplar remains unknown. Therefore, it is fitting that we be learned-in-ignorance beyond our understanding so that we may at least be led to seeing that there is a precise truth which we cannot now comprehend.[6]

The 'images', 'approximations', 'likenesses' and 'contractions' available to us only give provisional and conjectural access to the divine 'exemplars'. Indeed, all our knowledge is conjectural. Immediately after his *De docta ignorantia* Cusanus wrote a treatise, *De coniecturis* (*On Conjectures*, or *On Surmises*), emphasising that our limited mental powers will always fall short of absolute truth. Mind has limits that cannot be transcended within its own rules of operation (like a kind of Gödel theorem).

Humans may be excluded from absolute truth, but via Christ they occupy a privileged 'in-between' position in the universe.

> It would not be possible that more than one true human being [Christ] could ascend to union with Maximality. And, assuredly, this being would be a man in such way that He was also God and would be God in such way that He was also a man. He would be the perfection of the universe and would hold pre-eminence in all respects. In Him the least, the greatest, and the in-between things of the nature that is united to Absolute Maximality would so coincide that He would be the perfection of all things; and all things, *qua* contracted, would find rest in Him as in their own perfection. The measure of this man would also be the measure of an angel (as John says in the Book of Revelation) and of each thing.[7]

This is in keeping with Protagoras's tag that 'man is the measure of all things'. We can use the precise sciences to measure things that take us close to God (but only so close). The inaccessibility of the absolute truth does not absolve us from heroic striving to analyse the images with which we are presented.

In a section that begins 'Mathematics assists us very greatly in apprehending various divine [truths]', Cusanus indicates that there is an infinite perfectibility for our understanding: 'although every image seems to be like its exemplar ... no image is so similar or equal to its exemplar that it cannot be infinitely more similar and equal'.[8] The precise sciences provide the best access to God's ultimate inaccessibility.

> In creating the world, God used arithmetic, geometry, music, and likewise astronomy ... For through arithmetic God united things. Through geometry He shaped them, in order that they would thereby attain firmness, stability, and mobility in accordance with their conditions ... He proportioned things in such way that there is not more earth in earth than water in water, air in air, and fire in fire, so that no one element is altogether reducible to another.[9]

We can follow the magisterial logic of God's creation, but there is always the unbridgeable gap.

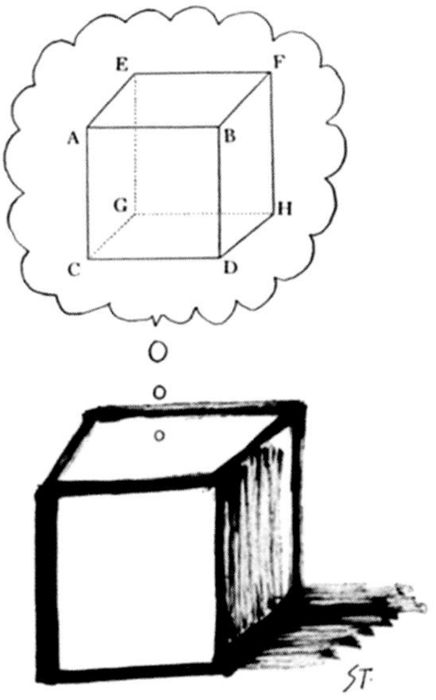

116 Saul Steinberg, *Cube's Dream*, 1960, ink on paper, 36.5 × 27.9 cm (14 3/8 × 11 3/8 in), private collection. Originally published in *The New Yorker*, July 30, 1960.

> The intellect, which is not truth, never comprehends truth so precisely that truth cannot be comprehended infinitely more precisely. For the intellect is to truth as [an inscribed] polygon is to [the inscribing] circle. The more angles the inscribed polygon has the more similar it is to the circle. However, even if the number of its angles is increased *ad infinitum*, the polygon never becomes equal [to the circle] unless it is resolved into an identity with the circle.[10]

As Cusanus knew, one of the time-honoured methods for squaring the circle – contriving a circle *precisely* equal in area to a given square, or vice versa – was by 'exhaustion'; that is to say by creating a polygon with as many sides as possible. But he realised that this method produced only an approximation. We may recall that the ultimate failure of Dante's faculties at the very end of the *Divina Commedia* was compared to the mathematician who aspires 'to measure the area of a circle, and, pondering, is unable to think of the rule he lacks'.

This conception of infinite perfectibility is nicely realised by Saul Steinberg's material cube (fig.116), with its sketchy graphics and insecure perspective, which can dream of the notion of a perfect cube. But in Cusanus's terms, even this 'perfect' cube remains conjectural as an approximate 'likeness', compared to the true archetype or 'exemplar' in the Platonic realm of God. The sphere inscribed in the cube is equally conjectural, but because of its endless roundness stands as a useful symbol of the infinite.

Even in the material world, where we think we have a grip of what is at the centre and what is at the periphery, this conviction is a subjective matter of our placement in the system and what we call 'our perspective'. Cusanus's account is not an easy ride.

> To understand something about the motion of the universe, you must merge the centre and the poles, aiding yourself as best you can by your imagination. For example, if someone were on the earth but beneath the north pole [of the heavens] and someone else were actually at the north pole [of the heavens], then just as to the one on the earth it would appear that the pole is at the zenith [from that point], so to the one at the actual pole it would appear that the centre is at the zenith [from that point]. And just as antipodes have the sky above, as do we, so to those who are at either pole the earth would appear to be at the zenith [from their point]. And at whichever [of these] anyone would be, he would believe himself to be at the centre. Therefore, merge these different imaginative pictures so that the centre is the zenith and vice versa. Thereupon you will see – through the intellect, to which only learned ignorance is of help, that the world and its motion and shape cannot be apprehended. For [the world]

will appear as a wheel in a wheel and a sphere in a sphere – having its centre and circumference nowhere, as was stated.[11]

This 'learned ignorance' – the realisation that all our knowledge is provisional, partial and relative to our situation – does not mean that we are absolved from the profound investigation of the world that is available to us.

> Who would not admire this Artisan, who with regard to the spheres, the stars, and the regions of the stars used such skill that there is – though without complete precision – both a harmony of all things and a diversity of all things? He considered in advance the sizes, the placing, and the motion of the stars in the one world; and He ordained the distances of the stars in such a way that unless each region were as it is, it could neither exist nor exist in such a place and with such an order – nor could the universe exist. Moreover, He bestowed on all stars a differing brightness, influence, shape, colour, and heat … And He established the interrelationship of parts so proportionally that in each thing the motion of the parts is oriented toward the whole. With heavy things [the motion is] downward toward the centre, and with light things it is upward from the centre and around the centre…
>
> With regard to these objects, which are so worthy of admiration, so varied, and so different, we recognise – through learned ignorance and in accordance with the preceding points – that we cannot know the rationale for any of God's works but can only marvel; for the Lord is great, whose greatness is without end. Since He is Absolute Maximality: as He is the Author and Knower of all His works, so He is also the End; thus, all things are in Him and nothing is outside Him. He is the Beginning, the Middle, and the End of all things, the Centre and the Circumference of all things – so that He alone is sought in all things; for without Him all things are nothing.[12]

This is an extreme philosophy of the unknowability of God, and the ultimate provisionality of our rational understanding of his creation of the universe, but if we place the emphasis upon 'learned' rather than 'ignorance', Cusanus sets requirements on possible knowledge of a very high order. Someone who can write a learned dialogue on the elaborate science of a ball game (*De ludo globi*) takes the knowledge of physics very seriously. Almost needless to say the game has its metaphysical dimension. As his discussant says, 'the comparison of the bowling-ball to the body and of its motion to the soul is especially pleasing'.[13]

In our present context, it is appropriate to end our collage of Cusanus quotations with one that takes us back to light.

> Earth is to fire as the world is to God. For fire, in its relation to earth, has many resemblances to God. The is no limit to fire's power; and fire acts upon, penetrates, illumines, distinguishes, and forms all earthly things through the medium of air and of water, so that, as it were, in all the things which are begotten from earth there is nothing except fire's distinct activities. Hence, the forms of things are different as a result of a difference in fire's brightness. But fire is intermingled with things; it does not exist without them.[14]

And we need to remember that 'things' as we see them are provisional: 'God alone is absolute. Hence, God, who is light and in whom there is no darkness, is spoken of by the ancients as absolute consuming fire and as absolute brightness'.[15]

Cusanus's texts on light could accompany Gaulli's heavenly conflagration, even though the chance of the painter knowing Cusanus's treatise is close to zero. What is shared by Cusanus, Gaulli, Dante and all those we have encountered as proponents of divine light is a conjoined awe in what is known, what might be known and what cannot be known. This awe is a central motivation in science, literature and art. Human creativity begins where knowledge ends.

Abbreviations

THE BIBLE

References are by book, chapter and verse (where relevant) and are from the Cambridge edition, *c.*1900, of the original translation of the King James Bible of 1611, which has a power and beauty that can stand beside Dante's texts. Where appropriate the Latin Vulgate is also cited.

The online reference used in this book is the King James Bible (Standard and 1911) in: https://www.kingjamesbibleonline.org/

WORKS BY DANTE: VN, CONV, INF, PURG AND PARA

For the *Vita N(u)ova* (*VN*) and *Convivio* (*Conv*), see *Opere minori*, ed. D. De Robertis and C. Vasoli, 2 vols., Milan and Naples, 1984 and 1995.

The translations I have mainly used and edited are: *Vita Nuova*, trs. M. Musa, Oxford, 2008; and the *Convivio*, trs. R. Lansing, New York and London, 1990.

For the *Divine Comedy* – *Inferno* (*Inf*), *Purgatorio* (*Purg*) and *Paradiso* (*Para*) – see *Divina Commedia*, ed. G. Petrocchi, 4 vols., Milan 1966–7.

The translation of the *Divine Comedy* to which I have had most recourse is: Dante Alighieri, *The Divine Comedy*, trs. C. Sisson, intro. and notes by D. Higgins, Oxford, 2008.

See also the very useful online resources on page 224.

I have on occasion adjusted the most favoured translations to clarify a particular sense in relation to the topics I am covering rather than aspiring to literary quality.

EUCLID

H. Burton, 'The Optics of Euclid', *Journal of the Optical Society of America*, vol.XXXV, 1945, pp 357–72.

DE ASP (DE ASPECTIBUS)

The Optics of Ibn al-Haytham, Books I–III on Direct Vision, ed. and trs. A. I. Sabra, 2 vols., London, 1989.

PECHAM

John Pecham and the Science of Optics: Perspectiva Communis, ed. D. Lindberg, Madison, Milwaukee and London, 1970.

CRONACA

G. Santi, *Federigo da Montefeltro, Duca d' Urbino: Cronaca*, ed. H. Holtzinger, Stuttgart, 1893.

FESTE D'OLTRARNO

N. Newbiggin, *Feste d'Oltrarno: Plays in Churches in Fifteenth-Century Florence*, 2 vols., Florence, 1996.

CUSANUS

N. Cusanus (von Kues or Cusa), *De docta ignorantia* (1440), trs. J. Hopkins, *Complete Philosophical and Theological Treatises of Nicholas of Cusa*, Minneapolis, 2001.

Notes

1 DIVINE OPTICS, CHRISTIAN AND ISLAMIC: THE OPTICAL DIMENSIONS

1 Genesis 1: 1–5:
In principio creavit Deus cælum et terram.
Terra autem erat inanis et vacua, et tenebræ erant super faciem abyssi: et spiritus Dei ferebatur super aquas.
Dixitque Deus: Fiat lux. Et facta est lux.
Et vidit Deus lucem quod esset bona: et divisit lucem a tenebris.
Appellavitque lucem Diem, et tenebras Noctem.
2 Exodus 24: 15–17
3 John 1: 4–5
4 John 8: 12
5 John 9: 5
6 James 1: 16–7
7 Matthew 17: 2–5
8 Gulielmus Durandus, *Rationale divinorum officiorum*, I. 24, in J. M. Neale and B. Webb (ed. and trs.), *The Symbolism of Churches and Church Ornaments*, London, 1893, *proeme* 24–5, p.23
9 Quran, 24: 35–6
10 Euclid, first postulate
11 *De Asp* I, 1 19
12 *De Asp* III, 3 12; and III, 7 83
13 *De Asp* I, 4 1–2
14 *De Asp* I, 1 19
15 *De Asp* I, 6 20
16 *Opus majus*, ed. Bridges, I, pt. V, pp 41–2
17 Pecham, Proemium, p.60
18 Leonardo da Vinci, Milan, Biblioteca Ambrosiana, Codice Atlantico 543r
19 Pecham I, 9
20 Pecham II, 11
21 *Roman de la rose*, II, 18004–18006, pp 40–1 (Gilson, *Mediaeval Optics*, p.33, n.60)

2 DANTE'S DAZZLE

1 This is my estimate from C. H. Sisson's translation, *The Divine Comedy*, Oxford, 2008
2 *VN* II, 1–8
3 *VN* XIX
4 *VN* V
5 *Conv* III, ix 6
6 *Conv* II, xiii 26–7
7 *Conv* II, 3 6
8 Wisdom 11: 20
9 *Conv* III, xiv 4
10 *Conv* III, xiv 5
11 Albertus Magnus, *De intellectu et intelligibili* I, 3
12 *Conv* III, vii
13 *Conv* III, canzone 2
14 *Conv* III, xv 8
15 *Conv* III, ix 15–16
16 *Conv* III, ix 7–9
17 *Conv* II, ix 4–5
18 *De Anima*, II, 12.42a 17–24
19 *Inf* XV, 16–21
20 *Inf* V, 51
21 *Inf* III, 133–5
22 *Inf* XXXI, 19–22
23 *Purg* I, 13–24
24 *Purg* II, 22–39
25 *Purg* VIII, 25–6
26 *Purg* IX, 82–4
27 *Purg* XVII, 53–7
28 *Purg* XXIV, 137–8
29 *Purg* XV, 10–24
30 *Purg* III, 19–27
31 *Purg* XXVIII, 52–4 and 62–6

32 *Purg* XXIX, 64–6
33 *Purg* XXIX, 73–5
34 Ptolemy, *Optics*, II, 96
35 Leonardo MS A, Paris, Institut de France, 27v
36 *Purg* XXXII, 1–18
37 *Purg* XXXIII, 145
38 *Para* I, 46–54
39 *Para* II, 31–6
40 *Para* II, 58 ff, for the lengthy dispute
41 *Para* II, 94–6
42 *Para* II, 109–11
43 *Para* III, 10–22
44 *Para* V, 133–7
45 *Para* XIV, 55–7
46 Augustine, *City of God*, XXII, 29
47 *Para* XIV, 100–103
48 *Para* XIV, 111–177
49 Lucretius, *De rerum natura*, II, 113–21
50 Isidore of Seville, *Etymologiarum*, lib III, c 2, no.107. Gilson, *Mediaeval Optics*, p.95, n.40
51 *Para* XXI, 4–6
52 *Para* XXI, 11–12
53 *Para* XXIII, 31–3
54 E.g. *Para* XXIII, 118–20; XXVIII, 16–18; XXX, 79–81; XXXIII, 52–84
55 *Para* XXV, 118 – XXVI, 79
56 *Para* XXVIII, 16 ff
57 *Para* XXX, 25–123
58 *Para* XXXI, 76–8
59 *Para* XXXI, 13–15
60 *Para* XXXI, 130–32
61 *Para* XXXIII, 106
62 *Para* XXXIII, 115–45

3 ILLUMINATED AND ILLUSTRATED

1 Rome, Casa di Dante, Dante, *Divina Commedia*, ed. Pietro da Figino and C. Landino, Florence, Pietro Piasi, 1491; facsimile, Salerno Editrice, Rome, 2014: https://www.facsimilefinder.com/facsimiles/dante-divina-commedia-facsimile
2 D. Laurenza and M Kemp (eds.), *Leonardo da Vinci: A New Edition of the Codex Leicester of Leonardo da Vinci*, 4 vols, Oxford, 2019–20
3 *Purg* IX
4 *Para* I, 1–6
5 *Para* I
6 Fol. 189
7 *Para* XXXIII, 94–7
8 *Comento di Cristophoro Landino Fiorentino sopra la Comedia di Danthe Alighieri poeta Fiorentino*, Florence, Nicolaus Laurentii, 1481, preface: *Questo solo affermo, havere liberato el nostro cittadino dalla barbarie di molti externi idiomi, ne' quali da' comentatori era stato corropto; et al presente chosì puro et semplice è paruto mio officio apresentarlo ad voi illustrissimi signor nostri, acciochè per le mani di quel magistrato, el quale è sommo nella fiorentina rep., sia dopo lungo exilio restituito nella sua patria, et riconosciuto nè Romagnuolo essere nè Lombardo, nè degli idiomi di quegli che l'hanno comentato, ma mero fiorentino. La quale lingua quanto tutte l'altre italiche avanzi manifesto testimonio ne sia, che nessuno nel quale apparisca o ingegno o doctrina, nè versi scripse mai nè prosa, che non si sforzassi usa el fiorentino idioma.*
9 *Para* III, 10–22

4 DANTESQUE DRAMAS: FROM GIOTTO TO TITIAN

1 *Purg* XI, 94–6
2 *Para* XXVIII, 16–18
3 *Conv* III, vii
4 Leon Battista Alberti, *On Painting*, 49
5 Leon Battista Alberti, *On Painting*, 47
6 Para XIV, 111–117
7 Matthew: 17 2–5
8 *Laudato sie, mi Signore cum tucte le Tue creature,*
spetialmente messor lo frate Sole,
lo qual è iorno, et allumini noi per lui.
Et ellu è bellu e radiante cum grande splendore:
de Te, Altissimo, porta significatione.
9 Acts 9: 1–8
10 *Cronaca* 89–90
11 *Cronaca* 113–155
12 C. D'Onofrio, *Visitiamo Roma mille anni fa: la città dei mirabilia*, Rome, 1988, XI
13 Acts 12: 6–9
14 Matthew 17: 14–18; similar description in Mark 9: 17–27
15 https://digital.library.sydney.edu.au/nodes/view/7505
16 Isaiah 7.14; also see a version in Matthew 1: 23

5 DANTESQUE DRAMAS: FROM CORREGGIO TO RUBENS

1 Revelation 1: 7
2 *Purg* XV, 10–24
3 M. Spagnolo, *Coreggio, geografico e storia della fortuna*, Correggio, 2005, p.174
4 For the printed booklet, see https://archive.org/details/gri_dichiarationoorosi/page/n13/mode/2up. For the translation by Simona Albinese, see: https://simonaalbanese.blogspot.com/2010/03/triumph–of–divine–providence–by–pietro.html
5 Weil, 'The Devotion of the Forty Hours', p.227
6 Weil, p.230 n.36
7 https://archive.org/details/trattatodellapitoootto/mode/2up
8 Ottonelli, *Il trattato*, p.23

9 Ottonelli, *Il trattato*, p.200–201
10 Philippians 2: 9–11
11 I. Lavin, *Bernini and the Unity of the Visual Arts*, New York and Oxford, 1980
12 Teresa of Ávila, *The Life of Teresa of Jesus: The Autobiography of Teresa of Ávila*, ed. and trs. E. A. Peers, New York, 1991, pp 274–5
13 Kemp, *The Science of Art: The Science of Art: Optical Themes in Western Art from Brunelleschi to Seurat*, p.139, and proemio
14 IGNEM VENI MITTERE IN TERRA, Luke 12: 49

6 PARADISE PERFORMED: FROM THE RENAISSANCE TO THE BAROQUE

1 G. Vasari, *Le vite de' più eccellenti pittori, scultori e architettori italiani, da Cimabue insino a' tempi nostri*, Florence, 1568, ed. P. Barocchi, Pisa, 1999, III, p.454
2 *Feste d'Oltrarno*, II, p.291
3 *Feste d'Oltrarno*, I, p.7
4 *Feste d'Oltrarno*, I, p.3
5 *Feste d'Oltrarno*, I, p.6
6 *Feste d'Oltrarno*, I, p.6
7 *Feste d'Oltrarno*, I, p.4
8 *Feste d'Oltrarno*, I, p.7
9 *Feste d'Oltrarno*, I, pp 62–3
10 A sagene is a Russian unit of measurement equal to about 7 feet.
11 *Feste d'Oltrarno*, I, pp 60–1
12 *Feste d'Oltrarno*, I, pp 62–3
13 Matteo Palmieri, *La città di vita*, Firenze, Biblioteca Medicea Laurenziana, Plut. 40.53
14 http://www.nuovaricerca.org/leonardo_inf_e_par/BELLINCIONI.pdf; and E. Solmi, 'La festa del Paradiso di Leonardo da Vinci e Bernardo Bellincore (13 Gennaio, 1490)'. *Archivo storico lombardo: giornale della Società, Storica Lombarda, Serie Quarta*, I 1904, pp 75–89
15 E. Solmi and A. Solmi, *Scritti vinciani*, Florence, 1924, pp 12–13
16 Buccheri, *The Spectacle of Clouds*, p.43
17 *Feste d'Oltrarno*, p.223
18 *Feste d'Oltrarno*, II, pp 281–2
19 Vasari, *Le vite*, III, pp 188–91
20 https://warburg.sas.ac.uk/pdf/dch2208k.pdf
21 Florence, Uffizi, Gabintetto dei disegni e stampe, 8951F and 123201. For the engraving, see https://www.britishmuseum.org/collection/object/P_1873–0809–460
22 For an imaginative reconstruction of the *intermezzi*, see https://www.youtube.com/playlist?list=PL1145D2CEC1ECC20C

7 LIMITS OF THE KNOWABLE

1 Robert Grosseteste, *On Light* (*De luce*), trs. C. Riedl, Milwaukee, 1942. See http://www.boscarol.com/wikipdf/Riedel_1942_Grosseteste_On_Light.pdf
2 For a rudimentary but effective demonstration, see https://www.youtube.com/watch?v=IS9qAUc0WG8
3 D. Castelvecchi, 'Machine Learning Comes up Against Unsolvable Problem', *Nature*, 17 January 2019, p.277
4 M. Dalivalle, M. Kemp and R. Simon, *Leonardo's Salvator Mundi, and the Collecting of Leonardo in the Stuart Courts*, Oxford, 2019, pp 81–2
5 Cusanus I, 2 5
6 Cusanus I, 11 30
7 Cusanus III, 3 199
8 Cusanus I, 11 30
9 Cusanus II, 13 175
10 Cusanus I, 3 10
11 Cusanus, II, 11 161
12 Cusanus II, 13 178–9
13 Cusanus, *De ludo globi*, I, 25
14 Cusanus II, 13 177
15 Cusanus II, 13 177

Online Resources and Further Reading

There is a vast body of literature on Dante and I have drawn selectively upon what seemed to be most relevant for my current theme. I am all too conscious that I am not a Dante specialist. The bibliography is also shaped, or rather hindered, by writing the book during the COVID-virus lockdown without access to libraries that hold out-of-print texts not available online. These circumstances have exaggerated my customary inefficiency as a bibliographer, for which I apologise, above all to authors of relevant works that I have overlooked. At least I can claim close attention to the primary sources, most notably the writings of Dante.

I have limited the note references in the predecing section to primary sources or to publications quoting primary sources. The annotated list of further reading is ordered so that it runs parallel to the text and is laid out by chapter.

ONLINE RESOURCES FOR DANTE

https://digitaldante.columbia.edu
a wide-ranging resource with the edition by Giorgio Petrocchi (1966-7), and translations by Longfellow and Mandelbaum, Lansing and Frisardi

https://etcweb.princeton.edu/dante/index.html
a comprehensive resource for Dante's writings, with the Petrocchi edition

https://dantelab.dartmouth.edu/reader
with tools to explore text and commentaries

http://www.danteonline.it/english/codici_frames/elencocodici.asp,
for manuscript editions

https://www3.nd.edu/~italnet/Dante/
for printed editions 1472–1629

INTRODUCTION

M. Kemp, 'In the Light of Dante: Meditations on Natural Light and Divine Light in Piero della Francesca, Raphael and Michelangelo', in *Ars naturam adiuvans: Festschrift für Matthias Winner*, ed. V. von Flemming and S. Schütze, Mainz am Rhein, 1996, pp 160–77

M. Kemp, *Christ to Coke: How Image Becomes Icon*, Oxford, 2011

CHAPTER 1

References to the Bible are by book, chapter and verse (where relevant) and are from the Cambridge edition, *c.*1900, of the King James Bible of 1611, which has a power and beauty that can stand beside Dante's texts. Where appropriate the Latin Vulgate is also cited.

For a very fine history of colour and light in various artistic media, see J. Gage, *Colour in Culture*, London, 1993

For a perceptive essay on the Sinai *Transfiguration*, see C. Mango: https://fortnightlyreview.co.uk/2014/07/mango-sinai-mosaic/

Gulielmus Durandus, *Rationale divinorum officiorum*, I. 24, in J. M. Neale and B. Webb (ed. and trs.), *The Symbolism of Churches and Church Ornamments*, London, 1893

A. Lidov, 'Hierotopy and Iconicity: Spatial Icons versus Iconographic Devices', *Icons of Space, Icons in Space, Iconography or Hierotopy? International Congress of Byzantine Studies*, Belgrade, August 2016, pp 2–8, for space and light in Hagia Sofia

H. Belting, *Florence and Baghdad*, trs. D. Schneider, Cambridge (Mass.), 2011, for a sustained compare-and-contrast

V.-S. Schulz, 'Intricate Letters and the Reification of Light: Prolegomena on the Pseudo-Inscribed Haloes in Giotto's *Madonna di San Giorgio alla Costa* and Masaccio's San Giovenale triptych', *Mitteilungen des Kunsthistorischen Institutes in Florenz*, vol.LVIII, 2016, pp 59–94; and 'From Letter to Line: Artistic Experiments with Pseudo-Script in Late Medieval Italian Painting, Preliminary Remarks', *The Power of Line*, ed. M. Faietti and G. Wolf, Munich 2015, pp 144–61

The fundamental treatment of Mediaeval and Renaissance optics is by D. Lindberg, *Theories of Vision from Al-Kindi to Kepler*, Chicago, 1976

A. M. Smith, *Ptolemy and the Foundations of Ancient Mathematical Optics: A Source Based Guided Study*, Philadelphia, 1999

A. M. Smith, *From Sight to Light: The Passage from Ancient to Modern Optics*, Chicago and London, 2014

M. Kemp, *The Science of Art: Optical Themes in Western Art from Brunelleschi to Seurat*, London, 1990 and 1992

R. Bacon, *Opus majus*, ed. J. Bridges, 2 vols., Oxford, 1897, I, pt. V, *De scientia perspectiva*

https://archive.org/details/opusmajusofroger02bacouoft/page/n7/mode/2up

D. Lindberg (ed.), *Roger Bacon and the Origins of Perspectiva in the Middle Ages: A Critical Edition and English Translation of Bacon's Perspectiva*, Oxford, 1996

S. Gilson, *Medieval Optics and Theories of Light in the Works of Dante*, Lampeter, 2000, a key work that underpins my discussion of Dante's science of optics in this and the next chapter

R. Librandi, 'Dante e la lingua della scienza', in *Dante e la lingua italiana*, ed. M. Tavoni, *Letture classensi*, vol.XLI, Ravenna, 2013, pp 61–87, especially for Mediaeval sources for Dante's cosmology

M. De Mey, 'Artistic and Intellectual Factors in Scientific Discovery: Ocular Anatomical Drawings', *Scientiarum Historia*, vol.XXIII, Ghent, 1997, pp 73–108, for a wide conspectus of early images of the eye

CHAPTER 2

E. Gardiner (ed.), *Visions of Heaven and Hell Before Dante*, New York, 2009. A useful anthology of early texts

A. Minnis, *From Eden to Eternity: Creations of Paradise in the Later Middle Ages*, Philadelphia, 2016

A. Minnis, *Hellish Imaginations from Augustine to Dante: An Essay in Metaphor and Materality*, Oxford, 2020

Z. Baranski and S. Gilson (eds.), *The Cambridge Companion to Dante's 'Commedia'*, Cambridge, 2018. For the dating of Dante's work, see:
doi:10.1017/9781108367769

P. Boyde, *Perception and Passion in Dante's Comedy*, Cambridge, 1993, for a fine analysis of vision and feeling in Dante's writing

S. Gilson, *Mediaeval Optics* (see ch. 1 above)

The Oxford Handbook of Dante, ed. Manuele Gragnolati, Elena Lombardi and Francesca Southerden, Oxford, 2021

M. Camille, 'Before the Gaze: The Internal Senses and Late Medieval Practices of Seeing', in *Visuality Before and After the Renaissance: Seeing as Others Saw*, ed. Robert Nelson, Cambridge, 2000, pp 197–223

M. Ariani, *Lux inaccessibilis: metafore e teologia della luce nel 'Paradiso' di Dante*, Rome, 2010

For the eagle and the sun, see Cambridge, Corpus Christi College, Parker Library, Isidore of Seville, *Isidori etymologiae et synonyma, bestiarius etc.*, CCCC MS 22, fol. 166v

Albertus Magnus, *Opera omnia*, ed. A. Borgnet, Paris, 1890, I, *De intellectu et intelligibili*, pp 527–584

For the fallibility of vision, see M. Kemp, 'In the Beholder's Eye: Leonardo and the "Errors of Sight" in Theory and Practice' (Hammer Prize Lecture), *Achademia Leonardi Vinci*, vol.V, 1992, pp 153–62

E. M. Longen, 'The Grammar of Apotheosis: Paradiso XXXIII', *Dante Studies, with the Annual Report of the Dante Society*, no.XCIII, Baltimore, 1975, pp 209–214

CHAPTER 3

M. Gill, *Angels and the Order of Heaven in Medieval and Renaissance Italy*, Cambridge, 2014

P. Brieger, M. Meiss and C. S. Singleton, *Illuminated Manuscripts of the Divine Comedy*, 2 vols., Princeton, 1969

R. Owen, 'Dante's Reception by 14th- and 15th-century Illustrators of the *Commedia*', *Reading Medieval Studies*, vol.XXVII, 2001, pp 163–225

For the Holkham manuscript, see https://digital.bodleian.ox.ac.uk/inquire/Discover/Search/#/?p=c+4,t+Dante%20Holkham,rsrs+0,rsps+100,fa+,so+ox%3Asort%5Easc,scids+,pid+10974934-30a5-4495-857e-255760e5c5ff,vi+

and https://library280projects.wordpress.com/2012/03/25/manuscript-study-libr-280-12/#Introduction%20and%20Historical%20Overview

For the Yates Thompson manuscript in the British Library with Giovanni di Paolo's illuminations, see https://www.bl.uk/catalogues/illuminatedmanuscripts/record.asp?MSID=6468

M. Meiss, 'The Yates Thompson Dante and Priamo dell Quercia', *The Burlington Magazine*, vol.CVI, London, 1964, pp 403–412

For apposite remarks on Botticelli and Dante, see M. Marmor, 'From Purgatory to the "Primavera": Some Observations on Botticelli and Dante', *Artibus et Historiae*, vol.XXI, 2003, pp 199–212

J. Pope-Hennessy, *Paradiso: The Illuminations to Dante's Divine Comedy by Giovanni di Paolo*, London, 1993

For the Botticelli illustrations, see http://www.worldofdante.org/gallery_botticelli.html

R. Lightbown, *Sandro Botticelli*, 2 vols., Berkeley, 1978, pp 196–205

B. J. Watts, 'Sandro Botticelli's Drawings for Dante's "Inferno": Narrative Structure, Topography and Manuscript Design', *Artibus et Historiae*, vol.XVI, Krakow, 1995, pp 163–201

H. Webb, 'Botticelli's Illustrations of Dante's *Paradiso*: The Construction of Conjoined Vision', *I Tatti Studies in the Italian Renaissance*, vol.XXII, Chigaco, 2019, pp 187–208

For the Urbino Manuscript in the Vatican, see https://spotlight.vatlib.it/humanist-library/catalog/Urb_lat_365 and https://digi.vatlib.it/view/MSS_Urb.lat.365

R. Eitel-Porter, 'Drawings for the Woodcut Illustrations to Alessandro Vellutello's 1544 Commentary on Dante's Comedia', *Print Quarterly*, vol.XXXVI, London, March 2019, pp 3–17

CHAPTER 4

The Cambridge Companion to Giotto, ed. A. Derbes and M. Sandona, Cambridge, 2004

For the 'portrait', see E. H. Gombrich, 'Giotto's Portrait of Dante', in *New Light on Old Masters*, Oxford, 1986, pp 10–31

L. Jacobus, *Giotto and the Arena Chapel: Art, Architecture and Experience*, London, 2008

G. Pisani, 'Dante e Giotto: la Commedia degli Scrovegni', in *Dante fra il settecentocinquantenario della nascita (2015) e il settecentenario della morte (2021)*. Atti delle Celebrazioni in Senato, del Forum e del Convegno internazionale di Roma, 2015, ed. E. Malato and A. Mazzucchi, Rome, 2016, vol.2, pp 799–815, looking particularly at Giotto's images of the Virtues and Vices

Fra Angelico: Heaven on Earth, exh.cat., ed. Nathaniel Silver, Isabella Stewart Gardner Museum, Boston, 2018

G. Didi-Huberman, *Fra Angelico: Dissemblance and Figuration*, Chicago, 1995

For an informative exploration of Giovanni di Paolo's, *Madonna and Child*, see https://www.nortonsimon.org/learn/multimedia/videos-podcasts-and-lectures/branchini-madonna/

Leon Battista Alberti, *On Painting*, C. Grayson (trs.), M. Kemp (intro.), London, 1991

Leon Battista Alberti, *On Painting*, ed. and trs. R. Sinisgalli, Cambridge, 2011

D. R. Edward Wright, *Il De pictura di Leon Battista Alberti e i suoi lettori 1435–1600*, Florence, 2010

Piero della Francesca, *De propspectiva pingendi*, ed. G. Nicco-Fasola, intro. E. Battisti, Florence, 1984

C. Bertelli, *Piero della Francesca*, London, 1992

R. Lightbown, *Piero della Francesca*, New York, 1992

M. Aronberg Lavin, *Piero della Francesca: The Flagellation*, Chicago, 1972

For Piero della Francesca and light, see M. Kemp, *The Science of Art* (see ch. 1 above) and 'In the Beholder's Eye' (see ch. 2 above); also:

M. Kemp, 'New Light on Old Theories: Piero della Francesca and the Transmission of Light', in *Piero della Francesca tra arte e scienza*, ed. M. Dalai Emiliani and V. Curzi, Venice, 1996, pp 33–46

R. Goffen, *Giovanni Bellini*, London, 1989

S. Rutherglen and C. Hale, *In a New Light: Giovanni Bellini's 'St. Francis in the Desert'*, Frick Collection, New York and London, 2015, with close-focus essays and close-focus reproductions

For the Frick *St Francis*, see also https://www.frick.org/exhibitions/past/2011/bellini

For the Canticle of the Sun, see http://faculty.webster.edu/barrettb/cantico.htm

R. Hatfield, 'Botticelli's *Mystic Nativity*, Savonarola and the Millenium', *Journal of the Warburg and Courtauld Institutes*, vol.LVIII, London, 1995, pp 88–114

J. Riess, *The Renaissance Antichrist: Luca Signorelli's Orvieto Frescoes*, Princeton, 1995

C. Gilbert, *How Fra Angelico and Signorelli Saw the End of the World*, Pennsylvania, 2002

For Michelangelo, see the collection of essays in G. Massimo (ed.), *The Sistine Chapel*, with contributions by C. Pietrangeli, A. Chastel, J. Shearman, John O'Malley, S. J., P de Vecchi, M. Hirst, F. Mancinelli, G. Colalucci and F. Bernabei, New York, 1984

L. Steinberg, *Michelangelo's Last Paintings: The Conversion of St Paul and the Crucifixion of St Peter in the Cappella Paolina, Vatican Palace*, Oxford, 1975

For the spirituality of Leonardo's last paintings, see M. Dalivalle, M. Kemp and R. Simon, *Leonardo's Salvator Mundi and the Collecting of Leonardo in the Stuart Courts*, Oxford, 2019, ch. 2

For Giovanni Santi's *Cronaca rimata*, 1492, in the Biblioteca Vaticana, Holtzinger (ed.), see C. Gilbert, *Italian Art 1400–1500: Sources and Documents*, New Jersey, 1980; and

K. B. Wingfield, 'La Cronaca Rimata di Giovanni Santi e Raffaello', in *Raffaello e Urbino: la formazione giovanile e i rapporti con la città natale*, ed. L. Onori, exh.cat., Milan, 2009, pp 38–43

For Giovanni Santi's career, see R. Dubos, *Giovanni Santi*, Bordeaux, 1971

For his paintings, see *Giovanni Santi: 'Da poi … me dette alla mirabil arte de pictura'*, exh.cat., ed. M. Valazzi and A. Vastano, Gallerie Nazionale della Marche, Urbino, 2018–19

P. Taylor, 'Julius II and the Stanza della Segnatura', *Journal of the Warburg and Courtauld Institutes*, vol.LXXII, 2009, pp 103–41

J. Shearman, *The Vatican Stanze: Functions and Decorations*, Oxford, 1972

D. Riser, *Raphael's Poetics: Art and Poetry in High Renaissance Rome*, Amsterdam, 2012

J. Shearman, *Raphael in Early Modern Sources 1483–1602*, New Haven, 2003, pp 134–5 and pp 136–7

A. Aceto, 'Appendix: Two Sonnets. Raphael as a Poet-Lover', in C. Whistler and B. Thomas, *Raphael: The Drawings*, Oxford, 2017, p.249

M. Sensi, 'La "Madonna di Foligno" e il suo committente Sigismondo dei Conti di Antignano', *Bolletino storico della città di Foligno*, vol.XXXVII, 2014, pp 75–187. See also other essays in the same volume

P. Emison, 'Raphael's Dresden Cherubs', *Zeitschrift für Kunstgeschichte*, vol.LXV, 2002, pp 242–50

E. H. Gombrich, 'The Ecclesiastical Significance of Raphael's *Transfiguration*', in *New Light on Old Masters*, Oxford, 1986, pp 143–6

C. King, 'The Liturgical and Commemorative Allusions in Raphael's *Transfiguration* and Failure to Heal', *Journal of the Warburg and Courtauld Institutes*, vol.XLV, 1982, pp 148–59

S. Hale, *Titian: His Life and the Golden Age of Venice*, London, 2012

M. Loh, *Titian's Touch: Art, Magic and Philosophy*, London, 2109, especially for paint into light

D. Bohde, 'Titian's Three-Altar Project in the Venetian Church of San Salvador: Strategies of Self-Representation by Members of the Scuola Grande di San Rocco', *Renaissance Studies*, vol.XV, 2001, pp 450–72

R. Mellinkoff, *The Devil at Isenheim: Reflections of Popular Belief in Grunewald's Altarpiece*, Berkeley, 1988

G. Bryda, 'The Exuding Wood of the Cross at Isenheim', *The Art Bulletin*, vol.C, 2018, pp 6–36

CHAPTER 5

S. Gilson, 'Optics in and Through Dante: Notes on Visual and Optical Theory in the *Lezioni* on Dante by Cosimo Bartoli and Benedetto Varchi', *Letteratura Italiana antica*, vol.XX, 2019, pp 501–16

For a wide-ranging and finely illustrated survey, see D. Stephenson and V. Hammond, *Visions of Heaven: The Dome in European Architecture*, New York, 2005

A. Buccheri, *The Spectacle of Clouds, 1439–1650: Italian Art and Theatre*, Farnham, 2014, which has richly informed both this and the following chapter

D. Ekserdjian, *Corrgeggio*, London, 1997

A. Buccheri and M. Spagnolo, *Correggio*, Milan, 2004

M. Spagnolo, *Coreggio, geografico e storia della fortuna*, Correggio, 2005

J. Shearman, 'Correggio's Illusionism', in *La propspettive rinascimentale: codificazione e trasgressioni*, ed. M. Emiliani, Florence, 1980, pp. 282–95

J. Shearman, 'Raphael's Clouds and Correggio's', in *Studi su Raffaelo: atti del congresso internazionale di studi*, ed. M. Sambucco, 2 vols., Urbino, 1987, II, p. 657 ff.

J. Shearman, *Only Connect: Art and the Spectator in the Italian Renaissance*, Princeton, 1992, especially ch. IV, 'Domes'

M. Kemp, 'From Different Points of View: Correggio, Copernicus & the Mobile Observer', in *Coming About … A Festschrift for John Shearman*, ed. L. Jones and L. Matthew, Cambridge (Mass.), 2001, pp 207–13.

F. Haskell, *Patrons and Painters: A Study in the Relations between Italian Art and Society in the Age of the Baroque*, New Haven, 1963; as *Patrons and Painters: Art and Society in Baroque Italy*, London, 1980

J. Scott, *Images of Nepotism: The Painted Ceilings of the Palazzo Barberini*, Princeton, 1991

For a lively account of the Pietro da Cortona vault, see this translation of *Declaration of the Paintings* by Mattia Rosichino: https://simonaalbanese.blogspot.com/2010/03/triumph-of-divine-providence-by-pietro.html

For Pietro's co-author, see https://scholar.harvard.edu/files/jconnors/files/connors_1998_ottonelli_in_cortona_atti_english_1.pdf

For the treatise G. Domenico Ottonelli e Pietro Berrettini [Pietro da Cortona] *Il trattato della pittura e scultura, uso et abuso loro* (1652), ed. V. Casale, Florence, 1973: https://archive.org/details/trattatodellapitoootto/page/n5/mode/2up

J. Imorde, 'Francesco Barberini Vice-Chancellor: The Quarant'Ore Decorations in San Lorenzo in Damaso 1633', in *Pietro da Cortona*, ed. C. Frommel and S. Schüze, Milan, 1998, pp 53–61

M. Weil, 'The Devotion of the Forty Hours and Roman Baroque Illusions', *Journal of the Warburg and Courtauld Institutes*, vol.XXXVII, 1974, pp 218–48

A. Buccheri, 'I teatri delle Quarantore: il popolo testimone dell'epifania del divino', in *La 'Sovrabbondanza' nel Barocco*, ed. V. Viola, R. La Delfa and C. Scordato, Leonforte, 2019, pp 190–207

R. Enggass, *The Painting of Baciccio: Giovanni Battista Gaulli 1639–1709*, Pennsylvania, 1964

M. Fagiolo dell'Arco, D, Graf and F. Petrucci, *Giovan Battista Gaulli, Il Baciccio (1639–1709)*, Milan, 1999

L. Wolk-Simon and C.Johns, *The Holy Name: Art of the Gesù. Bernini and His Age*, exh.cat., Philadelphia, 2018

S. Ostrow, 'Bernini, Baciccio, and the Dome Fresco in the Gesù: A Reconsideration', *Artibus et Historiae*, vol.LXXIX, Krakow, 2019, pp 287–306, which also contains a good set of bibliographical references.

R. Palmer, 'All is very plain, upon inspection of the figure: the visual method of Andrea Pozzo's *Perspectiva pictorum et architectorum*', in *The Rise of the Image*, ed. R. Palmer and T. Frangenberg, Aldershot, 2003

M. Kemp, *The Science of Art* (see ch. 1 above)

F. Camerota, 'Exactitude and Extravagence: Andrea Pozzo's "Viewpoint"', in *Imagine Math: Between Culture and Mathematics*, ed. M. Emmer, Milan, 2012

St Teresa of Ávila, *El Libro de la Vida (1565): The Life of Teresa of Jesus: The Autobiography of Teresa of Ávila*, ed. and trs. E. A. Peers, New York, 1991

I. Lavin, *Bernini and the Unity of the Visual Arts*, New York and Oxford, 1980

F. Fehrenbach, 'Bernini's Light', *Art History*, vol.XXVIII, 2005, pp 1–42

A good number of primary sources are cited in S. Landre, 'The Bel Composto in Gian Lorenzo Bernini's Cornaro Chapel', *Theses and Dissertations* at the University of Wisconsin, Milwaukee, 2015, https://dc.uwm.edu/etd/1008

See also: Roma, Biblioteca Apostolica Vaticana, Chig. D III fol. 52r, trs. T. Montanari, in 'A Contemporary Reading of Bernini's "Maraviglioso Composto": Unpublished Poems on the Four River Fountain and the Cornaro Chapel', *Poetry on Art: Renaissance to Romanticism*, ed. T. Frangenberg, Donington, 2003, pp 193–7

M. Weil, 'The relationship of the Cornaro Chapel to Mystery Plays and Italian Court Theatre', in '*All the World's a Stage...': Art and Pageantry in the Renaissance and Baroque*, ed. B. Wisch and S. Scott Munshower, Pennsylvania, 1990, pp 459-84

François de Aquilón (Aguilonius), *Opticorum libri sex: philosophiis juxta ac mathematicis utiles*, Antwerp, 1613

J. Martin, *The Ceiling Paintings for the Jesuit Church in Antwerp (Corpus Rubenianum Ludwig Burchard)*, London, 1968

A good set of essays is in *Innovation and Experience in the Early Baroque in the Southern Netherlands: The Case of the Jesuit Church in Antwerp, ed.* P. Lombaerde, Turnhout, 2008.

R. Fabri and P. Lombaerde, *Architecture and Architectural Sculpture: The Jesuit Church of Antwerp (Corpus Rubenianum Ludwig Burchard)*, London, 2018

C. Boeckl, 'Plague Imagery as Metaphor for Heresy in Rubens' *The Miracles of Saint Francis Xavier*', *The Sixteenth Century Journal*, vol. XXVII, 1996, pp 979–95

CHAPTER 6

A. Buccheri, *The Sepectacle of Clouds* (see ch. 5 above)

L. Zorzi, 'La scenotecnica brunelleschiana: problemi filalogici et interpretativi', *Filippo Brunelleschi: La sua opera e il suo tempo*, Florence, 1980, pp 161–71

N. Newbigin, 'Greasing the Wheels of Heaven: Recycling, Innovation and the Question of "Brunelleschi's" Stage Machinery', *I Tatti: Studies in the Italian Renaissance*, vol.XI, Cambridge, (Mass.), 2007, pp 201–41

M. Fabbri, E. Garbero Zorzi and A. M. Petrioli Tofani, *Il luogo: teatrale a Firenze: Brunelleschi, Vasari, Buontalenti, Parigi*, Milan, 1975

A. Ferraro, 'Matteo Palmieri's City of Life: The Original Idea of Three Opportunities for Salvation', *International Journal of Literature and Arts*, vol.II, no.6, New York, 2014, pp 230–39

J. Sliwka, *Visions of Paradise: Botticini's Palmieri Altarpiece*, exh. cat., National Gallery, London, 2015; and for the film made for the exhibition see https://www.youtube.com/watch?v=ZUXa1nDtOBo

C. King, 'The Dowry Farms of Niccolosa Serragli and the Altarpiece of the Assumption in the National Gallery, London (1126). Ascribed to Francesco Botticini', *Zeitschrift für Kunstgeschichte*, vol.L, 1987, pp 275–78

R. Begemihl, 'Francesco Botticini's Palmieri Altar-Piece', *The Burlington Magazine*, vol.CXXXVIII, London, 1996, pp 308–14

A. Blumenthal, *Theatre Art of the Medici*, Dartmouth, 1980

E. Garbero Zorzi and M. Sperenzi, *Teatro e spettacolo nella Firenze dei Medici*, Florence, 2001

J. Saslow, *The Medici Wedding of 1589: Florentine Festival as Theatrum Mundi*, London, 1996

A. Fara, *Buontalenti: archittetura e teatro*, Florence, 1979

A. Blumenthal, *Giulio Parigi's Stage Designs: Florence and the Early Baroque Spectacle*, New York, 1986

S. Mamone, 'Drammaturgia di macchine nel teatro granducale fiorentino: il teatro degli Uffizi da Buontalenti ai Parigi', *Drammaturgia*, vol.XII, Florence, 2016, pp 17–43

S. Rinaldi, 'Due disegni di Giulio Parigi per gli allestimenti fiorentini del 1608', *Paragone. Parte arte*, vol.CXXXIV, 2017, Florence, pp 63–72

M. Kemp, 'Ludovico Cigoli on the Origins and Rationale of Painting', *Mitteilungen des Kunsthistorischen Institutes in Florenz*, vol.XXXV, Florence, 1991, pp 133–52

F. Camerota, *Linear Perspective in the Age of Galileo: Lodovico Cigoli's 'Prospettiva pratica'*, Florence, 2010

M. Fabbri et al., in *Il luogo: teatrale* (see above) for Cigoli, no. 8.18

For the *Lucifer* designs, see M. Chappell, *Disegni di Lodovico Cigoli (1559–1613)*, exh.cat., Uffizi, Gabinetto Disegni e Stampe, Florence, 1992, pp 7–9, no.4; and 'Cigoli, *Lucifero*', in Ministero dei Beni e delle Attivita' Culturali e del Turismo, *Acquisizioni e donazioni 2001-2011: arte dal Medioevo al XXI secolo*, Rome, 2014, pp 182–3.

For the Galle engraving after Cigoli, see https://www.britishmuseum.org/collection/object/P_1873-0809-460

S. Ostrow, *Art and Spirituality in Counter-Reformation Rome: The Sistine and Pauline Chapels in S. Maria Maggiore*, Cambridge and New York, 1996

S. Ostrow, 'Cigoli's Immacolata and Galileo's Moon: Astronomy and the Virgin in Early Seicento Rome', *The Art Bulletin*, vol. LXXVIII, 1996, pp 218–35

J. Bell, 'The Life and Works of Matteo Zaccolini (1574–1630)', *Regnum Dei*, vol.XLI, 1985, pp 237–58

M. Fagiliolo dell'Arco and S. Carandini, *L'effimero baracco: strutture della festa nella Roma del '600*, 2 vols, Rome, 1977–8

M. Weil, *Baroque Theatre and Stage Design*, St Louis, Missouri, 1983

Theatricality in Early Modern Art and Architecture, ed. C. van Eck and S. Bussels, *Art History*, XXXIII, 2011

For a facsimile edition of Zuccari's illustrations, see *Dante historiato da Federigo Zuccaro: Firenze, Gabinetto disegni e stampe degli Uffizi*, ed. A Massucchi, Rome, 2005.

G. Balass, 'Five Hierarchies of Intercessors for Salvation: The Decoration of the Angels' Chapel in the Gesù', *Artibus et Historiae*, vol.XXIV, Krakow, 2003, pp 177–208

CHAPTER 7

Robert Grosseteste, *On Light (De luce)*, trs. C. Riedl, Milwaukee, 1942

A. Sparavigna, 'The Light Linking Dante Alighieri to Robert Grosseteste', *Philica*, 2016, pp 1–9

J. Barrow, *Impossibility: The Limits of Science and the Science of Limits*, London, 1999: for Heisenberg, see pp 23–4; and for Gödel, pp 209–10 and pp 214–5. Although the physics has changed a good deal since 1999, Barrow's underlying questions retain their cogency

W. Heisenberg, 'Über den anschaulichen Inhalt der quantentheoretischen Kinematik und Mechanik' (On the perceptual content of quantum theoretical kinematics and mechanics), *Zeitschrift für Physik*, vol.XLIII, 1927, pp 172–98

K. Gödel, 'Über formal unentscheidbare Sätze der Principia Mathematica und verwandter Systeme 1' (On formally undecidable propositions of *Principia Mathematica* and related systems I) (1931) in *Kurt Gödel: Collected works*, ed. S. Feferman, 2 vols, Oxford, I, 1986, pp 144–95

J. Hopkins, *Complete Philosophical and Theological Treatises of Nicholas of Cusa*, Minneapolis, 2001

See also for translated texts by Cusanus, https://www.jasper-hopkins.info

A good account of Cusanus is in https://plato.stanford.edu/entries/cusanus/

C. Carman, *Leon Battista Alberti and Nicholas Cusanus*, Farnham, 2014

Picture Credits

The author and publishers wish to thank the following for their kind permission to reproduce the illustrations:

FRONTISPIECE: Vatican, Pinacoteca. © 2020. Photo Scala, Florence.

CHAPTER 1 OPENER: akg-images / Erich Lessing; 1 By permission of Saint Catherine's Monastery, Sinai, Egypt; 2 © photo by Andrea Paoletti; 3 ©2020. Manuel Cohen/Scala, Florence; 4 Metropolitan Museum of Art, gift of J. Pierpont Morgan, 1917; 5 Eth-Bibliothek Zurich/Science Photo Library.

CHAPTER 2 OPENER: akg-images / De Agostini / G. Cigolini; 6 © British Library Board. All Rights Reserved/Bridgeman Images; 7 The Master and Fellows of Corpus Christi College, Cambridge.

CHAPTER 3 OPENER AND 30: Rare Book & Manuscript Library, Columbia University in the City of New York, Rare Book B85DL B44; 8, 9, 10, 11 Photo Bodleian Libraries, Ms Holkham Misc. 48 (pp.74, 116, 145, 147); 12, 13, 14, 15, 16, 17 © British Library Board. All Rights Reserved / Bridgeman Images; 18, 19, 20, 21, 22 Philipp Allard/BPK, Berlin © 2020 Scala, Florence; 23, 24, 25, 26 by permission of Biblioteca Apostolica Vaticana, with all rights reserved; 27, 28, 29 Rare Book & Manuscript Library, Columbia University in the City of New York, Rare Book B85DL B44.

CHAPTER 4 OPENER: Vatican, Pinacoteca. © 2020. Photo Scala, Florence; 31, 32 ©2020. Photo Scala, Florence; 33 Google Art Project/Wikimedia Commons (CC0); 34 © 2020 Photo Scala, Florence/bpk, Bildagentur fuer Kunst, Kultur und Geschichte, Berlin; 35 Google Art Project/Wikimedia Commons (CC0); 36 Wikimedia Commons (CC0.1.0); 37 Luisa Ricciarini / Bridgeman Images; 38 © 2020. Photo Scala, Florence; 39, 40 Album / Alamy Stock Photo; 41 Granger Historical Picture Archive / Alamy Stock Photo; 42, 43 classicpaintings / Alamy Stock Photo; 44 © 2020. DeAgostini Picture Library/Scala, Florence; 45 akg-images / Ghigo Roli; 46 imageBROKER / Alamy Stock Photo; 47 akg-images / Erich Lessing; 48 The Picture Art Collection / Alamy Stock Photo; 49 akg-images / Erich Lessing; 50, 51 Heritage Image Partnership Ltd / Alamy Stock Photo; 52 Dennis Hallinan / Alamy Stock Photo; 53, 54 Album / Alamy Stock Photo; 55 Daniele Ciuffardi/Wikimedia Commons (CC0); 56 Heritage Image Partnership Ltd / Alamy Stock Photo; 57 Art Library / Alamy Stock Photo; 58 Album / Alamy Stock Photo; 59 © 2020. Photo Scala, Florence; 60 akg-images / Cameraphoto; 61 Heritage Image Partnership Ltd / Alamy Stock Photo; 62 classicpaintings / Alamy Stock Photo; 63 The Print Collector / Alamy Stock Photo; 64 Colmar, Musée d'Unterlinden. © 2020. Photo Scala, Florence; 65 Bridgeman Images; 66 Godong / Alamy Stock Photo.

CHAPTER 5 OPENER: Author; 67 imageBROKER / Alamy Stock Photo; 68 © 2020. Photo Scala, Florence; 69, 70 Album / Alamy Stock Photo; 71, 72 Ghigo Roli / Bridgeman Images; 73 Arthur Becker; 74 © 2020. Photo Scala, Florence; 75 Courtesy of the Gallerie Nazionali di Arte Antica, MIBACT - Bibliotheca Hertziana, Istituto Max Planck for the History of Art/Enrico

Fontolan; 76 Artexplorer / Alamy Stock Photo; 77 Courtesy of the Gallerie Nazionali di Arte Antica, MIBACT - Bibliotheca Hertziana, Istituto Max Planck for the History of Art/Enrico Fontolan; 78 Royal Collection Trust/© Her Majesty Queen Elizabeth II, 2020; 79, 80 Arthur Becker; 81 Jozef Sedmak / Alamy Stock Photo; 82 Arthur Becker; 83 Vito Arcomano / Alamy Stock Photo; 84 ho visto nina volare from Italy / Wikimedia Commons (CC BY-SA/2.0); 85 EnriquePSans / Alamy Stock Photo; 86 isogood / Alamy Stock Photo; 87 akg-images/Pirozzi; 88 © 2020. Photo Scala, Florence/ Fondo Edifici di Culto-Min.dell'Interno; 89 Paolo Romiti / Alamy Stock Photo; 90 © 2020.Photo Scala, Florence/ Fondo Edifici di Culto-Min. dell'Interno; 91 Firenze, BNC, Palat.10.8.6.15, vol.1 (1693) f.XCIX, by permission of MiBACT / Biblioteca Nazionale Centrale di Firenze; 92 Hemis / Alamy Stock Photo; 93 Arthur Becker; 94 isogood / Alamy Stock Photo; 95 mauritius images GmbH / Alamy Stock Photo; 96, 97 Firenze, BNC, Palat.10.8.6.15, vol 1 (1693) f.XCIV and f.CVIII, by permission of MiBACT / Biblioteca Nazionale Centrale di Firenze; 98 © The Trustees of the British Museum; 99 akg-images / Andrea Jemolo; 100, 101 Author; 102 Piet Lombaerde; 103 Album /Alamy Stock Photo; 104 Wikimedia Commons (CC BY-SA 3.0).

CHAPTER 6 OPENER, 107 and 108: © 2020. Copyright The National Gallery, London/Scala, Florence; 105 PRISMA ARCHIVO / Alamy Stock Photo; 106 Firenze, BNC, Banco Rari 228, f.115r by permission of MiBACT / Biblioteca Nazionale Centrale di Firenze; 109 Metropolitan Museum of Art, bequest of Phyllis Massar, 2011; 110 Goran Bogicevic /Alamy Stock Photo; 111, 112 Gallerie degli Uffizi, Florence; 113 Russell Mountford / Alamy Stock Photo; 114, 115 Alessandra Buccheri.

CHAPTER 7 OPENER: Bridgeman Images; 116 © The Saul Steinberg Foundation/Artists Rights Society (ARS), NY/ DACS, London 2020.

Index

Works of art are listed under the name of the artist.
Page numbers of illustrations are indicated in *italic*.